STRENGTHENING PROFESSIONAL AND SPIRITUAL EDUCATION
THROUGH 21ST CENTURY SKILL EMPOWERMENT IN PANDEMIC
AND POST-PANDEMIC ERA

Discover a treasure trove of knowledge in the proceedings of the First International Conference on Education (ICEdu). This meticulously curated collection of research papers delves into the transformative landscape of education in the 21st century, offering insights, solutions, and inspiration for educators, researchers, and policymakers alike.

Explore a diverse range of subject areas, from pedagogical innovations to the challenges of digital learning and the impact of the COVID-19 pandemic on education. With 28 scholarly papers contributed by experts from around the world, this volume offers a comprehensive understanding of the multifaceted issues in contemporary education.

Whether you're an academic seeking fresh perspectives or an educator navigating the complexities of modern pedagogy, these proceedings provide invaluable guidance. Join us in shaping the future of education by harnessing the power of 21st-century skills, professional development, and spiritual growth.

This book is an essential resource for anyone passionate about the advancement of education in the pandemic and post-pandemic era.

PROCEEDINGS OF THE 1ST INTERNATIONAL CONFERENCE ON EDUCATION (ICEDU 2022), SEPTEMBER 28, 2022, MALANG, INDONESIA

Strengthening Professional and Spiritual Education through 21st Century Skill Empowerment in Pandemic and Post-Pandemic Era

Edited by

Syamsul Arifin, Ahmad Fauzi, Triastama Wiraatmaja, Eggy Fajar Andalas and Nafik Muthohirin

Routledge
Taylor & Francis Group
LONDON AND NEW YORK

First published 2024
by Routledge
4 Park Square, Milton Park, Abingdon, Oxon OX14 4RN

and by Routledge
605 Third Avenue, New York, NY 10158

Routledge is an imprint of the Taylor & Francis Group, an informa business

British Library Cataloguing-in-Publication Data
A catalogue record for this book is available from the British Library

Library of Congress Cataloging-in-Publication Data
A catalog record has been requested for this book

ISBN: 978-1-032-45243-2 (hbk)
ISBN: 978-1-032-45244-9 (pbk)
ISBN: 978-1-003-37612-5 (ebk)

DOI: 10.1201/9781003376125

Typeset in Times New Roman
by MPS Limited, Chennai, India

Table of Contents

Preface

We are delighted to present the proceedings of the First International Conference on Education (ICEdu) on the theme "Strengthening Professional and Spiritual Education through 21st Century Skill Empowerment in Pandemic and Post-Pandemic Era." This conference, organized jointly by the Faculty of Teacher Training and Education and the Faculty of Islamic Studies at Universitas Muhammadiyah Malang, marked a significant milestone in the world of education.

The COVID-19 pandemic has had an unprecedented and profound impact on the field of education worldwide. The sudden closure of schools and universities, coupled with the shift to remote and online learning, disrupted traditional educational systems and highlighted the need for adaptability and resilience. Educators, students, and policymakers found themselves facing unprecedented challenges, from the digital divide to the psychological and social effects of isolation. It became clear that the pandemic was not merely a health crisis but also an educational crisis, one that demanded innovative solutions and a reevaluation of educational practices.

In this context, ICEdu emerged as a crucial platform for the global education community to come together and address these challenges head-on. Recognizing the urgency of the situation, ICEdu was designed to explore the intersection of professional and spiritual education, guided by the empowerment of 21st-century skills. By fostering a collaborative environment for scholars, practitioners, and policymakers, the conference aimed to facilitate the exchange of ideas and best practices that could shape the future of education, both during and after the pandemic.

This seminar featured the participation of three keynote speakers: Prof. Te-Sheng Chang from National Dong Hwa University, Taiwan; Assoc. Prof. Dennis Alonzo, Ph.D. from the University of New South Wales, Australia; and Prof. Muhamad Ali from the University of California, Riverside, United States. Additionally, we were honored to have three invited speakers: Prof. Dr. Tobroni, M.Si., Prof Dr. Dwi Priyo Utomo, M.Pd., and Prof. Dr. Ribut Wahyu Eriyanti, M.Si., M.Pd., all from Universitas Muhammadiyah Malang. Their insights and expertise enriched the discourse on education in the 21st century.

The proceedings presented here are a testament to the collective commitment to finding innovative and sustainable solutions for education in these unprecedented times. In total, this volume includes 28 papers, contributed by scholars and researchers from diverse corners of the globe, including Indonesia, the Philippines, the United States, Pakistan, South Korea, China, India, Nepal, and Mozambique. Their research papers contribute to a deeper understanding of the multifaceted challenges and opportunities in education today.

We hope that the papers presented in this volume will inspire further research, dialogue, and collaboration in the field of education. Together, we can continue to strengthen professional and spiritual education through the empowerment of 21st-century skills in the pandemic and post-pandemic era.

Acknowledgements

We extend our heartfelt gratitude to the individuals and organizations whose support and contributions made the First International Conference on Education (ICEdu) and the publication of these proceedings possible.

First and foremost, we would like to express our sincere appreciation to the esteemed rector of Universitas Muhammadiyah Malang for their unwavering support and commitment to the success of this seminar. Your leadership and vision have been instrumental in making this event a reality.

We also wish to extend our warm thanks to the dedicated team at the Lembaga Pengembangan Publikasi Ilmiah (Institution for the Development of Academic Publications) at Universitas Muhammadiyah Malang for their tireless efforts in coordinating all aspects of this international seminar, including ICEdu. Your meticulous planning and execution ensured the smooth and effective organization of this event.

We are deeply grateful to our keynote speakers, Prof. Te-Sheng Chang from National Dong Hwa University, Taiwan; Assoc. Prof. Dennis Alonzo, Ph.D. from the University of New South Wales, Australia; and Prof. Muhamad Ali from the University of California, Riverside, United States, for generously sharing their expertise and insights. Their contributions have enriched our understanding of education in the 21st century.

We would like to express our heartfelt gratitude to the Scientific Committee and Organizing Committee members for their tireless efforts in reviewing and selecting high-quality papers and ensuring the smooth conduct of the conference.

Our appreciation also goes to the authors of the 28 selected full papers, who contributed their valuable research and findings to this publication. Your scholarly work has enriched our understanding of education in the 21st century and its response to the challenges posed by the pandemic.

Lastly, we extend our thanks to all contributors, participants, and sponsors who made this conference possible. Your support has been instrumental in advancing the discourse on education in these extraordinary times.

We hope that the papers presented in this volume will inspire further research, dialogue, and collaboration in the field of education. Together, we can continue to strengthen professional and spiritual education through the empowerment of 21st-century skills in the pandemic and post-pandemic era.

Malang, August 31, 2023
Organizer of The First International Conference on Education (ICEdu)
Universitas Muhammadiyah Malang
Indonesia

Scientific committee

Prof. Akhsanul In'am, Ph.D.
Universitas Muhammadiyah Malang, Malang, Indonesia

Prof. Siti Nur Hidayati, Ph.D.
Middle Tennessee State University, Murfreesboro, Tennessee, USA

Prof. Dr. Yus Mochamad Cholily, M.Si.
Universitas Muhammadiyah Malang, Malang, Indonesia

Prof. Dr. Tobroni, M.Si.
Universitas Muhammadiyah Malang, Malang, Indonesia

Prof. Nobuyasu Katayama
Tokyo Gakugei University, Koganei, Japan

Assoc. Prof. Milan Kubiatko, Ph.D.
J.E. Purkyne University in Usti nad Labem, Czech Republic

Assoc. Prof. Bello Ganiyu
University of Ilorin, Nigeria

Assoc. Prof. Dr. Trisakti Handayani, MM
Universitas Muhammadiyah Malang, Malang, Indonesia

Assoc. Prof. Dr. Sugiarti, M.Si.
Universitas Muhammadiyah Malang, Malang, Indonesia

Prof. Dr. Abdulkadir Rahardjanto, M.Si.
Universitas Muhammadiyah Malang, Malang, Indonesia

Assoc. Prof. Dr. M. Syaifuddin, M.Si.
Universitas Muhammadiyah Malang, Malang, Indonesia

Assoc. Prof. Bayu Hendro Wicaksono, Ph.D.
Universitas Muhammadiyah Malang, Malang, Indonesia

Organizing committee

General Chair
Fuad Jaya Miharja, M.Pd.
Universitas Muhammadiyah Malang, Malang, Indonesia

Treasurer
Erlyna Abidasari, MA., M.Ed.
Universitas Muhammadiyah Malang, Malang, Indonesia

Technical Program & Publication Chair
Ahmad Fauzi, M.Pd.
Triastama Wiraatmaja, M.Si.
Eggy Fajar Andalas, M.Hum.
Nafik Muthohirin, MA., M.Hum.
Universitas Muhammadiyah Malang, Malang, Indonesia

Publicity and Sponsorship Chair
Kharisma Naidi Warnanda, M.Pd.
Reni Dwi Susanti, M.Pd.
M. Novi Rifa'i, MA., ME.
Fahdian Rahmandani, M.Pd.
Universitas Muhammadiyah Malang, Malang, Indonesia

Program Chair
Moh Mirza Nuryady, M.Si.
Fida Pangesti, MA.
Hasnan Bachtiar, S.HI., MIMWAdv.
Universitas Muhammadiyah Malang, Malang, Indonesia

Registration and Secretariat Chair
Diani Fatmawati, M.Pd.
Moh. Wahyu Kurniawan, M.Pd.
Adityo, MA.
Rizal Dian Azmi, M.Sc.
Universitas Muhammadiyah Malang, Malang, Indonesia

Facilities and Local Arrangement Chair
Alimin Adi Waloyo, M.App. Ling.
Abdurrohman Muzakki, M.Pd.
Murdiono, M.PdI.
Bramy Biantoro, M.Ed.
Universitas Muhammadiyah Malang, Malang, Indonesia

Editor Biographies

Prof. Dr. Syamsul Arifin, M.Si. is a full professor in Islamic studies at the University of Muhammadiyah Malang, where he has been employed since October 1991. He holds a Bachelor's Degree in Islamic Education from Universitas Islam Negeri Sunan Ampel, a Master's Degree in Sociology from Universitas Muhammadiyah Malang, and a Doctorate in Islamic Studies from Universitas Islam Negeri Sunan Ampel. Throughout his career, Arifin has been involved in numerous research projects, including studies on human rights, democracy, multiculturalism, and religious fundamentalism. His work has contributed significantly to the understanding of these topics within the context of Indonesian society.

Ahmad Fauzi, S.Pd., M.Pd. is a lecturer in the Department of Biology Education at the Faculty of Teacher Training and Education, Universitas Muhammadiyah Malang, Indonesia. He earned his bachelor's and master's degrees from Universitas Negeri Malang. His research interests encompass biology education, science education, genetics education, instrument development, and learning assessment. He has made significant contributions to his field, with a total of 1500 citations since 2018, an h-index of 19, and an i10-index of 34. His research continues to have a significant impact on the field of biology education. Additionally, he serves as an editor for several national journals and is actively involved as a reviewer for various international journals.

Triastama Wiraatmaja, S.S., M.Si. is Assistant Professor in the English Education Language Department, Faculty of Teacher Training and Education, University of Muhammadiyah Malang. He completed his Bachelor Degree majoring in English Linguistics and Literature in the State University of Malang in 2013, and he continued his Master Degree majoring in American Studies which was completed in 2016. Currently, he also a member of Translator and Interpreter Team in University of Muhammadiyah Malang who deals with international accreditation program since 2021. His research addresses sociolinguistics and psycho-linguistics contexts with a focus on race, class, and ethnicities relationship among language learners, and language and identity development in diasporic and language learners' context. His theoretical work is set in empirical ethnographic contexts using various methods, including Critical Discourse Analysis, sociolinguistics surveys, interview, and narrative approaches. He received numerous grants from the university which dealt with socio-linguistics and psycholinguistics contexts among language learners in Indonesia. Currently, he is working on a project that explores the language well-being of language learners in various universities in Indonesia, and community services programs engaging young learners from diverse suburbs in Malang. He also supervises Bachelor Degree students research projects, and a member of the Editorial Board for the following journals; (1) Celtic: A Journal of Culture, English Language Teaching, Literature and Linguistics, and (2) Notion: Journal of Linguistics, Literature, and Culture.

Eggy Fajar Andalas, S.S., M. Hum was born in Malang, East Java on August 11, 1989. In 2014, he graduated with a Bachelor's degree in the Indonesian Language and Literature program from Universitas Negeri Malang. In 2016, he completed the Master's program in Literary and Cultural Studies at the Faculty of Humanities, Universitas Airlangga, achieving the highest distinction. His expertise and primary focus have been in literature and culture. Currently, he holds a position as a lecturer in the Department of Indonesian Language and Literature Education, Faculty of Teacher Training and Education, Universitas Muhammadiyah Malang. He is actively involved as an editor for Jurnal Satwika: Studies in

Cultural Science and Social Change, Jurnal Inovasi Pembelajaran, Jurnal Genre, and Journal of Regional and Disaster Studies, as well as a reviewer for several national and international journals. In addition to contributing to scholarly journals, he has authored 19 books in the fields of education, literature, and culture.

Nafik Muthohirin, S.Pd.I., MA, Hum. is a lecturer at the Faculty of Islamic Religion and program director at RBC Institute Abdul Malik Fadjar – Universitas Muhammadiyah Malang (UMM), Indonesia. He was active at the Center for Islamic and Philosophical Studies (PSIF) UMM, and previously as a program manager at the Center for Religious and Multiculturalism Studies (PUSAM) UMM. His research interests are centered on the themes of Islam and peace; Islamic education; radicalism and violent extremism.

Strengthening Professional and Spiritual Education through 21st Century Skill Empowerment in Pandemic and Post-Pandemic Era – Arifin et al. (Eds)
© 2024 The Author(s), ISBN: 978-1-032-45243-2

Strengthening professional development with an instructional design for an interdisciplinary undergraduate-level engineering course

Te-Sheng Chang
National Dong Hwa University, Taiwan

ABSTRACT: Faculty professional development has long been a critical component of higher education. The 1950s and 1960s were the eras of scholars with a focus on research skills and productivity. In the 1970s, development moved into the era of the teacher, focusing on improving teaching skills and abilities. The 1980s were the era of the developer, where development departed, and faculty-centric programs (teaching and research) began to emerge. The 1990s were the era of the learner, with the focus shifting from teaching to learning. Today, we are in the era of teamwork/network, which focuses on "collaboration across faculty to encourage interdisciplinarity. There were two folds of this study. This study explored the impact of project-oriented problem-based learning on university students' engineering creativity through a quasi-experimental design. The experimental curriculum was designed and put into practice by three professors from different professional fields and incorporated three key concepts: participatory design, future thinking, and visual communication. Design thinking was the course's main axis. The experimental group consisted of 19 undergraduate students in the Engineering Design for Society course, while the control group of 23 Civil Engineering undergraduates participated in the Civil Engineering Design course. The findings are: (1) The experimental group received significantly higher creativity scores on fluency, flexibility, originality, and usefulness. (2) The control group's scores regressed on the post-test. (3) The experimental group's higher scores indicated that interdisciplinary teaching combined with innovative pedagogy can promote engineering creativity through solving problems from multi-faceted perspectives. The implications of this study for engineering creativity learning apropos future engineering demands are discussed.

Keywords: Engineering creativity, future thinking, interdisciplinary course, participatory design, project-oriented problem-based learning, visual communication

1 INTRODUCTION

The need for creativity, problem solving, and innovation in education is an urgent, global issue. This is specifically emphasized in engineering education, where today's students will be facing unprecedented challenges in their professional careers due to climate change and demographic changes. The goal of engineering education is to cultivate students' creativity and to develop their problem-solving skills in the wake of a nearly unknown, future society (Blizzard 2013; Charyton 2013). Hence, engineering students cannot only address engineering, but interdisciplinary skills which manage several issues at once. Miller (2010) stressed that students could improve teamwork, communication, and critical thinking skills through interdisciplinary courses which emphasis knowledge and critical thinking. Students in such a class would be asked to design innovative solutions for practical problems by

DOI: 10.1201/9781003376125-1

applying interdisciplinary knowledge (Miller 2010). Such an approach is necessary for today's engineering students.

Currently, many institutions have implemented project-oriented problem-based learning (POPBL) courses in undergraduate engineering curricula to implement a diverse set of engineering teaching to address tomorrow's challenges (Fini *et al.* 2018; Meehan *et al.* 2014). POPBL allows different groups of students in a course to work together to solve practical problems and to present and defend their approaches and solutions. The work requires them to actively participate in the process of acquiring and applying knowledge. Yasin *et al.* (2009) indicated that POPBL not only focuses on deriving solutions that have practical influence on social issues, but also promotes students' creativity. Thus, interdisciplinary POPBL curricula is one of the powerful ways to cultivate students' critical thinking and engineering creativity. Students improve communication, social, and leadership skills through teamwork such creativity requires (Fini *et al.* 2018).

Although POPBL has been the subject of numerous studies focusing on teaching in engineering education, comparatively little empirical research has been devoted to exploring the effects of POPBL in an interdisciplinary course on students' engineering creativity. A sound framework to design and integrate POPBL in an interdisciplinary course specifically addressing students engineering creativity towards future society design remains to be developed. This study describes the framework of teaching and learning by using the POPBL in an interdisciplinary course in Taiwan as well as to investigate the impact of the course on students' engineering creativity.

2 LITERATURE REVIEW

2.1 *Definitions of engineering creativity*

Guilford (1950) proposed the definition of creativity as a mental task demanding novel ideas, sparking a wave of creativity research that has been scrutinized ever since. Torrance (1974) applied Guilford's creativity theory to draw a framework for creative thinking processes that consisted of four aspects: fluency, flexibility, originality, and elaboration. Fluency refers to the production of a great number of ideas or alternate solutions to a problem. Flexibility refers to the production of ideas that show multiple possibilities or realms of thought. Originality involves the production of ideas that are novel. Elaboration is the process of enhancing ideas by providing more detail. Further, Sternberg and Lubart (1998) stressed that creativity produces content that is novel while being appropriate to the situational demands. Hence, originality and functionality intertwine.

Creativity can be defined as something new, valuable or useful for a particular group. Engineers achieve creativity more explicitly through "functional creativity" (Cropley and Cropley 2005). Functional creativity means that products designed by engineers serve a functional and pragmatic purpose. Thus, engineering problem identification is one of the key steps in the process of problem-solving; both of which fit the definition of increasing creative production (Srinivasan and Kraslawski 2006). Hence, engineers not only need to address aesthetics like artists, but they also need to solve problems, prevent potential problems, and address utility within the constraints and parameters that have been designated (Charyton 2013). How to develop such attributes in creative engineering programs needs to be assessed and further developed through educational innovation (Cropley and Cropley 2005). This study has adapted Torrance's four dimensions (fluency, flexibility, originality, and elaboration) and usefulness as the central theoretical framework of engineering creativity. The aim is to identify educational interventions which can enhance student's engineering creativity.

2.2 *POPBL within an interdisciplinary course*

The basic principles of POPBL are as follows: (1) Student-centered programs which motivate and gain commitment among students; (2) Problem-oriented and not subject-oriented;

(3) A solution is found through the learning process rather than recalling knowledge; (4) Project-Based which has a goal and action component to derive change; (5) Exemplarity instead of generality; (6) Promote group team work, social and communication skills (Yasin and Rahman 2011). Implementing a POPBL interdisciplinary course starts with the analysis of a research problem followed by project design which implements interdisciplinary activity to derive a solution (Yasin and Rahman 2011).

An interdisciplinary course complements the professional knowledge among different professional teachers to develop innovative pedagogy (Wang and Lo 2014). One of the most common ways of developing an interdisciplinary course is to focus on addressing practical problems in society (Wu and Yeh 2003). Teachers identifying the most pressing problems for engineering students to solve creates a focused environment for students. The related concepts of each discipline are horizontally and vertically integrated with the thematic concept of a societal problem as the center. The project theme (i.e., the central problem identified) can be executed by teachers in different professional fields, while the teaching-concepts from interdisciplinary subjects are mainly used to integrate the differing professional knowledge.

One of the effective methods to teach POPBL is the design thinking approach. Design thinking refers to the human-oriented problem-solving methodology, seeking innovative solutions for various issues and creating more possibilities through human needs (Brown 2008). The Hasso-Plattner Institute of Design at Stanford defined the processes of design thinking as following: (1) Empathize: Human-centered and divergent thinking; (2) Define: Converging the problems of the previous stage, identifying the core needs of users, and then defining core issues; (3) Ideate: Creating various ways to solve problems and help users solve problems; (4) Prototype: Using existing resources to test and start making prototypes; (5) Test: Looking for subjects to experience and complete the project. The model of Design Thinking originates from Herbert Simon's The Sciences of the Artificial, in which he originally indicated that design thinking was divided into two parts: firstly, in the empathy phase, people from different fields think divergently and explore various issues; secondly, in the ideate phase, everyone from different fields think to find possible solution, propose various possible solutions, integrate different solutions and find the most suitable way to present the prototype. Design thinking is a process of combining the two main elements of creativity: divergent thinking and convergent thinking (Yasin et al. 2009). This study employed the design thinking approach into an interdisciplinary course with POPBL to cultivate undergraduates' engineering creativity.

3 METHODS

3.1 Participants and procedure

A quasi-experimental design was used in this study. The researchers employed a control group to compare with the experimental group. The participants were not randomly selected or assigned to the groups due to the organizational system of classes at the university. The participants were 41 undergraduate students in a public university in Taipei, Taiwan. The experimental group consisted of 19 students who took the "Engineering Design for Society" course during the 2019 spring semester and were instructed with the POPBL in interdisciplinary activities. The control group of 23 civil engineering students took another course titled "Civil Engineering Design" and received the standard engineering instruction.

3.2 Teaching design

The POPBL with interdisciplinary activities curriculum delivered in the experimental group was designed and taught by three professors from different fields: Civil engineering, future studies, and architecture. The design thinking approach was applied in the course to promote

3

students' team work and critical thinking. The students were asked to complete a social-space problem solution project for a real-world field task.

The real-world geographic locations in this course were the Nanfuli (南福里) and Longfuli (龍福里) areas in the Zhongzheng District of Taipei City. These local areas used to be a Japanese civil servant residential area before 1945. Historic sites, traditional Chinese buildings, art and historic museums, and numerous business stores such as vintage postal stores, old book stalls and furniture houses, are located in these areas. The students were asked to work as a team to design a city plan to remodify these sensitive, multicultural, and historical areas. The instructors guided the students to integrate futures thinking methods and participatory design to think about the problems. Students had to observe how residents of these areas moved about and functioned in life in order to meet the requirement of participatory design; resident's behavior had to be a factor in their design. Students had to think 30–50 years ahead while keeping today's residents in-mind. Residents needed enough space to live, but also enough innovation to enhance their living standards. At the end of the semester, students were asked to make city plan proposals for their social-space problem solutions. Experts were invited to give suggestions and comments on students' proposals.

3.3 Instrument and data collection

Students' engineering creativity was assessed by the Engineering Creativity Scale (ECS). In order to avoid the carry-over effect of pre-test on the participants, this study created two parallel ECS forms: Form A and Form B. Form A was applied as the pre-test and Form B as the post-test. Form A consisted of two sub-tests: "Design a product that generates sound" and "Design a car." Form B consisted of two sub-tests: "Design a product for communication" and "Design a bus stop". The theoretical framework for assessment was based on Torrance 1974 to identify fluency, flexibility, originality, and elaboration. Questions needed to address aesthetic and functional needs while also solving problems and preventing problems (Charyton 2013).

"Design a product that generates sound" was designed to ask participants to draw two designs (Design 1 and Design 2) based on two 3-dimension images. The participants were asked to describe each of their two designs by answering the following questions: (1) What is your design? (2) What are the materials of your designs? (3) What are the problems solved with your designs? (4) Who will be users of your designs? The second subtest, "Design a car", required participants to draw a car with their imagination. Concurrently, the participants were asked to describe the features and specifics of the car they designed. The test was meant for group administration and asked the participants to draw their creative products by pens. The test time allotted was 30 minutes: 10 minutes for "Design a product that generates sound" and 20 minutes for "Design a car". Form B's testing system was the same as Form A, only with different tasks: "Design a product for communication," and "Design a bus stop."

The participants' answers were scored by four engineering experts. The following procedural steps were used to score each subject's answer. The (A) "Design a product that generates sound" and (B) "Design a product for communication," assessments consisted of four dimensions: fluency, flexibility, originality, and usefulness. Fluency was computed by the number of ideas on the sketch, description, materials, problems solved, and users. Flexibility was counted by the number of different categories, types, or classifications of responses. Originality was scored on an 11-point scale. The Usefulness is scored by a 5-point scale. At first, Design 1 and Design 2 were scored separately, and then the sum of Design 1 and Design 2 was computed for each dimension, separately.

The (A) "Design a Car" and (B) "Design a bus stop" assessments included four dimensions: fluency, flexibility, originality, and elaboration. The fluency score was given simply by counting all of the valid responses given by the subjects. The flexibility score was given by counting the total number of feature categories that were on the car. The originality score was developed from a tabulation of the frequency of all of the responses obtained. Frequencies and percentages of each response were computed. Among all answers, 2 points were given to a special answer for the originality score when the probability of this answer being given on the assessment was smaller than 1.99%. One point was given to an answer of which the probability being given on the assessment is between 2% and 4.99%. The elaboration score was obtained by counting the numbers of specific car details provided by the subjects.

The total score for (A) "Design a product that generates sound" and (B) "Design a product for communication," respectively, for each participant was computed by summing individuals' T scores for fluency, flexibility, originality, and usefulness. The total score for (A) "Design a car" and (B) "Design a bus stop," respectively, was computed by summing the T scores of fluencies, flexibility, originality, and elaboration. The total score for engineering creativity for each subject was computed by averaging scores of these two subtests' scores.

The coefficients of inter-rater reliability were between .47-.97, $p < .001$ and the test/re-test reliability coefficients were between .44-.56, $p < .05$).

3.4 Analytic strategy

The one-way analysis of covariance with $\alpha = .05$ (pre-test score as covariate) was employed to explore the difference between the experimental group and control group in each dimension of the ECS scores.

4 RESULTS

The means and standard deviations of the pre-test and post-test scores on each dimension of the CTS in the experimental and control group are presented. The results of ANCOVA are also indicated. Significant differences were demonstrated between groups in the dimensions of fluency ($F = 12.23$, $p < .05$), flexibility ($F = 4.37$, $p < .05$), originality ($F = 18.56$, $p < .001$), and usefulness ($F = 10.38$, $p < .05$). However, no significant difference was found between the experimental group and control group on the elaboration dimension ($F = .52$). The overall adjusted mean showed the experimental group reported significantly higher scores ($F = 10.38$, $p < .01$).

Notably, on the pre-test, the control group performed better. However, on the post-test, not only did the experimental group perform better, but the control group's scores dropped so sharply the adjusted mean for both tests showed that the experimental group had significantly higher scores on the above-mentioned dimensions. Hence, the experimental group was working from 'less' engineering creativity in the beginning. This carries implications for the success of the interdisciplinary course to deliver creativity and, urgently, the lack thereof for standardized civil engineering design courses. The results revealed that the "Interdisciplinary Social Engineering Design for Society in this study could promote participants" fluency, flexibility, fluency, flexibility, and originality.

5 DISCUSSION

The study results provide important contributions to the theory and practice of innovation in teaching creativity. Moreover, reflections on innovating 'regular' engineering courses to ensure they include original creativity are also important to making pragmatic changes in courses; moving successful 'experimental' courses into regular course work.

The first contribution pertains to the applicability and validity of the ECS assessment for capturing learning outcomes pertaining to creativity in engineering. Using both pre-test and post-test data, our empirical findings suggest that the ECS assessment is a reliable instrument for assessment of student learning outcomes. Students' responses reflected the attributes of creativity (Torrance 1974) and not necessarily the 'right' engineering answer. This can be seen in the fact the Civil Engineering Design students score's dropped after a semester – had the assessment been invalid, scores in both courses would have stagnated. Furthermore, expert engineers scored the assessment to confirm that the designs were practical engineering items, not only 'creative' items that lacked the required engineering functionality.

The second contribution of the study pertains to the impact of POPBL on the improvement of key dimensions of engineering student's creativity and learning outcomes. While previous studies have shown improvement in student learning outcomes by using POPBL in civil engineering courses (Yasin and Rahman 2011), this study was able to show the effect of POPBL in the context of city planning; a practical and pragmatic end of an engineering course. Our empirical findings show significant improvement in student learning outcomes in engineering creativity through the application of teamwork and communication skills, both on the student's and teacher's ends. This could help instructors to more effectively apply POPBL in conjunction with other pedagogical practices to enhance student learning outcomes.

Moreover, there is a negative and positive aspect to the outcomes. Not only did the experimental students' show higher creativity on the end assessment, they surpassed the original scores of the Civil Engineering students. However, the Civil Engineering student's creativity scores sharply dropped below the pre-test scores of the experimental class. The most significant reason this could be is the engineering students were seeking to provide the 'textbook' answer to the ECS assessment. Current Engineering Design courses thus may be stifling creativity and encouraging students to provide uniform answers. This hypothesis is supported in the post-test originality score, which was the lowest score (Control: $M = 45.47$, Experimental: $M = 52.89$) of all scores for the control group. Not only this, but the standard deviation was 4.56, the smallest SD in both groups pre- and post-tests. That is, students in the traditional engineering class gave fewer original answers after taking the course and provided more homogenous answers; all evidence of students giving 'textbook' answers instead of showcasing practical creativity. Considering the challenges tomorrow engineer's will face, it is thus imperative engineering courses adopt an interdisciplinary and problem-based approach.

The third contribution of this study pertains directly to the success of the experimental group. Creating a multi-disciplinary learning environment on improvement of students' teamwork, collaboration, and communication while encouraging students to look outside of a standard 'set' answers improved student's engineering creativity. Creativity was not only improved on the aesthetic attributes, but the functional too. The highest score for both groups on both tests was in-fact the experimental group's Usefulness score ($M = 53.41$). Particularly beneficial was likely the future studies aspect which encouraged 'participatory design.' Students had to directly solve for problems that demanded fluency (i.e., variety in the area's future designs), flexibility (i.e., willingness to adjust for the historical nature of the areas; architecture flexible to withstand change in time), originality (i.e., designs which were fresh to older districts yet were future-problem oriented), elaboration (i.e., explaining their designs comprehensively), and usefulness (i.e., ensuring it was useful for the future-city as well as today's residents). Engineering teachers should consider teaching these merits of engineering education instead of focusing on delivering classically 'correct' answers to presented problems that have already been answered.

The result corresponds with the previous studies that an interdisciplinary course with problem-oriented and project-based learning could improve students' engineering creativity (e.g., Yasin et al. 2009). However, this study went a step further in identifying the specific dimensions which creativity improves. Students not only had to focus on creating something that was beneficial to their lives, but to the community. That is, this project moved students out of the classroom and into the public arena where they had to consider public opinion while focusing on the pull of the past, present, and future in a historical area of Taipei. Teachers hardly agree upon what constitutes 'creativity' and how to assess it (Jahnke et al. 2017). Yet, one of the reservations on creativity is coursework often focuses on only producing something that can be used for a non-specific audience, thus leaving students to reflect on how this item may affect them. Creativity, as this study shows, cannot be thought of in an abstract, isolated vacuum. Creative items are truly creative when they break the box of self-conventional concepts and consider others' needs, both in the present and future.

6 CONCLUSION AND IMPLICATIONS

This study was designed to assess the improvement in students' learning outcomes in the area of creative engineering by using POPBL in an interdisciplinary course combined with real-world field studies. Educators can use the proposed platform to improve students' learning and creativity while enhancing content coverage. Furthermore, POPBL in a teamwork framework improves students' teamwork skills. This suggests that POPBL is an effective teaching and learning method that helps students relate course materials to functional practice while improving their level of understanding about the subject matter. Additionally, POPBL is a tool that increases students' interest and their awareness of a subject. The POPBL intervention left students with improved confidence in their ability to assess practical problems. Students were engaged in future studies and future thinking, which will be essential for engineers of the future to give attention to. Hence, it is highly recommended to be considered in various engineering courses; even more so as this study suggests conventional engineering courses may be stifling creativity.

One of the limitations of the study is the sample size. Future studies should use a larger sample size to examine the impact of POPBL intervention in improving student learning outcomes. While increasing the sample size may not be practical due to the limitation on the number of students in a class, increasing the sample size through administering the survey to several courses or over several semesters could provide the required sample size to conduct a more robust statistical analysis. Action research may offer pragmatic follow through for such a creativity course focused on interdisciplinary learning.

Another limitation was student willingness to participate. Student recruitment into the experimental group was difficult due to the course requiring rigorous involvement. Originally there were over 20 students. Many dropped the course leading to the 19 students listed in this study. Future studies should take into consideration how the course is offered, incentives, and target groups, specifically because engineering design courses are rigorous and demand dedication.

Moreover, future studies can integrate qualitative data, such as classroom observation, instructors' logs, and students' learning portfolios, to explore the different aspects of POPBL in an interdisciplinary course on students' engineering creativity. This data will be essential to showcasing the finer details of how POPBL generates teamwork, course satisfaction, and interpersonal skills. A course cannot be thought of as only teaching the subject material, but all of the tangible and intangible skills necessary for students to take action on the material.

This study highlighted that student's engineering creativity is improved through interdisciplinary, POPBL teaching. Ancillary data also suggests conventional courses may hinder creativity. Engineering students will face unprecedent challenges that demand rigorous problem-solving and daring creativity. Ecological crisis highlights the urgent demands of the skills. POPBL ought to be implemented in classrooms, and future studies, so that engineering students are equipped with the skills which will be demanded of them.

REFERENCES

Blizzard, J. (2013) *Design Thinkers Can Save The World: How Understanding Their Interests, Goals, and Motivations Can Inform Engineering Educators.* Clemson University. Available at: https://tigerprints. clemson.edu/cgi/viewcontent.cgi?article=2135&context=all_dissertations.

Brown, T. (2008) *Design Thinking*. Harvard Business Review. Available at: https://readings.design/PDF/Tim%20Brown,%20Design%20Thinking.pdf (Accessed: 3 September 2023).

Charyton, C. (2013) *Creative Engineering Design Assessment: Background, Directions, Manual, Scoring Guide and Uses*. Springer Science & Business Media. Available at: http://hozekf.oerp.ir/sites/hozekf.oerp.ir/files/kar_fanavari/manabe%20book/Thinking/Creative%20Engineering%20Design%20Assessment_%20Background%2C%20Directions%2C%20Manual%2C%20Scoring%20Guide%20and%20Uses-Springer-Verlag%20London%20%20%2820.pdf.

Cropley, D. and Cropley, A. (2005) *Engineering Creativity: A Systems Concept of Functional Creativity*. Psychology Press. Available at: https://www.taylorfrancis.com/chapters/edit/10.4324/9781410611925-15/engineering-creativity-systems-concept-functional-creativity-david-cropley-arthur-cropley.

Fini, E.H. *et al.* (2018) 'The impact of project-based learning on improving student learning outcomes of sustainability concepts in transportation engineering courses', *European Journal of Engineering Education*, 43(3), pp. 473–488. Available at: https://doi.org/10.1080/03043797.2017.1393045.

Guilford, J.P. (1950) 'Creativity.', *American Psychologist*, 5(9), pp. 444–454. Available at: https://doi.org/10.1037/h0063487.

Jahnke, I., Haertel, T. and Wildt, J. (2017) 'Teachers' conceptions of student creativity in higher education', *Innovations in Education and Teaching International*, 54(1), pp. 87–95. Available at: https://doi.org/10.1080/14703297.2015.1088396.

Meehan, A., Lawlor, B. and McLoone, S. (2014) 'On project oriented problem based learning (POPBL) for a first year engineering circuits project', in *25th IET Irish Signals & Systems Conference 2014 and 2014 China-Ireland International Conference on Information and Communities Technologies (ISSC 2014/CIICT 2014)*. Institution of Engineering and Technology, pp. 386–391. Available at: https://doi.org/10.1049/cp.2014.0719.

Miller, R.K. (2010) 'From the ground up: Rethinking engineering education for the 21st Century', in *Symposium on Engineering and Liberal Education*. New York. Available at: https://www.ateaonline.org/resources/Documents/Rethinking%20Engineering%20from%20the%20Ground%20Up,%20Richard%20Miller%20President,%20Olin%20College%20of%20Engineering.pdf.

Srinivasan, R. and Kraslawski, A. (2006) 'Application of the TRIZ creativity enhancement approach to design of inherently safer chemical processes', *Chemical Engineering and Processing: Process Intensification*, 45(6), pp. 507–514. Available at: https://doi.org/10.1016/j.cep.2005.11.009.

Sternberg, R.J. and Lubart, T.I. (1998) 'The concept of creativity: prospects and paradigms', in *Handbook of Creativity*. Cambridge University Press, pp. 3–15. Available at: https://doi.org/10.1017/CBO9780511807916.003.

Torrance, E.P. (1974) *Torrance Tests of Creative Thinking. Directions Manual and Scoring Guide, Verbal Test Booklet B*. Scholastic Testing Service. Available at: https://books.google.co.id/books/about/Torrance_Tests_of_creative_thinking_Dire.html?id=BUDnAQAACAAJ&redir_esc=y (Accessed: 3 September 2023).

Wang, H.-R. and Lo, W.-H. (2014) 'Applying interdisciplinary teaching to the course of gender education', *Taiwan Journal of General Education*, 14, pp. 59–86.

Wu, Y.-S. and Yeh, Y.-C. (2003) 'The relationship between thematic integrated instruction, grade level, parental socio-economic status and pupil's technological creativity', *Journal of National Taiwan Normal University*, 48(2), pp. 239–260.

Yasin, R.M., Mustapha, R. and Zaharim, A. (2009) 'Promoting creativity through problem oriented project based learning in engineering education at Malaysian polytechnics: Issues and challenges', in *Proceedings of the 8th WSEAS International Conference on Education and Educational Technology*, pp. 253–258. Available at: http://www.wseas.us/e-library/conferences/2009/genova/EDU/EDU-42.pdf (Accessed: 3 September 2023).

Yasin, R.M. and Rahman, S. (2011) 'Problem oriented project-based learning (POPBL) in promoting education for sustainable development', in *Procedia – Social and Behavioral Sciences*, pp. 289–293. Available at: https://doi.org/10.1016/j.sbspro.2011.03.088.

Strengthening Professional and Spiritual Education through 21st Century Skill Empowerment in Pandemic and Post-Pandemic Era – Arifin et al. (Eds)
© 2024 The Author(s), ISBN: 978-1-032-45243-2
Open Access: www.taylorfrancis.com, CC BY-NC-ND 4.0 license

Shifting the focus of professional development from teachers to students: Building students as teacher partners

D.A. Alonzo
University of New South Wales Sydney, Australia

ABSTRACT: The role of professional development in improving learning, assessment, and teaching is highly supported in the literature. It is a critical component of teacher development to better support teachers for continuous improvement. However, there is a mismatch between the content of teacher PD and the fundamental needs for effective learning. Most of the content is teacher-centric knowledge and skills, which is contrary to the most appropriate content of PD. As shown in the literature, 50% of the variance observed in student outcomes is due to themselves. This means that students are the main contributors to their learning. Hence, we must ensure that students have the knowledge and skills to effectively engage in their learning, including assessment, behaviour management, self-reflection, and others. To achieve this, teachers must build students' capacity as classroom partners. The disruption brought upon by the COVID-19 pandemic highlighted the importance of students' capacity for self-directed learning. Those who can engage in their learning independently have a better chance of success. Thus, we need to leverage this lesson to better prepare our students in the emerging context of the post-pandemic era.

1 INTRODUCTION

1.1 *Background*

Professional development is an integral part of teacher education and development. It is used to deliver new content and knowledge for teachers as one of the mechanisms to ensure teaching quality. Many educational bureaucracies have mandated PD programs or the required number of hours for teachers to engage (Asih *et al.* 2022). Although most PD programs reported in the literature highlight their positive impacts on increasing teachers' knowledge and skills (Popova *et al.* 2022), their direct link to student learning is contentious (Fischer *et al.* 2018). There is opposing evidence suggesting that whilst other PD programs resulted in increased student engagement and learning gains, there are other PD programs that have negligible impacts on students.

Establishing the direct or indirect effects of PD programs on student learning is a critical enquiry that needs further exploration. However, a more critical investigation is lacking in the literature. There is a paucity in the literature about PD content and design that enhances students' capacity to partner with teachers to ensure effective learning, assessment and teaching.

In this paper, I present a theorization of the content and design of PD programs that build students' capacity to learn, engage in assessment, and take an active role in the teaching process.

1.2 *The key to effective learning and teaching*

The current emphasis on teacher roles in improving student learning and performance is rooted in the evidence that student achievement is significantly associated with the competence of teachers (Ferguson and Brown 2000). Research shows that high-performing teachers create a learning environment that supports and engages students. The contribution of teachers to student learning explains roughly 30% of the variance observed in student performance. However, not everything teachers do in the classroom brings about the desired learning improvement (Hattie 2008). This raises the issue of what then really matters inside the classroom or, simply put, what teachers need to do to ensure effective learning, which consequently increases student outcomes.

Whilst the contribution of teachers is relatively significant, the students contribute mainly to their learning, where 50% of the variance observe is due to themselves, whilst school environment/culture and other factors contribute the remaining 20% (Hattie 2008). Thus, to optimize student learning outcomes, it is vital to focus efforts on improving the specific teaching competencies that positively impact learning. That is the ability of the teachers to optimize students' contribution to their learning. In addition, if schools and the whole system are committed to supporting the key teacher functions that help students to learn effectively, the focus of performance evaluation and professional development for continuous improvement should be on those teacher functions that are known to impact the improvement of student learning and achievement most positively.

1.3 *Students as teacher partners in learning, assessment and teaching*

Whilst the roles of teachers in student learning are critically important, students' active role in their learning remains the most significant factor in ensuring effective learning, assessment and teaching. Thus, one concept that highlights the intersection between teacher roles and student roles in learning and teaching is a student as a partner (Alonzo 2016; Zdravković *et al.* 2018). The ability of the teachers to establish a strong partnership with students in all facets of their learning is highly cited in the literature (Alonzo 2020; Alonzo *et al.* 2021; Bird and Yucel 2015) but least operationalized in the actual classroom setting.

The concept of *students as partners* of teachers in the classroom is implied in many concepts used in the literature to highlight the roles of students. Table 1 presents some of these concepts.

Table 1. Concepts that highlight students as partners in learning and teaching.

Concept	Description
Student engagement	A student must engage with the learning process on behavioral, affective, and cognitive levels. To engage at a behavioral level, the learner must have some degree of participation or effort and be persistent in the learning process. At the affective level of engagement, the learner must have a level of interest in the experience that results in improved motivation and enjoyment, thus establishing a level of commitment. Lastly, the learner must engage on a cognitive level displaying a degree of mental activity, processing thought about the experience that should result in the ability to cognitively process the experience and establish linkages to previous experiences (Groccia 2018, pp. 13–14).
Student agency	"How individuals, in the context of schooling, are able to influence and exert influence and create opportunities in the learning context through intentions, decisions, and actions … how the in-dividual works to enact their agency in relation to the social context (Vaughn *et al.* 2020, p. 727)."
Student responsibility	"Students' causal attributions regarding their learning processes and outcomes (Lau *et al.* 2018, p. 604)." Students view them-selves as responsible to achieve the learning outcomes.
Co-creation	A pedagogical approach that empowers students (Ryan and Tilbury 2013), "occupying the space in between student engagement and partnership, to suggest a meaningful collaboration between students and staff, with students becoming more active participants in the learning process, constructing understanding and resources with academic staff (Bovill *et al.* 2016, p. 197)."

There are many other concepts (e.g., student involvement, student participation, student partnership) that highlight the need for students' active role in learning, assessment and teaching processes. However, many author (Cook-Sather *et al.* 2014; Lau *et al.* 2018; Ryan and Tilbury 2013) argue that for effective learning to occur, we need to go beyond involvement and participation. Rather, teachers need to build the capacity of students to partner with them in learning, assessment and teaching. (Cook-Sather *et al.* 2014) define partnership in learning and teaching as 'a collaborative, reciprocal process through which all participants have the opportunity to contribute equally, although not necessarily in the same ways, to curricular or pedagogical conceptualization, decision making, implementation, investigation, or analysis (pp. 6–7)."

2 ISSUES WITH THE CURRENT FOCUS OF PROFESSIONAL DEVELOPMENT

2.1 *The focus of professional development*

Professional development programs pay great attention to building teacher capability. Whilst it is critically important that teachers build critical contextual skills, defined by teacher professional standards, greater emphasis must be given to teaching skills that build students' capacity to learn, engage in assessment and reflect on their overall experiences. As noted above, teachers contribute 30% only to the observed variance in student learning. Although this figure is just more than half of what students contribute to their learning, teacher contribution can be optimized to support students in developing their critical knowledge and skills in learning, assessment and teaching.

2.2 *Inconsistency in building effective learning environment*

As argued above, building an effective learning environment requires strong partnerships with students and teachers. Thus, the ability of teachers to establish and sustain partnerships with students should be an explicit content of professional development, if not of the teaching standards. The incoherence of skills between what is needed by teachers and what are delivered in PD poses significant issues on the effectiveness of teacher development and actual teaching practices.

A large number of research evidence points to the effectiveness of students as partners of teachers in ensuring learning outcomes. Thus, this construct needs to be operationalized and translated into actual pedagogical and assessment approaches to realize its potential. There has been a continuous theorization of this construct. However, there is paucity in the theorization on how this construct is translated in professional development programs for students and teachers.

3 PRACTICES AND POLICY REQUIREMENTS

3.1 *Professional development for students*

There is emerging research evidence that building students' ability to learn (Mantle 2019; Engeness 2020) and to engage in assessment (Carless and Boud 2018) has significant positive impacts on their learning. These reported studies have explicitly built students' capacity through training or workshop.

The content of the student professional development should be carefully selected to ensure that students will develop theoretical knowledge and practical skills to engage in learning, assessment and teaching activities effectively. Firstly, students need to understand the nature of learning (REFS). Students need to understand the why and how of learning, including learning strategies, approaches to learning, and evidence-based learning practices. Secondly, students need to develop their assessment knowledge and skills, known as assessment literacy, to engage in assessment actively. This assessment literacy covers general assessment knowledge, development of strategies to engage in assessment, active engagement in assessment, monitoring learning progress, engagement in reflective practice, and dispositions (Hannigan *et al.* 2022, p. 1). Thirdly, students need to understand the roles of social-emotional factors in their learning (REFS). The social-emotional constructs include may include but are not limited to adaptability (Holliman *et al.* 2019), buoyancy and goal setting (Burns *et al.* 2019), sense of efficacy (Dorfman and Fortus 2019), burnout (Bakker and Demerouti 2017), and many other constructs. Students' understanding of these factors will develop their capacity to draw on these social-emotional resources when engaging in their learning, particularly when they face a difficult learning situation. This is also particularly important to increase their motivation and sustain their engagement.

3.2 *Professional development for teachers*

To achieve coherence between what knowledge and skills students need to learn effectively and how teachers can support students to acquire those knowledge and build those skills, the content of teacher PD program needs to be reoriented towards building the capacity of students take active role in their learning, engage in assessment and monitor their learning. This does not mean that these knowledge and skills are the only focus of the PD program, but instead, they should form a big part along with other knowledge and skills that ensure effective teaching.

The focus of teacher PD programs should shift from building teacher knowledge and skills for effective teaching to building teacher knowledge and skills for effective student learning. This shift calls for positioning students as teachers' partners and active participants in learning, assessment, and teaching. The PD program should build teachers' capacity to include but not be limited to enhancing students' autonomy, building their learning capacity, increasing their responsibility, and sustaining engagement.

3.3 *Policy support*

Whilst developing a student professional development program can be done by teachers, contextual and policy support is needed to ensure its effectiveness. A cultural shift for a whole-school approach (Alonzo 2020; Alonzo *et al.* 2021) is needed such that school leaders, teachers, students, parents and other stakeholders understand and support the program. A common language about student professional development programs should be clearly agreed upon and established. This language includes the program's principles, aims, content, design, implementation, and evaluation. More importantly, school leaders should develop accessible policy that supports teachers and students develop their partnership in learning, assessment and teaching. A specific framework for student-teacher partnership is needed to develop policy and practice (Starkey 2019). The framework will also inform the content and delivery of PD programs for students and teachers.

4 CONCLUSION

This paper argues for shifting the focus of professional development from teachers to students to build the capacity of students to take active roles in learning, assessment, and teaching. As argued, effective learning requires students to take an active role and higher autonomy in their learning. This means they need to be considered partners in the classroom rather than passive recipients of content and passive participants in learning, assessment, and teaching activities.

We must acknowledge the long-standing argument that we cannot engage students in their learning unless they know how to engage. Also, we have to recognize that students' beliefs, knowledge and skills in learning, assessment and teaching impact their learning outcomes. Hence, like teachers, we need to develop the capacity of students to be proficient in their learning. We need to go beyond telling our students what to do, but instead build their capacity to set and achieve their learning goals, monitor their learning, manage their behaviour, draw on their social-emotional resources to enhance their motivation and engagement, and reflect on their learning experiences to identify areas, both learning contents and learning skills, needing improvement to further improve their learning.

Given the arguments presented above on the role of students in their learning, three provocations that will expand our discourse around effective learning, assessment, and teaching:

- When do we start (year level) building students to engage effectively in learning, assessment and teaching?
- For younger students (or even for all), do we really need explicit training, or can this be embedded whilst learning and teaching?
- If we have an explicit professional development programme for students, how does it look like (design, implementation and evaluation)?

REFERENCES

Alonzo, D. (2016) *Development and Application of a Teacher Assessment for Learning (AfL) Literacy Tool*. University of New South Wales. Available at: http://unsworks.unsw.edu.au/fapi/datastream/unsworks:38345/SOURCE02?view=true.

Alonzo, D. (2020) "Teacher education and professional development in industry 4.0. The case for building a strong assessment literacy," in J.P. Ashadi, A.T. Basikin, and N. Putor (eds.) *Teacher Education and Professional Development in Industry 4.0. 4th International Conference on Teacher Education and Professional Development (InCoTEPD 2019)*. Taylor & Francis Group, pp. 3–10. Available at: https://www.taylorfrancis.com/chapters/edit/10.1201/9781003035978-1/teacher-education-professional-development-industry-4-0-case-building-strong-assessment-literacy-alonzo.

Alonzo, D. *et al.* (2021) "The policy-driven dimensions of teacher beliefs about assessment," *Australian Journal of Teacher Education*, 46(3), pp. 36–52. Available at: https://doi.org/10.14221/ajte.2021v46n3.3.

Alonzo, D., Leverett, J. and Obsioma, E. (2021) "Leading an assessment reform: Ensuring a whole-school approach for decision-making," *Frontiers in Education*, 6. Available at: https://doi.org/10.3389/feduc.2021.631857.

Asih, R., Alonzo, D. and Loughland, T. (2022) "The critical role of sources of efficacy information in a mandatory teacher professional development program: Evidence from Indonesia's underprivileged region," *Teaching and Teacher Education*, 118, p. 103824. Available at: https://doi.org/10.1016/j.tate.2022.103824.

Bakker, A.B. and Demerouti, E. (2017) "Job demands–resources theory: Taking stock and looking forward.," *Journal of Occupational Health Psychology*, 22(3), pp. 273–285. Available at: https://doi.org/10.1037/ocp0000056.

Bird, F.L. and Yucel, R. (2015) "Feedback codes and action plans: building the capacity of first-year students to apply feedback to a scientific report," *Assessment & Evaluation in Higher Education*, 40(4), pp. 508–527. Available at: https://doi.org/10.1080/02602938.2014.924476.

Bovill, C. *et al.* (2016) "Addressing potential challenges in co-creating learning and teaching: overcoming resistance, navigating institutional norms and ensuring inclusivity in student–staff partnerships," *Higher Education*, 71(2), pp. 195–208. Available at: https://doi.org/10.1007/s10734-015-9896-4.

Burns, E.C., Martin, A.J. and Collie, R.J. (2019) "Understanding the role of personal best (PB) goal setting in students' declining engagement: A latent growth model.," *Journal of Educational Psychology*, 111(4), pp. 557–572. Available at: https://doi.org/10.1037/edu0000291.

Cook-Sather, A., Bovill, C. and Felten, P. (2014) *Engaging Students as Partners in Learning and Teaching: A Guide for Faculty*. San Francisco: Jossey Bass. Available at: https://www.wiley.com/en-us/Engaging+Students+as+Partners+in+Learning+and+Teaching:+A+Guide+for+Faculty-p-9781118434581.

Dorfman, B. and Fortus, D. (2019) "Students' self-efficacy for science in different school systems," *Journal of Research in Science Teaching*, 56(8), pp. 1037–1059. Available at: https://doi.org/10.1002/tea.21542.

Engeness, I. (2020) "Teacher facilitating of group learning in science with digital technology and insights into students' agency in learning to learn," *Research in Science & Technological Education*, 38(1), pp. 42–62. Available at: https://doi.org/10.1080/02635143.2019.1576604.

Ferguson, R.F. and Brown, J. (2000) "Certification test scores, teacher quality, and student achievement," in D. Grissmer and M. Ross (eds.) *Analytic Issues in the Assessment of Student Achievement*. National Center for Education Statistics.

Fischer, C. *et al.* (2018) "Investigating relationships between school context, teacher professional development, teaching practices, and student achievement in response to a nationwide science reform," *Teaching and Teacher Education*, 72, pp. 107–121. Available at: https://doi.org/10.1016/j.tate.2018.02.011.

Groccia, J.E. (2018) "What is student engagement?," *New Directions for Teaching and Learning*, 2018(154), pp. 11–20. Available at: https://doi.org/10.1002/tl.20287.

Hattie, J. (2008) *Visible Learning: A Synthesis of Over 800 Meta-Analyses Relating to Achievement*. New York: Routledge. Available at: https://apprendre.auf.org/wp-content/opera/13-BF-References-et-biblio-RPT-2014/Visible Learning_A synthesis or over 800 Meta-analyses Relating to Achievement_Hattie J 2009...pdf.

Holliman, A.J. *et al.* (2019) "Adaptability: Does students' adjustment to university predict their mid-course academic achievement and satisfaction?," *Journal of Further and Higher Education*, 43(10), pp. 1444–1455. Available at: https://doi.org/10.1080/0309877X.2018.1491957.

Lau, C. *et al.* (2018) "Perceived responsibility for learning, self-efficacy, and sources of self-efficacy in mathematics: a study of international baccalaureate primary years programme students," *Social Psychology of Education*, 21(3), pp. 603–620. Available at: https://doi.org/10.1007/s11218-018-9431-4.

Mantle, M.J.H. (2019) "How different reflective learning activities introduced into a postgraduate teacher training programme in England promote reflection and increase the capacity to learn," *Research in Education*, 105(1), pp. 60–73. Available at: https://doi.org/10.1177/0034523718775436.

Popova, A. *et al.* (2022) "Teacher professional development around the world: The gap between evidence and practice," *The World Bank Research Observer*, 37(1), pp. 107–136. Available at: https://doi.org/10.1093/wbro/lkab006.

Ryan, A. and Tilbury, D. (2013) *Flexible Pedagogies: New Pedagogical Ideas*. York. Available at: https://www.advance-he.ac.uk/knowledge-hub/flexible-pedagogies-new-pedagogical-ideas.

Starkey, L. (2019) "Three dimensions of student-centred education: a framework for policy and practice," *Critical Studies in Education*, 60(3), pp. 375–390. Available at: https://doi.org/10.1080/17508487. 2017.1281829.

Vaughn, M. *et al.* (2020) "Student agency in literacy: A systematic review of the literature," *Reading Psychology*, 41(7), pp. 712–734. Available at: https://doi.org/10.1080/02702711.2020.1783142.

Zdravković, M. *et al.* (2018) "Students as partners: Our experience of setting up and working in a student engagement friendly framework," *Medical Teacher*, 40(6), pp. 589–594. Available at: https://doi.org/10.1080/0142159X.2018.1444743.

Strengthening Professional and Spiritual Education through 21st Century Skill Empowerment in Pandemic and Post-Pandemic Era – Arifin et al. (Eds)

Educational institutions policy in times of pandemic: A comparative study between Middle Tennessee State University and Universitas Muhammadiyah Malang

Siti Nur Hidayati
Middle Tennessee State University, USA

Elly Purwanti* & Ahmad Fauzi
Universitas Muhammadiyah Malang, Indonesia

ABSTRACT: The current COVID-19 pandemic has changed the teaching process suddenly and dramatically. Policy formulation needs to be carried out by all educational institutions in dealing with education during the pandemic. The purpose of this study was to describe and compare the policies implemented by Middle Tennessee State University (MTSU) in the United States with the Universitas Muhammadiyah Malang (UMM) in Indonesia. This comparative research used policy documents as data sources. The results of the study informed that all courses at MTSU and UMM switched to distance teaching in March 2020. Limited face-to-face lectures have been implemented at MTSU since August 2020, while at UMM since April 2021. Prior to the pandemic, both MTSU and UMM provided LMS, although both used different platforms (Brightspace at MTSU and CANVAS at UMM). Apart from LMS, lecturers at both campuses may use other platforms, such as Zoom. With the help of the health department, both MTSU and UMM provided the opportunity for COVID-19 vaccination to serve the academic community. Furthermore, at MTSU, a mask mandate is not required for individuals who are fully vaccinated, while UMM instructs every individual on campus to always wear a mask. Financial aids were also distributed by MTSU and UMM for both lecturers and students, although the amount is different. In conclusion, although there are differences in the details, the two campuses have issued policies related to the form of lectures, learning platforms, implementation of health protocols, to financial aid in order to optimize the learning process during the COVID-19 pandemic.

Keywords: College education, COVID-19 pandemic, education policy

1 INTRODUCTION

The COVID-19 pandemic has affected various sectors of human life, including the education sector (Daniel 2020; Rulandari 2020). To minimize the rate of transmission of COVID-19, health protocols are applied in all daily activities and everyone is expected to keep their distance from each other (Chu *et al.* 2020; Yuki *et al.* 2020). Facing these conditions, learning activities have undergone drastic changes, from face-to-face activities to distance learning activities (Azhari and Fajri 2021; Sparrow *et al.* 2020). Online learning is the best alternative in designing distance learning designs in today's digital era (Basilaia and Kvavadze 2020; Kim 2020).

---

*Corresponding Author: purwantielly@ymail.com

DOI: 10.1201/9781003376125-3

Unfortunately, online learning raises other problems in various countries (Abuhammad 2020; Chiu *et al.* 2021). One of the main challenges of online learning is the lack of literacy and skills in implementing educational information technology (Churiyah and Sakdiyyah 2020). Low literacy and skills in using technology will have an impact on the low quality of learning. In addition, online learning is also reported to reduce students' learning motivation and students' engagement with the learning process (Tan 2020). In the end, learning achievement and student academic achievement are less than optimal (Al-Kumaim *et al.* 2021).

Learning without face to face will also have an impact on practicum-based subjects (Holmberg and Bakshi 1982). In practicum-based learning, competency empowerment is not only based on the cognitive domain but also psychomotor. Students are trained to use various laboratory equipment, process some materials, and perform several experimental procedures. Such activities are difficult to realize in online learning because students cannot access the laboratory and materials directly (Gamage *et al.* 2020). One of the programs that involve a lot of practical activities is the biology program.

Several studies were conducted to identify the quality (Vadakalu Elumalai *et al.* 2020; Nugroho *et al.* 2021) or student response to online learning (Ahmad *et al.* 2021; Bączek *et al.* 2021). In addition, most studies are still discussing the negative impacts and barriers to learning during the COVID-19 pandemic in developing countries. Therefore, the purpose of this study is to describe the policy differences between developed countries and Indonesia. This research will provide an overview of the comparison of policies and the application of online learning between developing and developed countries. In addition, the information obtained from this research will provide benefits for institutions in developing countries to adopt policies and lecture designs carried out in developed countries.

2 METHODS

This descriptive study aimed to describe the policy implemented during the COVID-19 pandemic at the Middle Tennessee University, USA and Universitas Muhammadiyah Malang, Indonesia. Data collection was carried out from February 2019 to August 2021. The scope of the study focused on policies issued by campuses related to changes in the lecture process in the pandemic era, changes in lecture design, and policies for providing financial assistance. Research data collection was conducted by direct observation and reviewing documents. The collected data were then grouped and described.

3 RESULTS

3.1 *General policy*

In these challenging times due to the pandemic, Middle Tennessee State University (MTSU) reaffirms its commitment to maintaining quality in its academic programs and services, maximizing options for study and work, and minimizing risks to the health of students, faculty, staff, and society. Like most universities, in March 2020 all courses at MTSU switched to distance teaching to slow the spread of the virus. However, on April 30, 2020, Dr. Sydney McPhee, president of MTSU announced that the campus will resume on-campus learning for the Fall 2020 semester. He formed the COVID-19 Task Force to make recommendations on how to continue the teaching and learning process while maintaining the quality of education and minimizing risk to the community. The task force, which consists of faculty, staff, administrators, and community members, is divided into three committees: Academic, Student Affairs and Services, and Administration and Operations.

March 2020, Spring Break extended from March 9-14 to March 9-22, and March 23 classes resumed online. During this Spring break extension, lecturers prepare for the transition to distance teaching. The Department of Information and Technology provides online teaching short course services for lecturers who need it. Video training can be accessed by lecturers at any time. Only essential personnel are allowed to enter campus. Everyone who enters the building on campus is required to wear a mask. There were three phases in MTSU. Phase 1 (June): Restoring On-Campus Services/Campus Partially Occupied. Phase 2 (July): Increasing On-Campus Services and Campus Employee Footprint. Phase 3 (August): Full Service. On August–November (Fall semester), Offline: Science lab classes, performances, or other activities that need to be done in a special room or involve collaboration with other people. Other classes are conducted online (~60% classes). The laboratory can only be filled at 50% of its original capacity. On January–May 2021, Science lab classes, performances, or other activities that need to be done in a special room or involve collaboration with other people. (~10% offline). The laboratory can only be filled at 50% of its original capacity. Other classes are conducted online (~90% classes). On February, Health Services started to provide COVID-19 vaccination opportunities to serve MTSU faculty, staff, students and retirees. On May–August, Mask mandate is not required for fully vaccinated individual.

At UMM, face-to-face learning was suddenly stopped and changed to distance learning in March 2020. This policy was issued in the middle of the even semester period so that the preparation of lecturers to transform their learning to online learning was not optimal. In the next semester, learning was also conducted online and lecturers were recommended to use the LMS provided by UMM. The limited face-to-face learning policy was implemented in the even semester of 2021. During the pandemic, all people who enter the campus area were required to wear masks even though there are no strict sanctions if anyone violates this policy. For students who enter the campus area, they must show a health certificate UMM also formed a COVID-19 Task Force and held vaccination programs for lecturers and students. The use of masks is still instructed even though the academic community has received the vaccine.

3.2 *Learning design*

Prior to the pandemic, the campus had provided Brightspace, which is a Learning Management System (LMS) software for online learning and teaching for each class. However, not all lecturers use LMS. During the pandemic, besides Brightspace, the campus also provides Zoom and Panopto which are compatible with Brightspace. To complete the Spring semester (March–May, 2020), all lecture materials are delivered via zoom which automatically records all conversations and uploads them to Brightspace. Meanwhile, other homework assignments, such as writing papers, discussions, and discussing current issues, can be collected via ropbox.

Entering the new academic year (August 2020 to May 2021), lectures are divided based on the maximum number of students in each class, and the level and topic. There are five kinds of classes: conventional, web assisted, remote, hybrid, and online. Unlike previous semesters, class types will not change after students register for each semester for the 2020–2021 school year. Students can view their class schedule and type by identifying the location, meeting type, or attribute in the Pipeline.

In the conventional learning, all instructions are carried out at the designated place and in person. In the Pipeline, these classes will have scheduled days/times and assigned classrooms. Class content will be codified or notes provided for students who are unable to attend class due to illness. In the web-assisted learning, instruction is a combination of in person and online. All in-person instruction is carried out during the scheduled class day/time. Students will meet face-to-face for at least 15 hours for grade 3 credits. In Pipeline, these classes will have scheduled days/times and assigned classrooms. The instructor will tell you what day and time the student must be present within the specified class time. Face-to-face class content should be recorded or notes provided for students who are unable to attend class due to illness. In the remote learning, all instructions are delivered online via Zoom, D2L, and/or other university-approved platforms (Microsoft Teams, etc.). In the Pipeline, the class will show the scheduled day/time for the class session but the location will be listed as REMOTE. Class content for synchronous classes will be recorded or notes provided for students who are unable to attend class due to illness.

In the hybrid learning, instruction is a combination of in person and online. All direct instruction is carried out on the scheduled class day/time. Classes will meet in person for no more than 15 hours for class 3 credits. In Pipeline, these classes will have scheduled days/times and assigned classrooms. These classes begin with the letter "D" in the number section. Face-to-face class content should be recorded or notes provided for students who are unable to attend class due to illness. In the online learning, completely online instructions at D2L. In Pipeline, these classes have no scheduled days/times or assigned classrooms. These classes begin with the letter "D" in the number section.

At UMM, online learning is the main alternative for learning during the pandemic. In the even semester of 2020, the campus instructs all lectures to be conducted online. Lecturers are not required to use certain online learning platforms. Before the pandemic occurred, UMM had conducted several online learning trainings. The campus also has LMS that support online learning, i.e. Moodle-based and Canvas-based LMS. However, because the majority of UMM lecturers have not been able to take part in the training, many lecturers have never designed and practiced LMS-based online learning. As a result, in that semester, many lecturers implemented WhatsApp-based learning, although not a few used Zoom or Google meet. In the next semester, online learning still applied at UMM. However, before the semester starts, the lecturers are retrained to implement LMS-based online learning. In the even semester of 2021, UMM began to apply limited face-to-face learning. Lecturers may hold face-to-face learning but the number of students attending is limited to less than 50% of the room's capacity.

3.3 *Aid/stimulus*

On March 25, 2020 United State Congress passed the Coronavirus Aid, Relief, and Economic Security (CARES) Act (2020) to provide fast and direct economic assistance for American workers, families, small business, and industries. As of March 2021, MTSU received $17,299,411 from US Department of Education pursuant to the Certification and Agreement for Emergency Financial Aid Grants to students, one-half of which (8,649,709) has disbursed directly to students in the form of emergency grants. Students received between $500–$1390, based on the eligibility criteria. The other half allowed for institutional expenses such as: (1) Issued refunds to students for housing totaling $1,269,730; (2) Issued refunds to students for meals totaling $631,667; (3) Continued paying student workers who were no longer able to come onto the campus to work for the months of April and May. The students were paid a total of $776,088 for those two months based on their average earnings from January 1, 2020 to March 15, 2020; (4) Technology purchases totaling $269,918, which included the following items used for the transition to remote learning: (a) Zoom license, (b) VPN license, (c) headsets, (d) webcams, (e) computers for use by students; and (6) Purchasing, leasing, or renting additional equipment or software to enable distance learning, or upgrading campus Wi-Fi access or extending open networks to parking lots or public spaces.

UMM also provides financial aid, both to students and lecturers. The students were given a tuition fee discount of Rp. 500,000.00/semester. Students also get internet quota assistance from the government. Lecturers also get internet quota assistance from the government. In addition, lecturers also receive health funding assistance issued every semester. Campus funds are also spent to develop LMS facilities to support the lecture process.

4 DISCUSSION

The COVID-19 pandemic has brought up new problems and challenges in the education field (Daniel 2020; Rulandari 2020). The high rate of transmission of COVID-19 (Ciotti *et al.* 2020; Pascarella *et al.* 2020) causes face-to-face learning activities to be limited to avoidance (Azhari and Fajri 2021; Basilaia and Kvavadze 2020). The application of distance learning using information and communication technology is the main alternative in solving these problems. Unfortunately, the unpreparedness of educational institutions, teacher competencies, student skills, and public facilities has led to new problems in distance learning implementation in the pandemic era.

Although there are various obstacles and limitations, online learning is the best alternative for learning in the pandemic era (Faizah *et al.* 2021; Gamage *et al.* 2020). To optimize the implementation of online learning, clear policies need to be issued by the local government or educational institutions regarding the implementation of online learning activities. The existence of policies can be a basic guide that can help lecturers understand what to do or what not to do.

Similar to policy, learning design is also considered as the main variable determining the quality of learning during a pandemic (Faizah *et al.* 2021; Vadakalu Elumalai *et al.* 2020). Learning design will determine learning activities and evaluation of learning outcomes carried out by lecturers (Ramdiah *et al.* 2019). A good learning design has a clear syntax and still focuses on student learning, even though learning is carried out remotely. Lecturers should also be able to optimize the integration of information and communication technology in the design of learning designs (Manco-Chavez *et al.* 2020).

However, even though policies have been issued by educational institutions and learning designs have been designed by lecturers, various obstacles and challenges can still emerge. The main obstacles and challenges of learning in the pandemic era are often caused by the unpreparedness of lecturers and students to migrate to online learning. This problem is due to the lack of frequency of online learning training before the pandemic occurred and the lack of optimal provision of online learning facilities from institutions and the government. Not surprisingly, many students, teachers, and guardians of students feel the weight of implementing online learning in the current pandemic era.

5 CONCLUSION

The COVID-19 pandemic has caused a transformation in lecture form in various countries, including the United States and Indonesia. Several policies have been issued by campuses, including Middle Tennessee State University and the University of Muhammadiyah Malang, to transform face-to-face lectures into online lectures.

REFERENCES

Abuhammad, S. (2020) "Barriers to distance learning during the COVID-19 outbreak: A qualitative review from parents' perspective," *Heliyon*, 6(11), p. e05482. doi: 10.1016/j.heliyon.2020.e05482.

Ahmad *et al.* (2021) "Student responses during online learning in the Covid-19 pandemic period," in *Journal of Physics: Conference Series*, p. 012125. doi: 10.1088/1742-6596/1764/1/012125.

Al-Kumaim, N. H. *et al.* (2021) "Exploring the impact of the COVID-19 pandemic on university students' learning life: An integrated conceptual motivational model for sustainable and healthy online learning," *Sustainability*, 13(5), p. 2546. doi: 10.3390/su13052546.

Azhari, B. and Fajri, I. (2021) "Distance learning during the COVID-19 pandemic: School closure in Indonesia," *International Journal of Mathematical Education in Science and Technology*. Taylor and Francis Ltd., pp. 1–21. doi: 10.1080/0020739X.2021.1875072.

Bączek, M. *et al.* (2021) "Students' perception of online learning during the COVID-19 pandemic," *Medicine*, 100(7), pp. 1–6. doi: 10.1097/MD.0000000000024821.

Basilaia, G. and Kvavadze, D. (2020) "Transition to online education in schools during a Sars-Cov-2 Coronavirus (COVID-19) pandemic in Georgia," *Pedagogical Research*, 5(4), p. em0060. doi: 10.29333/pr/7937.

Chiu, T. K. F., Lin, T.-J. and Lonka, K. (2021) "Motivating online learning: The challenges of COVID-19 and beyond," *The Asia-Pacific Education Researcher*, 30(3), pp. 187–190. doi: 10.1007/s40299-021-00566-w.

Chu, D. K. *et al.* (2020) "Physical distancing, face masks, and eye protection to prevent person-to-person transmission of SARS-CoV-2 and COVID-19: a systematic review and meta-analysis," *The Lancet*, 395 (10242), pp. 1973–1987. doi: 10.1016/S0140-6736(20)31142-9.

Churiyah, M. and Sakdiyyah, D. A. (2020) "Indonesia education readiness conducting distance learning in COVID-19 pandemic situation," *International Journal of Multicultural and Multireligious Understanding*, 7(6), pp. 491–507. doi: 10.18415/ijmmu.v7i6.1833.

Ciotti, M. *et al.* (2020) "COVID-19 outbreak: An overview," *Chemotherapy*, 64(5–6), pp. 215–223. doi: 10.1159/000507423.

Daniel, S. J. (2020) "Education and the COVID-19 pandemic," *Prospects*. Springer Netherlands, 49(1), pp. 91–96. doi: 10.1007/s11125-020-09464-3.

Faizah, U., Ambarwati, R. and Rahayu, D. (2021) "From offline to online learning: various efforts to secure the learning process during covid-19 outbreaks," *Journal of Physics: Conference Series*, 1747(1), p. 012002. doi: 10.1088/1742-6596/1747/1/012002.

Gamage, K. A. A. *et al.* (2020) "Online delivery of teaching and laboratory practices: Continuity of university programmes during COVID-19 pandemic," *Education Sciences*, 10(10), p. 291. doi: 10.3390/educsci10100291.

Holmberg, R. G. and Bakshi, T. S. (1982) "Laboratory work in distance education," *Distance Education*, 3(2), pp. 198–206. doi: 10.1080/0158791820030203.

Kim, J. (2020) "Learning and teaching online during COVID-19: Experiences of student teachers in an early childhood education practicum," *International Journal of Early Childhood*. Springer, 52(2), pp. 145–158. doi: 10.1007/s13158-020-00272-6.

Manco-Chavez, J. A. *et al.* (2020) "Integration of ICTS and digital skills in times of the pandemic COVID-19," *International Journal of Higher Education*, 9(9), p. 11. doi: 10.5430/ijhe.v9n9p11.

Nugroho, Y. S. *et al.* (2021) "Analysis of learning quality with internet-based distance learning during the COVID-19 pandemic," *IJORER: International Journal of Recent Educational Research*, 2(1), pp. 96–110. doi: 10.46245/ijorer.v2i1.81.

Pascarella, G. *et al.* (2020) "COVID-19 diagnosis and management: A comprehensive review," *Journal of Internal Medicine*, 288(2), pp. 192–206. doi: 10.1111/joim.13091.

Ramdiah, S. *et al.* (2019) "Understanding, planning, and implementation of HOTS by senior high school biology teachers in Banjarmasin-Indonesia," *International Journal of Instruction*, 12(1). Available at: http://www.e-iji.net/dosyalar/iji_2019_1_28.pdf.

Rulandari, N. (2020) "The impact of the COVID-19 pandemic on the world of education in Indonesia," *Ilomata International Journal of Social Science*, 1(4), pp. 242–250.

Sparrow, R., Dartanto, T. and Hartwig, R. (2020) "Indonesia under the new normal: Challenges and the way ahead," *Bulletin of Indonesian Economic Studies*. Taylor and Francis Ltd., 56(3), pp. 269–299. doi: 10.1080/00074918.2020.1854079.

Tan, C. (2020) "The impact of COVID-19 on student motivation, community of inquiry and learning performance," *Asian Education and Development Studies*, 10(2), pp. 308–321. doi: 10.1108/AEDS-05-2020-0084.

Vadakalu Elumalai, K. *et al.* (2020) "Factors affecting the quality of e-learning during the COVID-19 pandemic from the perspective of higher education students," *Journal of Information Technology Education: Research*, 19, pp. 731–753. doi: 10.28945/4628.

Yuki, K., Fujiogi, M. and Koutsogiannaki, S. (2020) "COVID-19 pathophysiology: A review," *Clinical Immunology*, 215(April). doi: 10.1016/j.clim.2020.108427.

Strengthening Professional and Spiritual Education through 21st Century Skill Empowerment in Pandemic and Post-Pandemic Era – Arifin et al. (Eds)
© 2024 The Author(s), ISBN: 978-1-032-45243-2
Open Access: www.taylorfrancis.com, CC BY-NC-ND 4.0 license

Knowledge and attitudes of university students toward COVID-19 pandemic: Analysis based on the background of the science clusters

Utsav Nepal
Kathmandu University, Nepal

Poncojari Wahyono*, H. Husamah, Dwi Setyawan & Ahmad Fauzi
Universitas Muhammadiyah Malang, Indonesia

Diani Fatmawati
Kyung Hee University, Republic of Korea
Universitas Muhammadiyah Malang, Indonesia

ABSTRACT: Education plays a vital role in knowledge achievement to intervene learners' attitude, particularly in dealing with the COVID-19 outbreak. This research aims at describing students' knowledge and attitude levels toward COVID-19 pandemic in Indonesia. The data from this research were collected between March 2020 and April 2020. Malang was the chosen location, which is one of the education cities that was declared a red zone during the pandemic. The respondents were 555 students from one of the private universities in Malang who were studying exact science, social humanity science, as well as biology at the time when research was being conducted. The questionnaire used to gain the data was divided into five parts, i.e., 1) respondents' identity profile, 2) information attaining time, 3) the trust level toward information source, 4) knowledge level, and 5) attitude level. ANOVA was used to analyze the effect of science clusters on students' knowledge and attitude levels toward COVID-19. The results implied that science clusters had significant effect on knowledge and attitude levels. Moreover, majority of students possessed high-level knowledge about COVID-19 as well as had positive attitude toward health authority in gaining COVID-19-related information. Thus, it was suggested to promote more massive information about COVID-19 to the wider society to get a better understanding about the pandemic.

Keywords: Knowledge and attitude level, students' science cluster, COVID-19

1 INTRODUCTION

Everyone must be able to prepare themselves to face the possible outbreak and pandemic (Kain and Fowler 2019; Saravara 2007; World Health Organization 2010), to avoid transmission and other dangerous things (Annas *et al.* 2008; Malm *et al.* 2008; Yang *et al.* 2019). Public awareness and preventive behavior adoption are related to the recent pandemic (Barennes *et al.* 2010; Takahashi *et al.* 2017).

Considering this outbreak and pandemic conditions, the education field plays a vital role (Bakhtiar 2016; Barennes *et al.* 2010; Ernst and Harris 2012; Karlsen *et al.* 2015; Pogreba-Brown *et al.* 2019). Education has the most effective contribution in controlling the pandemic as it has greater and longer effects on disease management compared to technology intervention (Bakhtiar 2016; Kouadio *et al.* 2012; Taylor *et al.* 2015). In the countries-prone infectious diseases, intensive and effective education has been becoming a strong prevention,

---

*Corresponding Author: poncojari@umm.ac.id

DOI: 10.1201/9781003376125-4

detection, and response mechanisms toward the epidemic as soon as the condition occurs (Jones-Konneh *et al.* 2017). This kind of societal health intervention has potentially decreased the incidence and death rate (Albright and Allen 2018). Not only does the limited knowledge about health risks at the time the pandemic occurred contribute to the low awareness, but it also exaggerates the occurrence of infectious diseases which, actually can be avoided. Educational institutions, including all its components as well as students can be the agents to spread health information so that society will be more aware with the health risk along with their efforts to conduct health practices such as prevention, response, and recovery (Jafari *et al.* 2011; Pascapurnama *et al.* 2016, 2018).

Education contributes to an individual's knowledge and attitudes to deal with infectious diseases (Adou *et al.* 2019; Davies *et al.* 2017; Wang *et al.* 2018). The low level of knowledge can be a considerable hindrance to preventive efforts and a caring attitude (Li *et al.* 2019; Della Polla *et al.* 2020; Spjeldnæs *et al.* 2014). Health literacy is the minimum knowledge that must be enacted by people to cope with the pandemic condition, to be aware of the worst situation, and to understand the way they protect themselves and others through basic treatments (Batterham *et al.* 2016; Griffey *et al.* 2014; Okan *et al.* 2020; Sørensen *et al.* 2012)

By knowledge, attitude, and health literacy, several pieces of research addressed these points possessed by students in general. The findings implied that health literacy and self-efficacy are correlated with health behaviors (Barsell *et al.* 2018). Moreover, health literacy is also determined by individual background and department (Elsborg *et al.* 2017), besides demographic characteristics (Rababah *et al.* 2019). Intrapersonal factors and sociocultural environment are also reported as the responsible aspects that support or hinder health literacy (Rosario *et al.* 2017). The provision of health material is positively correlated with the health-promotion-domain-based competence of students (Sukys *et al.* 2017). Likewise, the gender factor has significantly correlated with health literacy level (Uysal *et al.* 2020).

In these two last decades, several pieces of research focused on students' knowledge and attitude were conducted in accordance with various pandemic, i.e., HIV/AIDS (Maswanya 2000; Petros *et al.* 1997; Santos *et al.* 2017; Terry *et al.* 2006), influenza (Akan *et al.* 2010; Huapaya *et al.* 2015; Suresh *et al.* 2011; Zhang 2018), swine flu (Bharadva *et al.* 2018; Rukmanee *et al.* 2014), MERS-CoV (Al-Hazmi *et al.* 2018; Asaad *et al.* 2019), ebola (Koralek *et al.* 2016), tuberculosis (Tachfouti *et al.* 2012), and another infectious diseases in general (Wang *et al.* 2018). However, there was only research related to the knowledge and attitude toward COVID-19 (Zhong *et al.* 2020) in which the research subjects were limited to Chinese residents. In that research, Zhong *et al.* (2020) found that education/health literacy which addressed improving COVID-19 knowledge was helpful for Chinese residents to have an optimistic attitude and conduct appropriate treatment.

Therefore, this research aimed to investigate students' knowledge and attitudes toward the COVID-19 pandemic in Indonesia. The findings of this research are expected to be a reference in formulating steps, planning, and policies to improve society's health literacy, especially those related to the COVID-19 pandemic.

2 METHODS

2.1 *Study design and respondent selection*

This survey research explored the knowledge level as well as students' attitudes toward COVID-19. The students of one of the greatest Indonesian private universities were involved. The data collection was conducted from March until April 2020 when COVID-19 entered Indonesia. The chosen location to conduct this research was Malang, East Java, Indonesia. The respondents were students at a private university in Malang. There were three groups of students chosen as the research respondents, i.e., students from the exact science cluster, students from social science and humanity, and students from Biology Education.

2.2 Data collection instruments and procedures

The questionnaire designed by the authors was used to collect students' COVID-19 knowledge and attitude data. The questionnaire contained five parts, i.e., (1) respondent identity, (2) attaining time profile of COVID-19 related information, (3) respondent's trust level toward information sources, (4) respondent's knowledge level about COVID-19, (5) respondent's attitudes level toward COVID-19.

There were 18 items of knowledge part. In more detail, 14 items accessed respondents' knowledge based on the respondent's rightness in answering the questions. To answer these 14 items, respondents were asked to choose their answer in which the options available were correct, incorrect, and "No idea" answers. Respondents were required to choose the options based on their knowledge. For the correct answer, a score of 1 was given for that item. For the incorrect answer, a score of 0 was given for that item. In addition, the "No idea" answer was categorized as an incorrect answer. The underlying premise for this grouping is that "No idea" response indicated that the respondent does not know the information asked. This is a conservative strategy. Besides the 14 items mentioned, three items in the knowledge part addressed the respondent's knowledge about transmissions, symptoms, and self-protective procedures of COVID-19. Respondents were demanded to choose options available in the three items. There were no wrong choices in the three items as the information contained in the items has been developing to date. The last item was aimed at collecting data about the possible COVID-19-related information expected respondents to gain in advance. Furthermore, in the attitude part, there were 12 items aimed at obtaining respondents' opinions toward COVID-19. The respondents were grouped into positive and negative based on their choice in answering each item. Furthermore, the positive attitude was given a score of 1, and the negative one was given a score of 2.

2.3 Data analysis

The survey analysis data was downloaded in .csv format. The data was then checked by researchers before the Microsoft-Excel-and-SPSS-aided analysis data was performed. The frequency of the information source data was calculated and served in table and radar chart forms. After the responses were scored based on the determined procedure, the profile of information attaining time, knowledge level, and attitude level were presented through crosstab. The Chi-square analysis was performed to observe the significant association between the variable of students' science cluster differences and their responses to the question asked. The Fisher-Freeman-Halton exact test was used as the cell with its expected count less than five. The scores of the 14 items in knowledge level were summed. Likewise, the scores of the 12 attitude items proceeded with the same procedure. The student's knowledge and attitude were grouped into "good", "moderate", and "low" based on Bloom's cut-off point. As the students were able to give the appropriate response for a minimum of 80% of the asked knowledge, the students were categorized as "good". For those whose response properness reached between 60 and 79% were categorized as "moderate", and the "low" level of knowledge was given to those who reached no more than 60% of the appropriate responses given. The frequency of three knowledge level groups of each science cluster was presented in a pie chart. To go further, the student's knowledge scores were analyzed using one-way analysis of variance (ANOVA) to analyze the effect of science clusters on the knowledge and attitude of students toward COVID-19. The significant results were tested using the Least Significant Difference (LSD) with a significance level of 5%.

3 RESULTS

3.1 *Respondent characteristics*

Table 1 presents the number and the identity distribution of respondents. Of 598 respondents who filled the questionnaire, there were 555 which could be the data source. This is because the 43 remaining respondents fulfilled the questionnaire with an inappropriate identity as was instructed in the questionnaire. The 555 respondents comprised 118 exact students, 290 Biology Education students, and 147 social humanity students. The student's years of respondents were similar, i.e., 25.9% of the year 2016, 25.2% of the year 2017, 27.2% of the year 2018, and 21.6% of the year 2019. In addition, the percentage of male students was 24.3% and the female students was 75.7%.

Table 1. The demographic profile of respondents.

Variable	Cluster			Total n (%)
	Exact Science	Biology Education	Social Humanity	
Student's year				
2016	14 (11.9%)	76 (26.2%)	54 (36.7%)	144 (25.9%)
2017	31 (26.3%)	85 (29.3%)	24 (16.3%)	140 (25.2%)
2018	28 (23.7%)	80 (27.6%)	43 (29.3%)	151 (27.2%)
2019	45 (38.1%)	49 (16.9%)	26 (17.7%)	120 (21.6%)
Gender				
Male	48 (40.7%)	42 (14.5%)	45 (30.6%)	135 (24.3%)
Female	70 (59.3%)	248 (85.5%)	102 (69.4%)	420 (75.7%)

3.2 *The profile of information attaining time*

Table 2 informs the time students gained the information about COVID-19. As many as 91.4% of students had heard about COVID-19 before the report of the first patient found in Indonesia. Moreover, 85.9% of students have obtained information about the preventive

Table 2. The profile of COVID-19 information attaining time of teacher candidate students.

Variable	Cluster			Total	*P*-value
	Exact science	Biology Education	Social Humanity		
Heard about COVID-19 before it entered Indonesia					0.07
No	4 (3.4%)	30 (10.3%)	14 (9.5%)	48 (8.6%)	
Yes	114 (96.6%)	260 (89.7%)	133 (90.5%)	507 (91.4%)	
Heard about the preventive procedure for COVID-19 transmission					0.003
No	26 (22.0%)	28 (9.7%)	24 (16.3%)	78 (14.1%)	
Yes	92 (78.0%)	262 (90.3%)	123 (83.7%)	477 (85.9%)	
Heard about the preventive protocol for COVID-19 transmission during traveling					0.565
No	52 (44.1%)	127 (43.8%)	72 (49.0%)	251 (45.2%)	
Yes	66 (55.9%)	163 (56.2%)	75 (51.0%)	304 (54.8%)	
Found unclear or bewildering information					0.001
No	53 (44.9%)	115 (39.7%)	85 (57.8%)	253 (45.6%)	
Yes	65 (55.1%)	175 (60.3%)	62 (42.2%)	3.2 (54.4%)	

procedure for disease transmission. However, only 54.8% of students have obtained information about traveling protocols in the COVID-19 pandemic situation. Furthermore, as many as 54.4% of students stated that they need more information about COVID-19. The percentage of students who have heard about preventive procedures for COVID-19 transmission was the only profile that was not significantly associated with student science clusters ($P = 0.565$).

3.3 *The profile of the information source*

The students' knowledge level about COVID-19 was explored in this research. The students need information sources to comprehend this new disease. Social media was the greatest source referred by students of the three science clusters to gain information about COVID-19 (78.6%) (Figure 1). 58.9% of students preferred the internet as the source to get COVID-19 information, while 37.8% voted for television as the media they chose.

The interesting feature of the results gained was that social media was the highest frequent source chosen by students, but only 27.6% of students trusted the information they gained from this source. The most reliable source for the students was health workers (64.7%) followed by television (41.6%) and internet (19%). This trend was also obviously shown as the students responded to the question about the information source, they would choose in case they have questions about COVID-19. Moreover, it is also an interesting fact that even though health workers were the most reliable source for students, only 3.6% of them gained COVID-19 information from this source.

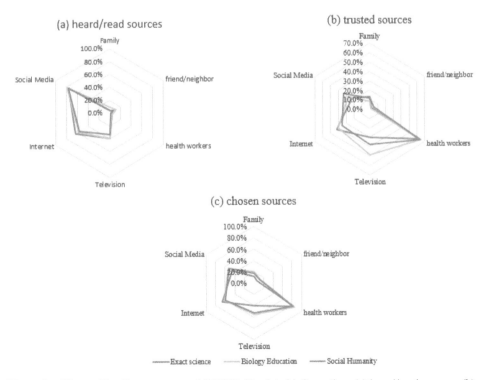

Figure 1.   The profile of source types of COVID-19 related information: (a) heard/read sources; (b) trusted sources; (c) chosen sources for further expected COVID-19 information (n = 555, each respondent was allowed to choose more than one option).

3.4 Student knowledge about COVID-19

Table 3 shows the results of one-way ANOVA about the effect of students' science clusters on the student's knowledge level about COVID-19. The results of the analysis informed that the science cluster differences had a significant effect on their knowledge level [F (2,552) = 6.038, P = 0.003, $\eta p2$ = 0.021]. The results of the post hoc test informed that the exact science cluster students have significantly higher knowledge than the other clusters. Contrarily, the students of the social humanity cluster possessed the lowest knowledge level even though that was insignificantly different compared to Biology Education students.

Table 3. The summary of one-way ANOVA test results of the effect of science clusters on COVID-19 knowledge level.

	Sum of Squares	df	Mean Square	F	Sig.	Partial Eta Squared
Between Groups	42.266	2	21.133	6.038	0.003	0.021
Within Groups	1931.940	552	3.500			
Total	1974.205	554				

3.5 Students' attitude toward COVID-19

Table 4 shows the ANOVA test results of the effect of science clusters on students' attitudes. The analysis results informed that the science cluster differences gave significant differences toward their attitudes [F(2,552) = 3.197, P = 0.042, $\eta p2$ = 0.011]. Meanwhile, the post hoc test results implied that the highest knowledge was possessed by the students of the exact science cluster even though there was no significant difference among biology education students. Contrarily, social humanity cluster students were placed in the lowest position in terms of their attitude compared to the other science clusters.

Table 4. The summary of one-way ANOVA test results of the effect of science clusters on student's attitude level.

	Sum of Squares	df	Mean Square	F	Sig.	Partial Eta Squared
Between Groups	14.799	2	7.400	3.197	0.042	0.011
Within Groups	1277.752	552	2.315			
Total	1292.551	554				

4 DISCUSSION

Higher education institution has a great number of students which is potentially the centre of disease during the pandemic period. Thus, students' knowledge and attitudes during this period are important to be suited to the guidance of the Ministry of Health Authority. This study investigated students' knowledge and attitudes related to COVID-19. It is expected to give scientific support in terms of aiding health sector authority to develop the strategy and health education campaign to prevent COVID-19 transmissions. The respondents of this study showed that the number of female respondents was higher than male (Table 1). This is in line with the previous study which focused on COVID-19 (Zhong *et al.* 2020) and addressed other outbreaks (Akan *et al.* 2010; Al-Hazmi *et al.* 2018; Latiff *et al.* 2012; Lin *et al.* 2011). Meanwhile, Akan *et al.* (2010) stated that in the health education field, gender difference is not a variable that is connected with disease infection risk. In addition, this research also compared students' knowledge and attitude levels based on three different science clusters, i.e., biology education, exact, as well as social humanity sciences. This was supported by several previous studies which have a similar topic and different subject (Akan *et al.* 2010; Huapaya *et al.* 2015; Suresh *et al.* 2011; Zhang 2018).

The majority of students know that the world has been facing the COVID-19 pandemic, even though this majority also did not have adequate knowledge about preventive protocol for COVID-19. Moreover, there was several bewildering information for them to find. Generally, the students had heard the information about the COVID-19 outbreak before the first case was found in Indonesia. This is due to the rapid development of information contained in various sources such as mass media (Kamate *et al.* 2009; Paek *et al.* 2008) as well as social media. Paek *et al.* (2008) inferred that in their endeavor to spread pandemic-related information, the government should cooperate with mass media as well as television to educate society. Furthermore, today's generation is familiar with social media so influencer can be an effective alternative partner for the government to spread important information related to the COVID-19 pandemic in social media. This is due to the massive development of social media in this era (Al-Aufi *et al.* 2017; Khan and Idris 2019; Moon and Bai 2020). The ability to gain information about the disease is one of health literacy. This ability is vital to verify if the information gained is valid and referred from credible sources (Ghaddar *et al.* 2012; Khan and Idris 2019).

COVID-19-related information often appears on the front page every platform of social media like X (previously Twitter), Instagram, Line, and so forth. Yet, not all students care to access that information. Students' major subject affects their care in accessing information related to the disease. Biology Education is the social major in which the scope is education, yet the students get exact courses. This is the underlying reason for the good knowledge about COVID-19 preventive procedures possessed by Biology Education students. On the other hand, most of the exact science students knew about COVID-19-related information before the disease entered Indonesia (96.6%). This is because exact and biology education students have a good ability to read and process scientific information (Budd 2020) compared to social science students. However, the students, at the same time, experienced a lack of knowledge of preventive procedures for COVID-19. In addition, some students are confused about comprehending information. This should be one of governmental concern as well as higher institutions to be able to provide important and clear information about COVID-19 as the crucial role of higher education in educating students facing nowadays' outbreak condition (Sarma and Oliveras 2013; Van *et al.* 2010).

The next finding of this research implied that the COVID-19-related information source referred to by students was social media. In accordance with the fact that the Indonesian government through the Ministry of Education has replaced the teaching-learning system in the classroom with online learning, the students have much more time to interact online which enabled them to gain COVID-19-related information from social media. The development of digital technology has inevitably made social media more popular among youths (Halsall *et al.* 2019; Moon and Bai 2020; Tezci and İçen 2017). Moreover, students are keen on gaining information from social media as its interesting visualization (text combinations, images, videos, and audio) (Oelze 2019; Paulsen and Taekke 2013; Tezci and İçen 2017). Generally, students realize that the information obtained from social media is not reliable. The most reliable as their information source was health workers. This is an indicator of the success of health literacy in terms of students' ability to choose credible and trusted information sources (Sørensen *et al.* 2012).

Choosing a trusted information source is an aspect of health literacy even though there are also other important aspects such as comprehending, assessing, and using information which should be mastered by an individual (DeWalt *et al.* 2004; Ranaweera 2017; Sørensen *et al.* 2012). The exact major students showed the highest correct percentage in. nine of the 13 questions (Table 3) compared to biology education and social humanity students. This can be connected with students' exact backgrounds who already have basic concepts about science compared to social students who never get the materials in their field. Similarly, the research results served in Table 4 showed that the exact students possessed a significant difference in knowledge level about COVID-19 compared to social humanity students. Sukys, Cesnaitiene, and Ossowsky (2017) claimed that the administration of health materials has positively correlated with the health-promotion-domain-based competence of students. Besides, students' academic ability is the other determinant factor that influences their knowledge (Banik and Kumar 2019; Erich and Popescu 2010; Shao and Purpur 2016; Soleymani 2014) as well as intrapersonal and socio-cultural factors of the institution which can be support or hindrance in health literacy.

The student's knowledge level of COVID-19 cases shows that, generally, the students had moderate knowledge about COVID-19. Poorly, Biology Education and social humanity students have a similarly low level of COVID-19 knowledge. This study's results showed that Biology Education and social humanity students could not understand COVID-19-related information. In other words, the health knowledge of these two science clusters' students was low, yet the students had enough knowledge about COVID-19. Good health literacy is a minimum knowledge that should be possessed by an individual in facing a pandemic situation the awareness of the worst situation and the ability to comprehend self-and-others protection procedures (Batterham et al. 2016; Griffey et al. 2014; Okan et al. 2020; Sørensen et al. 2012). Health literacy and self-efficacy are correlated to health behaviors (Barsell et al. 2018), individual backgrounds and departments (Elsborg et al. 2017), as well as demographic characteristics (Rababah et al. 2019). Thus, education institution has a great responsibility to direct students to improve their health literacy in dealing with the recent COVID-19 outbreak in Indonesia.

Furthermore, the average students have a good understanding of the cause, symptoms, and self-protection. As high as 87.9% of students agreed that COVID-19 transmissions can occur through cough and sneeze with the symptoms of fever (96.8%) and sore throat (80%). This has influenced the way students do self-protection by avoiding crowded places (91.2%), more often hand washing (90.3%), and using a mask in traveling (85.4%). This also related to the success of health promotion conducted by both central and district governments through mass media, television (Akan et al. 2010), and even social media influencers, which were coordinated by the Ministry of Communication and Information and cooperated with related ministries such as the Health Ministry. The information served by the government contained suggestions about preventive steps. For instance, do not go outside as no important thing to do, implement social distancing, use a mask, and more often wash hands, as well as explain the symptoms that appear in a COVID-19-infected person. Likewise, Zhong et al. (2020) reported that the use of masks outside the house and avoiding crowded places during the COVID-19 period in China has been well obeyed by the citizens. This indicated that the students' attitude has been cultured by the government suggestions which widely spread through social media.

This study also revealed that science and biology education students expected to gain more information about the consequences and treatment after being infected by COVID-19 compared to the social humanity students. The underlying premise for this is that the exact and Biology Education students learn closer topics to COVID-19 compared to those who learned in social humanity science so they have more interest in learning about this disease (Sukys et al. 2017). Conversely, social humanity science students have lower curiosity about this topic as they do not tend to gain the information.

The majority of students either from exact science or biology education stated that they needed further information about COVID-19, while 70% of students from social humanity science gave a negative attitude. The negative attitude shown by social humanity cluster students about their curiosity toward the COVID-19 issue was caused by the lack of health literacy empowerment in the learning process of social humanity science students. Health literacy is considerably correlated with the education process in school (Gazmararian et al. 2005; Kickbusch and Maag 2008; Peterson et al. 2001). Besides that, the other interesting negative attitude was their ignorance to avoid their infected friends (52.8%). This is harmful if the students still interact with the COVID-19-positive patient as it will exaggerate the condition. Therefore, the knowledge of self-protective procedure to avoid this disease need to be improved. Moreover, the results of the students' attitude assessment showed that the average students performed positive attitude. This proved that the students' attitude toward COVID-19 in Indonesia has been good even though it needs to be improved in terms of knowledge aspect (Zhong *et al.* 2020).

Finally, all students had a positive attitude with a percentage of more than 50%. However, each group of science clusters showed a significant difference. A significant difference was shown in the attitude of social humanity cluster students towards COVID-19 compared to those who took exact science as their major field. This proved that attitude is strongly affected by knowledge (Zhong *et al.* 2020). Hence, the results of this study showed that the intervention in health education will be more effective if it is targeted to students from various clusters so that it increases COVID-19 knowledge as the program is designed specifically by the government through higher education. The success of understanding implementation and attitude toward COVID-19 will considerably determine the success of Indonesia in facing the recent COVID-19 pandemic.

5 CONCLUSION

Students from the exact science cluster performed better understanding of COVID-19 compared to biology education and social humanity science clusters. Yet, the social humanity science cluster was placed at the lowest level in both knowledge and attitudes. Furthermore, the better the COVID-19 comprehension owned by students; the more positive attitude arises to deal with the recent COVID-19 pandemic. Thus, it is suggested to promote more massive information about COVID-19 to wider society so that they will get a better understanding of this disease and have a better attitude in coping with this pandemic.

REFERENCES

Adou, A. A. *et al.* (2019) "Travelers' knowledge, attitudes, and behavior related to infectious diseases in Italy," *PLoS ONE*, 14(4), pp. 1–12. doi: 10.1371/journal.pone.0215252.

Akan, H. *et al.* (2010) "Knowledge and attitudes of university students toward pandemic influenza: a cross-sectional study from Turkey," *BMC Public Health*, 10(1), p. 413. doi: 10.1186/1471-2458-10-413.

Al-Aufi, A. S., Al-Azri, H. M. and Al-Hadi, N. A. (2017) "Perceptions of Information Literacy Skills among Undergraduate Students in the Social Media Environment," *International Information and Library Review*. Taylor and Francis Ltd., 49(3), pp. 163–175. doi: 10.1080/10572317.2017.1293416.

Al-Hazmi, A. *et al.* (2018) "Knowledge, attitude and practice of secondary schools and university students toward Middle East Respiratory Syndrome epidemic in Saudi Arabia: A cross-sectional study," *Saudi Journal of Biological Sciences. King Saud University*, 25(3), pp. 572–577. doi: 10.1016/j.sjbs.2016.01.032.

Albright, A. E. and Allen, R. S. (2018) "HPV misconceptions among college students: The role of health literacy," *Journal of Community Health*. Springer US, 43(6), pp. 1192–1200. doi: 10.1007/s10900-018-0539-4.

Annas, G. J., Mariner, W. K. and Parmet, W. E. (2008) *Pandemic Preparedness: The Need for a Public Health Approach.* Washington, D.C.

Asaad, A. M. *et al.* (2019) "Exploring knowledge and attitude toward middle east respiratory syndrome-coronavirus (MERS-CoV) among university health colleges' students, Saudi Arabia: A cross-sectional study," *Revista Brasileira de Gestao e Desenvolvimento Regional*, 15(1), pp. 37–43. doi: 10.3844/ajidsp.2019.37.43.

Bakhtiar, T. (2016) "Optimal intervention strategies for cholera outbreak by education and chlorination," *IOP Conference Series: Earth and Environmental Science*, 31(1). doi: 10.1088/1755-1315/31/1/012022.

Banik, P. and Kumar, B. (2019) "Impact of Information Literacy Skill on Students' Academic Performance in Bangladesh," *International Journal of European Studies*, 3(1), p. 27. doi: 10.11648/j.ijes.20190301.15.

Barennes, H. *et al.* (2010) "Paradoxical risk perception and behaviours related to Avian Flu outbreak and education campaign, Laos," *BMC Infectious Diseases*, 10(March 2006). doi: 10.1186/1471-2334-10-294.

Barsell, D. J. *et al.* (2018) "Examining health behaviors, health literacy, and self-efficacy in college students with chronic conditions," *American Journal of Health Education*. Routledge, 49(5), pp. 305–311. doi: 10.1080/19325037.2018.1486758.

Batterham, R. W., Beauchamp, A. and Osborne, R. H. (2016) *Health literacy*. Second Edi, *International Encyclopedia of Public Health*. Second Edi. Elsevier. doi: 10.1016/B978-0-12-803678-5.00190-9.

Bharadva, N. *et al.* (2018) "Knowledge, attitude and practice regarding swine flu (H1N1) among people accompanying patients of a tertiary health care," *National Journal of Community Medicine*, 9(1), pp. 1–4.

Budd, S. (2020) *Science Literacy in a Changing World: Covid-19 and CitySprouts Youth, CitySprouts.*

Davies, C. *et al.* (2017) "'Is it like one of those infectious kind of things?' The importance of educating young people about HPV and HPV vaccination at school," *Sex Education*. Routledge, 17(3), pp. 256–275. doi: 10.1080/14681811.2017.1300770.

DeWalt, D. A. *et al.* (2004) "Literacy and health outcomes: A systematic review of the literature," *Journal of General Internal Medicine*, 19(12), pp. 1228–1239. doi: 10.1111/j.1525-1497.2004.40153.x.

Elsborg, L., Krossdal, F. and Kayser, L. (2017) "Health literacy among Danish university students enrolled in health-related study programmes," *Scandinavian Journal of Public Health*, 45(8), pp. 831–838. doi: 10.1177/1403494817733356.

Erich, A. and Popescu, C. (2010) "The impact of information literacy in the academic education environment," *Library and Information Science*, (14), pp. 150–161.

Gazmararian, J. A. *et al.* (2005) "Public health literacy in America: An ethical imperative," *American Journal of Preventive Medicine*, 28(3), pp. 317–322. doi: 10.1016/j.amepre.2004.11.004.

Ghaddar, S. F. *et al.* (2012) "Adolescent health literacy: The importance of credible sources for online health information," *Journal of School Health*, 82(1), pp. 28–36.

Griffey, R. T. *et al.* (2014) "Is low health literacy associated with increased emergency department utilization and recidivism?," *Academic Emergency Medicine*, 21(10), pp. 1109–1115. doi: 10.1111/acem.12476.

Halsall, T. *et al.* (2019) "Evaluation of a Social Media Strategy to Promote Mental Health Literacy and Help-Seeking in Youth," *Journal of Consumer Health on the Internet*. Routledge, 23(1), pp. 13–38. doi: 10.1080/15398285.2019.1571301.

Huapaya, J. A. *et al.* (2015) "Knowledge, practices and attitudes toward volunteer work in an influenza pandemic: cross-sectional study with Peruvian medical students," *Medwave*, 15(04), pp. e6136–e6136. doi: 10.5867/medwave.2015.04.6136.

Jafari, N. *et al.* (2011) "Prevention of communicable diseases after disaster: A review," *Journal of Research in Medical Sciences*, 16(7), pp. 956–962.

Jones-Konneh, T. E. C. *et al.* (2017) "Intensive education of health care workers improves the outcome of ebola virus disease: Lessons learned from the 2014 outbreak in Sierra Leone," *Tohoku Journal of Experimental Medicine*, 243(2), pp. 101–105. doi: 10.1620/tjem.243.101.

Kain, T. and Fowler, R. (2019) "Preparing intensive care for the next pandemic influenza," *Critical Care*. Critical Care, 23(1), pp. 1–9. doi: 10.1186/s13054-019-2616-1.

Kamate, S. K. *et al.* (2009) "Public knowledge, attitude and behavioural changes in an Indian population during the Influenza A (H1N1) outbreak," *The Journal of Infection in Developing Countries*, 4(01), pp. 007–014. doi: 10.3855/jidc.501.

Karlsen, H. *et al.* (2015) "Teaching outbreak investigation to undergraduate food technologists," *British Food Journal*, 117(2), pp. 766–778. doi: 10.1108/BFJ-02-2014-0062.

Khan, M. L. and Idris, I. K. (2019) "Recognise misinformation and verify before sharing: a reasoned action and information literacy perspective," *Behaviour and Information Technology*. Taylor and Francis Ltd., 38 (12), pp. 1194–1212. doi: 10.1080/0144929X.2019.1578828.

Kickbusch, J. and Maag, D. (2008) "Health Literacy," *International Encyclopedia of Public Health*, 3, pp. 204–211.

Koralek, T. *et al.* (2016) "Lessons from Ebola: Sources of outbreak information and the associated impact on UC Irvine and Ohio University College students," *PLoS Currents Outbreaks*, 1, pp. 1–18. doi: 10.1371/currents.outbreaks.f1f5c05c37a5ff8954f38646cfffc6a2.

Kouadio, I. K. *et al.* (2012) "Infectious diseases following natural disasters: Prevention and control measures," *Expert Review of Anti-Infective Therapy*, 10(1), pp. 95–104. doi: 10.1586/eri.11.155.

Latiff, L. A. *et al.* (2012) "Pandemic influenza a (H1N1) and its prevention: A cross sectional study on patients' knowledge, attitude and paractice among patients attending Primary Health Care Clinic in Kuala Lumpur, Malaysia," *Global Journal of Health Science*, 4(2). doi: 10.5539/gjhs.v4n2p95.

Li, L. *et al.* (2019) "Evaluation of health education interventions on Chinese factory workers' knowledge, practices, and behaviors related to infectious disease," *Journal of Infection and Public Health.* King Saud Bin Abdulaziz University for Health Sciences, 12(1), pp. 70–76. doi: 10.1016/j.jiph.2018.09.004.

Lin, Y. *et al.* (2011) "Knowledge, Attitudes and Practices (KAP) related to the Pandemic (H1N1) 2009 among Chinese general population: a Telephone survey," *BMC Infectious Diseases*, 11(1), p. 128. doi: 10.1186/1471-2334-11-128.

Malm, H. *et al.* (2008) "Ethics, pandemics, and the duty to treat," *American Journal of Bioethics*, 8(8), pp. 4–19. doi: 10.1080/15265160802317974.

Maswanya, E. (2000) "Knowledge and attitudes toward AIDS among female college students in Nagasaki, Japan," *Health Education Research*, 15(1), pp. 5–11. doi: 10.1093/her/15.1.5.

Moon, S. J. and Bai, S. Y. (2020) "Components of digital literacy as predictors of youth civic engagement and the role of social media news attention: the case of Korea," *Journal of Children and Media.* Routledge. doi: 10.1080/17482798.2020.1728700.

Oelze, M. (2019) "#HashtagPedagogies: Improving Literacy and Course Relevance through Social Media Metaphors," *Change: The Magazine of Higher Learning.* Informa UK Limited, 51(6), pp. 8–16. doi: 10.1080/00091383.2019.1674076.

Okan, O., Sørensen, K. and Messer, M. (2020) *COVID-19: A Guide to Good Practice on Keeping People Well Informed, The Conversation.*

Paek, H.-J. *et al.* (2008) "Public support for government actions during a Flu Pandemic: Lessons learned from a statewide survey," *Health Promotion Practice*, 9(4_suppl), pp. 60S–72S. doi: 10.1177/1524839908322114.

Pascapurnama, D. N. *et al.* (2016) "Prevention of tetanus outbreak following natural disaster in Indonesia: Lessons learned from previous disasters," *Tohoku Journal of Experimental Medicine*, 238(3), pp. 219–227. doi: 10.1620/tjem.238.219.

Pascapurnama, D. N. *et al.* (2018) "Integrated health education in disaster risk reduction: Lesson learned from disease outbreak following natural disasters in Indonesia," *International Journal of Disaster Risk Reduction.* Elsevier Ltd, 29(July 2017), pp. 94–102. doi: 10.1016/j.ijdrr.2017.07.013.

Paulsen, M. and Taekke, J. (2013) "Social media and teaching: Education in the new media environment," in *Defending democracy.* Oslo and Akershus University College, pp. 1–13.

Peterson, F. L., Cooper, R. J. and Laird, J. M. (2001) "Enhancing teacher health literacy in school health promotion: A vision for the new millennium," *Journal of School Health*, 71(4), pp. 138–144. doi: 10.1111/j.1746-1561.2001.tb01311.x.

Petros, B., Belayneh, S. and Mekonnen, Y. (1997) "AIDS and college students in Addis Ababa: a study of knowledge, attitude and behavior," *Ethiopian Journal of Health Development*, 11(2), pp. 115–123. 22 ref.

Pogreba-Brown, K., Ernst, K. and Harris, R. (2012) "Teaching epidemiology concepts experientially: A 'real' foodborne outbreak in the classroom," *Public Health Reports*, 127(5), pp. 549–555. doi: 10.1177/003335491212700512.

Della Polla, G. *et al.* (2020) "Knowledge, attitudes, and practices towards infectious diseases related to travel of community pharmacists in Italy," *International journal of environmental research and public health*, 17(6). doi: 10.3390/ijerph17062147.

Rababah, J. A. *et al.* (2019) "Health literacy: Exploring disparities among college students," *BMC Public Health.* BMC Public Health, 19(1), pp. 1–11. doi: 10.1186/s12889-019-7781-2.

Ranaweera, P. (2017) "Importance of information literacy skills for an information literate society," *National Institute of Library & Information Sciences, University of Colombo*, pp. 1–13. doi: 10.1017/CBO9781107415324.004.

Rosario, C. *et al.* (2017) "An examination of ecological predictors of health literacy in black college students," *Journal of American College Health.* Taylor & Francis, 65(6), pp. 423–431. doi: 10.1080/07448481.2017.1341894.

Rukmanee, N. *et al.* (2014) "Knowledge, attitudes and practices (KAP) regarding influenza a (H1N1) among a population living along Thai-Myanmar border, Ratchaburi Province, Thailand," *Southeast Asian Journal of Tropical Medicine and Public Health*, 45(4), pp. 825–833.

Santos, V. P. *et al.* (2017) "Is there a relationship between students' knowledge of HIV/AIDS ways of transmission and their responses regarding their proximity to people living with HIV/AIDS?," *Ciencia e Saude Coletiva*, 22(8), pp. 2745–2752. doi: 10.1590/1413-81232017228.25892015.

Saravara, S. I. I. I. J. (2007) "Business continuity planning in higher education due to pandemic outbreaks business continuity planning in higher education due to pandemic outbreaks: A faculty perspective," *Journal of Security Education*, 2(3), pp. 41–51. doi: 10.1300/J460v02n03.

31

Sarma, H. and Oliveras, E. (2013) "Implementing HIV/AIDS Education: Impact of teachers' training on HIV/AIDS education in Bangladesh," *Journal of Health, Population and Nutrition*, 31(1), pp. 20–27. doi: 10.3329/jhpn.v31i1.14745.

Shao, X. and Purpur, G. (2016) "Effects of information literacy skills on student writing and course performance," *Journal of Academic Librarianship*. Elsevier Ltd, 42(6), pp. 670–678. doi: 10.1016/j.acalib.2016.08.006.

Soleymani, M. R. (2014) "Investigating the relationship between information literacy and academic performance among students," *Journal of Education and Health Promotion*. Medknow Publications & Media Pvt Ltd, 3, p. 95. doi: 10.4103/2277-9531.139677.

Sørensen, K. *et al.* (2012) "Health literacy and public health: A systematic review and integration of definitions and models," *BMC Public Health*. BioMed Central Ltd, 12(1), pp. 1–13. doi: 10.1186/1471-2458-12-80.

Spjeldnæs, A. O., Kitua, A. Y. and Blomberg, B. (2014) "Education and knowledge helps combating malaria, but not degedege: A cross-sectional study in Rufiji, Tanzania," *Malaria Journal*, 13(1), pp. 2–11. doi: 10.1186/1475-2875-13-200.

Sukys, S., Cesnaitiene, V. J. and Ossowsky, Z. M. (2017) "Is health education at university associated with students' health literacy? evidence from cross-sectional study applying HLS-EU-Q," *BioMed Research International*, 2017. doi: 10.1155/2017/8516843.

Suresh, P. S., Thejaswini, V. and Rajan, T. (2011) "Factors associated with 2009 pandemic influenza A (H1N1) vaccination acceptance among university students from India during the post-pandemic phase," *BMC Infectious Diseases*, 11, pp. 1–8. doi: 10.1186/1471-2334-11-205.

Tachfouti, N. *et al.* (2012) "The impact of knowledge and attitudes on adherence to tuberculosis treatment: A case-control study in a moroccan region," *Pan African Medical Journal*, 12(1), pp. 1–8. doi: 10.11604/pamj.2012.12.52.1374.

Takahashi, S. *et al.* (2017) "Public preventive awareness and preventive behaviors during a major influenza epidemic in Fukui, Japan," *Journal of Infection and Public Health*. King Saud Bin Abdulaziz University for Health Sciences, 10(5), pp. 637–643. doi: 10.1016/j.jiph.2017.04.002.

Taylor, D. L. *et al.* (2015) "The impact of water, sanitation and hygiene interventions to control cholera: A systematic review," *PLoS ONE*, 10(8), pp. 1–19. doi: 10.1371/journal.pone.0135676.

Terry, P. E. *et al.* (2006) "An examination of knowledge, attitudes and practices related to HIV/AIDS prevention in Zimbabwean university students: Comparing intervention program participants and non-participants," *International Journal of Infectious Diseases*, 10(1), pp. 38–46. doi: 10.1016/j.ijid.2004.10.007.

Tezci, E. and İçen, M. (2017) "High school students' social media usage habits," *Journal of Education and Practice*. Online, 8(27), pp. 99–108.

Uysal, N., Ceylan, E. and Koç, A. (2020) "Health literacy level and influencing factors in university students," *Health and Social Care in the Community*, 28(2), pp. 505–511. doi: 10.1111/hsc.12883.

Van, D. *et al.* (2010) "University life and pandemic influenza: Attitudes and intended behaviour of staff and students towards pandemic (H1N1) 2009," *BMC Public Health*, 10(130), pp. 1–9. doi: 10.1186/1471-2458-10-130.

Wang, M. *et al.* (2018) "Impact of health education on knowledge and behaviors toward infectious diseases among students in Gansu Province, China," *BioMed Research International*, 2018(6397340), pp. 1–12. doi: 10.1155/2018/6397340.

World Health Organization (2010) *Pandemic influenza preparedness and response: A WHO guidance document.* Geneva, Switzerland: World Health Organization: Global Influenza Programme.

Yang, J. *et al.* (2019) "Associations between hand hygiene education and self-reported hand-washing behaviors among Korean adults during MERS-CoV outbreak," *Health Education and Behavior*, 46(1), pp. 157–164. doi: 10.1177/1090198118783829.

Zhang, Z. (2018) "Knowledge, attitudes and practices towards seasonal influenza and vaccine among private high school students in Connecticut," *ACM International Conference Proceeding Series*, pp. 12–17. doi: 10.1145/3290818.3290829.

Zhong, B.-L. *et al.* (2020) "Knowledge, attitudes, and practices towards COVID-19 among Chinese residents during the rapid rise period of the COVID-19 outbreak: A quick online cross-sectional survey," *International Journal of Biological Sciences*, 16(10), pp. 1745–1752. doi: 10.7150/ijbs.45221.

Strengthening Professional and Spiritual Education through 21st Century Skill Empowerment in Pandemic and Post-Pandemic Era – Arifin et al. (Eds)
© 2024 The Author(s), ISBN: 978-1-032-45243-2
Open Access: www.taylorfrancis.com, CC BY-NC-ND 4.0 license

Unveiling health-related knowledge, attitude, and practice among school principals in the post-pandemic landscape

Atok Mitachul Hudha*
Universitas Muhammadiyah Malang, Indonesia

Mahomed Sidique Abdul Cadar Dadá
Universidade Eduardo Mondlane, Mozambique

H. Husamah, Moh. Mirza Nuryady & Ahmad Fauzi
Universitas Muhammadiyah Malang, Indonesia

ABSTRACT: Amid the evolving landscape of the post-pandemic era, understanding the COVID-19 knowledge, attitude, and practice (KAP) levels among school principals assumes critical importance. This research examines the COVID-19-related knowledge, attitude, and practice (KAP) levels of school principals in Indonesia. A survey involving 251 principals utilized the SKAPCOV-19 questionnaire. Findings indicated predominant "good" knowledge but variations in attitudes and practices. Gender and educational background significantly impacted practice levels; females and higher-educated principals exhibited better adherence. While no substantial differences emerged in knowledge and attitude across demographics, these insights highlight the imperative of bridging the knowledge-practice gap. Tailored educational strategies, leveraging demographic strengths, can amplify pandemic management. Collaborative efforts among institutions are essential for fostering a resilient educational environment and broader community health.

Keywords: health literacy, pandemic management, school principals

1 INTRODUCTION

In an ever-changing landscape marked by the global outbreak and subsequent shift away from the pandemic status (Cucinotta and Vanelli 2020), the preparedness of individuals has emerged as a crucial factor, necessitating a proactive approach to mitigate potential outbreaks (Kain and Fowler 2019). This entails not only the avoidance of transmission but also a comprehensive understanding of associated risks and the cultivation of preventive measures (Tang *et al.* 2020; Yang *et al.* 2019). The significance of public consciousness and the embrace of precautionary behaviors has particularly resonated in the wake of recent pandemic experiences (Barennes *et al.* 2010; Takahashi *et al.* 2017).

As these global shifts prompt a reevaluation of preparedness strategies in the post-pandemic era, it becomes evident that key figures within communities play a paramount role. Among these, school principals stand out as pivotal decision-makers, responsible for shaping policies that directly influence the safety and well-being of their students and staff (Reyes-Guerra *et al.* 2021). Navigating the complex landscape of the pandemic, these educational leaders not only contribute to transmission reduction but also guide the implementation of preventive measures and risk management (Dare and Saleem 2022). Their leadership gains particular significance in light of the public awareness imperative and the embrace of precautionary behaviors,

---

*Corresponding Author: atok1964@gmail.com

underscoring the essential role they play in fostering a secure learning environment amid evolving health challenges (Dare and Saleem 2022; Reyes-Guerra *et al.* 2021).

Amid the complexities of disease management, the nexus of Knowledge, Attitude, and Practice (KAP) has consistently emerged as a linchpin in effective response strategies (Saefi *et al.* 2020). The intimate interplay between these three components underpins the ability to navigate health challenges with precision. A robust Knowledge base empowers individuals with accurate information, dispelling misconceptions and promoting informed decision-making (Beca-Martínez *et al.* 2022; Gupta *et al.* 2021). Concomitantly, cultivating a proactive Attitude fosters a culture of vigilance and compliance, propelling the adoption of recommended preventive measures. However, it is the translation of this awareness into Practice that forges a tangible impact, fortifying not only personal protection but collectively influencing the trajectory of an outbreak. In the context of the post-pandemic landscape, the significance of KAP resonates deeply, serving as an enduring framework for disease preparedness and response.

The proactive involvement of school principals in shaping effective pandemic response strategies underscores the critical importance of Knowledge, Attitude, and Practice (KAP) in decision-making processes. An astute understanding of the virus's dynamics, transmission vectors, and preventive protocols equips educational leaders with the insight needed to craft comprehensive policies that safeguard the well-being of their school communities. In this context, an informed Knowledge base enables leaders to anticipate challenges, while a positive Attitude cultivates a culture of adherence to protocols and a resilient outlook. This, coupled with sound Preventive Practices, forms the bedrock for informed policy formulation, reinforcing the value of KAP as a guiding framework across diverse contexts beyond educational institutions.

As scholarly inquiries surged over the past two decades, a multitude of investigations delved into students' awareness and dispositions within the context of diverse pandemics, such as HIV/AIDS (Maswanya 2000; Santos *et al.* 2017; Terry *et al.* 2006), (Akan *et al.* 2010; Huapaya *et al.* 2015; Zhang 2018), swine flu (Bharadva *et al.* 2018; Rukmanee *et al.* 2014), MERS-CoV (Al-Hazmi *et al.* 2018; Asaad *et al.* 2019), and Ebola (Koralek *et al.* 2016), (Tachfouti *et al.* 2012). However, despite this extensive body of work, a notable research gap remains: there is a dearth of comprehensive investigations that scrutinize the knowledge and attitudes surrounding COVID-19 across broader populations. This glaring gap prompts our current research endeavor, which seeks to transcend geographical confines and intricately examine the knowledge, attitudes, and practices of school principals in relation to COVID-19 within a post-pandemic landscape.

2 METHODS

2.1 *Study design and respondent selection*

This research employs a survey approach conducted in Indonesia, involving school principals as the primary respondents. To ensure a sample that is both representative and aligned with the research objectives, purposive sampling is adopted as the sampling technique. The inclusion criteria for this study sample were Indonesian citizens, assigned to schools in the Indonesian region, not currently suffering from a serious illness, and willing to voluntarily become research respondents. The school principals involved are principals assigned to elementary to high school. On the other hand, the exclusion criteria in this study were principals who had been dismissed, retired, suspended, had their schools closed, and did not provide complete demographic information. The research location encompasses various regions across Indonesia, facilitating the collection of diverse data that can effectively capture a broader contextual perspective. Because this research was a quick survey assessing knowledge and perception, the target population is 1000 school principals (estimated based on data held by the head of the Department of Biology Education Masters). Therefore, the minimum sample size was 214 (a confidence level of 90% and alpha 0.1).

2.2 Data collection instrument and procedures

The research utilized the SKAPCOV-19 questionnaire, which was developed by Saefi et al. (2020)and has been validated in that studies. The questionnaire is structured into four distinct sections: (a) Demographic Profile, (b) knowledge domain, (c) attitude domain, and (d) practice domain. The analysis of the instrument revealed noteworthy findings. All items in the SKAPCOV-19 questionnaire exhibited a CVI (Content Validity Index) exceeding 0.80, signifying their indispensable role in measuring KAP. Factor analysis further affirmed the significance of each item, with all demonstrating a significant value of λ ($p < 0.05$). The item reliability within the three domains was robust, with Real RMSE values of 0.97 for attitudes, 0.98 for knowledge, and 0.99 for practices, accompanied by a separation index value > 0.20. The rating scale diagnostic affirmed that response choices didn't bewilder respondents. The Andrich threshold and logit values of response categories displayed a monotonic increase in line with anticipated trends. Additionally, the instrument exhibited favorable infit and outfit MNSQ fit statistics, indicative of its overall reliability. The questionnaire was transformed into an online questionnaire using Google Form. After that, the Google form link was distributed to school principals via WhatsApp. Based on the minimum sample size that has been calculated and taking into account the possibility that all questionnaires will not be filled out, the questionnaire link was sent to at least around 300 school principals.

2.3 Data analysis

For the purpose of analysis, the obtained knowledge, attitudes, and practice scores underwent summation across all respective items, subsequently transformed into a scale ranging from 0 to 100. These cumulative scores were then dichotomized into two categories, namely "good" and "poor," employing the Bloom cut-off point as a reference. A respondent's score was deemed "good" if they demonstrated accuracy in answering at least 80% of the items, while scores falling below this threshold were classified as "poor." To ascertain disparities in mean scores predicated on demographic characteristics, a one-way ANOVA was conducted. The predetermined significance level for this study was set at 0.05, underscoring the threshold for determining statistically significant variations.

2.4 Ethical approval

This research has been approved by the Department of Biology Education Masters, Universitas Muhammadiyah Malang. Respondents' involvement in the survey was voluntary. The personal information of the respondents was kept confidential and anonymous. In addition, participants have confirmed their willingness to participate in this KAP survey.

3 RESULTS

3.1 Respondent characteristics

A total of 251 school principals completed the questionnaire, constituting the study's respondent base. Based on the estimated number of school principals who have received the questionnaire link, the response rate for this survey was 83.67%. The demographic profile of the respondents, as outlined in Table 1, indicates a balanced gender distribution, with 123 (49.0%) males and 128 (51.0%) females participating. In terms of age, 78 (31.1%) respondents were aged 50 years or younger, while 173 (68.9%) were above 50 years old. Regarding educational background, 168 (66.9%) respondents held Bachelor's degrees, while 83 (33.1%) possessed Master's or Doctoral degrees. Furthermore, the years of experience as a school principal varied, with 116 (46.2%) having served for 0–5 years, 82 (32.7%) for 6–10 years, and 53 (21.1%) for over 10 years. As for school characteristics, the distribution indicated 53.0% (n = 133) were from elementary schools, 17.9% (n = 45) from middle schools, and

Table 1. The demographic profile of respondents.

Variables	Group	Frequency (n)	Percentage (%)
Gender	Male	123	49.0
	Female	128	51.0
Age	less than equal to 50 years	78	31.1
	more than 50 years	173	68.9
Last education	Bachelor	168	66.9
	Master/Doctoral	83	33.1
Years as School Principal	0–5 years	116	46.2
	6–10 years	82	32.7
	above 10 years	53	21.1
School Level of Service	Elementary School	133	53.0
	Middle School	45	17.9
	High School	73	29.1
School Status	Private School	108	43.0
	Public School	143	57.0
School Location	City	130	51.8
	District	121	48.2

29.1% (n = 73) from high schools. In terms of school status, 43.0% (n = 108) represented private schools, while 57.0% (n = 143) were from public schools. Additionally, the location of the schools revealed a fairly even split, with 51.8% (n = 130) situated in cities and 48.2% (n = 121) in districts. These demographics provide a comprehensive snapshot of the respondent profile, enabling a nuanced exploration of the subsequent results.

3.2 The profile of KAP scores

The analysis of the respondents' Knowledge, Attitude, and Practice (KAP) categories, as presented in Table 2, reveals that 81.70% of school principals demonstrated a "good" level of knowledge, while 18.30% fell into the "poor" category. In terms of Attitude, 47.00% exhibited a "good" disposition, whereas 53.00% displayed a "poor" attitude. Additionally, concerning Practice, 34.70% showcased "good" implementation of health protocols, while a notable 65.30% demonstrated a "poor" practice level. These findings offer valuable insights into the distribution of KAP among school principals, laying the foundation for a comprehensive assessment of their responses and behaviors within the context of the pandemic.

Table 2. Distribution of School Principals' Knowledge, Attitude, and Practice (KAP) Categories.

	Category	
Variables	Good	Poor
Knowledge	81.70%	18.30%
Attitude	47.00%	53.00%
Practice	34.70%	65.30%

3.3 The effect of demographic variables on KAP scores

The ANOVA results investigating the influence of demographic variables on the knowledge, attitude, and practice (KAP) scores of school principals are summarized in Table 3. In terms of knowledge, the ANOVA results reveal that none of the demographic variables yielded statistically significant differences in the knowledge scores. This suggests that factors such as gender, age, last education, years of experience as a school principal, school level of service, school status, and location did not significantly influence the variation observed in knowledge scores among the school principals.

Table 3. ANOVA results for knowledge, attitude, and practice scores (* $p < 0.05$).

		Mean			F		
Variables	Group	Knowledge	Attitude	Practice	Knowledge	Attitude	Practice
Gender	Male	72.13	73.33	82.22	0.077	2.033	5.509*
	Female	71.74	69.69	87.30			
Age	less than equal to 50 years	72.93	70.77	80.61	0.931	0.136	6.809*
	more than 50 years	71.48	71.79	86.71			
Last education	Bachelor	72.12	71.07	83.04	0.148	0.199	5.426*
	Master/Doctoral	71.55	72.29	88.40			
Years as School Principal	0 – 5 years	70.35	71.38	84.16	6.873	0.662	0.543
	6 – 10 years	75.54	73.17	86.43			
	above 10 years	69.81	69.06	83.73			
School Level of Service	Elementary School	73.18	70.68	85.71	1.980	0.217	0.682
	Middle School	71.23	72.44	82.22			
	High School	70.09	72.33	84.76			
School Status	Private School	70.83	70.37	83.80	1.899	0.560	0.649
	Public School	72.77	72.31	85.58			
School Location	City	72.22	72.46	87.69	0.183	0.638	7.656*
	District	71.63	70.41	81.71			

Moving on to the attitude domain, the ANOVA outcomes indicate that gender, age, last education, years of experience as a school principal, school level of service, school status, and location did not have a statistically significant impact on the attitude scores of the school principals. These findings suggest that these demographic variables did not lead to substantial differences in the attitudes displayed by school principals regarding COVID-19.

However, within the practice domain, the ANOVA analyses present a distinct picture. Gender, age, and last education emerged as noteworthy factors influencing the variation in practice scores among school principals. Specifically, female principals exhibited higher practice scores compared to their male counterparts. Additionally, school principals aged more than 50 years and those with a Master's or Doctoral education demonstrated higher practice scores. The location of the school also played a significant role, with those situated in cities showcasing higher practice scores. In contrast, variables such as years of experience as a school principal, school level of service, and school status did not contribute significantly to the observed differences in practice scores.

4 DISCUSSION

The insights gleaned from the finding in this study offer valuable perspectives into the knowledge, attitude, and practice (KAP) levels among school principals concerning COVID-19. While the WHO has declared the end of the COVID-19 pandemic, this research remains crucial. Besides, surveys involving school principals have been challenging to come by during the pandemic, especially in Indonesia. The data from such surveys can provide valuable insights into both education and public health. The COVID-19 pandemic has presented both challenges and opportunities to evaluate and document unprecedented conditions. By examining the KAP among school principals, information regarding the effectiveness of public health communication, policy translation and implementation, and crisis management within educational institutions can be explored. These findings can serve as fundamental knowledge to prepare for the future, ensuring the readiness of educational institutions in responding to future pandemics. The survey findings can also serve as a basis for the development of targeted training programs aimed at enhancing the capacity of school principals to respond to health emergencies.

The predominance of a "good" knowledge category among school principals regarding COVID-19 underscores a commendable understanding of essential facets related to the disease (Saefi et al. 2020). This robust knowledge base can be attributed to concerted educational efforts, information dissemination, and training initiatives that have effectively equipped school leaders with the necessary insights to comprehend the virus's transmission, symptoms, and preventive measures (Fauzi et al. 2020). However, the presence of a "poor" knowledge category necessitates targeted interventions to address specific knowledge gaps that may hinder effective decision-making and communication.

The prevalence of a "good" knowledge category among school principals is pivotal in shaping informed decision-making and policy formulation. An adept understanding of COVID-19 transmission dynamics, symptoms, preventive measures, and risk factors empowers school leaders to make timely and well-informed choices (Saefi et al. 2020). A robust knowledge foundation serves as a basis for crafting effective communication strategies, instituting appropriate health protocols, and accurately assessing risks (Beca-Martínez et al. 2022; Gupta et al. 2021). Furthermore, it bolsters confidence in both administrative actions and interactions with staff, students, and parents, fostering a sense of trust and credibility.

Within the realm of attitude, the near-even split between "good" and "poor" categories signifies a diversity of perceptions and sentiments among school principals. This variation in attitude can be influenced by a myriad of factors, including personal beliefs, cultural contexts, and information sources (Saefi et al. 2020). While "good" attitudes reflect an optimistic and proactive stance towards the pandemic, "poor" attitudes might stem from concerns about uncertainties, misconceptions, or challenges associated with its management. Addressing this divergence warrants tailored communication strategies and targeted interventions to foster a more unified and informed attitude towards COVID-19.

The varied distribution between "good" and "poor" attitudes among school principals holds implications for fostering a conducive environment within educational institutions. A "good" attitude signifies an optimistic and proactive stance, which in turn influences interactions and decision-making processes. A positive attitude can drive proactive efforts in adopting and promoting health protocols, thereby inspiring a collaborative and unified approach to pandemic management (Sondakh et al. 2022). On the other hand, addressing the "poor" attitude category is crucial to dispel misconceptions, address concerns, and encourage alignment with recommended guidelines.

The distribution of practice scores, with a substantial proportion categorized as "poor," signals potential challenges in translating knowledge and attitudes into tangible actions. Factors such as resource constraints, logistical barriers, or even resistance to change might contribute to this divergence between knowledge and practice. Recognizing that "good" practice levels signify a willingness to implement health protocols effectively, efforts should be directed towards addressing the barriers that hinder consistent practice among the "poor" category.

The observed distribution of "good" and "poor" practice scores underscores the necessity of translating knowledge and attitudes into tangible actions (Saefi et al. 2020). Implementing health protocols consistently and effectively is instrumental in safeguarding the well-being of students, staff, and the wider community. "Good" practice reflects a commitment to operationalizing policies, thereby reducing the risk of transmission and fostering a safe and secure learning environment (Beca-Martínez et al. 2022). Addressing the challenges within the "poor" practice category demands targeted interventions to overcome barriers, enhance resource availability, and promote behavioral change.

Collectively, these findings underscore the need for a comprehensive approach to enhance KAP levels among school principals. This involves not only strengthening knowledge dissemination but also fostering a conducive environment for translating knowledge and attitudes into impactful practices. Targeted interventions should address specific knowledge gaps, dispel misconceptions, and promote consistent practice adherence. Additionally, engaging school principals in open dialogues and collaborative decision-making processes can help align attitudes and actions, fostering a shared sense of responsibility in mitigating the pandemic's impact within the educational sphere.

The insights gleaned from the findings presented in Table 3 offer valuable perspectives into the potential influence of various demographic variables on the knowledge, attitude, and practice (KAP) scores of school principals concerning COVID-19. The absence of statistically significant differences in knowledge scores across demographic variables suggests that factors such as gender, age, educational background, years of experience as a school principal, school level of service, school status, and location did not yield discernible variations in knowledge levels. This could be attributed to the effectiveness of uniform educational campaigns and information dissemination strategies that have successfully equipped school principals with consistent levels of COVID-19-related knowledge. The uniformity in knowledge underscores the efficacy of equitable educational interventions aimed at ensuring a foundational understanding of the pandemic's various dimensions.

Similarly, the absence of significant differences in attitude scores across demographic variables suggests that gender, age, educational background, years of experience as a school principal, school level of service, school status, and location did not significantly influence the formation of attitudes towards COVID-19. This could point towards a shared sense of responsibility and collective understanding of the pandemic's gravity across diverse demographic groups. The uniformity in attitudes emphasizes the potential impact of unified communication efforts in fostering a collective awareness and response to the challenges posed by the pandemic.

The identification of statistically significant differences in practice scores across certain demographic variables highlights intriguing patterns in the implementation of health protocols. The findings indicate that female school principals, those aged more than 50 years, and those with higher educational levels exhibited "good" practice levels to a greater extent. This could be attributed to a range of factors including heightened awareness, adherence to guidelines, and a sense of responsibility stemming from life experiences and educational attainment. Furthermore, the geographic context appears to play a role, as urban schools demonstrated higher practice scores. This could be indicative of better resource availability, heightened risk perception, or community dynamics in urban settings.

The statistically significant difference in practice scores based on gender introduces an intriguing dimension to the study. The finding that female school principals exhibited higher "good" practice levels compared to their male counterparts suggests a potential gender-related variation in the implementation of health protocols. This might be attributed to factors such as attention to detail, communication, and empathy—traits often associated with effective crisis management. Female school principals' heightened engagement in practice aligns with broader discussions around gender roles in caregiving and community well-being. Previous research outside of the pandemic context also provides information that gender can influence learning leadership (Ross *et al.* 2020). In addition, gender is also reported to have an effect on the coping dimension (Graves *et al.* 2021). Addressing this discrepancy could involve exploring tailored approaches to encouraging male school principals to enhance their practice adherence through targeted communication and awareness initiatives.

The observation of statistically significant differences in practice scores based on the educational background of school principals adds an additional layer of complexity. The finding that those with higher educational levels (Master's/Doctoral degrees) exhibited higher "good" practice levels underscores the potential influence of educational attainment on behavior during the pandemic. This finding is in line with previous reports which stated that education is closely related to the level of health knowledge which has a positive impact on a healthy lifestyle (Hoffmann and Lutz 2019). Other studies have also found that higher educational attainment will have a better level of health than people whose education level is below them (Raghupathi and Raghupathi 2020). Individuals with advanced degrees might possess a heightened ability to comprehend the gravity of health protocols, translate knowledge into action, and effectively communicate guidelines to their school communities. Addressing the gap between practice levels of different educational backgrounds could involve tailored educational interventions that ensure that school principals across various educational levels are equally equipped to lead in times of crisis.

The observed variations in practice scores underscore the multifaceted nature of adherence to health protocols and highlight the importance of tailoring interventions based on demographic characteristics. Incorporating gender-sensitive and education-specific approaches into intervention strategies can foster equitable and effective practice adherence, ultimately contributing to a safer and more resilient educational environment in the face of the pandemic.

5 CONCLUSION

In conclusion, the comprehensive examination of school principals' knowledge, attitude, and practice (KAP) levels in relation to COVID-19 yields valuable insights into the challenges and opportunities in pandemic management within educational contexts. The uniformity in knowledge and attitudes highlights the success of widespread educational initiatives, while the observed variations in practice underscore the importance of targeted interventions to bridge the gap between knowledge and action. To enhance KAP levels, tailored approaches should be employed, capitalizing on the strengths of female school principals in practice adherence and harnessing the potential of those with higher educational backgrounds.

This study calls for ongoing collaborative efforts among educational institutions, health authorities, and policy makers to reinforce the dissemination of accurate and timely information, fostering a collective sense of responsibility in pandemic response. Recognizing the potential of school principals as pivotal figures in influencing their school communities, implementing gender-sensitive strategies and educational interventions that promote the translation of knowledge and attitudes into effective practices is paramount. By cultivating a unified understanding of COVID-19, fostering proactive attitudes, and enabling consistent practice, educational institutions can not only navigate the current challenges more effectively but also build a resilient foundation for future health crises.

REFERENCES

Akan, H. *et al.* (2010) "Knowledge and attitudes of university students toward pandemic influenza: a cross-sectional study from Turkey," *BMC Public Health*, 10(1), p. 413. doi: 10.1186/1471-2458-10-413.

Al-Hazmi, A. *et al.* (2018) "Knowledge, attitude and practice of secondary schools and university students toward Middle East Respiratory Syndrome epidemic in Saudi Arabia: A cross-sectional study," *Saudi Journal of Biological Sciences*. King Saud University, 25(3), pp. 572–577. doi: 10.1016/j.sjbs.2016.01.032.

Asaad, A. M. *et al.* (2019) "Exploring knowledge and attitude toward middle east respiratory syndrome-coronavirus (MERS-CoV) among university health colleges' students, Saudi Arabia: A cross-sectional study," *Revista Brasileira de Gestao e Desenvolvimento Regional*, 15(1), pp. 37–43. doi: 10.3844/ajidsp.2019.37.43.

Barennes, H. *et al.* (2010) "Paradoxical risk perception and behaviours related to Avian Flu outbreak and education campaign, Laos," *BMC Infectious Diseases*, 10(March 2006). doi: 10.1186/1471-2334-10-294.

Beca-Martínez, M. T. *et al.* (2022) "Compliance with the main preventive measures of COVID-19 in Spain: The role of knowledge, attitudes, practices, and risk perception," *Transboundary and Emerging Diseases*, 69 (4). doi: 10.1111/tbed.14364.

Bharadva, N. *et al.* (2018) "Knowledge, attitude and practice regarding swine flu (H1N1) among people accompanying patients of a tertiary health care," *National Journal of Community Medicine*, 9(1), pp. 1–4.

Cucinotta, D. and Vanelli, M. (2020) "WHO declares COVID-19 a Pandemic," *Acta Bio-Medica: Atenei Parmensis*, 91(1), pp. 157–160. doi: 10.23750/abm.v91i1.9397.

Dare, P. S. and Saleem, A. (2022) "Principal leadership role in response to the pandemic impact on school process," *Frontiers in Psychology*, 13. doi: 10.3389/fpsyg.2022.943442.

Fauzi, A. *et al.* (2020) "Exploring COVID-19 literacy level among biology teacher candidates," *Eurasia Journal of Mathematics, Science and Technology Education*, 16(7), p. em1864. doi: 10.29333/ejmste/8270.

Graves, B. S. *et al.* (2021) "Gender differences in perceived stress and coping among college students," *PLoS ONE*. Edited by A. R. Dalby, 16(8), p. e0255634. doi: 10.1371/journal.pone.0255634.

Gupta, P. K., Kumar, A. and Joshi, S. (2021) "A review of knowledge, attitude, and practice towards COVID-19 with future directions and open challenges," *Journal of Public Affairs*, 21(4). doi: 10.1002/pa.2555.

Hoffmann, R. and Lutz, S. U. (2019) "The health knowledge mechanism: evidence on the link between education and health lifestyle in the Philippines," *The European Journal of Health Economics*, 20(1), pp. 27–43. doi: 10.1007/s10198-017-0950-2.

Huapaya, J. A. *et al.* (2015) "Knowledge, practices and attitudes toward volunteer work in an influenza pandemic: cross-sectional study with Peruvian medical students," *Medwave*, 15(04), pp. e6136–e6136. doi: 10.5867/medwave.2015.04.6136.

Kain, T. and Fowler, R. (2019) "Preparing intensive care for the next pandemic influenza," *Critical Care*. Critical Care, 23(1), pp. 1–9. doi: 10.1186/s13054-019-2616-1.

Koralek, T. *et al.* (2016) "Lessons from Ebola: Sources of outbreak information and the associated impact on UC Irvine and Ohio University College students," *PLoS Currents Outbreaks*, 1, pp. 1–18. doi: 10.1371/currents.outbreaks.f1f5c05c37a5ff8954f38646cfffc6a2.

Maswanya, E. (2000) "Knowledge and attitudes toward AIDS among female college students in Nagasaki, Japan," *Health Education Research*, 15(1), pp. 5–11. doi: 10.1093/her/15.1.5.

Raghupathi, V. and Raghupathi, W. (2020) "The influence of education on health: an empirical assessment of OECD countries for the period 1995–2015," *Archives of Public Health*, 78(1), p. 20. doi: 10.1186/s13690-020-00402-5.

Reyes-Guerra, D. *et al.* (2021) "Confronting a compound crisis: The school principal's role during initial phase of the COVID-19 pandemic," *Frontiers in Education*, 6. doi: 10.3389/feduc.2021.617875.

Ross, P. T. *et al.* (2020) "Considerations for using race and ethnicity as quantitative variables in medical education research," *Perspectives on Medical Education*, 9(5), pp. 318–323. doi: 10.1007/S40037-020-00602-3.

Rukmanee, N. *et al.* (2014) "Knowledge, attitudes and practices (KAP) regarding influenza a (H1N1) among a population living along Thai-Myanmar border, Ratchaburi Province, Thailand," *Southeast Asian Journal of Tropical Medicine and Public Health*, 45(4), pp. 825–833.

Saefi, M. *et al.* (2020) "Validating of Knowledge, Attitudes, and Practices questionnaire for prevention of COVID-19 infections among undergraduate students: A RASCH and factor analysis," *Eurasia Journal of Mathematics, Science and Technology Education*, 16(12), p. em1926. doi: 10.29333/ejmste/9352.

Santos, V. P. *et al.* (2017) "Is there a relationship between students' knowledge of HIV/AIDS ways of transmission and their responses regarding their proximity to people living with HIV/AIDS?," *Ciencia e Saude Coletiva*, 22(8), pp. 2745–2752. doi: 10.1590/1413-81232017228.25892015.

Sondakh, J. J. S. *et al.* (2022) "Indonesia medical students' knowledge, attitudes, and practices toward COVID-19," *Heliyon*, 8(1), p. e08686. doi: 10.1016/j.heliyon.2021.e08686.

Tachfouti, N. *et al.* (2012) "The impact of knowledge and attitudes on adherence to tuberculosis treatment: A case-control study in a moroccan region," *Pan African Medical Journal*, 12(1), pp. 1–8. doi: 10.11604/pamj.2012.12.52.1374.

Takahashi, S. *et al.* (2017) "Public preventive awareness and preventive behaviors during a major influenza epidemic in Fukui, Japan," *Journal of Infection and Public Health*. King Saud Bin Abdulaziz University for Health Sciences, 10(5), pp. 637–643. doi: 10.1016/j.jiph.2017.04.002.

Tang, D., Comish, P. and Kang, R. (2020) "The hallmarks of COVID-19 disease," *PLoS Pathogens*, 16(5), pp. 1–24. doi: 10.1371/journal.ppat.1008536.

Terry, P. E. *et al.* (2006) "An examination of knowledge, attitudes and practices related to HIV/AIDS prevention in Zimbabwean university students: Comparing intervention program participants and non-participants," *International Journal of Infectious Diseases*, 10(1), pp. 38–46. doi: 10.1016/j.ijid.2004.10.007.

Yang, J. *et al.* (2019) "Associations between hand hygiene education and self-reported hand-washing behaviors among Korean adults during MERS-CoV outbreak," *Health Education and Behavior*, 46(1), pp. 157–164. doi: 10.1177/1090198118783829.

Zhang, Z. (2018) "Knowledge, attitudes and practices towards seasonal influenza and vaccine among private high school students in Connecticut," *ACM International Conference Proceeding Series*, pp. 12–17. doi: 10.1145/3290818.3290829.

Strengthening Professional and Spiritual Education through 21st Century Skill Empowerment in
Pandemic and Post-Pandemic Era – Arifin et al. (Eds)
© 2024 The Author(s), ISBN: 978-1-032-45243-2
Open Access: www.taylorfrancis.com, CC BY-NC-ND 4.0 license

Biotechnology hands-on activity concept: Is it easy to conquer?

Diani Fatmawati
Universitas Muhammadiyah Malang, Indonesia
Kyung Hee University, South Korea

Arce D. Bellere
Kyung Hee University, South Korea
Central Bicol State University of Agriculture, Philippines

Moh. Mirza Nuryady*
Universitas Muhammadiyah Malang, Indonesia

ABSTRACT: Mastering basic concepts of biotechnology laboratory work is a crucial competency to be achieved by biology education students. This research is aimed at observing the competency level of biology education students in comprehending their basic concepts of biotechnology laboratory work. The population of this survey research was students in the sixth semester of the Department of Biology Education, University of Muhammadiyah, Malang. The sample was 71 students comprising 14 male and 57 female students. The collected data were analyzed descriptively to determine student ability in mastering basic concepts of biotechnology laboratory work. Moreover, the differences among sample groups based on two parameters (gender and academic level) were determined using Kruskal Walis and Mann-Whitney Tests as the prerequisite for parametric statistics were not met. The findings showed that the basic competency of the majority of biology education students was low (no more than 40% of students answered the question correctly). In addition, even though there was no difference between male and female students in mastering biotechnology laboratory work concepts, they were significantly different based on an academic level. Based on the findings, it was suggested for lecturers as well as laboratory instructors to design a proper learning strategy to boost student ability in achieving basic concepts of biotechnology laboratory work.

Keywords: Biology Education Student, Biotechnology Knowledge, Biotechnology Laboratory Concept

1 INTRODUCTION

Biotechnology is a subject that involves great areas in terms of the concepts undergirding the competencies to enact. Discussing bread, *Tempe* (a food made from fermented soybean), vinegar, and other fermentation products, students are introduced to the very basic and simple techniques to proceed with biomaterials to the products that benefit human beings. On the other hand, comprehending genetic engineering, for example, encompasses new aspects (Harms 2002), which is also accompanied by new problems arising from the ambivalence of the biotechnology topics. Moreover, biotechnology needs to deal with multidisciplinary concepts, including molecular biology, in which its level of difficulty is even higher (Harms 2002; Southard *et al.* 2016). This is a particular responsibility of schools to inform students the ways of the scientific and technical aspects of biotechnology, besides, qualify them to be decision-makers to cope with the problems that will potentially arise in the future.

---

*Corresponding Author: mirzanuryady@umm.ac.id

DOI: 10.1201/9781003376125-6

To enact expected learning goals, biotechnology basic concepts are critical to be mastered, particularly those that are related to laboratory work skills. The concepts enable students to arrange and design their cutting-edge laboratory works (Black 2020) correctly by avoiding the errors that may occur due to the lack of mastering concepts. Laboratory exercise is often used as a learning method to gain a deeper understanding of a wide spectrum of biological sciences (Almroth 2015). The wrong step taken in the laboratory will determine the validity of the data gained.

In several countries, biotechnology laboratory work is studied at elementary, middle, and higher education levels (Harms 2002). The important role of laboratory work in achieving students' comprehension of life sciences, many researchers proposed laboratory applications to replace laboratory learning with the emergence of COVID-19 which enables students to do their real laboratory practices (Aripin and Suryaningsih 2020). It is undeniable that laboratory knowledge is an indispensable competency of fundamental science that needs to be achieved by students (Gökmen *et al.* 2021; Halimah 2019). Thus, initial identification is needed. Thus, this study aimed to investigate the competency level of Biology Education students in comprehending their basic concepts of Biotechnology laboratory work.

The findings of this research will contribute to future research to design the most proper learning or teaching techniques as well as to generate a good curriculum for Biotechnology learning.

2 METHODS

This survey research aimed at investigating the competency level biology education students in biotechnology laboratory work basic concepts. The competencies observed in this research were limited to basic knowledge as well as error analysis of biotechnology laboratory work procedures. The population of this research was all students in the sixth semester of the Department of Biology Education, Faculty of Teacher Training and Education,

Table 1. The instrument used in measuring biotechnology laboratory work knowledge of biology education students.

No	Case Statement	Skill Measured
1	One day, Amel isolated a whole genome of mammals. She found that in the procedure of buffer lysis making, she needed to use SDS buffer with a concentration of 2%. Thus, she mixed 0.2 grams of SDS powder into 500 ml of distilled water. Poorly, she did not get any DNA bands at all when she checked the extract qualitatively. According to your knowledge of biotechnology laboratory work,	Error analysis Generating solution Using proper formula (1), Calculation (2)
	(a) Why did not Amel get the DNA isolate? (b) How can she correct her mistake to get the DNA isolate? (c) She corrected her mistake, did a re-extraction of the DNA, and obtained the data of the absorption value was 0.080 (Note: the measurement was done using a spectrophotometer in 260 nm with a dilution of 250 times). Thus, what is the concentration of DNA isolation she obtained?	
2	Aldina conducted cytochrome b gene amplification of *Drosophila melanogaster*. She forgot to add dNTPs into the PCR mixture.	Error analysis Using proper formula (1), Calculation (2)
	(a) At which stage of the PCR process could not be completed? 2) Why it could not be completed? (b) If Aldina re-mixed the PCR mixture properly and set the PCR cycle to 34 cycles, how many amplicons would be obtained from Aldina?	

University of Muhammadiyah Malang. The sample was 71 students which comprised 14 male and 57 female students. They were randomly chosen from A, B, C, and D classes. All students involved have attended general biology, biochemistry, general bio laboratory introduction, genetics, and biotechnology subjects.

The data collection was conducted by using an instrument that contained two cases with several questions in each. The students were required to analyze the error procedure that occurred and give the solution. The quantitative data collected were the information on how many items of the test were correctly answered by students. The data were then analyzed using descriptive statistics in terms of percentage and served as a bar chart.

Moreover, this research scrutinized the difference in students' competency in the bio-technology laboratory works concept based on their academic competency levels. Related to this purpose, the subjects were classified into three academic groups, i.e., low, fair, and high based on their academic record. Hence, there were 11 students grouped in the high academic level, 51 of them were grouped in the fair level, and 9 students were grouped in the low level. Therefore, the Kruskal Walis Test was performed to ensure that the three academic groups were significantly different in conquering the biotechnology laboratory work concept. Furthermore, the Mann-Whitney Test was also performed to ensure the difference in stu-dents' knowledge based on their gender. These tests were conducted after the prerequisite tests of parametric statistics (i.e., normality (Shapiro-Wilk) and homogeneity (Levene tests) were done and did not meet the requirements needed.

3 RESULTS

Generally, biotechnology laboratory work comprises three stages: preparation, laboratory work, and data interpretation. Preparation including preparing all materials needed in lab work. In the preparation processes, students need to calculate all materials needed to make good solutions. The calculation made, the wrong concentration of the solution, and the laboratory work will fail. Hence, the measurement of students' ability to calculate laboratory materials was measured and served in Figure 1. Based on the results, it can be seen that the highest percentage was achieved in calculation skills in question 2b2 (58%). Interestingly, question number 1c2 which also measured calculation skills was not solved even by one student (0%). This is probably because of the complexity of the formula. The formula needed to be written by students to answer question number 2b1 is only "2n", moreover, students were allowed to not calculate the final results as they were not allowed to bring any

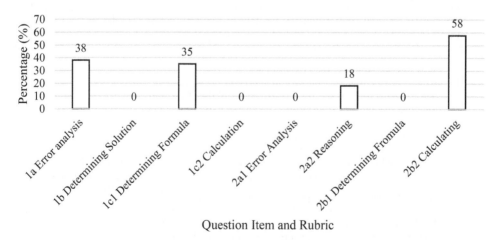

Question Item and Rubric

Figure 1.   Student competency in analyzing procedural error in Biotechnology laboratory work.

44

calculation devices into the examination room. Thus, they only need to substitute the numbers to replace the "n" notation. On the other hand, the calculation employed in question number 1c2 was more complex. The formula was supposed to be "[DNA] = Åλ260 × dilution factor × 50" which is the answer the question number 1c. Notwithstanding that as many as 35% of students could correctly write the formula, it could not guarantee that they could complete the calculation properly which is proven by the 0% of students correctly answering question number 1c2. In addition, the existence of students who succeeded in answering question number 2b2, yet, they failed to determine the formula used (question number 2b1) in which the percentage was 0%. This is because the students jumped to do the calculation without writing the formula.

A similar data pattern occurred in students' responses to error analysis questions (1a and 2a1). There were as many as 38% of students who answered question number 1a correctly, but not with 2a1 (0%). These two error analysis questions were responded to differently. This is probably because question number 1a required simple language, and no difficult technical terms were used. Contrarily, question number 2a1 asked students to use specific terms in English (i.e., extension or elongation) which is not their mother tongue language. Thus, the probability of wrongly mentioning and bewildering terms was higher.

Table 2. The results of the Kruskal Wallis test based on student academic levels.

	Score
Chi-Square	27.342
df	2
Asymp. Sig.	.000

To make the findings of the research more meaningful, further analysis was performed in terms of the Kruskal Walis test based on student academic levels. The Kruskal Walis test was employed as the data were not normally distributed. The results of the Kruskal Wallis test are depicted in Table 2. Table 2 revealed that there is a significant difference in students' biotechnology laboratory concepts knowledge based on their academic levels [Chisq. = 27.342, $p > .001$]. While there was a significant difference in students' mastery of biotechnology concepts based on their academic levels, their knowledge showed no significant difference based on their gender [U. = 350.5, $p = .450$] as shown in Table 3.

Table 3. The results of the Mann-Whitney U test based on gender.

	Score
Mann-Whitney U	350.500
Wilcoxon W	455.500
Z	−.756
Asymp. Sig. (2-tailed)	.450

4 DISCUSSION

The students with high academic levels tended to achieve higher scores on the tests given. This is in line with the findings of Lee et al. (2012) who stated that students who did not attend laboratory classes tended to achieve higher scores in exams that required rote memorization compared to those who attended laboratory classes. However, they were less likely to generate high-quality research proposals. Similarly, Tonissen et al. (2014) reported that laboratory activity enables students to generate report writing well.

At a certain point, academic level is a parameter of students' knowledge and literacy. Hence, this is crucial basic information for lecturers or instructors to determine a starting point to train students in laboratory skills (Mistry and Gorman 2020). Furthermore, students' metacognitive knowledge determines their habits, and cognition, as considerably as their attitude (Hamiddin and Saukah 2020). In other words, students who gain concepts understanding undergird laboratory works will ease to comprehend their laboratory works and even find alternative solutions as they find hindrances in the laboratory. This self-regulated thinking, which is encompassed in higher-order thinking skills (Husamah *et al.* 2018), is needed by biology students who work in the laboratory.

Acknowledging the crucial role of hands-on activities, researchers even designed many techniques, methods, and even applications to facilitate students to do that during a pandemic or limited conditions. Barthet (2021) designed molecular laboratory practices that can be done safely from home; Azizah and Aloysius (2021) concluded that, from 2009 to 2019, there were 12 articles published in international journals that focused on the development of virtual laboratory; Udin *et al.* (2020) assessed the impact of the virtual laboratory on students' cognitive, affective, and psychomotor; and the other researchers who revealed Tian *et al.* (2020) suggested to implement Ausubel Cognitive Assimilation Theory (A's CAT) to overcome student difficulties in learning molecular.

Although there was a significant difference in students' biotechnology mastering concepts based on their academic levels, their knowledge was insignificantly different based on their gender. This is assumed that the resources accessed by students are identical and even they share their study notes, thus, they have homogenous concepts mastered in terms of hands-on Biotechnology materials. Even though some researchers found a significant difference in knowledge between male and female students in science subjects (Ayub *et al.* 2017), there are also identical findings reported by previous researchers (Reddy 2017; Yamtinah *et al.* 2017). Based on these findings, it can be suggested that instructors need to do an initial analysis of the students they teach before training them in further laboratory skills. The initial test can be done simply using a pretest and analyzing the results. In case a difference between male and female students is significant, the instructors need to treat them differently and vice versa.

5 CONCLUSION

Based on data analysis results, it can be seen that laboratory work basic competency of the majority of biology education students was still low. However, a significant difference occurred between students with high, fair, and low academic levels. Hence, it is recommended to do further detailed analysis in terms of students' academic levels before deciding on teaching or training methods used in Biotechnology laboratory work.

REFERENCES

Almroth, B. C. (2015). The importance of laboratory exercises in biology teaching; Case study in an ecotoxicology course. *Pedagogical Development and Interactive Learning, september,* 1–11. https://pil.gu.se/publicerat/texter

Aripin, I., & Suryaningsih, Y. (2020). Developing BTEM-based virtual biology laboratory to improve students' critical thinking skills on the concept of bacteria. *Scientiae Educatia, 9*(2), 216. https://doi.org/10.24235/sc.educatia.v9i2.7379

Ayub, A. F. M., Yunus, A. S. M., Mahmud, R., Salim, N. R., & Sulaiman, T. (2017). Differences in students' mathematics engagement between gender and between rural and urban schools. *AIP Conference Proceedings, 1795*(January 2017). https://doi.org/10.1063/1.4972169

Azizah, N., & Aloysius, S. (2021). The effects of virtual laboratory on biology learning achievement: A literature review. *Proceedings of the 6th International Seminar on Science Education (ISSE 2020)*, *541*(Isse 2020), 107–116. https://doi.org/10.2991/assehr.k.210326.015

Barthet, M. M. (2021). Teaching molecular techniques at home: Molecular biology labs that can be performed anywhere and enable hands-on learning of restriction digestion/ligation and …. *Biochemistry and Molecular Biology Education*, *49*(4), 598–604. https://doi.org/10.1002/bmb.21517

Black, P. N. (2020). A revolution in biochemistry and molecular biology education informed by basic research to meet the demands of 21st century career paths. *Journal of Biological Chemistry*, *295*(31), 10653–10661. https://doi.org/10.1074/jbc.AW120.011104

Gökmen, A., Gürkan, B., & Katırcıoğlu, H. T. (2021). Preservice biology teachers' knowledge and usage level regarding lab equipment and materials. *Journal of Education and Learning (EduLearn)*, *15*(3), 397–405. https://doi.org/10.11591/edulearn.v15i3.20018

Halimah, M., Rahmat, A., & Redjeki, S. (2019). Biotechnology learning profile biology in FKIP Biology Education Study Program Pasundan University Bandung Indonesia. *International Conference on Mathematics and Science Education*, *1521*, 42031. https://doi.org/10.1088/1742-6596/1521/4/042031

Hamiddin, H., & Saukah, A. (2020). Investigating metacognitive knowledge in reading comprehension: The case of Indonesian undergraduate students. *Indonesian Journal of Applied Linguistics*, *9*(3), 608–615. https://doi.org/10.17509/ijal.v9i3.23211

Harms, U. (2002). Biotechnology education in schools. In *Electronic Journal of Biotechnology* (Vol. 5, Issue 3).

Husamah, H., Fatmawati, D., & Setyawan, D. (2018). OIDDE learning model: Improving higher order thinking skills of biology teacher candidates. *International Journal of Instruction*, *11*(2), 249–264. https://doi.org/10.12973/iji.2018.11217a

Lee, S. W. Y., Lai, Y. C., Yu, H. T. A., & Lin, Y. T. K. (2012). Impact of biology laboratory courses on students' science performance and views about laboratory courses in general: Innovative measurements and analyses. *Journal of Biological Education*, *46*(3), 173–179. https://doi.org/10.1080/00219266.2011.634017

Mistry, N., & Gorman, S. G. (2020). What laboratory skills do students think they possess at the start of University? *Chemistry Education Research and Practice*, *21*(3), 823–838. https://doi.org/10.1039/c9rp00104b

Reddy, L. (2017). Gender differences in attitudes to learning science in grade 7. *African Journal of Research in Mathematics, Science and Technology Education*, *21*(1), 26–36. https://doi.org/10.1080/18117295.2017.1279450

Southard, K., Wince, T., Meddleton, S., & Bolger, M. S. (2016). Features of knowledge building in biology: Understanding undergraduate students' ideas about molecular mechanisms. *CBE Life Sciences Education*, *15*(1), 1–16. https://doi.org/10.1187/cbe.15-05-0114

Tian, Z., Zhang, K., Zhang, T., Dai, X., & … (2020). Application of Ausubel cognitive assimilation theory in teaching/learning medical biochemistry and molecular biology. *… and Molecular Biology …*, *48*(3), 202–219. https://doi.org/10.1002/bmb.21327

Tonissen, K. F., Lee, S. E., Woods, K. J., & Osborne, S. A. (2014). Development of scientific writing skills through activities embedded into biochemistry and molecular biology laboratory courses. *International Journal of Innovation in Science and Mathematics Education*, *22*(4), 1–14. https://openjournals.library.sydney.edu.au/index.php/CAL/article/view/7564/8365

Udin, W. N., Ramli, M., & Muzzazinah. (2020). Virtual laboratory for enhancing students' understanding on abstract biology concepts and laboratory skills: A systematic review. *Journal of Physics: Conference Series*, *1521*(4). https://doi.org/10.1088/1742-6596/1521/4/042025

Yamtinah, S., Masykuri, M., & Syahidul Shidiq, A. (2017). Gender differences in student's attitudes toward science: an analysis of students' science process skill testlet instrument. *AIP Conference Proceedings*, *4*, 030003-1-030003–030006. https://doi.org/10.1063/1.4995086

Strengthening Professional and Spiritual Education through 21st Century Skill Empowerment in
Pandemic and Post-Pandemic Era – Arifin et al. (Eds)
© 2024 The Author(s), ISBN: 978-1-032-45243-2
Open Access: www.taylorfrancis.com, CC BY-NC-ND 4.0 license

Profiling metacognitive awareness in Arabic learners

Diana Nur Sholihah
Universitas Islam Tribakti Lirboyo Kediri, Indonesia

Nur Ila Ifawati & Kartika Ratna Sari
Universitas Islam Negeri Maulana Malik Ibrahim, Indonesia

Diani Fatmawati*
Universitas Muhammadiyah Malang, Indonesia
Kyung Hee University, South Korea

ABSTRACT: Notwithstanding that metacognitive awareness plays a crucial role in determining student learning, in the context of Arabic learning, this matter is still receiving less
attention. The present research aims at observing students' metacognitive awareness of Arabic
learners. This descriptive research employed 100 students who were taking 1-year intensive
Arabic class in Language Center of Universitas Islam Negeri Maulana Malik Ibrahim
Malang, Indonesia. The participants comprised 60 female students and 40 male students. The
data were obtained by using the instrument Junior Metacognitive Inventory, which was then
analyzed descriptively. The results showed that the majority of students possessed very good
metacognitive knowledge (67%) and good metacognitive regulation (70%). Meanwhile, no
significant differences between male and female students in metacognitive knowledge [$t(98)$ =
1.56, p = .121] and metacognitive regulation [$t(98)$ = 1.26, p = .210]. It is suggested to treat
male and female students in the same way in terms of teaching and learning aspects, even
though a deeper analysis of each instrument item can be done if needed.

Keywords: Arabic learners, junior metacognitive inventory, metacognitive awareness

1 INTRODUCTION

Metacognition was introduced by Flavell in 1976 (Anderson 2012). It is known as someone's
knowledge of his/her process of cognition and its products or anything about them. The popu-
larity of this terminology triggered the emergence of numerous studies on exploring metacognition along with teaching and learning (Cubukcu 2009; Hashmi *et al.* 2019; Ijirana and Supriadi
2018; Jenkins and Jenkins 2018; Misu and Masi 2017; Schraw and Moshman 1995; Sengul and
Katranci 2012). In the context of foreign/second language learning, metacognitive has been
discussed together with four skills of language learning (i.e., listening, speaking, reading, and
writing). Kasim and Darus (2020) investigated the English as a Second Language (ESL) of
undergraduate students' metacognitive awareness in reading academic materials. Furthermore,
Umam *et al.* (2020) examined the correlation between metacognitive awareness and Islamic
secondary school students' achievement in listening comprehension. In different way, Sholihah
et al. (2021) described the metacognitive awareness profile of Chinese language learners.

Along with the studies that focused on metacognition, the roles of metacognitive awareness
in teaching and learning activities were also scrutinized. Beach, Anderson, Jacovidis, and
Chadwick 2020 claimed that metacognition plays an essential role in teaching and learning and

---

*Corresponding Author: fatmawati06@khu.ac.kr

DOI: 10.1201/9781003376125-7

is a main driver for self-regulation. It assists the learners in developing their learning plan, and concept understanding (Adadan 2020), achieving their goals, choosing the learning strategies, monitoring their learning progress (Sugita 2021), and reflecting on what they learned and how (Adadan and Oner 2018). In other words, metacognition allows the learner to understand their cognitive performance and regulate it (Jaleel and Premachandran 2016).

Numerous studies addressed metacognitive awareness, but it is only a few studies have explored the metacognitive awareness of Arabic language learners. Alhaqbani and Riazi (2012) as well as Alhaqbani and Riazi (2012) investigated reading metacognitive awareness of non-Arabic students who learn Arabic as a second language. The participants of their research were 122 King Saud University undergraduate students and 81 students of Arabic language and literature at Yarmouk University, respectively. Barnabas Rafli and Rasyid (2019) have focused their investigation on metacognitive in the frame of Arabic learning, but in the context of learning strategy not as an awareness. Yet, the information about it will positively contribute to providing adequate support for both learners and educators to conduct better teaching and learning processes. This study aimed to investigate the meta-cognitive awareness of Arabic learners of Universitas Islam Negeri Maulana Malik Ibrahim Malang in terms of metacognitive knowledge and regulation.

2 METHODS

This research was quantitative in terms of survey research. The participants were 100 university students of Universitas Islam Negeri Maulana Malik Ibrahim Malang who were learning Arabic as a second/foreign language in a 1-year Arabic intensive course program conducted by the university. A convenience/opportunity sampling technique was employed to select the participants. The participants' metacognitive awareness data were obtained using Junior metacognitive inventory (Jr. MAI) which was developed by Kim et al. 2016. The inventory consists of 18 items which are classified into two categories: metacognitive knowledge and metacognitive regulation. Confirmation of instrument validity was done by using the Chi-square test, Tocker-lewis index, comparative fit index, and root mean square error of approximation in which the values were 494.84, 0.89, 0.91, and 0.05, respectively. The reliability of the instrument was confirmed using Cronbach alpha in which the value was 0.64. The original instrument which was written in English translated into the Indonesian Language to minimize misunderstanding that might occur among participants as their mother tongue is Indonesian Language. Moreover, a clear explanation that the response given by the participants on the instrument would not affect their academic report was given as well. This step aimed to encourage the participants to complete every single item in the instrument freely and based on their real condition. Thus, the obtained data would describe the real metacognitive awareness belonging to the participants.

A descriptive quantitative was utilized to analyze the collected data by calculating items' score percentages. The item scores were analyzed in two classifications based on Jr. MAI categorization (metacognitive knowledge and metacognitive regulation) in which the classification criteria served in Table 1. Meanwhile, the difference between male and female learners' metacognitive was proven by using a t-test after performing the normality test (Kolmogorov-Smirnov) and the homogeneity test (Levene test) as the pre-requisite tests.

Table 1. The criteria of metacognitive awareness classification.

Criteria	Category
1–9	Very Lacking
10–18	Poor
19–27	Fair
28–36	Good
37–45	Very Good

3 RESULTS AND DISCUSSION

This study aimed to provide the profile of metacognitive awareness of Arabic Language learners. The data were collected using The Jr. MAI instrument in which the items were classified into two classifications, i.e., metacognitive knowledge and metacognitive regulation (Kim *et al.* 2016). Hence, the results and discussions conducted are also divided based on this classification after several analyses were performed.

3.1 *Metacognitive knowledge*

The first analysis of the metacognitive knowledge data gained was descriptive in terms of percentage. Figure 1 depicts the percentage of the metacognitive knowledge level of Arabic Language learners in Universitas Islam Negeri Maulana Malik Ibrahim Malang. It can be seen that among the five levels of metacognitive awareness (Table 1), the highest percentage of the students' metacognitive knowledge was at a good level (67%), followed by those who were classified at a very good level (27%) and fair level (6%). Interestingly, no one of the students has poor or even very lacking metacognitive knowledge. This means that the student's metacognitive knowledge is adequate to support them in learning Arabic as a second language. In addition, it is also important to consider the proper way to optimize this metacognitive to a very good level. Metacognitive knowledge is crucial to be possessed by learners as it plays an important role in dealing with their task achievement performance (Halamish 2018). Above that, for language learners, it has been proven to be strongly related to their vocabulary knowledge (Teng 2021).

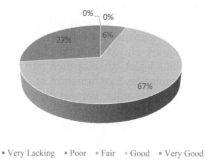

Figure 1.   Percentage of Arabic language learners' metacognitive knowledge.

Acknowledging the existence of students who still have fair metacognitive knowledge, the scientists suggested various alternative solutions. Herlanti *et al.* (2017) reported that PBL is one of the effective learning strategies to improve students' cognitive knowledge. Likewise, Nunaki, Damopolii, Kandowangko, and Nusantari (2019) suggested inquiry-based learning to train students' cognitive skills.

3.2 *Metacognitive regulation*

Metacognitive regulation is the other important part of metacognitive awareness. By possessing good metacognitive regulation, learners can regulate the essential things they need to accomplish their learning goals. Figure 2 shows the percentage of the metacognitive regulation level of Arabic language learners in Universitas Islam Negeri Maulana Malik Ibrahim Malang. The result analysis of metacognitive regulation indicated that 70% of learners were at a good level, 15% were at a very good level, and 15% were at a fair level. Meanwhile, no metacognitive regulation learners were in poor and very lacking level. On one hand, the phenomenon of the greatest percentage of good metacognitive regulation owned by students is reasonable by considering the good metacognitive knowledge they have. However, the fact that there were 15% of students who were in a fair level of meta-cognitive regulation needs to be coped with, unless, it will be worsened.

Students must comprehend whether they have adequate knowledge of the Arabic language or not. This will enable the students to organize their learning needs such as choosing the resources they need to access, determining the most proper learning strategies for themselves to achieve their goals, and so forth. Related to language learning, in terms of reading skills, Sugita (2021) reported that self-regulated reading, which is determined by metacognitive strategies, helps L2 learners achieve their comprehension in text reading. Erlin and Fitriani (2019) concluded that the higher the student's metacognitive awareness level, the greater their learning achievement they enact.

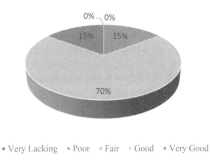

Figure 2.   The percentage of Arabic language learners' metacognitive regulation.

3.3   *Metacognitive difference between male and female learners*

To date, teachers keep questioning whether they need to differentiate their teaching treatment of male and female students. Hence, the basic information of students' cognitive is crucial to achieve. Generally, male and female students use their metacognitive skills in learning (Ciascai *et al.* 2011). However, the elaboration of their metacognitive skill in certain fields also needs to be considered as the different characteristics of the subjects themselves.

The recent study collected two groups of data i.e., knowledge of cognition and regulation of cognition of students who were learning Arabic as a second language during the research period. As the data were collected, several tests were conducted. The tests were: the normality test to ensure the data gained were distributed normally; the Levene test which was used to fulfill the requirement of data homogeneity; and the t-test to answer the research hypothesis.

Table 2 shows the results of the normality test of male student data. Based on the table, it can be seen that the data of male students were normally distributed, both knowledge of cognition [$D(40) = .106$, $p = .200$] and regulation of cognition [$D(40) = .079$, $p = .200$].

Table 2.   The results of the normality test of metacognitive knowledge and regulation of male students.

	Kolmogorov-Smirnov		
	Statistic	df	Sig.
Knowledge of Cognition	.106	40	.200[*]
Regulation of Cognition	.079	40	.200[*]

Table 3 depicts the results of the normality test of female student data. Based on the table, it also can be seen that the data of female students were normally distributed, both knowledge of cognition [$D(60) = .113$, $p = .054$] and regulation of cognition [$D(60) = .088$, $p = .200$].

Table 3.   The results of the normality test of metacognitive knowledge and regulation of female students.

	Kolmogorov-Smirnov[b]		
	Statistic	df	Sig.
Knowledge of Cognition	.113	60	.054
Regulation of Cognition	.088	60	.200[*]

Furthermore, the Levene test and t-test were carried out based on the dependent variable. Table 4 shows the analysis results of the Levene test as well as the t-test of students' knowledge of cognition. The table informs that the variance of students' knowledge is homogenous [$F(1,98) = .004$, $p = .947$].

In addition to the information on t-test results contained in Table 4, Table 5 completes that information. By referring the both tables, it can be inferred that students' knowledge of cognition between males ($M = 33.18$, $SD = 3.54$) and females ($M = 34.32$, $SD = 3.61$) was insignificantly different [$t(98) = 1.56$, $p = .121$].

Table 4.   The analysis results of the Levene test and t-test of students' knowledge of cognition.

		Levene's Test for Equality of Variances		t-test for Equality of Means						
								Std.	95% Confidence Interval of the Difference	
						Sig.	Mean	Error		
		F	Sig.	t	df	(2-tailed)	Difference	Difference	Lower	Upper
Knowledge of Cognition	Equal variances assumed	.004	.947	−1.563	98	.121	−1.142	.730	−2.591	.308
	Equal variances not assumed			−1.569	84.845	.120	−1.142	.728	−2.588	.305

Table 5.   The group statistics of students' knowledge of cognition.

	Sex	N	Mean	Std. Deviation	Std. Error Mean
Knowledge of Cognition	Male	40	33.18	3.537	.559
	Female	60	34.32	3.606	.465

Meanwhile, the information about the analysis results of students' regulation of cognition is served in Tables 6 and 7. In terms of homogeneity, Table 6 depicts the clear information that the variance of students' regulation is homogenous [$F(1,98) = 1.40$, $p = .240$]. By combining the information of t-test results of students' regulation of cognition (Table 6) and group statistics of students' regulation of cognition (Table 7), it can be stated that even though the male students' knowledge of cognition ($M = 31.58$, $SD = 4.80$) was lower compared to those of females' ($M = 32.70$, $SD = 4.06$), but this was statistically insignificantly different [$t(98) = 1.26$, $p = .210$]. This fact makes sense by considering the homogenous societal background experienced by the students as they are origins from Indonesia. This finding is in line with the previous studies which reported that there was no significant difference between and female students even in different education levels such as higher education (Gheith and Aljaberi 2015; Hashempour et al. 2015; Misu and Masi 2017), secondary school (Garzón et al. 2020; Jaleel and Premachandran 2016; Nunaki et al. 2019).

There might be several factors resulting in the similarity of metacognitive awareness between male and female students of UIN Maulana Malik Ibrahim students. One of the factors is the selection system used by the university to determine if the matriculants meet the university qualification standard or not. As a public university, Universitas Islam Negeri Maulana Malik

Table 6.   The Analysis results of Levene test and t test of students' knowledge of cognition.

| | | Levene's Test for Equality of Variances | | t-test for Equality of Means | | | | | | |
| | | | | | | | | | 95% Confidence Interval of the Difference | |
		F	Sig.	t	df	Sig. (2-tailed)	Mean Difference	Std. Error Difference	Lower	Upper
Regulation of Cognition	Equal variances assumed	1.400	.240	−1.262	98	.210	−1.125	.891	−2.894	.644
	Equal variances not assumed			−1.220	73.922	.226	−1.125	.922	−2.962	.712

Table 7.   The group statistics of students' knowledge of cognition.

	Sex	N	Mean	Std. Deviation	Std. Error Mean
Regulation of cognition	Male	40	31.58	4.798	.759
	Female	60	32.70	4.056	.524

Ibrahim Malang should determine certain standards of cognitive level to select the students. It means that the level of students' cognition was homogenized by this standard at the same time.

The interesting point of the findings is that there was no significant difference in metacognitive knowledge and regulation between male and female students, but it can be seen that the female students seem to have higher metacognitive awareness compared to females in both knowledge and regulation. This, somehow, was proven significantly different by previous researchers. Panda (2017) revealed that girls are significantly better than boys in metacognitive knowledge but not in metacognitive regulation. In addition, the findings showed no differences in metacognitive control and execution. Panchu et al. (2016) have compared the genders and noted that females have better metacognitive regulation, meanwhile, males' scores were significantly higher in metacognitive knowledge than females' scores. Accordingly, Abdelrahman (2020) stated that females attained significantly greater levels than males on the two scales of metacognitive awareness as considerable as metacognitive knowledge.

The insignificant difference in metacognitive awareness that occurred between males and females is presumably because elements that build their metacognitive awareness tended to be homogenous. Flavell (1979) argued that four elements build metacognitive awareness i.e., metacognitive knowledge, metacognitive experiences, goals (or tasks), and actions (strategies). Furthermore, various sub-elements determine each element such as declarative knowledge, procedural knowledge (Yorulmaz et al. 2021), and so forth. Hence, the more homogenous the factors, the insignificant difference between male and female metacognitive awareness presumably occurred. In the Indonesian context, there have been several reports that revealed that Indonesian students have low literacy rates (Kurnia and Astuti 2017; Novaristiana et al. 2019). Yet, literacy is a crucial aspect that determines one's good cognition, habits, and attitude (Hamiddin and Saukah 2020).

4 CONCLUSION

Based on the analysis results of the data collected from 100 participants, it can be concluded that the majority of students possessed good metacognitive knowledge (67%) and good metacognitive regulation (70%). Meanwhile, no significant differences between male and female students in metacognitive knowledge [$t(98) = 1.56$, $p = .121$] and metacognitive regulation [$t(98) = 1.26$, $p = .210$]. Hence, this information can be considered as one of the references to provide better teaching and learning management for students. Furthermore, the findings of this research are also useful for the authorities to regulate the better quality of education in terms of policy-making.

The limitation noticed in this study is that the participants of this study were only 100 learners and were selected from only one university. Lacking sufficiency and diversity data may affect the result of the depiction profile of the learners' metacognitive awareness, as the depiction is a pattern shaped by the results of data interpretation. Therefore, the greater quantity and various data in future research may direct to better results.

REFERENCES

Abdelrahman, R. M. (2020) 'Metacognitive awareness and academic motivation and their impact on academic achievement of Ajman University students', *Heliyon*, 6(May), p. e04192. doi: 10.1016/j.heliyon.2020.e04192.
Adadan, E. (2020) 'Analyzing the role of metacognitive awareness in preservice chemistry teachers' understanding of gas behavior in a multirepresentational instruction setting', *Journal of Research in Science Teaching*, 57(2), pp. 253–278. doi: 10.1002/tea.21589.
Adadan, E. and Oner, D. (2018) 'Examining preservice teachers' reflective thinking skills in the context of web-based portfolios: The role of metacognitive awareness', *Australian Journal of Teacher Education*, 43 (11), pp. 26–50. doi: 10.14221/ajte.2018v43n11.2.
Alhaqbani, A. and Riazi, A. M. (2012) 'Metacognitive awareness of reading strategy use in Arabic as a second language', *Reading in*, 24(2), pp. 231–255.
Anderson, N. J. (2012) 'Metacognition: awareness of language learning', in *Psychology for Language Learning*. Palgrave Macmillan, pp. 169–187. doi: http://dx.doi.org/10.1057/9781137032829_12.
Barnabas, R. A., Rafli, Z. and Rasyid, Y. (2019) 'Cognitive and metacognitive strategies in arabic listening learning and relationship with students' oersonality', *Arabiyat: Jurnal Pendidikan Bahasa Arab dan Kebahasaaraban*, 6(2), pp. 254–271. doi: 10.15408/a.v6i2.11771.
Beach, P. T. et al. (2020) 'Making the abstract explicit: the role of metacognition in teaching and learning', pp. 1–57.
Ciascai, Liliana and Lavinia, H. (2011) 'Gender differences in metacognitive skills: A study of the 8th grade pupils in Romania', *Procedia – Social and Behavioral Sciences*, (29), pp. 396–401. doi: doi.org/10.1016/j.sbspro.2011.11.255.
Cubukcu, F. (2009) 'Metacognition in the classroom', in *World Conference on Educational Science 2009*, pp. 559–563. doi: 10.1016/j.sbspro.2009.01.101.
Erlin, E. and Fitriani, A. (2019) 'Profile metacognitive awareness of biology education students in microbiology course', *Journal of Physics: Conference Series*, 1157(2). doi: 10.1088/1742-6596/1157/2/022066.
Flavell, J. H. (1979) 'Metacognition and Cognitive Monitoring', *American Psyological Association*, 34(10), pp. 906–911. doi: 10.1037/0003-066X.34.10.906.

Garzón, D. F. M., Bustos, A. P. H. and Lizarazo, J. O. U. (2020) 'Relationship between metacognitive skills, gender, and level of schooling in high school students', *Suma Psicológica*, 27(1), pp. 9–17. doi: doi.org/10.14349/sumapsi.2020.v27.n1.2.

Gheith, E. M. and Aljaberi, N. M. (2015) 'Pre-service classroom teachers' attitudes toward graphs and their ability to read and interpret them', *International Journal of Humanities and Social Science*, 5(7), pp. 113–124.

Halamish, V. (2018) 'Pre-service and in-service teachers' metacognitive knowledge of learning strategies', *Frontiers in Psychology*, 9(NOV), pp. 1–5. doi: 10.3389/fpsyg.2018.02152.

Hamiddin, H. and Saukah, A. (2020) 'Investigating metacognitive knowledge in reading comprehension: The case of Indonesian undergraduate students', *Indonesian Journal of Applied Linguistics*, 9(3), pp. 608–615. doi: 10.17509/ijal.v9i3.23211.

Hashempour, M., Ghonsooly, B. and Ghanizadeh, A. (2015) 'A study of translation students' self-regulation and metacognitive awareness in association with their gender and educational level', *International Journal of Comparative Literature & Translation Studies*, 3(3), pp. 60–69. doi: 10.7575/aiac.ijclts.v.3n.3p.60.

Hashmi, A., Khalid, M. and Shoaib, A. (2019) 'A cross-sectional study of assessing metacognitive knowledge and metacognitive regulatory skills among prospective teachers and its relation to their academic achievement', *Bulletin of Education and Research*, 41(2), pp. 215–234.

Herlanti, Y. *et al.* (2017) 'Discovering learning strategy to increase metacognitive knowledge in Biology learning in secondary school', *Jurnal Pendidikan IPA Indonesia*, 6(1), pp. 179–186. doi: 10.15294/jpii.v6i1.9605.

Ijirana and Supriadi (2018) 'Metacognitive skill profiles of chemistry education students in solving problem at low ability level', *Jurnal Pendidikan IPA Indonesia*, 7(2), pp. 239–245. doi: 10.15294/jpii.v7i2.14266.

Jaleel, S. and Premachandran, P. (2016) 'A study on the metacognitive awareness of secondary school students', *Universal Journal of Educational Research*, 4(1), pp. 165–172. doi: 10.13189/ujer.2016.040121.

Jenkins, A. and Jenkins, A. P. (2018) 'Gender and Subject Area Differences in Academic Metacognition and Motivation A Thesis submitted in partial fulfillment for the Bachelor's Degree in Psychology'.

Kasim, A. A. M. and Darus, N. A. (2020) 'Metacognitive awareness level and strategy use in academic reading among ESL undergraduates', *Social Science Learning Education Journal*, 5(July), pp. 180–186. doi: doi.org/10.15520/sslej.v5i06.2679.

Kim, B. *et al.* (2016) 'Establishing the factor structure of the 18-item version of the junior metacognitive awareness inventory', *Measurement and Evaluation in Counseling and Development*, pp. 1–11. doi: doi.org/10.1177%2F0748175616671366.

Kurnia, N. and Astuti, S. I. (2017) 'Peta Gerakan Literasi Digital di Indonesia: Studi tentang pelaku, ragam kegiatan, kelompok sasaran dan mitra yang dilakukan oleh Japelidi', *Informasi*, 47(2), p. 149. doi: 10.21831/informasi.v47i2.16079.

Misu, L. and Masi, L. (2017) 'Comparison of metacognition awareness of male and female students based on mathematics ability in Department of Mathematics Education of Halu Oleo University', *International Journal of Education and Research*, 5(6), pp. 43–50.

Novaristiana, R., Rinanto, Y. and Ramli, M. (2019) 'Scientific literacy profile in biological science of high school students', *Jurnal Pendidikan Biologi Indonesia*, 5(1), pp. 9–16. doi: 10.22219/jpbi.v5i1.7080.

Nunaki, J. H. *et al.* (2019) 'The effectiveness of inquiry-based learning to train the students' metacognitive skills based on gender differences', *International Journal of Instruction*, 12(2), pp. 505–516. doi: https://doi.org/10.29333/iji.2019.12232a.

Panchu, P. *et al.* (2016) 'Metacognitive awareness-evaluation and implications in medical students', *International Journal of Research in Medical Science*, 4(8), pp. 3570–3575. doi: http://dx.doi.org/10.18203/2320-6012.ijrms20162331.

Panda, S. (2017) 'Metacognitive awareness of college students: perspective of age and gender', *Scholarly Research Journal for Interdisciplinary Studies*, 4(49366), pp. 8402–8412. doi: doi.org/10.21922/srjis.v4i37.10551.

Schraw, G. and Moshman, D. (1995) 'Metacognitive theories', *Educational Psychology Review*, 7(4), pp. 351–371. doi: http://dx.doi.org/10.1007/BF02212307.

Sengul, S. and Katranci, Y. (2012) 'Metacognitive aspects of solving function problems', *Procedia – Social and Behavioral Sciences*, 46(507), pp. 2178–2182. doi: 10.1016/j.sbspro.2012.05.450.

Sholihah, D. N. *et al.* (2021) 'Mapping metacognitive awareness of Chinese language learners', *Journal of Education and Learning (EduLearn)*, 15(4), pp. 584–591. doi: 10.11591/edulearn.v15i4.20352.

Sugita, M. (2021) *The Role of Metacognitive Knowledge and Inference Making in Second Language Reading*. Temple University Graduate Board.

Teng, M. F. (2021) 'Exploring awareness of metacognitive knowledge and acquisition of vocabulary knowledge in primary grades: a latent growth curve modelling approach', *Language Awareness*. doi: 10.1080/09658416.2021.1972116.

Umam, C. *et al.* (2020) 'Metacognitive awareness and self-efficacy: do they contribute to indonesian efl students' listening comprehension achievement?', *Humanities & Social Sciences Reviews*, 8(4), pp. 138–146. doi: https://doi.org/10.18510/hssr.2020.8415.

Yorulmaz, A., Uysal, H. and Çokçaliskan, H. (2021) 'Pre-service primary school teachers' metacognitive awareness and beliefs about mathematical problem solving', *JRAMathEdu (Journal of Research and Advances in Mathematics Education)*, 6(3), pp. 239–259. doi: 10.23917/jramathedu.v6i3.14349.

Strengthening Professional and Spiritual Education through 21st Century Skill Empowerment in Pandemic and Post-Pandemic Era – Arifin et al. (Eds)

Bioinformatics-based genetics practicum: An innovative remote learning approach keeping pace with the evolution of biological science

Ahmad Fauzi*
Universitas Muhammadiyah Malang, Indonesia

Maryam Saleem
Government College University, Pakistan

Iin Hindun & Fuad Jaya Miharja
Universitas Muhammadiyah Malang, Indonesia

ABSTRACT: In addition to keeping up with the developments in the field of biology, the transformation of conventional genetics laboratory practices into bioinformatics-based laboratory practices has become essential in the digital learning era, which has emerged as a significant alternative form of education since the onset of the pandemic. The purpose of this research is to describe the form of bioinformatics-based genetics laboratory practices implemented in the Department of Biology Education. The study was conducted at a private university in Malang, Indonesia. The laboratory practices in the department spanned over 9 weeks, commencing with an introductory meeting, followed by five bioinformatics topics, and concluded with a project activity. The average scores for individual reports and tests in each laboratory topic for the students were excellent (95.51 and 81.79, respectively), as were their project report scores (93.77). Given the benefits and the importance of bioinformatics activities in biology laboratory practices, optimizing the curriculum design and enhancing both laboratory and theoretical teaching methods are necessary.

Keywords: Bioinformatics Skill Development, Learning Adaptation, Project-Based Learning, Remote Genetics Practical, Student Competence Enhancement

1 INTRODUCTION

Genetics holds a significant position in biology as it delves into principles related to the inheritance of traits, variations in traits, genetic diseases, and genetic engineering (Ekundayo and Bleichert 2019; Kilpinen and Dermitzakis 2012; Poczai and Santiago-Blay 2021). The field of genetics has also seen rapid growth due to its involvement in uncovering various biological phenomena and addressing contemporary human issues (Little and Colegrave 2016; Relethford 2008; Macaulay and Voet 2014). Alongside its crucial role in advancing biological knowledge, genetics is a focal point in biology education, given the challenging nature of the subject for students (Machová and Ehler 2023; Smith and Wood 2016). The complexity and abstract nature of genetic concepts are some of the reasons why genetics can be difficult to learn (Fauzi *et al.* 2021). To address these challenges, the incorporation of laboratory practices is considered a viable alternative in genetics education (Fauzi and Ramadani 2017).

Laboratory activities play a crucial role in the biology curriculum (Nurgaliyeva 2021), particularly in genetics courses. These laboratory activities provide students with the opportunity to

---

*Corresponding Author: ahmad_fauzi@umm.ac.id

DOI: 10.1201/9781003376125-8

directly and tangibly grasp genetic concepts. By engaging in laboratory work, students can observe various phenomena firsthand, understand the practical applications of the concepts they are learning, and enhance their critical thinking skills and research competencies (Hofstein 2017; Nurgaliyeva 2021). Moreover, through laboratory work, the bridge between theoretical concepts and real-world biological research or phenomena can be established. Therefore, the presence of laboratory sessions in genetics courses is an ideal condition, empowering students to become proficient biologists or future biology educators with extensive knowledge and the inspiration to design laboratory activities in the future (Fauzi and Ramadani 2017).

However, the emergence of the COVID-19 pandemic has disrupted conventional learning processes, leading to a shift towards remote education (Daniel 2020). The presence of the pandemic has compelled educators worldwide to design and implement innovative learning alternatives that aim to optimize the quality of education and students' competencies (Diaz 2021; Gultom 2022; Rehman and Fatima 2021). This unforeseen situation has posed significant challenges to the continuity of laboratory activities, as these often involve various equipment and materials available only in campus laboratories. Nevertheless, due to the impossibility of in-person lectures, the design of remote laboratory activities has become an alternative that must be considered (Delgado *et al.* 2021; Gamage *et al.* 2020).

The implementation of online-based laboratory practices has been reported as a viable alternative to maintain the quality of laboratory education during the pandemic era (Borish *et al.* 2022; Delgado *et al.* 2021; Gamage *et al.* 2020). Since conventional laboratory topics and activities are not feasible through online labs, the application of bioinformatics principles emerges as the appropriate solution for laboratory activities during the pandemic. Apart from enabling remote participation and not requiring various laboratory equipment, bioinformatics has become a crucial component of contemporary biology (Abdurakhmonov 2016; Banaganapalli and Shaik 2019; Shah *et al.* 2023). In an era where genomic and molecular information is advancing rapidly, the proficiency in various bioinformatics procedures and analyses has become a vital skill for biology students. Through bioinformatics-based laboratory practices, students are introduced to and trained in exploring various bioinformatics procedures applied in genetic research.

In line with the background presented, this paper highlights the implementation of online genetics laboratory practices that utilize bioinformatics-based procedures. This paper not only contributes to the advancement of knowledge concerning laboratory practices in the pandemic era but also addresses the needs of educators in the field of genetics in the modern biology and digital education era. While various other papers have reported on the implementation of laboratory practices during the pandemic (Borish *et al.* 2022; Delgado *et al.* 2021; Gamage *et al.* 2020) or the application of bioinformatics laboratory practices (O'Donnell *et al.* 2014, 2016; Oke *et al.* 2018), there is still no research that reports on the integration of bioinformatics activities into genetics laboratories, especially in Indonesia. Therefore, the aim of this research is to describe bioinformatics-based genetics laboratory practices conducted online at one of the private universities in Indonesia. By presenting a detailed account of laboratory activities, laboratory topics, and student outcomes, this paper is expected to contribute to providing a comprehensive understanding of how bioinformatics is integrated into genetics education.

2 METHODS

2.1 *Research design*

This study falls under the category of descriptive research conducted at the Universitas Muhammadiyah Malang, Indonesia. The research participants consisted of students from two classes in the Department of Biology Education who were enrolled in the Genetics course. The study was conducted from March 2021 to June 2021.

2.2 Research procedures

The genetics laboratory course comprises ten sessions spread over ten weeks. Each laboratory class is led by one instructor and two laboratory assistants. The first meeting serves as an introductory session that provides information on rules, various activities, topics, assignments, and the assessment process for the entire laboratory course, which will be followed by the students. Subsequently, students will engage in six laboratory topics spread from the second to the sixth meetings. These six topics include GenBank, BLAST, multiple sequence alignment, phylogenetic tree construction, and nucleotide analysis along with genetic distance using the MEGA software. Students receive a laboratory manual that outlines the steps for conducting various bioinformatics analyses. Additionally, the manual provides links to video tutorials on bioinformatics analysis prepared by the laboratory instructor.

At the beginning of each laboratory session, there will be a pretest assessing their understanding of the previous laboratory topic. Furthermore, in each laboratory topic, students independently create reports based on the bioinformatics analyses they have conducted. In the seventh and eighth meetings, students will form project groups. Over these two weeks, each group will have the opportunity to complete a project activity involving the preparation of a simple research report that incorporates the bioinformatics analyses they have learned. Finally, in the tenth meeting, each group will present their project report in front of the instructor and laboratory assistants.

2.3 Data collection and analysis

The main sources of data for this study include the pretest scores, individual reports, and project activities completed by the students. These three data sources serve as indicators of the students' understanding and skills related to the various analyses they have learned. Subsequently, this data is analyzed using descriptive statistical analysis techniques, specifically the mean. The first two data sources are processed for each laboratory topic, while the last data source is analyzed once, as it is specifically related to the tenth meeting's project activity.

3 RESULTS AND DISCUSSION

The genetics laboratory course at the Universitas Muhammadiyah Malang is conducted online. The average scores for the pretest, individual report, and project activity are presented in Table 1. Based on Table 1, students' pretest scores in each laboratory session are generally good, although there are two topics with average scores below 80. Nevertheless, the overall average pretest scores for students are excellent, as they exceed 80.

Table 1. Mean pretest scores, self-reports, and project assessments in genetics practicum.

Topic	Pretest	Report	Project Assessment
GenBank	82.63	96.57	–
BLAST	79.21	97.49	–
Multiple Sequence Alignment	84.21	96.32	–
Phylogenetic Tree	83.16	90.43	–
Nucleotide Analysis and Genetic Distance	79.74	96.76	–
Final assignment	–	–	93.79
Average	81.79	95.51	93.79

The pretest questions are based on the principles, procedures, and theoretical foundations underlying the laboratory topics covered in the previous meetings. Through the pretest, the students' level of understanding regarding bioinformatics analysis from the previous week can be assessed. The presence of pretests in each laboratory topic provides valuable information for educators as it serves as a formative assessment. Through formative assessment, educators can evaluate the gradual progress of students' understanding and competence (Heritage 2007). Additionally, the presence of pretests ensures that students genuinely comprehend, study, and engage in laboratory work to achieve optimal grades.

The pretest activities in the bioinformatics laboratory practice utilize the Google Forms application. While the primary purpose of this platform is not for educational assessment, the features provided by Google Forms support educators in conducting formative assessments (Lailaturrahmi *et al.* 2020). Google Forms is also reported to be frequently used by educators during the pandemic era due to its convenience and the utility it offers (Perwitasari *et al.* 2021; Pantiwati *et al.* 2022).

In addition to the pretests, students' competence during the laboratory practice is also assessed through the individual reports prepared by each student for each laboratory topic. A summary of the average individual report scores is presented in Table 1. Consistent with the pretest data, students' scores in the individual reports are also categorized as good. In these individual reports, students provide data on the gene names they used, the analyses conducted, the software or websites utilized, and the results of their analyses. The high average scores in the individual reports indicate the students' success in carrying out and reporting the laboratory practice results.

In addition to assessing students' competence, the presence of the individual report assignment also serves to enhance their critical thinking and research methodology skills. In each laboratory session, students are given the freedom to choose the gene they will analyze, thus empowering their critical and creative thinking skills. These skills are essential in the 21st century and are required by both future researchers and educators (Dwyer *et al.* 2014; Newton and Newton 2014; ŽivkoviĿ 2016). Moreover, the systematic preparation of reports also facilitates students in honing their scientific reporting skills.

After completing the five laboratory topics, students collaborate in groups to undertake a project activity. Students, together with their groups, are guided to design and report on a simple research project based on the bioinformatics analyses they have learned. Subsequently, in the final meeting, they present their project results as if it were a presentation in a scientific forum. The average scores for their projects are also presented in Table 1. Based on the table, similar to the other two assessments, the average project scores are also categorized as good.

The presence of project activities in genetics education is expected to optimize the learning process for students, as this type of learning is recommended by researchers. Through project-based learning, students' critical thinking skills are further enhanced (Mutakinati *et al.* 2018; Sasson *et al.* 2018). Additionally, because the projects are conducted in groups, students' collaboration skills can also be facilitated to develop (Bell 2010; Kokotsaki, Menzies and Wiggins 2016). Communication skills can also significantly improve as they are trained to communicate their project results in both written and oral forms (Magleby and Furse 2007). These two skills are also considered essential in the 21st century. Alongside critical and creative thinking skills, collaboration and communication skills are part of the 4C skills that are touted as essential skills to navigate the current era (Astuti *et al.* 2019; Geisinger 2016).

Furthermore, the selection of bioinformatics topics for the laboratory practice is based on the frequency and utility of these analyses in various genetics research. Through the GenBank topic, students are introduced to and taught how to utilize the genetic information database of various organisms on Earth. GenBank is one of the largest databases providing information on nucleotide sequences, exon-intron distribution, as well as the names of researchers and research references reporting such genetic information (Benson *et al.* 2012). In the next topic, students delve into BLAST, a tool frequently used by genetic researchers to compare biological sequence information of one organism with various other organisms (Ye *et al.* 2006; Johnson *et al.* 2008). Subsequently, in the following laboratory session, students learn how to perform multiple sequence alignment. This tool is employed by researchers to study closely related genes and understand the evolutionary relationships between them

(Edgar and Batzoglou 2006). Next, students learn how to construct phylogenetic trees. Phylogenetic trees are diagrams that illustrate the evolutionary relationships among species or biological entities and are often featured in researchers' reports (De Bruyn *et al.* 2014; Challa and Neelapu 2019). Finally, students also explore nucleotide analysis and genetic distance analysis, which are frequently conducted analyses in the field of genetics. Students use software like MEGA, which is considered vital in various genetic research endeavors (Kumar *et al.* 2008; Sohpal *et al.* 2010).

In today's modern biology era, bioinformatics has become an inseparable component of the field of biology (Abdurakhmonov 2016; Banaganapalli and Shaik 2019; Shah *et al.* 2023). The skills of acquiring and processing bioinformatics data have become crucial competencies for students to support their future careers in biology and education. In the current era, information related to genomics and other molecular aspects has rapidly evolved. Therefore, bioinformatics-based skills have become fundamental competencies that need to be emphasized in biology education. Moreover, by applying various bioinformatics analyses, students can gain firsthand experience in processing molecular data and data related to the evolution of organisms, experiences that would be challenging to obtain through conventional laboratory practices alone. Thus, equipping biology education students through genetics laboratory practices is both urgent and highly beneficial.

4 CONCLUSION

This paper has described the implementation of bioinformatics-based genetics laboratory practices at the University of Muhammadiyah Malang. Based on the results and discussions presented in this paper, the transition from conventional laboratory practices to online bioinformatics-based practices has successfully empowered student competencies. Data from pretest scores and individual reports confirm that despite the remote nature of the laboratory practices, students are able to learn and engage in bioinformatics analyses effectively. Furthermore, the high project activity scores serve as an indication of the development of critical thinking, collaboration, and communication skills among the students. The selection of laboratory practice topics has also been based on bioinformatics analyses frequently employed by researchers in the field of genetics.

Based on this paper, the adaptation of laboratory activities to accommodate bioinformatics topics is necessary, both in the pandemic and post-pandemic era. As the field of biology continues to evolve, bioinformatics-based competencies are required by both future researchers and biology educators. Additionally, by incorporating bioinformatics, instructors can provide students with opportunities to explore various biological phenomena that might be challenging to study using conventional laboratory practices.

REFERENCES

Abdurakhmonov, I.Y. (2016) 'Bioinformatics: Basics, development, and future', in *Bioinformatics – Updated Features and Applications*. InTech. Available at: https://doi.org/10.5772/63817.

Astuti, A.P. *et al.* (2019) 'Preparing 21st century teachers: Implementation of 4C character's pre-service teacher through teaching practice', *Journal of Physics: Conference Series*, 1233(1), p. 012109. Available at: https://doi.org/10.1088/1742-6596/1233/1/012109.

Banaganapalli, B. and Shaik, N.A. (2019) 'Introduction to bioinformatics', in *Essentials of Bioinformatics, Volume I*. Cham: Springer International Publishing, pp. 1–18. Available at: https://doi.org/10.1007/978-3-030-02634-9_1.

Bell, S. (2010) 'Project-based learning for the 21st Century: Skills for the future', *The Clearing House: A Journal of Educational Strategies, Issues and Ideas*, 83(2), pp. 39–43. Available at: https://doi.org/10.1080/00098650903505415.

Benson, D.A. *et al.* (2012) 'GenBank', *Nucleic Acids Research*, 41(D1), pp. D36–D42. Available at: https://doi. org/10.1093/nar/gks1195.

Borish, V. *et al.* (2022) 'Undergraduate student experiences in remote lab courses during the COVID-19 pandemic', *Physical Review Physics Education Research*, 18(2), p. 020105. Available at: https://doi.org/ 10.1103/PhysRevPhysEducRes.18.020105.

Challa, S. and Neelapu, N.R.R. (2019) 'Phylogenetic trees: Applications, construction, and assessment', in *Essentials of Bioinformatics, Volume III*. Cham: Springer International Publishing, pp. 167–192. Available at: https://doi.org/10.1007/978-3-030-19318-8_10.

Daniel, S.J. (2020) 'Education and the COVID-19 pandemic', *PROSPECTS*, 49(1–2), pp. 91–96. Available at: https://doi.org/10.1007/s11125-020-09464-3.

De Bruyn, A., Martin, D.P. and Lefeuvre, P. (2014) 'Phylogenetic reconstruction methods: An overview', in, pp. 257–277. Available at: https://doi.org/10.1007/978-1-62703-767-9_13.

Delgado, T., Bhark, S. and Donahue, J. (2021) 'Pandemic teaching: Creating and teaching cell biology labs online during COVID-19', *Biochemistry and Molecular Biology Education*, 49(1), pp. 32–37. Available at: https://doi.org/10.1002/bmb.21482.

Diaz, C.M., Linden, K. and Solyali, V. (2021) 'Novel and innovative approaches to teaching human anatomy classes in an online environment during a pandemic', *Medical Science Educator*, 31(5), pp. 1703–1713. Available at: https://doi.org/10.1007/s40670-021-01363-2.

Dwyer, C.P., Hogan, M.J. and Stewart, I. (2014) 'An integrated critical thinking framework for the 21st century', *Thinking Skills and Creativity*, 12, pp. 43–52. Available at: https://doi.org/10.1016/j. tsc.2013.12.004.

Edgar, R.C. and Batzoglou, S. (2006) 'Multiple sequence alignment', *Current Opinion in Structural Biology*, 16 (3), pp. 368–373. Available at: https://doi.org/10.1016/j.sbi.2006.04.004.

Ekundayo, B. and Bleichert, F. (2019) 'Origins of DNA replication', *PLOS Genetics*, 15(9), p. e1008320. Available at: https://doi.org/10.1371/journal.pgen.1008320.

Fauzi, A. *et al.* (2021) 'The difficulty index of biology topics in Indonesian Senior High School: Biology undergraduate students' perspectives', *JPBI (Jurnal Pendidikan Biologi Indonesia)*, 7(2), pp. 149–158. Available at: https://doi.org/10.22219/jpbi.v7i2.16538.

Fauzi, A. and Ramadani, S.D. (2017) 'Learning the genetics concepts through project activities using Drosophila melanogaster: A qualitative descriptive study', *JPBI (Jurnal Pendidikan Biologi Indonesia)*, 3 (3), pp. 238–247. Available at: https://doi.org/10.22219/jpbi.v3i3.4897.

Gamage, K.A.A. *et al.* (2020) 'Online delivery of teaching and laboratory practices: Continuity of university programmes during COVID-19 pandemic', *Education Sciences*, 10(10), p. 291. Available at: https://doi.org/ 10.3390/educsci10100291.

Geisinger, K.F. (2016) '21st century skills: What are they and how do we assess them?', *Applied Measurement in Education*, 29(4), pp. 245–249. Available at: https://doi.org/10.1080/08957347.2016.1209207.

Gultom, F., Hernawaty, H. and Simanullang, P. (2022) 'Implementation of innovative learning models in chemistry lessons during the COVID-19 pandemic', *Jurnal Penelitian Pendidikan IPA*, 8(3), pp. 1443–1446. Available at: https://doi.org/10.29303/jppipa.v8i3.1658.

Heritage, M. (2007) 'Formative assessment: What do teachers need to know and do?', *Phi Delta Kappan*, 89 (2), pp. 140–145. Available at: https://doi.org/10.1177/003172170708900210.

Hofstein, A. (2017) 'The role of laboratory in science teaching and learning', in *Science Education*. Rotterdam: SensePublishers, pp. 357–368. Available at: https://doi.org/10.1007/978-94-6300-749-8_26.

Johnson, M. *et al.* (2008) 'NCBI BLAST: a better web interface', *Nucleic Acids Research*, 36(Web Server), pp. W5–W9. Available at: https://doi.org/10.1093/nar/gkn201.

Kilpinen, H. and Dermitzakis, E.T. (2012) 'Genetic and epigenetic contribution to complex traits', *Human Molecular Genetics*, 21(R1), pp. R24–R28. Available at: https://doi.org/10.1093/hmg/dds383.

Kokotsaki, D., Menzies, V. and Wiggins, A. (2016) 'Project-based learning: A review of the literature', *Improving Schools*, 19(3), pp. 267–277. Available at: https://doi.org/10.1177/1365480216659733.

Kumar, S. *et al.* (2008) 'MEGA: A biologist-centric software for evolutionary analysis of DNA and protein sequences', *Briefings in Bioinformatics*, 9(4), pp. 299–306. Available at: https://doi.org/10.1093/bib/bbn017.

Lailaturrahmi, L. *et al.* (2020) 'Google Forms as a useful tool for online formative assessment of a pharma-cotherapy course in Indonesia', *Pharmacy Education*, 20(2), pp. 5–6. Available at: https://doi.org/10.46542/ pe.2020.202.56.

Little, T.J. and Colegrave, N. (2016) 'Caging and uncaging Ggenetics', *PLOS Biology*, 14(7), p. e1002525. Available at: https://doi.org/10.1371/journal.pbio.1002525.

Macaulay, I.C. and Voet, T. (2014) 'Single cell genomics: Advances and future perspectives', *PLoS Genetics*, 10(1), p. e1004126. Available at: https://doi.org/10.1371/journal.pgen.1004126.

Machová, M. and Ehler, E. (2023) 'Secondary school students' misconceptions in genetics: origins and solutions', *Journal of Biological Education*, 57(3), pp. 633–646. Available at: https://doi.org/10.1080/00219266.2021.1933136.

Magleby, A. and Furse, C. (2007) 'Improving communication skills through project-based learning', in *2007 IEEE Antennas and Propagation Society International Symposium*. IEEE, pp. 5403–5406. Available at: https://doi.org/10.1109/APS.2007.4396769.

Mutakinati, L., Anwari, I. and Kumano, Y. (2018) 'Analysis of students' critical thinking skill of middle school through STEM education project-based learning', *Jurnal Pendidikan IPA Indonesia*, 7(1), pp. 54–65. Available at: https://doi.org/10.15294/jpii.v7i1.10495.

Newton, L.D. and Newton, D.P. (2014) 'Creativity in 21st-century education', *PROSPECTS*, 44(4), pp. 575–589. Available at: https://doi.org/10.1007/s11125-014-9322-1.

Nurgaliyeva, A. (2021) 'The role of teaching practicum in the future biology teachers' professional training', in *Challenges of Science*. Institute of Metallurgy and Ore Beneficiation, Satbayev University, pp. 61–66. Available at: https://doi.org/10.31643/2021.09.

O'Donnell, L., Andrick, B. and Meng, W. (2014) 'Design of a bioinformatics practicum aimed at integrating concepts in immunology, virology, and pharmaceutical sciences in pharmacy curricula (EDU1P.253)', *The Journal of Immunology*, 192(1_Supplement), pp. 49.7-49.7. Available at: https://doi.org/10.4049/jimmunol.192.Supp.49.7.

O'Donnell, L.A. *et al.* (2016) 'A bioinformatics practicum to develop student understanding of immunological rejection of protein drugs', *American Journal of Pharmaceutical Education*, 80(9), p. 147. Available at: https://doi.org/10.5688/ajpe809147.

Oke, M. *et al.* (2018) 'Design and implementation of structural bioinformatics projects for biological sciences undergraduate students', *Biochemistry and Molecular Biology Education*, 46(5), pp. 547–554. Available at: https://doi.org/10.1002/bmb.21169.

Pantiwati, Y., Sari, T.N.I. and Nurkanti, M. (2022) 'Learning assessment model in biology education during the COVID-19 pandemic', *JPBI (Jurnal Pendidikan Biologi Indonesia)*, 8(3), pp. 265–274. Available at: https://doi.org/10.22219/jpbi.v8i3.22992.

Perwitasari, F., Astuti, N.B. and Atmojo, S. (2021) 'Online learning and assessment: Challenges and opportunities during pandemic COVID-19', in. Available at: https://doi.org/10.2991/assehr.k.210423.077.

Poczai, P. and Santiago-Blay, J.A. (2021) 'Principles and biological concepts of heredity before Mendel', *Biology Direct*, 16(1), p. 19. Available at: https://doi.org/10.1186/s13062-021-00308-4.

Rehman, R. and Fatima, S.S. (2021) 'An innovation in flipped class room: A teaching model to facilitate synchronous and asynchronous learning during a pandemic.', *Pakistan journal of medical sciences*, 37(1), pp. 131–136. Available at: https://doi.org/10.12669/pjms.37.1.3096.

Relethford, J.H. (2008) 'Genetic evidence and the modern human origins debate', *Heredity*, 100(6), pp. 555–563. Available at: https://doi.org/10.1038/hdy.2008.14.

Sasson, I., Yehuda, I. and Malkinson, N. (2018) 'Fostering the skills of critical thinking and question-posing in a project-based learning environment', *Thinking Skills and Creativity*, 29, pp. 203–212. Available at: https://doi.org/10.1016/j.tsc.2018.08.001.

Shah, H., Chavda, V. and Soniwala, M.M. (2023) 'Applications of bioinformatics tools in medicinal biology and biotechnology', in *Bioinformatics Tools for Pharmaceutical Drug Product Development*. Wiley, pp. 95–116. Available at: https://doi.org/10.1002/9781119865728.ch6.

Smith, M.K. and Wood, W.B. (2016) 'Teaching genetics: Past, present, and future', *Genetics*, 204(1), pp. 5–10. Available at: https://doi.org/10.1534/genetics.116.187138.

Sohpal, V.K., Dey, A. and Singh, A. (2010) 'MEGA biocentric software for sequence and phylogenetic analysis: a review', *International Journal of Bioinformatics Research and Applications*, 6(3), p. 230. Available at: https://doi.org/10.1504/IJBRA.2010.034072.

Ye, J., McGinnis, S. and Madden, T.L. (2006) 'BLAST: improvements for better sequence analysis', *Nucleic Acids Research*, 34(Web Server), pp. W6–W9. Available at: https://doi.org/10.1093/nar/gkl164.

Živković, S. (2016) 'A model of critical thinking as an important attribute for success in the 21st century', *Procedia – Social and Behavioral Sciences*, 232, pp. 102–108. Available at: https://doi.org/10.1016/j.sbspro.2016.10.034.

Strengthening Professional and Spiritual Education through 21st Century Skill Empowerment in Pandemic and Post-Pandemic Era – Arifin et al. (Eds)
© 2024 The Author(s), ISBN: 978-1-032-45243-2
Open Access: www.taylorfrancis.com, CC BY-NC-ND 4.0 license

The influence of grade level on middle school students' metacognitive skills

Ali Usman Hali
Henan University, China

Eko Susetyarini*, Khairil Ikhwan, Nur Kholifatu Rohmah & Ahmad Fauzi
Universitas Muhammadiyah Malang, Indonesia

Ning Rahayu Handayani
Universitas Negeri Malang, Indonesia

Mujiati Perwita Sari
MTs Al Huda Bogo Nganjuk, Indonesia

ABSTRACT: Metacognitive skills represent pivotal competencies for students to align with the requirements of educational curricula across diverse countries. The metacognitive proficiencies exhibited by students can be gauged and comprehended by considering the distinctions arising from varying grade levels. This study is aimed at ascertaining the impact of grade levels on students' metacognitive skills within a selected public junior high school in Malang, Indonesia. The assessment of metacognitive skills entailed the utilization of an integrated essay-based metacognitive evaluation. Data analysis was executed through one-way ANOVA, utilizing a significance threshold of 5%. The research outcomes conclusively infer that a noteworthy variance exists in metacognitive skills among students in grades VII, VIII, and IX. Furthermore, the data underscore that the pedagogical process within schools has yet to fully harness the latent metacognitive skills of students. Consequently, it is anticipated that educators will actively embrace diverse instructional strategies and evaluative mechanisms to more effectively nurture the cultivation of metacognitive skills within the Indonesian educational landscape.

Keywords: curriculum impact, grade levels, junior high school students, metacognitive development, pedagogical strategies

1 INTRODUCTION

The current curriculum's core competencies demand students to possess metacognitive skills (Muna *et al.* 2017). This is because metacognition is one of the best predictors of academic achievement (Sarac *et al.* 2014) and plays a crucial role in learning success (Palennari *et al.* 2018). Metacognitive skills are identified as one of the three key principles of learning and are recommended to be integrated into the curriculum across various fields of study (Millis 2016). The emergence of metacognitive skills in the learning process is based on the assumption that this ability is effective in ensuring individuals acquire self-directed learning skills (Coşkun 2018).

Metacognitive skills are highly essential for the development of learners (Sart 2014). This is because metacognitive skills in students can guide them in developing a more meaningful

---

*Corresponding Author: susetyorini@umm.ac.id

DOI: 10.1201/9781003376125-9

learning environment, enhancing thinking skills, engaging in analysis/problem-solving processes, making generalizations, and selecting strategies to improve future cognitive performance (Hartman 2001; Lai 2011; Smith *et al.* 2017). For instance, instruction in metacognitive strategies enhances reading comprehension and vocabulary achievement for third-grade students (Fisher 1998; Fouché and Lamport 2011) as well as fourth and fifth-grade students (Fouché and Lamport 2011).

Through metacognitive skills, learners are guided toward abilities such as planning, self-monitoring, and self-evaluation (Lai 2011; García *et al.* 2015). In this regard, metacognitive skills assist students in becoming responsible, independent, and self-regulated (Listiana *et al.* 2016; Coşkun 2018), excelling in problem-solving (Muna *et al.* 2017) and generating and applying strategies to meet their learning needs (Corebima 2009; Jaleel and Premachandran 2016). Equipped with metacognitive skills, students develop self-confidence in their abilities, encouraging a positive approach to challenges rather than perceiving them as risks to avoid (Cera *et al.* 2013).

Several studies have uncovered factors influencing students' metacognitive skills, one of which is the difference in grade levels (Wahdah *et al.* 2016; Coşkun 2018). Grade level differences suggest that metacognitive skills increase with age and experience (Biggs 1987; Sart 2014). This is supported by research showing higher cognitive skills at higher grade levels (Wahdah *et al.* 2016). Other studies have yielded similar results, indicating that metacognitive skills measured through thinking skills, decision-making skills, and evaluation skills also improve with higher grade levels (Coşkun 2018).

However, many studies often apply specific teaching models or strategies in their treatments. Research exploring metacognitive skills of learners across different grade levels within natural learning conditions remains limited. Hence, the aim of this study is to investigate whether grade levels influence metacognitive skills among junior high school students. This research seeks to provide insights into the metacognitive skills at various grade levels in Junior High School.

2 METHODS

2.1 Study design and research participant

This research employs a descriptive and comparative study design with the objective of analyzing and comparing metacognitive skill levels among students based on their grade levels. The study was conducted at a public junior high school in Malang, East Java, Indonesia. The research sample consisted of students from 7th, 8th, and 9th grades, with each class consisting of 34, 32, and 34 students, respectively. Data collection took place in October 2018.

2.2 Data collection instrument and procedures

Metacognitive skills of the students were assessed using an integrated metacognitive assessment with essay tests (Corebima 2009). Before employing the essay tests as data collection instruments, the validity was tested using Pearson's Product-Moment correlation, and reliability was assessed using Cronbach's Alpha. Based on the results of both tests, all items in the assessment were deemed valid, and the instrument was considered reliable.

2.3 Data analysis

The collected metacognitive skill data were then subjected to one-way ANOVA with a significance level of 5%. Prior to conducting the ANOVA, tests for normality (Kolmogorov-Smirnov and Shapiro-Wilk tests) and homogeneity (Levene's test) were performed to ensure that data normality and homogeneity assumptions were met. Since the homogeneity assumption was not satisfied, the Games-Howell post hoc test was used for further analysis.

3 RESULTS

The collected research data is presented in Table 1. Based on Table 1, the average meta-cognitive skill scores for 7th, 8th, and 9th grade levels are 5.191, 8.324, and 19.351, respectively. The average metacognitive skill scores indicate that the highest level of metacognitive skill is possessed by the 9th-grade students, followed by the 8th-grade, and then the 7th-grade students.

Regarding the data distribution, the research data is found to be normally distributed (p-value = 0.200), but not homogeneous (p-value < 0.001). Hence, the homogeneity test was followed by an analysis of variance (ANOVA) with the Games-Howell post hoc test, as presented in Table 1. From Table 1, it is evident that there is a significant difference in the metacognitive skill scores among the 7th, 8th, and 9th grade levels [$F_{(3, 96)} = 35.972$, p-value = 0.000 < 0.05]. Thus, both the mean and the significance of the metacognitive skill scores across different grade levels exhibit substantial differences.

Table 1. Comparison of metacognitive skill scores across grade levels.

Grade	Mean Score
7th	5.191
8th	8.324
9th	19.351

4 DISCUSSION

Based on the conducted research, it is evident that the findings align with prior studies. Research conducted at the higher education level (Coşkun 2018) stated that significant differences in metacognitive skills exist based on the semester level at Kahramanmaras Sutcu Imam University, Turkey. Furthermore, research conducted at the high school level (Wahdah et al. 2016) also obtained similar results, showing significant differences in meta-cognitive skills among 10th and 11th-grade students at SMAN 1 Pringgarata, Mataram. Both studies demonstrate that as grade levels increase, metacognitive skills also improve.

Grade level emerges as a significant factor influencing students' metacognitive skills. These skills continue to develop throughout their maturation process. This is attributed to students becoming more conscious of their conscious thoughts as well as those of others (Wahdah et al. 2016). Older children grasp the capacity to remember and its limitations more comprehensively compared to younger children. The duration of learning and the accumulation of experiences significantly contribute to this phenomenon. Longer periods of learning enhance students' ability to determine effective learning methods for understanding

Table 2. Analysis of Variance (ANOVA) results for metacognitive skill scores by grade levels.

	Sum of Squares	df	Mean Square	F	Sig.
Between Groups	3052.124	2	1526.062	35.972	.000
Within Groups	3309.000	78	42.423		
Total	6361.124	80			

course material. Students with greater experience and intensity of learning (Expert learners) can adapt effective learning strategies to comprehend the concepts they are studying (Fouché and Lamport 2011). Metacognition plays a vital role in fostering students' personality development. In this context, students become more adept at using metacognitive strategies to gain confidence and independence, granting them the freedom to pursue their intellectual needs through independent information acquisition (Chauhan and Singh 2014).

The significant influence of grade levels on metacognitive skills can be attributed to the intricate interplay between cognitive development and educational experiences. As students' progress through higher grade levels, their cognitive abilities mature, allowing them to engage in more complex thinking processes. This maturation involves the enhancement of executive functions such as self-regulation, planning, and decision-making. Consequently, students in higher grade levels are better equipped to utilize metacognitive strategies effectively.

Furthermore, the accumulation of learning experiences and exposure to a wider range of academic challenges contribute to the variance in metacognitive skills across grade levels. With each academic year, students encounter progressively intricate subjects and assign-ments that demand greater cognitive flexibility, analytical thinking, and problem-solving capabilities. These challenges necessitate the deployment of metacognitive strategies to navigate through the learning process more efficiently. Students in higher grade levels, having dealt with a more diverse array of academic tasks, tend to possess a broader reper-toire of metacognitive strategies, enabling them to adapt to various learning situations.

Another key factor lies in the increasing academic demands placed on students as they advance through grade levels. The curriculum content becomes progressively intricate and multifaceted, requiring students to manage larger amounts of information, synthesize com-plex concepts, and engage in critical analysis. Such academic rigors foster the development of metacognitive skills, as students are compelled to strategize their learning approaches to handle the elevated cognitive demands. Consequently, higher grade levels become a training ground for students to refine their metacognitive strategies in order to succeed academically.

Empowering metacognitive skills necessitates educators' efforts to meet the demands of the curriculum. The empowerment of metacognitive skills is determined by the methods and learning strategies prepared by teachers. Several model that teachers can adopt include problem-based learning (Kevin 2011; Yuan et al. 2020) and project-based learning (Husamah 2015; Rumahlatu and Sangur 2019). Paired Problem Solving assists students in articulating their thoughts and those of their peers (Hargrove 2013). Cooperative learning, a method involving discussion, promotes students' metacognitive skills, as it encourages con-versation recall, discussion of subject matter, and the expression of opinions (Fouché and Lamport 2011).

In addition to the aforementioned methods and strategies, teachers can enhance students' metacognitive skills by guiding them on what to do during learning and problem-solving processes (Rahman et al. 2010). Furthermore, motivating students contributes to the development of metacognitive skills. This is consistent with research demonstrating a con-nection between students' metacognitive skills and their motivation (Muna et al. 2017). Teachers can also implement complex structured assessments or assignments involving various knowledge and skills, including recall and data processing abilities (Lai 2011). An example of an assessment for fostering metacognitive skills is a learning journal. Through a learning journal, students can identify strategies or learning models that suit their learning style, enhancing the effectiveness of understanding the material. The selection of such teaching methods or models is based on students' learning reflection within the learning journal (Wahdah et al. 2016).

Unfortunately, metacognitive awareness among students has yet to be comprehensively developed. Even at the university level, the majority of students remain unaware and lack an understanding of themselves as learners. Therefore, the role of educators as facilitators is crucial in fostering students' metacognitive skills. The capacity and creativity of educators in developing learning models as dominant supporters of improved metacognitive skills among students need to be further cultivated.

5 CONCLUSION

In light of the conducted research, it is evident that grade level differences significantly impact the metacognitive skills of junior high school students. This study has established that students in higher grade levels, particularly in the ninth grade, exhibit superior metacognitive skills compared to their counterparts in the seventh and eighth grades. This correlation underscores the progressive enhancement of metacognitive skills as students advance through different grade levels. Specifically, the results indicate that higher grade levels are associated with elevated levels of metacognitive proficiency. The findings contribute to a growing body of literature that highlights the connection between cognitive development and educational progression. The observed pattern emphasizes the role of grade levels as a significant factor in nurturing and refining metacognitive skills among students. This research underscores the importance of acknowledging and addressing these developmental nuances in educational practices.

Implications drawn from this study underscore the need for educators to recognize the varying metacognitive needs of students across different grade levels. As students ascend academically, their metacognitive skills demand greater attention and support. Instructors can employ innovative teaching methodologies, foster motivation, and design complex structured assessments to harness and enhance students' metacognitive capabilities effectively. Moreover, educational institutions should consider integrating metacognitive skill development as an integral component of the curriculum to ensure that students are equipped with essential cognitive tools to navigate the increasingly complex academic challenges they face.

REFERENCES

Biggs, J. (1987) "Reflective Thinking and School Learning: An Introduction to the Theory and Practice of Metacognition," *Set; n.2 item 10; 1987*. Wellington, New Zealand: New Zealand Council for Educational Research, (2). Available at: https://search.informit.org/doi/10.3316/aeipt.49826.

Cera, R., Mancini, M. and Antonietti, A. (2013) "Relationships between metacognition, self-efficacy and self-regulation in learning," *ECPS – Educational, Cultural and Psychological Studies*, (7), pp. 115–141. doi: 10.7358/ecps-2013-007-cera.

Chauhan, A. and Singh, N. (2014) "Metacognition: A conceptual framework," *International Journal of Education and Psychological Research (IJEPR)*, 3(3), pp. 21–22. Available at: http://ijepr.org/doc/V3_Is3_Oct14/ij4.pdf.

Corebima, A. D. (2009) "Metacognitive skill measurement integrated in achievement test," in *Third International Conference on Science and Mathematics Education (CoSMEd)*. Penang: SEAMEO Regional Centre for Education in Science and Mathematics. Available at: http://ftp.recsam.edu.my/cosmed/cosmed09/AbstractsFullPapers2009/Abstract/Science Parallel PDF/Full Paper/01.pdf.

Coşkun, Y. (2018) "A study on metacognitive thinking skills of university students," *Journal of Education and Training Studies*, 6(3), p. 38. doi: 10.11114/jets.v6i3.2931.

Fisher, R. (1998) "Thinking about thinking: Developing metacognition in children," *Early Child Development and Care*, 141(1), pp. 1–15. doi: 10.1080/0300443981410101.

Fouché, J. and Lamport, M. A. (2011) "Do metacognitive strategies improve student achievement in secondary science classrooms?," *Christian Perspectives in Education*, 4(2), pp. 1–25. Available at: https://digitalcommons.liberty.edu/cgi/viewcontent.cgi?referer=https://www.google.com/&httpsredir=1&article=1051&context=cpe.

García, T. *et al.* (2015) "Metacognitive knowledge and skills in students with deep approach to learning. Evidence from mathematical problem solving," *Revista de Psicodidactica*, 20(2), pp. 209–226. doi: 10.1387/RevPsicodidact.13060.

Hargrove, R. A. (2013) "Assessing the long-term impact of a metacognitive approach to creative skill development," *International Journal of Technology and Design Education*, 23(3), pp. 489–517. doi: 10.1007/s10798-011-9200-6.

Hartman, H. J. (2001) "Developing students' metacognitive knowledge and skills," in *Metacognition in Learning and Instruction*, pp. 33–68. doi: 10.1007/978-94-017-2243-8_3.

Husamah (2015) "Blended project based learning: Metacognitive awareness of biology education new students," *Journal of Education and Learning*, 9(4), pp. 274–281. doi: 10.11591/edulearn.v9.i4.2121.

Jaleel, S. and Premachandran, P. (2016) "A study on the metacognitive awareness of secondary school students," *Universal Journal of Educational Research*, 4(1), pp. 165–172. doi: 10.13189/ujer.2016.040121.

Kevin, D. (2011) "Impact of problem-based learning on student experience and metacognitive development," *Multicultural Education & Technology Journal*. Edited by N. Flora. Emerald Group Publishing Limited, 5(1), pp. 55–69. doi: 10.1108/17504971111121928.

Lai, E. R. (2011) *Metacognition: A literature review, Pearson's Research Report*. Available at: https://images.pearsonassessments.com/images/tmrs/Metacognition_Literature_Review_Final.pdf.

Listiana, L. *et al.* (2016) "Empowering students' metacognitive skils through new teaching strategy (group investigation integrated with think talk write) in biology classroom," *Journal of Baltic Science Education*, 15(3), pp. 391–400. Available at: http://www.scientiasocialis.lt/jbse/files/pdf/vol15/391-400.Listiana_JBSE_Vol.15_No.3.pdf.

Millis, B. J. (2016) "Using metacognition to promote learning," *IDEA Paper*, 63(December), pp. 1–9. Available at: http://www.ideaedu.org/Portals/0/Uploads/Documents/IDEAPapers/IDEAPapers/Paper IDEA_63.pdf.

Muna, K. et al. (2017) "Metacognitive skills and students' motivation toward chemical equilibrium problem solving ability: A correlational study on students of XI IPA SMAN 2 Banjarmasin," in *AIP Conference Proceedings*. AIP Publishing. doi: 10.1063/1.5016001.

Palennari, M., Taiyeb, M. and Saenab, S. (2018) "Profile of students' metacognitive skill based on their learning style," in *Journal of Physics: Conference Series*. doi: 10.1088/1742-6596/1028/1/012030.

Rahman, S. et al. (2010) "Metacognitive skills and the development of metacognition in the classroom," in *International Conference on Education and Educational Technologies*. Iwate, pp. 347–351. Available at: http://www.wseas.us/e-library/conferences/2010/Japan/EDU/EDU-58.pdf.

Rumahlatu, D. and Sangur, K. (2019) "The influence of project-based learning strategies on the metacognitive skills, concept understanding and retention of senior high school students," *Journal of Education and Learning (EduLearn)*, 13(1), p. 104. doi: 10.11591/edulearn.v13i1.11189.

Sarac, S., Onder, A. and Karakelle, S. (2014) "The relations among general intelligence, metacognition and text learning performance," *Egitim Ve Bilim-Education and Science*, 39(173), pp. 40–53. Available at: http://egitimvebilim.ted.org.tr/index.php/EB/article/viewFile/1111/657.

Sart, G. (2014) "The effects of the development of metacognition on project-based learning," *Procedia – Social and Behavioral Sciences*. Elsevier B.V., 152, pp. 131–136. doi: 10.1016/j.sbspro.2014.09.169.

Smith, A. K., Black, S. and Hooper, L. M. (2017) "Metacognitive knowledge, skills, and awareness: A possible solution to enhancing academic achievement in African American adolescents," *Urban Education*, pp. 1–15. doi: 10.1177/0042085917714511.

Wahdah, N. F., Jufri, A. W. and Zulkifli, L. (2016) "Jurnal belajar sebagai sarana pengembangan kemampuan metakognisi siswa," *Jurnal Pijar Mipa*, 11(1), pp. 70–74. Available at: https://jurnalfkip.unram.ac.id/index.php/JPM/article/view/65/65.

Yuan, K., Aftoni, A. and Çobanoğlu, Ö. (2020) "The effect of problem-based learning model and blended learning model to metacognitive awareness as a reflection towards a New Normal Era," *Jurnal Pendidikan Teknologi dan Kejuruan*, 26(2), pp. 183–188. doi: 10.21831/jptk.v26i2.32783.

Strengthening Professional and Spiritual Education through 21st Century Skill Empowerment in Pandemic and Post-Pandemic Era – Arifin et al. (Eds)
© 2024 The Author(s), ISBN: 978-1-032-45243-2
Open Access: www.taylorfrancis.com, CC BY-NC-ND 4.0 license

Critical thinking skills and metacognitive skills: Which holds more significance in biology learning outcomes?

Anjana Prusty
SR University, India

Iin Hindun*, Zaenul Muttaqin, Putri Nuril, Izzati Choirina, Rizqi Wildan Ab'ror, Lia Astuti & Ahmad Fauzi
Universitas Muhammadiyah Malang, Indonesia

ABSTRACT: In the context of biology education, the crucial link between metacognition, critical thinking, and learning outcomes has garnered increasing attention. This study examines the relationship between metacognitive skills, critical thinking abilities, and biology learning outcomes among high school students in Malang. Through integrated essay tests, the research evaluates metacognition and critical thinking, revealing a significant association between these cognitive dimensions (F = 12.828, p<0.05) that contributes to 28.6% of the variance in biology learning outcomes. The findings underscore the importance of fostering metacognitive and critical thinking strategies in biology education, providing students with effective learning tools and analytical approaches. Integrating these skills into curricula can cultivate adaptable learners capable of tackling academic challenges and real-world issues. This research informs educational practices and policies, offering a transformative approach to empower students with essential skills for their academic and personal growth.

Keywords: biology learning outcomes, high school students, higher-order thinking skills, metacognition

1 INTRODUCTION

In the realm of education, the assessment of learning outcomes holds immense significance as it provides insights into the effectiveness of instructional methods and curriculum design (Coates 2015; Ramdiah *et al.* 2019). Among the various subjects, the domain of biology education plays a pivotal role in shaping students' scientific understanding and critical thinking skills (Arsad *et al.* 2011; Firdaus and Darmadi 2017; Puig and Ageitos 2022). Biology not only imparts foundational knowledge about living organisms and their interactions but also fosters the development of analytical and problem-solving abilities that are crucial for informed decision-making in an increasingly complex world (Nainggolan *et al.* 2021; Slamet *et al.* 2019). The examination of students' performance in biology, therefore, goes beyond rote memorization; it delves into the mastery of concepts and the application of higher-order cognitive skills (Arsad *et al.* 2011; Ramdiah *et al.* 2019).

Moreover, metacognition holds paramount significance as a key factor in enhancing innovative behaviors, encompassing elements of planning, monitoring, and regulation for specific actions in generating and introducing novel ideas (Kim and Lee 2018). Metacognitive knowledge serves as the foundation for independent language learning (Ismael 2015). Metacognition plays a pivotal role in communication, reading comprehension, language acquisition, social cognition, attention, self-control, memory, self-instruction, writing, problem-solving, and personality development (Chauhan and Singh 2014). Therefore, empowering metacognitive thinking skills during the learning process needs to be taken into account to assist students in becoming accustomed to metacognitive thinking (Palennari and Hartati 2009). Furthermore, metacognition is intertwined with various other constructs, including critical thinking and motivation (Lai 2011).

---

*Corresponding Author: inhindun@umm.ac.id

DOI: 10.1201/9781003376125-10

Furthermore, in line with the importance of metacognition, critical thinking plays a pivotal role in shaping students' cognitive abilities. Critical thinking involves the capacity to think clearly and rationally about what should be done or believed (Sharples *et al.* 2017). It empowers learners to engage in focused assessment and self-regulation, enabling them to evaluate both external and internal arguments, leading to reasoned resolutions for complex issues and conflicts encountered in daily life (Shukri and Mukundan 2015). Teaching critical thinking to students is akin to training them to think like scientists (Schmaltz *et al.* 2017). It encompasses various skills, including argument analysis, drawing conclusions through inductive or deductive reasoning, evaluation, decision-making, and problem-solving (Lai 2011). Biology education, in particular, holds the promise of fostering these critical thinking skills effectively.

Biology education, as a scientific discipline, involves extensive exploration and constructivist activities that contribute to students' competencies. Within this context, the process of biology learning naturally guides students toward cultivating critical thinking skills through activity-based learning (Donald 2012; Schmaltz *et al.* 2017). The challenges presented by educators during biology lessons also possess the potential to enhance students' critical thinking abilities. In harmony with this notion, a plethora of research reports highlight the empowering role of biology education in fostering critical thinking skills among students (Croner 2003), spanning from secondary to tertiary levels (Addy and Stevenson 2014; Wilson 2017). Consequently, the possession of both variables, metacognitive awareness and critical thinking skills, during the learning process significantly contributes to a more focused educational journey, facilitating swifter attainment of competencies and desired learning outcomes.

In previous research, a positive relationship between metacognitive skills and cognitive learning outcomes of high school biology students was established within the context of scientific-based learning under the 2013 curriculum. In addition to metacognition, critical thinking has also contributed significantly to explaining learning outcomes, with several studies indicating a significant connection between critical thinking and cognitive learning outcomes. However, prior studies have been limited to investigating singular relationships between variables and seldom have simultaneously examined two variables such as metacognitive awareness and critical thinking skills in conjunction with cognitive learning outcomes within a specific instructional strategy.

Exploring the complex interplay between metacognitive skills and critical thinking skills in relation to learning outcomes within this research offers the potential for a more comprehensive understanding of how these two variables collectively elucidate cognitive learning outcomes in biology education. This prospect also holds the promise of yielding improved predictive insights into cognitive learning outcomes in the context of biology education. As such, the primary aim of this study is to ascertain which factor, between metacognitive awareness and critical thinking, exerts greater influence on biology learning outcomes among high school students in Malang. Through this investigation, we seek to bridge existing gaps in research by delving into the multifaceted dynamics of these cognitive constructs and their collective impact on biology learning outcomes.

2 METHODS

2.1 Study design and research participant

The participants in this study consisted of high school students from X grade in Malang, Indonesia. These students were selected from various schools in the area to ensure a diverse representation of backgrounds. The research procedure spanned several months. Subsequently, the integrated essay tests were administered in a controlled classroom setting. The students' demographic information, including age and gender, was also gathered for reference.

2.2 Data collection instrument and procedures

To gauge metacognitive skills and critical thinking abilities, a comprehensive assessment approach integrating essay tests was adopted. Specifically, the assessment of critical thinking skills utilized the essay test devised by Zubaidah *et al.* (2020), while the assessment of metacognitive skills employed the essay test formulated by Corebima (2009). Prior to employing the essay tests as data collection instruments, rigorous validation was conducted using Pearson's product-moment correlation to establish content and construct validity. Additionally, reliability was assessed using Cronbach's alpha. The robustness of the instruments was verified through both validity and reliability tests. By implementing an integrated essay-based assessment strategy for metacognitive skills and critical thinking abilities, this study intends to delve into the nuanced dynamics between these cognitive processes and biology learning outcomes. The distinctiveness of these constructs necessitates an analytical approach that can simultaneously account for their intricate interplay.

2.3 Data analysis

To explore the relationships between metacognitive skills, critical thinking abilities, and biology learning outcomes, a multiple regression analysis was conducted using specialized statistical software. This approach allows the simultaneous consideration of several independent variables in relation to a single dependent variable. Through this analysis, we aim to uncover the extent to which metacognitive skills and critical thinking abilities predict students' biology learning outcomes. A significance level of $p < 0.05$ was set for all statistical tests.

3 RESULTS

The statistical examination of the relationship between metacognitive skills and critical thinking abilities among students is illustrated in Tables 1–3. These tables provide a comprehensive overview of the ANOVA summary, presenting the calculated values that determine the significance level. A significance level of $p < 0.05$ was employed to evaluate the acceptance or rejection of the null hypothesis, thereby validating or dismissing the research hypotheses. The regression summary table further delineates the extent of metacognitive skills' contribution to critical thinking abilities, while the regression coefficient table unveils the precise regression equation defining the intricate interplay between metacognitive skills and critical thinking abilities. These tables collectively furnish an insightful understanding of the associations under investigation.

Table 1. Summary of correlation and determination coefficient calculations.

Model	R	R Square	Adjusted R Square	Std. Error of the Estimate
1	.557[a]	.310	.286	14.40168

Table 2. ANOVA summary of the relationship between metacognitive skills and critical thinking abilities among sudents.

	Model	Sum of Squares	df	Mean Square	F	Sig.
1	Regression	5321.427	2	2660.713	12.828	.000[b]
	Residual	11822.277	57	207.408		
	Total	17143.704	59			

Table 3. Regression coefficient summary of the relationship between metacognitive skills and critical thinking abilities among students.

		Unstandardized Coefficients		Standardized Coefficients		
	Model	B	Std. Error	Beta	T	Sig.
1	(Constant)	38.201	10.470		3.649	.001
	Critical thinking	1.101	.271	.478	4.070	.000
	Metacognitive	−.705	.166	−.499	−4.249	.000

71

Based on the analysis results presented in Tables 1 to 3, it is evident that the obtained F-value is 12.828, with a significance value of <0.001. This signifies the rejection of the null hypothesis and the acceptance of the research hypothesis. Therefore, a relationship exists between students' metacognitive skills and critical thinking abilities. The regression analysis results also reveal a correlation coefficient (R) value of 0.557 and a coefficient of determination (R2) value of 0.286. This indicates that Metacognitive Skills and Critical Thinking Abilities cumulatively account for 28.6% of the variance, while the remaining 70.4% is attributed to other unexamined variables in this study. The linear equation derived from the data analysis is Y = 1.101X1 − 0.705X2 + 38.201. From this equation, it can be observed that for every 1-point increase in metacognitive skill scores, there is a decrease of 0.705 in cognitive learning outcomes.

4 DISCUSSION

The results of this study shed light on the intricate relationship between metacognitive skills, critical thinking abilities, and biology learning outcomes among high school students. The identified significant correlation between metacognitive skills and critical thinking abilities underscores the interdependence of these cognitive processes in enhancing students' academic performance. This echoes the notion that metacognition serves as a cognitive scaffold that supports the development and application of critical thinking skills (Ku and Ho 2010; Magno 2010; Rivas et al. 2022). Metacognitive awareness empowers students to monitor, evaluate, and adjust their thinking, which in turn enables them to engage more effectively in critical thinking tasks (Emily R Lai 2011; Stanton et al. 2021).

The calculated correlation coefficient and coefficient of determination elucidate the extent to which metacognitive skills and critical thinking abilities collectively contribute to students' biology learning outcomes. The identified 28.6% variance highlights the substantive impact of these cognitive factors on academic achievement. However, the remaining unexplained variance, at 70.4%, emphasizes the multifaceted nature of learning outcomes, indicating the influence of unexamined variables. This reiterates the complexity of students' learning experiences, which are influenced by various individual, contextual, and instructional factors.

Critical thinking plays a pivotal role in shaping the quality of students' learning experiences, particularly in the domain of biology. The intricate relationship between critical thinking abilities and biology learning outcomes can be attributed to the inherently analytical and inquiry-driven nature of biological sciences (Peffer et al. 2020). Biology often requires students to comprehend complex concepts, analyze intricate systems, and synthesize information from various sources to formulate informed conclusions (Fauzi et al. 2021; Haambokoma 2007; Knippels 2005). By cultivating critical thinking skills, students are equipped with the cognitive tools necessary to navigate these complexities effectively (Behar-Horenstein and Niu 2011; Facione 2011; Staib 2003).

In the context of biology, critical thinking entails the ability to engage with empirical evidence, assess the validity of scientific claims, and construct well-reasoned arguments (Bailin 2002; Butcher et al. 2023; Emily R. Lai 2011). When students develop these skills, they become adept at evaluating the reliability of biological information, differentiating between credible and questionable sources, and making informed decisions based on evidence. Moreover, biology frequently presents students with real-world scenarios and ethical dilemmas (Nainggolan et al. 2021; Slamet et al. 2019), demanding them to apply critical thinking skills to assess potential consequences and propose solutions. As a result, students who possess robust critical thinking abilities are better prepared to comprehend the dynamic interplay of biological concepts and their implications in various contexts.

Furthermore, the alignment between critical thinking and the nature of scientific inquiry further accentuates the significant relationship between critical thinking abilities and biology learning outcomes. Scientific inquiry demands curiosity, skepticism, and the capacity to formulate and test hypotheses (Jirout 2020; Wu and Wu 2020). These essential components of scientific thinking mirror the cognitive processes intrinsic to critical thinking. Engaging with biology entails exploring the mechanisms underlying living organisms, investigating the effects of environmental factors, and drawing conclusions from empirical observations. Such endeavors necessitate critical thinking skills to decipher intricate relationships, identify patterns, and interpret data accurately (Amin *et al.* 2017; Breu 2008; Setiawati and Corebima 2017; Zion and Mendelovic 2012).

Incorporating critical thinking into biology education fosters a deeper engagement with the subject matter and cultivates a scientific mindset that extends beyond the classroom. By honing critical thinking skills, students are better equipped to grapple with the evolving landscape of biology, engage in evidence-based decision-making, and contribute meaningfully to scientific discourse. Consequently, the significant relationship between critical thinking abilities and biology learning outcomes underscores the imperative of integrating critical thinking instruction within biology curricula, offering students a comprehensive toolkit to excel in their academic pursuits and beyond.

Analyzing the regression equation derived from the analysis provides valuable insights into the nuanced dynamics between metacognitive skills, critical thinking abilities, and biology learning outcomes. Although the negative coefficient for metacognitive skills may initially appear counterintuitive, it suggests a complex interaction. This result might be attributed to the intricate interplay between metacognitive processes and other unmeasured variables that impact cognitive learning outcomes. Thus, it is vital to interpret this finding with caution and consider it as a starting point for further exploration.

The implications of these findings for biology education are substantial. Integrating metacognitive strategies and promoting critical thinking skills can be pivotal in enhancing students' academic achievement in biology. Educators can design curricula and instructional methods that encourage self-regulated learning, reflective practices, and analytical thinking. This approach not only empowers students to navigate complex biological concepts effectively but also equips them with transferable skills applicable across various domains. The correlation between critical thinking abilities and biology learning outcomes further underscores the significance of nurturing analytical thinking in the context of science education.

In light of the study's limitations, such as the specific context and sample size, further research could expand the investigation to different educational levels, diverse settings, and larger populations to enhance the generalizability of the findings. Ultimately, this study underscores the symbiotic relationship between metacognitive skills, critical thinking abilities, and successful biology learning outcomes, emphasizing the need for a comprehensive educational approach that nurtures both cognitive dimensions to empower students as confident and capable learners and thinkers.

5 CONCLUSION

In conclusion, this study sheds light on the intricate interplay between metacognitive skills, critical thinking abilities, and biology learning outcomes among high school students in Malang. The findings underscore the significance of both metacognition and critical thinking as influential factors in shaping students' success in biology education. The established relationship between metacognitive awareness and critical thinking highlights the holistic nature of cognitive development, where metacognition facilitates effective learning strategies and critical thinking empowers students to analyze, evaluate, and synthesize complex biological concepts.

Moving forward, educators should consider designing pedagogical approaches that explicitly cultivate metacognitive awareness and critical thinking skills in the context of biology education. Encouraging students to reflect on their learning processes, strategize their approaches, and critically evaluate biological information can enhance their overall academic performance and cognitive development. Additionally, educational policymakers should recognize the value of metacognitive and critical thinking instruction in fostering well-rounded, adaptable individuals capable of thriving in a knowledge-driven society.

REFERENCES

Addy, T. M. and Stevenson, M. O. (2014) "Evaluating biological claims to enhance critical thinking," *Journal of microbiology & biology education*, 15(1), pp. 49–50. doi: 10.1128/jmbe.v15i1.663.

Amin, A. M. *et al.* (2017) "The critical thinking skills profile of preservice biology teachers in Animal Physiology," in *Proceedings of the 3rd International Conference on Education and Training (ICET 2017)*, pp. 179–183. doi: 10.2991/icet-17.2017.30.

Arsad, N. M., Osman, K. and Soh, T. M. T. (2011) "Instrument development for 21st century skills in Biology," in *Procedia – Social and Behavioral Sciences*. Elsevier B.V., pp. 1470–1474. doi: 10.1016/j. sbspro.2011.03.312.

Bailin, S. (2002) "Critical thinking and science education," *Science & Education*, 11(4), pp. 361–375. doi: 10.1023/A:1016042608621.

Behar-Horenstein, L. S. and Niu, L. (2011) "Teaching critical thinking skills In higher education: A review of the literature," *Journal of College Teaching & Learning (TLC)*, 8(2). doi: 10.19030/tlc.v8i2.3554.

Breu, F., Guggenbichler, S. and Wollmann, J. (2008) *Implementation of Critical Thinking Exercises in Introductory Biology, Dissertation.* Available at: http://medcontent.metapress.com/index/A65RM03P487 4243N.pdf.

Butcher, K. R. *et al.* (2023) "Critical thinking during science investigations: what do practicing teachers value and observe?," *Teachers and Teaching*, pp. 1–21. doi: 10.1080/13540602.2023.2191186.

Chauhan, A. and Singh, N. (2014) "Metacognition: A conceptual framework," *International Journal of Education and Psychological Research (IJEPR)*, 3(3), pp. 21–22. Available at: http://ijepr.org/doc/V3_Is3_ Oct14/ij4.pdf.

Coates, H. (2015) "Assessment of learning outcomes," in *The European Higher Education Area.* Cham: Springer International Publishing, pp. 399–413. doi: 10.1007/978-3-319-20877-0_26.

Corebima, A. D. (2009) "Metacognitive skill measurement integrated in achievement test," in *Third International Conference on Science and Mathematics Education (CoSMEd)*. Penang: SEAMEO Regional Centre for Education in Science and Mathematics. Available at: http://ftp.recsam.edu.my/cosmed/ cosmed09/AbstractsFullPapers2009/Abstract/Science Parallel PDF/Full Paper/01.pdf.

Croner, P. (2003) "Developing critical thinking skills through the use of guided laboratory activities," *The Science Education Review*, 2(2), pp. 1–13.

Donald, G. M. (2012) "Teaching critical & analytical thinking in high school biology?," *The American Biology Teacher*, 74(3), pp. 178–181. doi: 10.1525/abt.2012.74.3.9.

Facione, P. a. (2011) "Critical thinking: What it is and why it counts," *Insight assessment*, (ISBN 13: 978-1-891557-07-1.), pp. 1–28. Available at: https://www.insightassessment.com/CT-Resources/Teaching-For-and-About-Critical-Thinking/Critical-Thinking-What-It-Is-and-Why-It-Counts/Critical-Thinking-What-It-Is-and-Why-It-Counts-PDF.

Fauzi, A. *et al.* (2021) "The difficulty index of biology topics in Indonesian senior high school: Biology undergraduate students' perspectives," *JPBI (Jurnal Pendidikan Biologi Indonesia)*, 7(2), pp. 149–158. doi: 10.22219/jpbi.v7i2.16538.

Firdaus, F. and Darmadi, D. (2017) "Shaping scientific attitude of biology education students through research-based teaching," in *AIP Conference Proceedings*. AIP Publishing, p. 100004. doi: 10.1063/ 1.4995214.

Haambokoma, C. (2007) "Nature and causes of learning difficulties in genetics at high school level in Zambia," *Journal of International Development and Cooperation*, 13(1), pp. 1–9. doi: 10.15027/28479.

Ismael, H. A. (2015) "The role of metacognitive knowledge in enhancing learners autonomy," *International Journal of Language and Linguistics*, 2(4), pp. 95–102. Available at: https://pdfs.semanticscholar.org/8e90/ 457970962cca26e977d23c063f913332ef31.pdf.

Jirout, J. J. (2020) "Supporting early scientific thinking through curiosity," *Frontiers in Psychology*, 11. doi: 10.3389/fpsyg.2020.01717.

Kim, D. and Lee, D. (2018) "Impacts of metacognition on innovative behaviors: Focus on the mediating effects of entrepreneurship," *Journal of Open Innovation: Technology, Market, and Complexity*, 4(2), p. 18. doi: 10.3390/joitmc4020018.

Knippels, M.-C. P. J., Arend, J. W. and Boersma, K. T. (2005) "Design criteria for learning and teaching genetics," *Journal of Biological Education*, 393(393), pp. 108–112. doi: 10.1080/00219266.2005.9655976.

Ku, K. Y. L. and Ho, I. T. (2010) "Metacognitive strategies that enhance critical thinking," *Metacognition and Learning*, 5(3), pp. 251–267. doi: 10.1007/s11409-010-9060-6.

Lai, E. (2011) *Motivation: A literature review, Alwasy Learning.* Available at: http://www.datec.org.uk/CHAT/ chatmetal.htm.

Lai, Emily R. (2011) *Critical thinking: A literature review, Pearson's Research Report.* Available at: https:// images.pearsonassessments.com/images/tmrs/CriticalThinkingReviewFINAL.pdf.

Lai, Emily R (2011) *Metacognition: A literature review, Pearson's Research Report.* Available at: https:// images.pearsonassessments.com/images/tmrs/Metacognition_Literature_Review_Final.pdf.

Magno, C. (2010) "The role of metacognitive skills in developing critical thinking," *Metacognition and Learning*, 5(2), pp. 137–156. doi: 10.1007/s11409-010-9054-4.

Nainggolan, V. A., Situmorang, R. P. and Hastuti, S. P. (2021) "Learning Bryophyta: Improving students' scientific literacy through problem-based learning," *JPBI (Jurnal Pendidikan Biologi Indonesia)*, 7(1), pp. 71–82. doi: 10.22219/jpbi.v7i1.15220.

Palennari, M. and Hartati (2009) "Pengaruh ekstrak tembakau sebagai insektisida botani terhadap perkem-bangan lalat buah (Drosophila melanogaster)," *Jurusan Biologi FMIPA Universitas Negeri Makassar*, 10 (2), pp. 79–83. Available at: https://ojs.unm.ac.id/bionature/article/download/1364/447.

Peffer, M. E. *et al.* (2020) "Learning analytics to assess beliefs about science: Evolution of expertise as seen through biological inquiry," *CBE—Life Sciences Education*. Edited by I. Davidesco, 19(3), p. ar47. doi: 10.1187/cbe.19-11-0247.

Puig, Blanca and Ageitos, N. (2022) "Critical thinking to decide what to believe and what to do regarding vaccination in schools. A case study with primary pre-service teachers," in Puig, B. and Jiménez-Aleixandre, M. P. (eds.) *Critical Thinking in Biology and Environmental Education. Contributions from Biology Education Research*. Cham: Springer, pp. 113–132. doi: 10.1007/978-3-030-92006-7_7.

Ramdiah, S. *et al.* (2019) "Understanding, planning, and implementation of HOTS by senior high school biology teachers in Banjarmasin-Indonesia," *International Journal of Instruction*, 12(1), pp. 425–440. doi: 10.29333/iji.2019.12128a.

Rivas, S. F., Saiz, C. and Ossa, C. (2022) "Metacognitive strategies and development of critical thinking in higher education," *Frontiers in Psychology*, 13. doi: 10.3389/fpsyg.2022.913219.

Schmaltz, R. M., Jansen, E. and Wenckowski, N. (2017) "Redefining critical thinking: Teaching students to think like scientists," *Frontiers in Psychology*, 8(MAR), pp. 2015–2018. doi: 10.3389/fpsyg.2017.00459.

Setiawati, H. and Corebima, A. D. (2017) "Empowering critical thinking skills of the students having different academic ability in biology learning of Senior High School through PQ4R – TPS Strategy," *The International Journal of Social Sciences and Humanities Invention*, 4(5), pp. 3521–3526. doi: 10.18535/ijsshi/v4i5.09.

Sharples, J. M. *et al.* (2017) "Critical thinking in healthcare and education," *BMJ (Online)*, 357, pp. 16–18. doi: 10.1136/bmj.j2234.

Shukri, N. A. and Mukundan, J. (2015) "A review on developing critical thinking skills through literary texts," *Advances in Language and Literary Studies*, 6(2), pp. 2–7. doi: 10.7575/aiac.alls.v.6n.2p.4.

Slamet, A., Taharu, F. I. and Hudha, A. M. (2019) "Developing genetic learning module based on blue eyes phenomenon in Buton Island, Southeast Sulawesi," *Jurnal Pendidikan Biologi Indonesia*, 5(1), pp. 69–76. doi: 10.22219/jpbi.v5i1.7071.

Staib, S. (2003) "Teaching and measuring critical thinking," *Journal of Nursing Education*, 42(11), pp. 498–508. doi: 10.3928/0148-4834-20031101-08.

Stanton, J. D., Sebesta, A. J. and Dunlosky, J. (2021) "Fostering metacognition to support student learning and performance," *CBE Life Sciences Education*, 20(2), pp. 1–7. doi: 10.1187/cbe.20-12-0289.

Wilson, J. S. (2017) "Promoting critical thinking in general biology courses: The case of the white widow spider," *Journal on Empowering Teaching Excellence*, 1(2). Available at: http://digitalcommons.usu.edu/jete%0Ahttp://digitalcommons.usu.edu/jete/vol1/iss2/9.

Wu, P.-H. and Wu, H.-K. (2020) "Constructing a model of engagement in scientific inquiry: investigating relationships between inquiry-related curiosity, dimensions of engagement, and inquiry abilities," *Instructional Science*, 48(1), pp. 79–113. doi: 10.1007/s11251-020-09503-8.

Zion, M. and Mendelovic, R. (2012) "Moving from structured to open inquiry: Challenges and limits," *Science Education International*, 23(4), pp. 383–399.

Zubaidah, S. *et al.* (2020) "Critical thinking embedded essay test," in, pp. 171–177. doi: 10.2991/absr.k.200807.036.

Strengthening Professional and Spiritual Education through 21st Century Skill Empowerment in Pandemic and Post-Pandemic Era – Arifin et al. (Eds)
© 2024 The Author(s), ISBN: 978-1-032-45243-2
Open Access: www.taylorfrancis.com, CC BY-NC-ND 4.0 license

Differences in metacognitive skills and critical thinking among male and female high school students

Louie P. Gula
Visayas State University, Philippines

Lud Waluyo*, Risca Suhariyanto, Novinda Dwi Septiana, Andri Ani Purwaning Rahayu, Astri Rizqi Amalia, Samsuji Bastian Bachtiar & Ahmad Fauzi
Universitas Muhammadiyah Malang, Indonesia

ABSTRACT: There is an emerging inquiry into the potential influence of gender on metacognitive skills and critical thinking in high school students. This study investigated the influence of gender on metacognitive skills and critical thinking among high school students. The research was conducted in Malang, Indonesia, with a sample of 56 science students, comprising 37 females and 19 males. Metacognitive skills and critical thinking abilities were assessed using an integrated essay-based assessment. The collected data were analyzed using one-way MANOVA. This study reveal that there is no significant gender-based difference in metacognitive and critical thinking skills. The study highlights the importance of integrating metacognitive and critical thinking skill development into educational curricula, irrespective of gender, and advocates for further exploration of individual cognitive traits and instructional strategies to enhance cognitive abilities.

Keywords: cognitive abilities, critical thinking, high school students, gender, metacognitive skills

1 INTRODUCTION

Learning, as a multifaceted process, is influenced by an array of factors, encompassing both internal and external elements (Li and Han 2022). In the realm of education and learning, fostering metacognitive skills among students has emerged as a pivotal factor in enhancing the quality of learning experiences (Rizkia and Zulfiani 2021). Metacognition, the ability to reflect upon and regulate one's own cognitive processes, plays a paramount role in enabling students to become proactive learners (Stanton *et al.* 2021). By understanding their own thinking patterns, setting learning goals, and monitoring their progress, students gain a profound awareness of their strengths and areas needing improvement. This heightened self-awareness empowers them to employ effective learning strategies, optimize their problem-solving approaches, and adapt flexibly to various learning contexts (Anthonysamy 2021). Furthermore, metacognitive skills involve the proficient assimilation of information through the lens of pre-existing knowledge, accompanied by the monitoring of personal competencies within the reading process (Lai 2011). Moreover, metacognition cultivates a sense of autonomy and ownership over learning, nurturing lifelong learners who can independently navigate the complexities of acquiring knowledge (Oates 2019). Thus, integrating metacognitive practices into educational frameworks equips students with essential skills not only for academic success but also for their personal and professional growth.

---

*Corresponding Author: ludwaluyo63@gmail.com

DOI: 10.1201/9781003376125-11

Furthermore, the integration of metacognition goes hand in hand with the cultivation of critical thinking skills, forging a comprehensive approach to effective learning. Critical thinking, characterized by the ability to analyze, evaluate, and synthesize information, serves as the bridge between metacognition and deep understanding (Scott 2015). Encouraging students to question assumptions, assess evidence, and engage in rigorous reasoning not only enriches their comprehension of subjects but also equips them to discern between reliable sources and misinformation (Rofieq and Fauzi 2022; Rupp 2019). The symbiotic relationship between metacognition and critical thinking compels students to reflect not only on what they are learning but also on how they are learning it. This, in turn, nurtures a culture of intellectual curiosity, open-mindedness, and a disposition for continuous learning. As students harness the power of critical thinking alongside metacognitive strategies, they fortify their cognitive toolset, positioning themselves to become astute problem-solvers and informed decision-makers in an ever-evolving knowledge landscape (Ku and Ho 2010; Magno 2010; Rivas Saiz and Ossa 2022).

Building upon the foundation of metacognition and critical thinking, it is also imperative to explore how the factor of gender intersects with the learning process. Gender differences in cognitive skills, as noted in psychological research, suggest that certain disparities can be mitigated through training. Likewise, both educational and psychological research emphasizes the influential role of motivational factors such as values, competency beliefs, ownership, and anxiety in shaping students' biology achievements and future learning attitudes (Reid and Tobin 2016). Gender is even perceived as linked to the development of an individual's thinking abilities (Siswati and Corebima 2017). Moreover, exploring the impact of peer effects offers valuable insights for effectively grouping students to attain specific equality goals or enhance educational outcomes (Cabezas 2010). It is noteworthy that students' thinking abilities naturally progress with age (Siswati and Corebima 2017).

The potential divergence in language abilities, often indicative of critical thinking skills, could potentially affect the critical thinking abilities between male and female students. Critical thinking, a cornerstone skill, enables individuals to think lucidly and rationally, crucial for decision-making and belief formation (Moalosi et al. 2016). Thus, learning processes are designed to foster skills that enable students to critically seek, process, and evaluate information (Sharples et al. 2017). Equipping students with critical thinking skills empowers them to evaluate, analyze, and interpret the information they encounter (Ali 2016). Importantly, biology education offers an ideal platform for cultivating students' critical thinking skills through inquiry-based learning (Schmaltz et al. 2017). This is corroborated by research revealing that metacognitive disparities do not stem significantly from developmental or gender-based differences (Chaudhary 2017). Notably, female students display heightened metacognitive awareness in comparison to their male counterparts (Misu and Masi 2017).

Further research findings report gender-related differences in academic resilience and achievements among high school students (Mwangi and Ireri 2017). Conversely, educational research underscores gender disparities in achievements, engagement, and participation (Reid and Tobin 2016). Despite numerous interventions aimed at learning enhancement, studies assessing metacognitive and critical thinking disparities between male and female students within natural learning environments are limited. Consequently, this study's objective is to investigate gender's influence on high school students' metacognitive skills and critical thinking abilities. The research aims to offer insights into enhancing metacognition and critical thinking skills in both genders during biology education, conducted by educators, while also addressing gender-based educational disparities.

2 METHODS

2.1 *Study design and research participant*

The present study adopts a comparative research design aimed at contrasting the attainment of metacognitive skills and critical thinking abilities between male and female high school students. The research was conducted in Malang, Indonesia, involving a sample of 56 science stream students from a local high school, comprising 37 females and 19 males.

2.2 Data collection instrument and procedures

To assess metacognitive skills and critical thinking abilities, an integrated assessment tool incorporating essay tests was employed. Specifically, the assessment of critical thinking skills utilized the essay test developed by Zubaidah (Zubaidah *et al.* 2020), while the assessment of metacognitive skills utilized the essay test developed by Corebima (2009). Prior to the utilization of the essay tests as data collection instruments, validity was established through Pearson's product-moment correlation, while reliability was assessed using Cronbach's alpha. The results of both validity and reliability tests confirmed the validity and reliability of all test items.

2.3 Data analysis

The gathered data on thinking skills were subjected to a MANOVA analysis, with a significance level set at 5%. Before conducting the MANOVA analysis, the normality and homogeneity of data were examined through the Kolmogorov-Smirnov test and Levene's test, respectively. This preliminary analysis served to ensure that the assumptions for conducting the subsequent MANOVA analysis were met.

3 RESULTS

3.1 Descriptive statistics

The analysis of results unveils the disparities in the mean scores of metacognitive skills and critical thinking abilities between female and male students. These findings are succinctly presented in Table 1. The differences in mean scores of metacognitive skills and critical thinking abilities between female and male students, as derived from this study, are presented in Table 1. As indicated in Table 1, the average metacognitive skill score for female students was 22.09, compared to 21.49 for male students. Additionally, the average score for critical thinking abilities among female students was 65, while it was 67 among male students.

Table 1. Mean scores of metacognitive skills and critical thinking abilities by gender.

Dependent Variable	Gender	Sum of Squares
Critical thinking skills	Male	67.00
	Female	65.00
Metacognitive skills	Male	21.49
	Female	22.09

Table 2. Multivariate analysis of variance (MANOVA) results for gender differences in metacognitive and critical thinking skills of high school students.

Source	Dependent Variable	Sum of Squares	df	Mean Square	F	Sig.
Gender	Critical thinking skills	58.430	1	58.430	.340	.562
	Metacognitive skills	4.517	1	4.517	.037	.848
Error	Critical thinking skills	9287.403	54	171.989		
	Metacognitive skills	6589.588	54	122.029		

a. R Squared = .006 (Adjusted R Squared = -.012)
b. R Squared = .001 (Adjusted R Squared = -.018)

3.2 *MANOVA results*

As the data followed a normal distribution (p-value = 0.200) and the variances of both male and female students' data in the metacognitive and critical thinking skill variables were homogenous (Metacognitive: p-value = 0.443; Critical Thinking: p-value = 0.953), the collected research data proceeded to be analyzed using MANOVA. A summary of the MANOVA test results is presented in Table 2. Based on Table 2, it can be observed that the critical thinking and metacognitive skills of female students did not significantly differ from their male counterparts in terms of Metacognition [F (4.02) = 0.037, p-value = 0.848 > 0.05] and Critical Thinking [F (4.02) = 0.340, p-value = 0.562 > 0.05] data. Therefore, despite the higher average critical thinking skills of male students compared to female students and the higher average metacognitive skills of female students compared to male students, no substantial differences were found. Furthermore, the multivariate table (Wilks' Lambda) indicates the absence of significant distinctions [F = 0.180, sig = 0.836].

4 DISCUSSION

The findings of this study align with several previous reports that have yielded similar results. Some research reports indicate that there is no gender influence on metacognitive skills (Siswati and Corebima 2017). In accordance with Heong, Yunos and Hassan (2011), gender, academic achievement, and socioeconomic status do not inherently impact students' thinking abilities. This is consistent with the current study's results, indicating that metacognitive and critical thinking skills are not influenced by gender. Metacognition pertains to knowledge, comprehension of learning outcomes, and awareness in the learning process. It encompasses higher-order thinking and closely interacts with cognitive processes that students employ to construct knowledge and develop understanding through their learning experiences (Thomas 2014).

Furthermore, the current study confirms that gender does not exert a significant influence on critical thinking skills. Critical thinking involves rational thinking about how to approach problems or phenomena (Sharples *et al.* 2017). It encompasses skills such as analyzing arguments, drawing conclusions using inductive or deductive reasoning, evaluating, and decision-making. Critical thinking is a cognitive skill paired with dispositions that reflect open and fair-mindedness, curiosity, flexibility, a tendency to seek reasons, a desire for information, and respect for diverse viewpoints (Lai 2011).

Empirical research has indicated that the development of critical thinking competencies begins at a young age. While adults often exhibit less rigorous reasoning, theoretically, everyone can be taught critical thinking. Bethel *et al.* (2018) suggest that critical thinking aims for assessment, self-regulation leading to interpretations, analysis, evaluation, and inferences, while explanations stem from the basis of these judgments. Dialogues, exposure to authentic problems and examples, and guidance positively impact critical thinking skills. Educators should use open-ended tasks to foster critical thinking, requiring students to provide evidence or logical arguments to support their assessments (Lai 2011). Teaching critical thinking is akin to teaching students to think like scientists (Schmaltz *et al.* 2017).

Moreover, the study by Mahanal (2012) revealed that while female students exhibit slightly higher critical thinking skills than male students, the difference lacks significance. This underpins the current research, suggesting that gender doesn't significantly influence critical thinking and metacognitive processes. Rather, individual differences in problem-solving abilities account for variations in metacognitive skills and critical thinking. This assertion finds consonance with Myers and Dyer (2006), reinforcing that gender does not lead to substantive differences in thinking skills. Overall, these findings contribute to the understanding of the role of gender in shaping metacognition and critical thinking skills among students.

5 CONCLUSION

This research has attempted to investigate the effect of gender on two important skills in students, namely metacognitive skills and critical thinking skills. The results of the analysis inform that gender has no significant effect on the two skills. Future research involving a larger sample and a more diverse population needs to be designed. Furthermore, other studies that analyze the influence of gender on various learning models also need to be considered.

REFERENCES

Ali, S. A. (2016) "Critical thinking in the information age: Helping students find and evaluate scientific information," *Teaching Innovation Projects*, 6(1). Available at: http://ir.lib.uwo.ca/tips/vol6/iss1/3%0AThis.

Anthonysamy, L. (2021) "The use of metacognitive strategies for undisrupted online learning: Preparing university students in the age of pandemic," *Education and Information Technologies*, 26(6), pp. 6881–6899. doi: 10.1007/s10639-021-10518-y.

Bethel, E. C. *et al.* (2018) *A systematic review of the effects of learning environments on student learning outcomes.* Melbourne. Available at: http://www.iletc.com.au/wp-content/uploads/2018/07/TR4_Web.pdf.

Cabezas, V. (2010) Gender peer effects in school: Does the gender of school peers affect student achievement? doi: 10.3389/fgene.2012.00057.

Chaudhary, V. (2017) "A comparative study on developmental and gender differences on metacognition," *International Journal for Innovative Research in Multidisciplinary Field*, 3(8), pp. 1–4. Available at: https://www.ijirmf.com/wp-content/uploads/2017/08/201708001.pdf.

Corebima, A. D. (2009) "Metacognitive skill measurement integrated in achievement test," in *Third International Conference on Science and Mathematics Education (CoSMEd)*. Penang: SEAMEO Regional Centre for Education in Science and Mathematics. Available at: http://ftp.recsam.edu.my/cosmed/cosmed09/AbstractsFullPapers2009/Abstract/Science Parallel PDF/Full Paper/01.pdf.

Heong, Y. M., Yunos, J. Bin and Hassan, R. Bin (2011) "The perception of the level of higher order thinking skills," *International Conference on Social Science and Humanity*, 5(IPEDR vol.5 (2011)), pp. 281–285. Available at: http://www.ipedr.com/vol5/no2/62-H10167.pdf.

Ku, K. Y. L. and Ho, I. T. (2010) "Metacognitive strategies that enhance critical thinking," *Metacognition and Learning*, 5(3), pp. 251–267. doi: 10.1007/s11409-010-9060-6.

Lai, E. (2011) *Motivation: A literature review, Alwasy Learning*. Available at: http://www.datec.org.uk/CHAT/chatmeta1.htm.

Lai, E. R. (2011) *Critical Thinking: A Literature Review, Pearson's Research Report*. Available at: https://images.pearsonassessments.com/images/tmrs/CriticalThinkingReviewFINAL.pdf.

Li, C. and Han, Y. (2022) "Learner-internal and learner-external factors for boredom amongst Chinese university EFL students," *Applied Linguistics Review*, 5. doi: 10.1515/applirev-2021-0159.

Magno, C. (2010) "The role of metacognitive skills in developing critical thinking," *Metacognition and Learning*, 5(2), pp. 137–156. doi: 10.1007/s11409-010-9054-4.

Mahanal, S. (2012) "Strategi pembelajaran biologi, pender dan pengaruhnya terhadap kemampuan berpikir kritis," in *Seminar Nasional IX Pendidikan Biologi FKIP UNS*, pp. 1–7. Available at: https://jurnal.fkip.uns.ac.id/index.php/prosbio/article/view/1040.

Misu, L. and Masi, L. (2017) "Comparison of metacognition awareness of male and female students based on mathematics ability in Department of Mathematics Education of Halu Oleo University," *International Journal of Education and Research*, 5(6), pp. 43–50. Available at: http://www.ijern.com/journal/2017/June-2017/04.pdf.

Moalosi, W. T. S., Mgawi, R. K. and Moeti, B. (2016) "Critical thinking among pre-service teacher trainees: A review using 5 – step framework," *Journal of Studies in Education*, 6(4), pp. 133–143. doi: 10.5296/jse.v6i4.10481.

Mwangi, C. N. and Ireri, A. M. (2017) "Gender differences in academic resilience and academic achievement among secondary school students in Kiambu County, Kenya," *Psychology and Behavioral Science International Journal*, 5(5), pp. 1–7. doi: 10.19080/PBSIJ.2017.05.555673.

Myers, B. E. and Dyer, J. E. (2006) "The Influence of student learning stye on critical thinking skill," *Journal of Agricultural Education*, 47(1), pp. 43–52. Available at: https://citeseerx.ist.psu.edu/document?repid=rep1&type=pdf&doi=164ee5803a31946f03960f46d407eb7035b8cb11.

Oates, S. (2019) "The importance of autonomous, self-regulated learning in primary initial teacher training," *Frontiers in Education*, 4. doi: 10.3389/feduc.2019.00102.

Reid, K. and Tobin, M. (2016) *Changing Minds: Discussions in Neuroscience, Psychology and Education*. Camberwell: Australian Council for Educational Research. Available at: https://research.acer.edu.au/cgi/viewcontent.cgi?article=1018&context=learning_processes.

Rivas, S. F., Saiz, C. and Ossa, C. (2022) "Metacognitive strategies and development of critical thinking in higher education," *Frontiers in Psychology*, 13. doi: 10.3389/fpsyg.2022.913219.

Rizkia, A. M. and Zulfiani, Z. (2021) "Fostering metacognitive skill: A means to improve students' academic achievement," *Biosfer*, 14(2), pp. 275–284. doi: 10.21009/biosferjpb.19839.

Rofieq, A. and Fauzi, A. (2022) "Students' knowledge and attitudes toward science: Its correlation on students' disbelief in non-scientific misinformation," *Jurnal Pendidikan IPA Indonesia*, 11(2), pp. 195–207. doi: 10.15294/jpii.v11i2.35768.

Rupp, M. T. (2019) "Encouraging students to challenge assumptions," *American Journal of Pharmaceutical Education*, 83(5), p. 7481. doi: 10.5688/ajpe7481.

Schmaltz, R. M., Jansen, E. and Wenckowski, N. (2017) "Redefining critical thinking: Teaching students to think like scientists," *Frontiers in Psychology*, 8(MAR), pp. 2015–2018. doi: 10.3389/fpsyg.2017.00459.

Scott, C. L. (2015) *The futures of learning 2: What kind of learning for the 21st century?* 14. Ireland. Available at: https://www.researchgate.net/profile/Dickson_Adom/post/How_to_develop_self_learning_skills_techniques_and_processes/attachment/5a8fa082b53d2f0bba53ba01/AS%3A597062399840261%401519362177920/download/242996e.pdf.

Sharples, J. M. *et al.* (2017) "Critical thinking in healthcare and education," *BMJ (Online)*, 357, pp. 16–18. doi: 10.1136/bmj.j2234.

Siswati, B. H. and Corebima, A. D. (2017) "The effect of education level and gender on students' metacognitive skills in Malang, Indonesia," *Advances in Social Sciences Research Journal*, 4(4), pp. 163–168. doi: 10.14738/assrj.44.2813.

Stanton, J. D., Sebesta, A. J. and Dunlosky, J. (2021) "Fostering metacognition to support student learning and performance," *CBE Life Sciences Education*, 20(2), pp. 1–7. doi: 10.1187/cbe.20-12-0289.

Thomas, G. P. (2014) "Metacognition and science learning," *Encyclopedia of Science Education*. Springer. doi: 10.1007/978-94-007-6165-0.

Zubaidah, S. *et al.* (2020) "Critical thinking embedded essay test," in, pp. 171–177. doi: 10.2991/absr.k.200807.036.

Strengthening Professional and Spiritual Education through 21st Century Skill Empowerment in Pandemic and Post-Pandemic Era – Arifin et al. (Eds)
© 2024 The Author(s), ISBN: 978-1-032-45243-2
Open Access: www.taylorfrancis.com, CC BY-NC-ND 4.0 license

Self-perceived action competence for sustainability of Indonesian prospective biology teachers

H. Husamah
Universitas Muhammadiyah Malang, Indonesia

Hadi Suwono*
Universitas Negeri Malang, Indonesia

Hadi Nur
Universitas Negeri Malang, Indonesia
Universiti Teknologi Malaysia, Malaysia

Agus Dharmawan
Universitas Negeri Malang, Indonesia

ABSTRACT: This study was aimed to analyze the Self-Perceived Action Competence for Sustainability (SPACS) of Indonesian biology teacher candidates. This study was a cross-sectional survey. The data collection process is carried out in June-August 2022. The target respondents are students of education study programs in the field of biology from various institutions in Indonesia. Gender, GPA, college status, and college status are positioned as respondents' characters whose impact on students' SPACS is analyzed in this study. The target population size for this survey is 1300 people, the minimum sample size with 95% confidence level and 5% margin of error is 1235 students. The inclusion criteria of respondents in this study were prospective biology teacher students, came from universities in Indonesia, Indonesian citizens, still active as students, and voluntarily wanted to be involved as research respondent. To determine the effect of gender, university status, and student status on SPACS, the Mann Whitney test was carried out. On the other hand, to determine the effect of GPA on SPACS, the Kruskal-Wallis test was carried out. The results show significant differences occur in the variables that have a p-value (Sig. value) below 0.05. It can be concluded that significant differences in SPACS scores occur in gender differences to KAP, differences in university status to COI and WTA, and differences in study status to COI and WTA.

Keywords: SPACS, Prospective biology teacher, Indonesia, Action Competence

1 INTRODUCTION

Education for Sustainable Development (ESD) or Education for Sustainability (EfS) is a vehicle needed by community members to act in the form of contributing to a sustainable lifestyle and to overcome today's global challenges, including climate change, environmental degradation, consumerism, and so forth (Bascopé *et al.* 2019; Glavič 2020; Paulauskaite-Taraseviciene *et al.* 2022). One way to understand learning in the context of ESD is through the development of action competence (Chen and Liu 2020; Sass *et al.* 2020, 2022). Action competence is the competence to act with reference to the environment or the concept of

---

*Corresponding Author: hadi.suwono.fmipa@um.ac.id

DOI: 10.1201/9781003376125-12

sustainability (Hedefalk *et al.* 2014; Ideland 2016; Jensen and Schnack 2006; Kalla *et al.* 2022).

The actions of people who have action competence are committed and enthusiastic to solve sustainable development problems, have relevant knowledge about the problems being faced, are involved in taking a critical attitude, are positive about various ways to solve problems and have confidence in the – their own skills and capacities to change the conditions at hand for the better (Pauw *et al.* 2019). An action competence framework has been developed to help teachers and students achieve this competency development (Eames 2010; Lohmann *et al.* 2021).

To measure the action competence in students, it can be done with the self-perceived action competence for sustainability questionnaire (SPACS-Q). SPACS-Q is a relatively recently introduced instrument, supported by adequate theory and empirically reliable. SPACS-Q has been analyzed and meets the criteria of validity and reliability. SPACS-Q needs to be continuously introduced and used to investigate people's action competence in various sustainability contexts (Olsson *et al.* 2020).

Because this instrument or questionnaire is relatively new, it is necessary to use it to measure the action competence of students in Indonesia, especially students of prospective biology teacher. In the context of the prospective teacher, there is only one article that has been written, and even then, in the form of a systematic literature review. The article was published by Husamah *et al.* (2022) which proposes eight ideas to be reflected by prospective teachers or teacher education providers (especially science) in educating prospective science teachers who care about action competence. Meanwhile, there is only one publication that tries to reveal SPACS, namely new knowledge of the effects of Sustainability Education on young people's SPACS, through a longitudinal design.

In this regard, this study was intended to analyze the Self-Perceived Action Competence for Sustainability (SPACS) of Indonesian biology teacher candidates. This will be the first study in Indonesia (and possibly in the world) to implement SPACS-Q to measure student action competence. The results of this cross-sectional survey will be the baseline and policy basis for the development of action competence of Indonesian biology teacher candidates and in relation to the implementation of ESD or EfS.

2 METHODS

2.1 *Research design and participants*

This research is a type of cross-sectional survey. This study was conducted with the aim of collecting SPACS data for prospective biology teachers' students in Indonesia. Our data collection was carried out from June to August 2022. The respondents who were targeted in this study were students of education in the field of biology who studied at various universities in Indonesia (both at the Faculty of Teacher Training and Education, College of Education), as well as the Faculty of Mathematics and Natural Sciences. Gender, GPA, college status, and respondent's lecture status are positioned as respondents' characters whose impact on the SPACS aspect becomes the aspect that is analyzed.

The target population size in this survey is 1300 students. Therefore, based on the Krejcie and Morgan tables, the minimum sample size with 95% confidence level and 5% margin of error is 1235 students. The inclusion criteria of respondents determined in this study are prospective biology teachers, currently active in studying at various universities in Indonesia, they are Indonesian citizens, and respondents voluntarily or willingly become respondents in the study. They are students taking Biology Education degree. The exclusion criteria that we set in this study were students with diploma and postgraduate status, not from educational study programs, had been dropped out, and they were incomplete in providing information about their characteristics as respondents.

2.2 Instruments and procedures for data collection

The data collection instrument used in this study was the self-perceived competence for sustainability questionnaire (SPACS-Q) (Olsson *et al.* 2020) which was validated by bilingual experts. This questionnaire consists of 12 items using a 5-point Likert scale, ranging from not important (score 1) to extremely important (score 5). This survey was conducted online with the consideration that at the time of data collection Indonesia was still in the COVID-19 pandemic. Another consideration is that the target respondents are quite large and broad, so online techniques will be easier and more cost-effective. Therefore, we transformed our SPACS-Q into an online questionnaire via Google Form.

2.3 Data processing and analysis

We first download the data collected through the survey in a comma separated value (csv) format. Then the data was checked and labeled using Microsoft Excel. After the inspection and labeling were carried out, the data were then analyzed using SPSS. Data or information about the characteristics of the respondents were analyzed using frequency and percentage. We calculated the score against the mean and standard deviation for each item. The comparison of two groups of students was analyzed using the Mann-Whitney U Test, while the comparison of more than two groups was analyzed using the Kruskal-Wallis H Test. We determined that the alpha value was 5% in this study.

3 RESULTS AND DISCUSSION

Information on the demographic distribution of respondents in this study is presented in Table 1.

Table 1. Demographic distribution of respondent.

Group		Frequency	Percentage (%)
Gender	Male	177	13.97
	Female	1090	86.03
GPA	< 3	52	4.10
3–3.5	552	43.57	
	3.6–4.0	663	52.33
University Status	State University	765	60.38
	Public University	502	39.62
Student Status	Have taken the "Environmental Science" course	1011	79.79
	Haven't taken the "Environmental Science" course	256	20.21

The average student answer scores for each SPACS item are presented in Table 2. Furthermore, to determine the effect of gender, PT status, and college status on SPACS, the independent samples t-test was carried out. On the other hand, to determine the effect of GPA on SPACS, a one-way ANOVA test was conducted. The summary of the results of the analysis of the four variables is presented in Table 3.

Significant differences occur in the variables that have a p-value (Sig. value) below 0.05. Based on Table 3, significant differences in SPACS scores occur in gender differences to KAP, differences in university status to COI and WTA, and differences in college status to COI and WTA.

Table 2. Average student answer scores in each SPACS item.

Item	Mean	SD
Knowledge of action possibilities (KAP)		
I can have a different point of view on an issue when people think differently.	3.71	0.96
I know how to take action on campus to contribute to sustainable development.	3.43	0.96
I know how to take action at home to contribute to sustainable development.	3.60	0.96
I know how to take action together with others to contribute to sustainable development.	3.52	0.95
Confidence in one's own influence (COI)		
I believe that my actions can have an impact on global sustainable development	3.57	0.98
I believe that my actions can have an impact on sustainable development in my community.	3.59	0.96
I believe that I have ample opportunity to participate in influencing our future together.	3.86	0.99
I believe that everyone's contribution is very important for sustainable development.	4.06	1.03
Willingness to act (WTA)		
I want to play a role in sustainable development in my community.	3.83	1.01
I want to play a role in global sustainable development.	3.84	1.02
I want to play a role in changing society towards sustainable development.	3.88	1.00
I want to do a lecture on how we can shape a sustainable future together.	3.98	1.03

Table 3. The difference in the mean SPACS scores in each group of students.

Group		KAP Average	SD	p-value	COI Average	SD	p-value	WTA Average	SD	p-value
Gender	Male	3.72	0.82	0.006	3.83	0.91	0.278	3.88	0.96	0.970
	Female	3.54	0.82		3.76	0.87		3.88	0.92	
GPA	< 3	3.57	0.95	0.076	3.60	1.11	0.074	3.75	1.14	0.069
	3–3.5	3.50	0.82		3.73	0.87		3.83	0.92	
	3.6–4.0	3.61	0.81		3.82	0.85		3.94	0.91	
University Status	State University	3.59	0.81	0.081	3.85	0.85	<0.001	3.96	0.90	<0.001
	Public University	3.51	0.84		3.64	0.89		3.76	0.95	
Student Status	Have taken the "Environmental Science" course	3.58	0.81	0.119	3.80	0.86	0.009	3.93	0.90	0.002
	Haven't taken the "Environmental Science" course	3.49	0.88		3.64	0.92		3.71	1.00	

Gender has an effect on Knowledge of action possibilities (KAP), which is one aspect of action competence. This is in line with the findings of previous researchers that gender equality is a central aspect of sustainable development. The development of action competence is a key element in ESD efforts (Biström and Lundström 2021). Gaps in knowledge about gender can cause problems in sustainable development (Kim 2017; Leal Filho *et al.* 2022; Manandhar *et al.* 2018; Mérida-Serrano *et al.* 2020; Zimm *et al.* 2018). Furthermore, it is said that environmental education must be separated from the gender gap, where awareness of the sustainability of men and women must be the same. The issue of whether gender gaps in environmental education can be identified is also necessary in ESD continuing education is a teaching approach that can play a key role in reducing gender disparities. However, the possible gender-specific effects of an ESD-oriented teaching approach have not been empirically tested (Olsson and Gericke 2017).

Differences in university status affect Confidence in one's own influence (COI) and Willingness to act (WTA), which are aspects of action competence. This finding indicates that university quality will affect the development of action competence. However, the university is uniquely placed to lead the cross-cutting implementation of the SDGs. This is the reason to build, strengthen and institutionalize university partnerships with government and society to achieve the SDGs. Therefore, it is necessary to change the mindset and culture in managing universities to face global challenges (El-Jardali et al. 2018). Universities can contribute a lot to achieve the sustainable development goals (SDGs). Involvement and attention to students is a broader form of work. Universities play a strategic role in generating innovations or new ways for the world, educating global citizens and bringing knowledge and innovation into society. Thus, universities can become engines of transformation for society, starting with the students they educate (Purcell et al. 2019).

In addition, the study status has an effect on aspects of Confidence in one's own influence (COI) and Willingness to act (WTA). Students' action competence must be taught and developed, particularly for prospective science teachers, to have a pedagogical perspective as environmental educators (Husamah et al. 2022). One way that can be done is by implementing environmental science courses. Environmental science is an amalgamation of scientific disciplines. The merging of scientific disciplines is important to overcome today's environmental challenges (Breiting et al 1999; Theobold and Hancock 2019; Valle and Berdanier 2012). The concepts of "environmental science" and "sustainable development" are commonly used because of their proximity (Beames et al. 2018; Houé and Duchamp 2021; Larsson 2021; Murzi et al. 2019; O'Neill 2015; Pussella 2022; Rudskaia 2021; Solá and Vilhelmson 2019; Surya et al. 2020; Thompson 2005). In clarifying the nature, meaning, and relationships between these alternative concepts, this paper helps interdisciplinary researchers to understand the opportunities and challenges associated with each of these concepts (Sauvé et al. 2016).

4 CONCLUSION

It can be concluded that significant differences in SPACS scores occur in gender differences with respect to Knowledge of action possibilities (KAP), differences in university status with respect to Confidence in one's own influence (COI) and Willingness to act (WTA), as well as differences in study status with respect to Confidence in one's own influence (COI) and Willingness to act (WTA). Thus, the factors that need to be considered in connection with the development of SPACS scores for prospective biology teacher students in Indonesia are gender, university status, and college status (Already taking the "Environmental Science" course).

Based on the aforementioned findings, some recommendations are addressed to further researches. First, teachers should pay attention to gender aspects in relation to the development of action competence and SPACS. Second, the status of universities (public or private) is still a key factor that describes the quality of each. Thus, the government needs to take policies to encourage even distribution of higher education quality. Third, environmental science courses as the embodiment of ESD and EfS in universities need to be taught appropriately, with appropriate strategies and methods, and managed by professional lecturers so as to encourage the achievement of the targets or objectives of these courses.

REFERENCES

Bascopé, M., Perasso, P. and Reiss, K. (2019) 'Systematic review of education for sustainable development at an early stage: Cornerstones and pedagogical approaches for teacher professional development', *Sustainability (Switzerland)*, 11(3). doi: 10.3390/su11030719.

Beames, A. *et al.* (2018) 'Amenity proximity analysis for sustainable brownfield redevelopment planning', *Landscape and Urban Planning*, 171, pp. 68–79. doi: https://doi.org/10.1016/j.landurbplan.2017.12.003.

Biström, E. and Lundström, R. (2021) 'Action competence for gender equality as sustainable development: Analyzing Swedish lower secondary level textbooks in biology, civics, and home and consumer studies', *Comparative Education Review*, 65(3), p. 236502079. doi: 10.1086/714607.

Breiting, S. *et al.* (1999) *Action Competence, Conflicting Interests and Environmental Education.* Research Programme for Environmental and Health Education, DPU, Aarhus University.

Chen, S. Y. and Liu, S. Y. (2020) 'Developing students' action competence for a sustainable future: A review of educational research', *Sustainability (Switzerland)*, 12(4), p. 1374. doi: 10.3390/su12041374.

Eames, C. (2010) *A framework for developing action competence in education for sustainability (EfS).* University of Waikato.

El-Jardali, F., Ataya, N. and Fadlallah, R. (2018) 'Changing roles of universities in the era of SDGs: Rising up to the global challenge through institutionalising partnerships with governments and communities', *Health Research Policy and Systems*, 16(1), pp. 1–5. doi: 10.1186/s12961-018-0318-9.

Glavič, P. (2020) 'Identifying key issues of education for sustainable development', *Sustainability (Switzerland)*, 12(16), pp. 1–18. doi: 10.3390/su12166500.

Hedefalk, M., Almqvist, J. and Lidar, M. (2014) 'Teaching for action competence', *SAGE Open*, 4(3), pp. 1–8. doi: 10.1177/2158244014543785.

Houé, T. and Duchamp, D. (2021) 'Relational impact of buyer–supplier dyads on sustainable purchasing and supply management: a proximity perspective', *The International Journal of Logistics Management*, 32(2), pp. 567–591. doi: 10.1108/IJLM-10-2019-0298.

Husamah, H. *et al.* (2022) 'Action competencies for sustainability and its implications to environmental education for prospective science teachers: A systematic literature review', *Eurasia Journal of Mathematics, Science & Technology Eduaction*, 18(8), p. em2138.

Ideland, M. (2016) 'The action-competent child: Responsibilization through practices and emotions in environmental education', *Knowledge Cultures*, 4(2), pp. 95–112.

Jensen, B. B. and Schnack, K. (2006) 'The action competence approach in environmental education', *Environmental Education Research*, 12(3–4), pp. 471–486. doi: 10.1080/13504620600943053.

Kalla, M. *et al.* (2022) 'Expanding formal school curricula to foster action competence in sustainable development: A proposed free-choice project-based learning curriculum', *Sustainability (Switzerland)*, 14(23). doi: 10.3390/su142316315.

Kim, E. M. (2017) 'Gender and the sustainable development goals', *Global Social Policy*, 17(2), pp. 239–244. doi: 10.1177/1468018117703444.

Larsson, M. (2021) 'Using environmental evaluation systems and their contribution to sustainable development', *Evaluation*, 27(4), pp. 453–472. doi: 10.1177/13563890211018411.

Leal Filho, W. *et al.* (2022) 'Promoting gender equality across the sustainable development goals', *Environment, Development and Sustainability*, (0123456789). doi: 10.1007/s10668-022-02656-1.

Lohmann, J. *et al.* (2021) 'Teachers' professional action competence in education for sustainable development: A systematic review from the perspective of physical education', *Sustainability*, 13(23), p. 13343. doi: 10.3390/su132313343.

Manandhar, M. *et al.* (2018) 'Gender, health and the 2030 Agenda for sustainable development', *Bulletin of the World Health Organization*, 96(9), pp. 644–653. doi: 10.2471/BLT.18.211607.

Mérida-Serrano, R. *et al.* (2020) 'Sustainable development goals in early childhood education. Empowering young girls to bridge the gender gap in science', *Sustainability (Switzerland)*, 12(22), pp. 1–14. doi: 10.3390/su12229312.

Murzi, H. *et al.* (2019) 'Measuring development of environmental awareness and moral reasoning: A case-study of a civil engineering course', *European Journal of Engineering Education*, 44(6), pp. 954–968. doi: 10.1080/03043797.2019.1566300.

O'Neill, D. W. (2015) 'The proximity of nations to a socially sustainable steady-state economy', *Journal of Cleaner Production*, 108, pp. 1213–1231. doi: https://doi.org/10.1016/j.jclepro.2015.07.116.

Olsson, D. *et al.* (2020) 'Self-perceived action competence for sustainability: The theoretical grounding and empirical validation of a novel research instrument', *Environmental Education Research*, 26(5), pp. 742–760. doi: 10.1080/13504622.2020.1736991.

Olsson, D. and Gericke, N. (2017) 'The effect of gender on students' sustainability consciousness: A nationwide Swedish study', *The Journal of Environmental Education*, 48(5), pp. 357–370. doi: 10.1080/00958964.2017.1310083.

Paulauskaite-Taraseviciene, A. *et al.* (2022) 'Assessing education for sustainable development in engineering study programs: A case of AI Ecosystem Creation', *Sustainability (Switzerland)*, 14(3), pp. 1–22. doi: 10.3390/su14031702.

Pauw, J. B. *et al.* (2019) *Action Competence in Sustainable Development*. University of Antwerp. Available at: http://enec-cost.eu/wp-content/uploads/2019/06/ACiSD-ENEC.pdf.

Purcell, W. M., Henriksen, H. and Spengler, J. D. (2019) 'Universities as the engine of transformational sustainability toward delivering the sustainable development goals: "Living labs" for sustainability', *International Journal of Sustainability in Higher Education*, 20(8), pp. 1343–1357. doi: 10.1108/IJSHE-02-2019-0103.

Pussella, N. I. (2022) 'Spatio and temporal dimensions for the public usage of Urban Green Parks in Colombo, Sri Lanka', *Indonesian Journal of Tourism and Leisure*, 03(2), pp. 84–99. doi: 10.36256/ijtl.v3i2.225.

Rudskaia, E. N. (2021) 'Environmental sustainability as the basis for urbanized ecosystems cluster projection', *IOP Conference Series: Earth and Environmental Science*, 937(4). doi: 10.1088/1755-1315/937/4/042015.

Sass, W. *et al.* (2020) 'Redefining action competence: The case of sustainable development', *The Journal of Environmental Education*, 51(4), pp. 292–305. doi: 10.1080/00958964.2020.1765132.

Sass, W. *et al.* (2022) 'Honing action competence in sustainable development: what happens in classrooms matters', *Environment, Development and Sustainability*, (0123456789), pp. 1–22. doi: 10.1007/s10668-022-02195-9.

Sauvé, S., Bernard, S. and Sloan, P. (2016) 'Environmental sciences, sustainable development and circular economy: Alternative concepts for trans-disciplinary research', *Environmental Development*, 17, pp. 48–56. doi: 10.1016/j.envdev.2015.09.002.

Solá, A. G. and Vilhelmson, B. (2019) 'Negotiating proximity in sustainable urban planning: A Swedish case', *Sustainability (Switzerland)*, 11(1), pp. 12–14. doi: 10.3390/su11010031.

Surya, B. *et al.* (2020) 'Land use change, spatial interaction, and sustainable development in the metropolitan urban areas, south Sulawesi province, Indonesia', *Land*, 9(3). doi: 10.3390/land9030095.

Theobold, A. and Hancock, S. (2019) 'How environmental science graduate students acquire statistical computing skills', *Statistics Education Research Journal*, 18(2), pp. 68–85. doi: 10.52041/serj.v18i2.141.

Thompson, I. H. (2005) 'The ethics of sustainability', *Landscape and Sustainability*, pp. 12–32. doi: 10.5840/du1998811/126.

Valle, D. and Berdanier, A. (2012) 'Computer Programming Skills for Environmental Sciences', *Emerging Technologies*, 2012(October), pp. 373–389.

Zimm, C., Sperling, F. and Busch, S. (2018) 'Identifying sustainability and knowledge gaps in socio-economic pathways vis-à-vis the sustainable development goals', *Economies*, 6(2). doi: 10.3390/economies6020020.

Strengthening Professional and Spiritual Education through 21st Century Skill Empowerment in Pandemic and Post-Pandemic Era – Arifin et al. (Eds)
© 2024 The Author(s), ISBN: 978-1-032-45243-2

Teaching science through English: Pre-service teachers' implementation of CLIL approach in primary school

K. Khoiriyah*, Mulya Fajar Bachtiar Idris, Aisyah Putri Rahma &
Ageng Hafizh Dhiya Ulhaq
Universitas Muhammadiyah Malang, Indonesia

ABSTRACT: In Indonesia, the CLIL (Content and Language Integrated Learning) approach has been adopted in various EFL settings. This research scrutinized the teaching practice of student teachers in implementing the CLIL approach in primary schools. Using a case study research design, three pre-service teachers participated purposefully. The data collection involved classroom observation, interviews, and document analysis (lesson plan and student's workbook). Results revealed that the CLIL approach implemented in teaching Science for primary graders seemed to corroborate with the framework of 4C (content, communication, cognition, and culture), such as providing rich input related to subject-specific vocabulary, using translanguaging as a means to scaffold students understanding, involving multimodality of learning recourses to engage students' interest, stimulating interaction and cooperation through learning activities, and addressing cross-cultural understanding. Further findings highlighted some insights and pedagogical implications for teaching Science through English in Islamic-affiliated primary schools.

Keywords: CLIL approach, teaching Science, primary school, student teachers

1 INTRODUCTION

Due to the importance of introducing English to primary school students, some primary schools in Indonesia have consistently provided English lessons as "enrichment" programs, meaning that English is taught in primary school to improve the student's competence. The models of English lesson delivery are varied. One of which is by teaching some content subjects using English. In other words, primary teachers are in an attempt to implement the Content and Language Integrated Learning (henceforth CLIL) approach. According to Sánchez et al. (2020), CLIL is a bilingual education approach that simultaneously teaches academic material and a second language. The implementation of CLIL is based on what is known as the "4C" principle: content (knowledge and understanding of the subject matter), communication (using the target language to communicate), cognition (or development of higher-order thinking skills), and culture (exposing learners to different points of view and achieving different cultural understandings) (Coyle et al. 2010; Czura 2017; Meyer 2017; Meyer et al. 2015).

Furthermore, since the CLIL approach is implemented for primary graders, teachers should also pay attention to the principles of teaching English to young learners. To teach young learners effectively, Mccloskey (2014) suggested several principles that primary school teachers should consider in their teaching practice. The teachers are highly recommended to fulfill some instructional aspects such as (1) offering young-age students enjoyable, active roles in the learning experience; (2) helping students develop and practice the language through collaboration; (3) integrating multi-dimensional, thematically organized activities;

---

*Corresponding Author: khoiriyah230693@umm.ac.id

DOI: 10.1201/9781003376125-13

(4) providing comprehensible input with several scaffolding techniques; (5) facilitating vocabulary learning; (6) integrating language with content; (7) validating and integrating home language and culture; and (8) providing clear goals and feedback on student's performance. Those principles seem in accordance with the framework of the CLIL approach as well.

Several studies have identified the various forms of CLIL approach for teaching Science. Take an example, Setyaningrum et al. (2020) narrated the experience of a grade-one CLIL Science teacher in teaching her students during the pandemic, meaning the learning activities were in online mode. The CLIL approach has been well-adopted in several schools in certain Indonesian regions since the teachers have already implemented the core feature of CLIL in their classes (Setyaningrum and Khoiriyah 2022). In a Taiwanese primary school, students were reported to have a meaningful learning experience and feel enjoyed in their CLIL classes (Huang 2020). Meanwhile, Pladevall-Ballester (2015) also highlighted that students and parents in several Catalonian primary schools had positive perspectives on implementing CLIL in science classes.

Further, the study of O Ceallaigh, Ní Mhurchú, and Ní Chróinín (2017) focuses on teachers' and students' interactions with a CLIL program in the Republic of Ireland, specifically physical education (PE) delivered in Irish (L2) in primary schools with an English-medium curriculum. The findings concluded that CLIL has potential since both teachers and students condemned their positive experiences. Teachers claimed that their pupils developed into highly motivated students who demonstrated improved self-assurance, satisfaction, and Irish language proficiency. Although numerous studies report on the implementation of CLIL for young learners in an EFL context (Andriani et al. 2018; Ellison 2015, 2019; Korosidou and Griva 2014; Yamano 2013; Wei and Feng 2015), research in the Indonesian context, particularly in formal Islamic affiliation schools, is still limited. Thus, this research aims to explore the implementation of CLIL in one of the Islamic-affiliated schools in Indonesia.

2 METHODS

A descriptive case study was employed since it sheds light on complex issues and describes natural phenomena in the context of the data under investigation (Karabassova and San Isidro 2020). The design is appropriate for this study because the researchers wanted to obtain a detailed description of the implementation of the CLIL approach in a primary school context. Further, a qualitative descriptive study is believed an effective approach to seeking the experiences of individuals or participants (Baxter and Jack 2008; Creswell 2013; Hartman et al. 2019). The participants were three student teachers who were joining the teaching practice program. They were delegated to teach English as an extracurricular in an Islamic-affiliated school. Based on the preliminary interview, the student teachers integrated several content subjects into their classes. Thus, the three research participants met the following criteria of this research: they have sufficient capability to teach English to young learners, have joined several professional development programs related to teaching English, and have implemented the CLIL approach in their teaching practices. Additionally, in terms of research ethics, participants were required to read, complete, and sign a consent form indicating that they willingly volunteered their time during the series of research data collection and that they reserved the right to withdraw their participation in any phase of the research. All in all, all participants submitted their research consent forms before proceeding to the data collection.

To conduct data collection, the researcher administered classroom observation and collected some related documents (lesson plans, handouts). The classroom observations were conducted several times until the data was saturated (7 meetings of 100-minute English lessons). The teaching and learning processes in English classes were audio-visually recorded and transcribed. Then, the result of the observation was analyzed to identify emerging themes associated with the 4C's CLIL framework proposed by Coyle, Hood, and Marsh (2010). Meanwhile, the interview was aimed at validating the results. The data, further, was triangulated and analyzed thematically. The direct observation and document analysis results were then analyzed using thematic analysis (Javadi and Zarea 2016; Maguire and Delahunt 2017; Peel 2020). Here, the rich verbal data was read and re-read, reduced into relevant content, coded, and classified based on the specified themes closely related to the research aims of the study. Four researchers analyzed the data separately to ensure the trustworthiness of the qualitative analysis results. Then, the research participants confirmed the last result through an interview session to validate the findings.

3 RESULTS

3.1 *Findings on the implementation of the CLIL approach in science classes*

The observed lessons and the interview results showed evidence of the integration of the CLIL frameworks in the teaching and learning process. The final results were analyzed using the following framework.

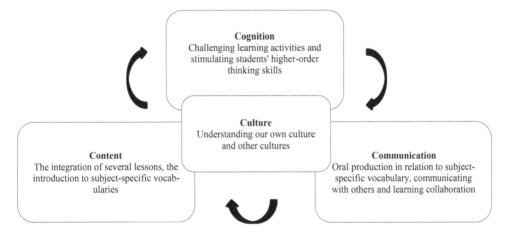

Figure 1.   The 4Cs framework of CLIL.

Figure 1 divided the findings into several subtopics, such as content, cognition, communication, and culture. In this research, content refers to integrating several lessons and introducing subject-specific vocabulary. Cognition can be depicted by challenging learning activities and stimulating students' higher-order thinking skills. Oral production is related to subject-specific vocabulary, communicating with others, and learning collaboration is categorized into communication aspects. Lastly, culture is defined as learning activities that provoke an understanding of our own culture and other cultures. The detailed findings are shown as follows.

3.2 *Providing rich input related to subject-specific vocabulary*

The lesson's topics were merely the integration of science and English, such as living things and non-living things, the life cycle, and parts of a plant. The topics were adapted from thematic books for fourth grade. It can be seen in the following mini-syllabus for the observed lessons.

Table 1.   The topics of the observed lessons.

Meeting	Topics
1	Introductions
2	Living things and non-living things
3	Animal classifications
4	Part of plans
5	Some animals mentioned in the Qur'an as surah

Table 1 illustrates the integration of several lessons in the observed classes. In several meetings, the English lesson was integrated into Natural Science. Based on the observation, during the lessons, several new vocabularies related to Science include "Amphibians can breathe through moist skin underwater". Within this sentence, the teacher tried to explain the characteristics of a fog. Another example is "leaves grow on the stems and branches. They are usually green due to the presence of chlorophyll, which helps them to prepare the food". Further, the teachers did some vocabulary drills and read aloud specific vocabularies.

Teacher: What do you know about living things? ..need to eat and drink or not?

Students: Yes need itu animal, itu living things

Teacher: Yes, that's right, animals need to eat and drink. An animal is categorized as a living thing. They can breathe, move, grow, and reproduce, and they all have senses. So, what are the characteristics of living things? *(The teacher did some drilling to the new vocabulary related to living things)*

Students: They can breathe, reproduce ... .

Interestingly, the teaching material was integrated with other content materials, such as religions. Take an example in the topic "Some animals mentioned in the Qur'an as surah", students were challenged to comprehend multifold materials such as English, Science, and Islamic Science.

3.3   *Using translanguaging as a means to scaffold students' understanding*

During the observed lessons, teachers tried to use the target language (English) as much as possible. In other topics, teachers preferred to use the students' L1 as a scaffolding tool, assisting students in making meaning, particularly regarding new vocabulary. It was found that students had little vocabulary related to animal classifications. Thus, teachers tried to assist students in understanding the materials using Bahasa Indonesia.

Students: *Itu apa* [what's that?]

Teacher: Okay, insects have three parts of body. First, a pair of feelers, then?

Students: head and thorax.

Teacher: Good. They also lay eggs. What "lay eggs" in Bahasa Indonesia?

Student: *bertelur.*

Not only in explaining the materials, the teacher also used Bahasa Indonesia in delivering the instructions. When it was indicated that the students did not understand particular instructions, the teacher switched to using the students' L1 or gave some hints to help the students comprehend the task.

3.4   *Involving multimodal learning recourses to engage students' interest*

The teacher distributed a "Fabulous" module later used for learning activities. Then, the teacher began to open the material to be taught that day, namely "Living Creatures" and the children listened carefully to the explanations given. Additionally, some videos related to materials were also shown during the class.

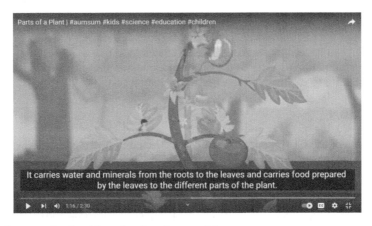

Figure 2. An example of a video related to the materials.

In grouping the students, the teacher used some sticks. Students are asked to choose an action picture to greet the teacher with at the start of class. The teacher then distributes colorful sticks. These sticks are used to form small groups of students. There are four groups: blue, red, green, and yellow. Each group has three to four students. Lastly, the teacher utilized some fun games as well using pictures. The pre-service teacher guided students through Eat Bulaga games to help them understand the previous material. The students are given some pictures and asked to guess the picture with their friends by asking questions and providing some hints in English.

3.5 *Stimulating interaction and cooperation through learning activities*

The students are given some pictures and asked to guess the picture with their friends by asking questions and providing some hints in English. Through small group discussions, the students were stimulated to practice their speaking. More importantly, they could collaborate with their friends to do the task and discuss the materials.

Figure 3. The students played games and worked with their friends using worksheet.

3.6 *Developing cross-cultural awareness*

During small group work, the co-teachers assisted students in discussing the materials and asked some questions related to the topic. Furthermore, teachers also introduced some cultural awareness during the discussion as it was described as follows.

Teacher: What animal is it?
Ss: a dog
Teacher: Yes, as a Muslim, is it halal or haram to eat a dog?
Ss: haram
Teacher: yes ... we are not allowed to consume it. What do you think?

93

S1: We cannot eat it.
Teacher: Exactly, we cannot eat it. It is okay for non-Muslims or maybe Western people.

From this, it can be seen that students already understood that as a Muslim it is prohibited to consume certain animals. The co-teacher then explained that it is forbidden to eat dogs because it is haram to eat them or assist others in eating them.

4 DISCUSSION

The first aspect of the CLIL approach that was reflected in observed classes was **content.** It was crystal clear that in the observed classes, the teacher integrated the language learning and science materials as it was congruent with the previous studies (Farah and Anggraeni 2022; Huang 2020; Khoiriyah 2022; Pladevall-Ballester 2015; Satayev *et al.* 2022). By exposing new vocabulary related to Science, students were stimulated to comprehend the content materials with high cognitive load (Coyle 2015; Lo and Fung 2018; Surdyanto and Kurniawan 2020; Vavelyuk 2015). The increased use of the foreign language to convey subject-specific information is expected to increase foreign language proficiency. Thus, given the authenticity of the input and the constant use of the target language, CLIL classrooms provide students with numerous opportunities to grow in their pragmatic competence. Due to the observations, little evidence proved the aspect of **cognition**. It might be justifiable since the lesson was only an "extracurricular". Thus, the learning outcomes should have been emphasized in increasing students' higher-order thinking skills.

In relation to **communication,** to improve language use, teachers used translanguaging in many ways, such as explaining materials, checking students' understanding, and giving instructions. It was also depicted that students tried to speak both in English and Bahasa Indonesia during the group discussion. From the excerpt, the implementation of trans-languaging coincided with previous studies (Karabassova and San Isidro 2020; Lin and Lo 2017; Setyaningrum *et al.* 2020). Translanguaging primarily occurs when students are constructing meaning about particular themes. Different from other EFL settings, the use of students' L1 in the CLIL setting was a promising support (Mahan 2022; Merino and Lasagabaster 2018; Nikula and Moore 2019; Nikula *et al.* 2017). When students were processing both language and material simultaneously in CLIL contexts, language-supportive scaffolding was likely to help them avoid cognitive overload. Thirdly, the aspect that should be inserted during the learning process in CLIL classes is communication. To boost the students' communication, the teacher grouped students into several small groups. By working in small groups, co-teachers assisted students to practice their speaking and comprehend the materials with their peers as suggested by Setyaningrum and Khoiriyah (2022) and Ordoñez and Vázquez (2015). By working in a group, students are stimulated to learn from other more capable peers as well. The teachers provided various learning materials and techniques such as using video, pictures, games, and colorful worksheets as it was highly suggested to teach young learners (Mccloskey 2014). Surprisingly, there was an interesting fact found in the research in relation to **cultural awareness**. Different from other studies that compare only their culture of own to others (Meyer *et al.* 2015, Coyle 2015), teachers tried to integrate Islamic Science and culture into their lessons. It can be said that the CLIL approach was also suitable for Islamic-affiliated schools. This finding is congruent with some prior studies (Banegas and Beamud 2020; Castillo-Rodriguez and Prat Fernández 2022; Mehisto 2012; Meyer 2017) stipulating that the CLIL approach provides a flexible framework. As a result, EFL teachers can implement the CLIL approach in various EFL settings.

5 CONCLUSIONS

This research might provide some insight into the teaching techniques used by English teachers in CLIL-oriented classes, particularly in teaching Science through English. The CLIL implementation was in line with the 4C frameworks and the principles of teaching English to young learners. There is a unique fact that the CLIL approach also can be implemented to integrate Islamic Science and culture instead of Western culture. Hence, it is projected to give some pedagogical reference for primary school teachers in Islamic-affiliated schools. Due to the limitation of this research, further studies are suggested to conduct experimental research to prove the effectiveness of the CLIL approach in students' learning outcomes.

REFERENCES

Andriani, P. F., Padmadewi, N. N. and Budasi, I. G. (2018) 'Promoting autonomous learning in English through the implementation of Content and Language Integrated Learning (CLIL) in science and maths subjects', *SHS Web of Conferences*, 42, p. 00074. doi: 10.1051/shsconf/20184200074.

Banegas, D. L. and Beamud, P. (2020) 'Content and Language Integrated Learning: A Duoethnographic Study about CLIL Pre-Service Teacher Education in Argentina and Spain'. doi: 10.1177/0033688220930442.

Baxter, P. and Jack, S. (2008) Qualitative Case Study Methodology: Study Design and Implementation for Novice Researchers, The Qualitative Report.

Castillo-Rodriguez, C. and Prat Fernández, B. (2022) 'Cooperative learning in the CLIL classroom: challenges perceived by teachers and recommendations for Primary Education', *Educatio Siglo XXI*, 40(1), pp. 79–106. doi: 10.6018/educatio.433411.

Coyle, D. (2015) 'Strengthening integrated learning: Towards a new era for pluriliteracies and intercultural learning', *Latin American Journal of Content and Language Integrated Learning*, 8(2), pp. 84–103. doi: 10.5294/laclil.2015.8.2.2.

Coyle, D., Hood, P. and Marsh, D. (2010) *Content and language integrated learning*. UK: Cambrigde.

Creswell, J. W. (2013) *Research Design: Qualitative, Quantitative, and Mixed Method Approaches*. SAGE Publications Inc.

Czura, A. (2017) 'Translation is not enough – the need for pedagogical adaptation in CLIL textbook development', *Porta Linguarum*, 27, pp. 35–46. doi: 10.30827/digibug.53950.

Ellison, M. (2015) 'CLIL: The added value to English Language Teacher Education for Young Learners', *Lingvarvm Arena*, 6, pp. 59–69.

Ellison, M. (2019) 'CLIL in the primary school context', in Garton, S. and Copland, F. (eds) *The Routledge Handbook of Teaching English to Young Learners*. Rouledge, pp. 247–268.

Hartman, R. J., Townsend, M. B. and Jackson, M. (2019) 'Educators' perceptions of technology integration into the classroom: a descriptive case study', *Journal of Research in Innovative Teaching & Learning*, 12(3), pp. 236–249. doi: 10.1108/jrit-03-2019-0044.

Huang, Y.-C. (2020) 'The Effects of Elementary Students' Science Learning in CLIL', *English Language Teaching*, 13(2), p. 1. doi: 10.5539/elt.v13n2p1.

Javadi, M. and Zarea, K. (2016) 'Understanding Thematic Analysis and its Pitfall', *Journal of Client Care*, 1(1). doi: 10.15412/j.jcc.02010107.

Karabassova, L. and San Isidro, X. (2020) 'Towards translanguaging in CLIL: a study on teachers' perceptions and practices in Kazakhstan', *International Journal of Multilingualism. Taylor & Francis*, 0(0), pp. 1–20. doi: 10.1080/14790718.2020.1828426.

Khoiriyah, K., Farah, R. R. and Anggraeni, L. (2022) 'Integrating Islamic values in CLIL materials: a syllabus design for Islamic primary school', *Journal of English Language Studies*, 7(1), pp. 12–26. Available at: https://jurnal.untirta.ac.id/index.php/JELS/article/view/3381.

Korosidou, E. and Griva, E. (2014) 'CLIL Approach in Primary Education: Learning about Byzantine Art and Culture through a Foreign Language', *Studies in English Language Teaching*, 2(2), p. 240. doi: 10.22158/selt.v2n2p240.

Lin, A. M. Y. and Lo, Y. Y. (2017) 'Trans/languaging and the triadic dialogue in content and language integrated learning (CLIL) classrooms', *Language and Education. Taylor & Francis*, 31(1), pp. 26–45. doi: 10.1080/09500782.2016.1230125.

Lo, Y. Y. and Fung, D. (2018) 'Assessments in CLIL: the interplay between cognitive and linguistic demands and their progression in secondary education', *International Journal of Bilingual Education and Bilingualism*, 9 March, pp. 1–19. doi: 10.1080/13670050.2018.1436519.

Maguire, M. and Delahunt, B. (2017) 'Doing a thematic analysis: A practical, step-by-step guide for learning and teaching Scholars.', *ALL Ireland Journal of Teaching and Learning in Higher Education (AISHE-J)*, 8 (3), pp. 3351–3365. doi: 10.1109/TIA.2014.2306979.

Mahan, K. R. (2022) 'The comprehending teacher: scaffolding in content and language integrated learning (CLIL)', *Language Learning Journal*. Taylor & Francis, 50(1), pp. 74–88. doi: 10.1080/09571736.2019.1705879.

Mccloskey, M. Lou (2014) 'Seven instructional principles for teaching young learners of English', *TESOL Symposium*, pp. 1–13.

Mehisto, P. (2012) 'Criteria for producing CLI learning material', *Encuentro*, 21, pp. 15–33.

Merino, J. A. and Lasagabaster, D. (2018) 'The effect of content and language integrated learning pro-grammes' intensity on English proficiency: A longitudinal study', *International Journal of Applied Linguistics (United Kingdom)*, 28(1), pp. 18–30. doi: 10.1111/ijal.12177.

Meyer, O. *et al.* (2015) 'A pluriliteracies approach to content and language integrated learning – Mapping learner progressions in knowledge construction and meaning-making', *Language, Culture and Curriculum*, 28(1), pp. 41–57. doi: 10.1080/07908318.2014.1000924.

Meyer, O. (2017) 'Introducing the CLIL-Pyramid: Key Strategies and Principles for CLIL Planning and Teaching Learnscaping: Creating next-gen environments for Pluriliteracies Teaching for Learning View project Pluriliteracies Teaching for Learning: conceptualizing learning', *Unpublished paper, Catholic University of Eichstaett-Ingolstadt*, (October). Available at: https://www.researchgate.net/publication/275887754.

Nikula, T. *et al.* (2017) 'Conceptualizing integration in CLIL and multilingual education', *International Journal of Bilingual Education and Bilingualism*. doi: 10.1080/13670050.2017.1416753.

Nikula, T. and Moore, P. (2019) 'Exploring translanguaging in CLIL', *International Journal of Bilingual Education and Bilingualism*. Taylor & Francis, 22(2), pp. 237–249. doi: 10.1080/13670050.2016.1254151.

O Ceallaigh, T., Ní Mhurchú, S. and Ní Chróinín, D. (2017) 'Balancing content and language in CLIL', *Journal of Immersion and Content-Based Language Education*, 5(1), pp. 58–86. doi: 10.1075/jicb.5.1.03oce.

Ordoñez, M. D. C. R. and Vázquez, V. P. (2015) 'Developing cooperative learning through tasks in Content and Language Integrated Learning', *Multidisciplinary Journal of Educational Research*, 5(2), p. 136. doi: 10.17583/remie.2015.1429.

Peel, K. L. (2020) 'A beginner's guide to applied educational research using thematic analysis', *Practical Assessment, Research and Evaluation*, 25(1), pp. 1–16. doi: 10.7275/ryr5-k983.

Pladevall-Ballester, E. (2015) 'Exploring primary school CLIL perceptions in Catalonia: students', teachers' and parents' opinions and expectations', *International Journal of Bilingual Education and Bilingualism*, 18 (1), pp. 45–59. doi: 10.1080/13670050.2013.874972.

Sánchez, O., Supervisor, L. and Ráez Padilla, J. (2020) Developing cooperative learning techniques in the CLIL classroom.

Satayev, M. *et al.* (2022) 'Content and Language Integrated Learning implementation through team teaching in Biology lessons: A quasi-experimental design with university students', *Frontiers in Education*, 7, pp. 1–11. doi: 10.3389/feduc.2022.867447.

Setyaningrum, R. W. *et al.* (2020) 'Content and Language Integrated Learning (CLIL) in Science class during covid-19 outbreak: A narrative inquiry', *English Review: Journal of English Education Volume*, 9(1), pp. 35–46.

Setyaningrum, R. W. and Khoiriyah (2022) 'Core features of Content and Language Integrated Learning (CLIL): An exploratory study in Indonesian primary schools', *Mextesol Journal*, 46(3), pp. 1–13.

Surdyanto, A. and Kurniawan, W. (2020) 'Developing critical reading module using integrated learning content and language approach', *Studies in English Language and Education*, 7(1), pp. 154–169. doi: 10.24815/siele.v7i1.15098.

Vavelyuk, O. (2015) 'To Integrate Successfully: Language and Subject Studies in ESP Teaching', *Procedia – Social and Behavioral Sciences*. Elsevier BV, 199, pp. 44–49. doi: 10.1016/j.sbspro.2015.07.485.

Wei, R. and Feng, J. (2015) 'Implementing CLIL for young learners in an EFL context beyond Europe', *English Today*, 31(1), pp. 55–60. doi: 10.1017/S0266078414000558.

Yamano, Y. (2013) 'Utilizing the CLIL approach in a Japanese primary school: A comparative study of CLIL and regular EFL lessons', *Content and Language Integrated Learning in Spanish and Japanese Contexts: Policy, Practice and Pedagogy*, 2(1), pp. 91–124. doi: 10.1007/978-3-030-27443-6_5.

Strengthening Professional and Spiritual Education through 21st Century Skill Empowerment in Pandemic and Post-Pandemic Era – Arifin et al. (Eds)

Application of Google Classroom as E-Learning media: Teachers' perspective

Nanda Kharisma Putri & A. Adityo*
Universitas Muhammadiyah Malang, Indonesia

ABSTRACT: E-Learning is one of the advanced technologies that uses media electronics to support online teaching and learning processes. One of the applications or learning management systems that assist the E-Learning process is Google Classroom. The purpose of this research is to determine a lecturer's perceptions about the use of Google Classroom as E-Learning media. To obtain the data from participants, the researcher used the descriptive qualitative method. The researcher used interviews and questionnaires as research instruments with six lecturers from English Language Education and Department at the University of Muhammadiyah, Malang. The interview and questionnaires were conducted from September 9 to 22, 2021 via WhatsApp call and Google Forms due to the COVID-19 pandemic. Based on the research findings and discussion, it was concluded that ELED lecturers had various perceptions about the use of Google Classroom for E-Learning media. In addition, the researcher found that the lecturers gained some benefits in using Google Classroom during their teaching practices. A benefit that lecturers experienced while using Google Classroom is the ease of delivering study material to students. Hence, it is good to use Google Classroom as E-Learning media for various teaching and learning processes.

Keywords: E-Learning, Google Classroom, perception

1 INTRODUCTION

Currently, the development of learning media has progressed significantly. With advanced technology, there is a modern media called E-Learning media. Arsyad (2011) stated that "E-Learning means learning by using electronic devices". With E-Learning media, the learning process is not limited to time and place because the teacher and student do not need to be in a face-to-face situation (Jonker *et al.* 2018) and it could save the cost incurred by an educational program (Atuahene *et al.* 2020). However, the utilization of E-Learning media could be also more expensive than face-to-face classes, especially when using multimedia that is more advanced and needs excellent network service and technical support (Fu 2022), but actually, the cost of network services and technical support can be cheaper than the class facilities, time spent, and the cost of travel used during conventional class-room learning sessions (Wani and Dalvi 2013). Technology, however, is an important part of learning and must be utilized in the classroom (Adityo 2015). In line with Sudiran *et al.* (2020), teaching media should be interactive and implement popular media to attract the students' attention. The implementation of E-Learning is also called a virtual class or online class that can perform a teaching and learning activity in interactive interaction.

One of the E-Learning media used to implement virtual classes in the English department of the University of Muhammadiyah Malang is Google Classroom. This application was made

---

*Corresponding Author: a.adityo1986@gmail.com

DOI: 10.1201/9781003376125-14
97

by Google to support the learning process. Prastiyo, Djohar, and Purnawan (2018) state that "Google Classroom is a network-based platform that integrates G Suite accounts for education with all G Suite services such as Google Docs, Gmail and Calendar". Google Classroom could be an alternative solution to solve the challenges in classroom learning. With this application, the lecturer can make a virtual class. This application will make it easier for lecturers to organize assignments, process students' grades, and open discussion forums (Izenstark and Leahy 2015; Rahmad *et al.* 2019; Shaharanee *et al.* 2016). Hence, by using this application the intensity of the teaching and learning process between lecturer and students will not be bound to the allocation of face-to-face time. Another efficiency of the Google Classroom application besides time is cost-efficiency. One of the features provided in this application is students are allowed to submit or upload assignments in the form of files or documents, videos, pictures, and links. So, these features will help students to reduce paper usage.

Perception is how a person interprets and responds to information from the surrounding environment. It means that someone can make any kind of response freely based on their feelings or point of view (Simbolon 2007). In making perception, someone can make positive or negative decisions to interpret an object (Parker *et al.* 2015) because perception always depends on their thinking. Someone's perception is usually used in qualitative research to get more information about the object being researched. According to the description above, the researcher is curious to investigate the lecturers's perception of the application of Google Classroom as an E-Learning media. Therefore, the researcher will conduct research about the application of Google Classroom in ELED (lecturer's perception) at the University of Muhammadiyah Malang.

1.1 *Definition of E-Learning*

E-Learning is the learning process that uses the internet, intranet, and other electronic networks to develop and deliver content provided to the learners through the networks (Hartley 2001). E-Learning can be defined as information technology in the form of cyberspace for the education field (Wijaya 2016). In addition, the use of E-Learning gives alteration into the learning process, from the teacher center to the student center which enables students to access material everywhere and at every time (Munir 2009; Sarker *et al.* 2019; Turnbull *et al.* 2021).

From those definitions above, we can conclude that E-Learning is one of the development technologies using media electronics to support teaching and learning processes and referring to the learning process delivered online. The utilization of E-Learning makes the learning process easier because the user still can share the material, discuss the material, and do quizzes online. Through E-Learning, the teacher can incorporate traditional teaching methods with modern technology (Szymkowiak *et al.* 2021) which has many advantages including cost efficiency, time flexibility, and place to get a measurable result.

Google Classroom is one of the best tools to improve and help teach in the learning process (Asnawi 2018). Google Classroom is a learning platform that a learning platform that can help to solve the difficulty of making assignments without using paper (paperless) (Iskandar *et al.* 2020). The paperless system in Google Classroom provides features that can allow students and teachers to access material anywhere and everywhere as long as there is an Internet connection. Through Google Classroom teachers can create an active, collaborative, and unforgettable lesson because it provides easy-to-use features for all students including adult learners (Nagele 2017). In conclusion, Google Classroom is a platform that can facilitate online classes. This application has some features which can be used by both teachers and students. Many experts have different meanings for the word perception. Perception is an individual's process of interpreting and organizing their impression to define something in their environment (Robbins 2005). In addition, Kinichi and Kreitner (2003:67) define perception as a cognitive process to interpret and understand surrounding conditions. Moreover, perception is the process of receiving and making sense of environmental information, including deciding what information to notice and how to categorize and define it

(McShane and von Glinow 2000). It can be summarized that perception is an individual's process to interpret something such as a problem, information, and experience that they see become something more meaningful.

2 METHODS

To conduct this research the researcher used a descriptive qualitative method. The descriptive qualitative method is that all aspects of the research such are the process, hypothesis, data analysis, and data conclusion, until the writing style uses non-numeric aspects, descriptive situational, in-depth interviews, content analysis, snowball, and story (Musianto 2004). The research subjects in this research are six lecturers of ELED. The researcher applied purposive convenience sampling to choose the participants and get the information based on the purpose of the research and theory from Andrade (2021). For purposive sampling, the researcher had criteria to be fulfilled by the participant. The criteria were the lecturers who are currently or ever used Google Classroom as their teaching media. For convenience sampling, the researcher chose the participants who were available at a given time or willingness to participate in this research. To collect the data from participants, the researcher used interviews and questionnaires. The possible questions asked by the researcher for the participants are as follows:

(a) What are your perceptions about the application of Google Classroom as E-Learning media?
(b) What are the benefits that you get from teaching using Google Classroom?
(c) What are the common problems that you find when you teach using Google Classroom?

3 RESULTS

The finding of this research was aimed to answer the research problem that has been stated in the first chapter. The data were gained from six lecturers as research subjects through interviews and questionnaires. The interview and questionnaires were conducted from September 9th until 22nd 2021 via WhatsApp call and Google Forms due to the COVID-19 pandemic.

3.1 *Lecturer's perception about the use of Google Classroom*

3.1.1 *Google Classroom is a Useful and Helpful Application*
Based on the point of view of the first respondent, Google Classroom was a platform that was very useful and helpful for teaching and learning activities, especially in the online platform. It can be seen from the result of the interview with the first interviewee below:

> "I believe the existence of Google Classroom is quite helpful for both the students and also the teachers in teaching and learning activities especially in the current era in which since the covid-19 pandemic. The teaching and learning process is suggested to conduct blended way, I mean we can have it not only in face-to-face or offline but also we can do it online. So, I believe that Google Classroom is very useful and helpful." (DM, Ln 22)

3.1.2 *Google Classroom is a user-friendly application*
The perception expressed by the second respondent regarding the use of Google Classroom. In the interview, the second interviewee stated that Google Classroom was user-friendly and

easy to use to help the teaching and learning process, as seen from the interview excerpt below:

> "I think using Google Classroom is quite user-friendly besides quite easy to use or the interface is quite easy to understand and the way how do we deliver the materials is quite easy for the students, and then as well as grading system and so on and so on." (TW, Ln 38)

The same perception also was shared by the third participant which Google Classroom was easy to use for students because the features of Google Classroom were accessible to understanding. It could be seen from the interview excerpt below:

> "Really good, because user friendly. So it's not hard to understand the features. The features are easy to use it. And students mostly do not problem in understanding or using the features. So it's very good." (NI, Ln 44)

The results of the questionnaire also support the previous answers. One participant stated that Google Classroom has an easy-to-use performance. As seen from the result of the questionnaire below:

> "I like using Google Classroom because of the easiness of its performance. It can facilitate the students in language learning process because through Google Classroom, students is easy to get information or announcement, do and submit their task or assignment, and also students can save their learning material and use it every time and everywhere." (KN)

3.2 *Some benefit from the use of Google Classroom*

This current research found that the lecturers gained various benefits from the use of Google Classroom during their teaching practices. The first respondent stated that some of the benefits were to keep the materials, access the assignments, and as a media to replace face-to-face meetings.

> " ... first I can store or keep the materials in there. So anytime students need to learn more, they can access the material that I have provided. Second, I can access my students' assignment as well, so anytime I can analyze and read my students' assignments and also I can give them feedback. And, in case I couldn't conduct face-to-face teaching and learning process and I have to give assignment to the students then I just simply put the assignment on there with the detailed explanation and the dateline that my students have to fulfill to finish the assignment." (DM, Ln 52)

The second participant also uttered the various benefits of using Google Classroom. The second participant argues that Google Classroom makes it easy to deliver the material and attach other resources related to the teaching material.

> " ... Easy for me to deliver the material and as well as pointing out what point that students need to improve or let say when I delivering the material they can understand easily because when I am using this platform sometimes I attach a video of the teaching because sometimes I record my teaching and then sometimes I attach a video and sometimes I use video from YouTube or other sources, and sometimes I attach a text as well. . So, this is easier for students as well to read and to understand about which part of the reading materials in the Google Classroom or the source for the days meeting and so on and so on." (TW, Ln 69)

The third respondent also said that the advantages of Google Classroom are that it is free and helps him integrate the material from another source.

> "The benefit is it free LMS. As I said before it easy to use, user friendly and it facilitate blended learning and also online learning. Very easy to integrate with other application or website." (NI, Ln 81)

Based on the result of the interview above, the most significant benefit of Google Classroom was the lecturers' ease of connecting it with other sources offside Google Classroom. Those statements above are closely related to the questionnaire result.

> "Organized teaching, organized assignment drive, useful features (link for video, file upload to other sources, etc.), easy assessment (Google form)." (RR)

3.3 *Some challenges in the use of Google Classroom*

However, challenges or problems when using Google Classroom during the teaching practices are still found by the lecturers. Each Lecturer has their challenges in using Google Classroom. The first interviewee stated that the appearance of Google Classroom is relatively unattractive to attract students' attention.

> "Some challenges from the use of Google Classroom from my point of view, I said first the display of Google Classroom is not really interesting to attract students' attention. It is quite simple. Also, since Google Classroom is usually connected to our Google Drive and encounter problem and also the Google Classroom will be affected. Sometimes, students not really active in accessing Google Classroom." (DM, Ln 87)

The second respondent revealed the problem of signing in, and some students were not familiar with this application and connection issues.

> " ... The students are having difficulty sign in if they don't have Google Email and then sometime maybe one until three students not familiar with the use of Google Classroom, and when they are facing poor connection sometimes I have to deliver the material using WhatsApp." (TW, Ln 109)

The third respondent stated both lecturers and students were challenged to respond fast.

> " ... No fast response either from the students and lecturers. Sometimes some students post something in the feed, for example and the other students and also the lecturers cannot or do not respond quickly or immediately." (NI, Ln 117)

3.4 *Lecturers' satisfaction with teaching using Google Classroom*

In this research, all of the respondents shared their satisfaction with the use of Google Classroom. All the respondents were quite satisfied with the use of Google Classroom as their media during their teaching practices, and also, explained the reason.

> " ... Of course I was satisfied and why because the existence of Google Classroom as E-Teaching Media it helped a lot in terms of scoring the material and if I could not meet my students directly due to some reason so we can communicating using WhatsApp and also I store the material in the Google Classroom." (DM, Ln 126)

" ... I am quite satisfied, but as I mention about the weaknesses of the Google Classroom in previously, so I think I am quite satisfied but there are some points need to be improve from Google Classroom." (TA, Ln 139)

"Yes, very satisfied. I think this user friendly and it also lite in terms of application, and it also a lot of product so it can integrate with other Google products such Google form, Google docs, YouTube, Google meet, etc." (NI, Ln 143)

The result of the questionnaire supported those statements above.

"Satisfied enough" (RR)

3.4.1 *Favorite features of Google Classroom*

In this research, the researcher asked about the features of menus in the Google Classroom that the respondents used or liked the most. The answers from the lecturers were pretty different and varied.

"The features that I use the most, I can upload the material so I can review or revise my students' work." (DM, Ln 153)

"I think the one that I use the most is the announcement setting in the dashboard. When I am giving the material and put some announcement there or I put attach-ment from Google drive and the students can access my drive as well to access the material." (TW, Ln 156)

" ... I think the delay post. So I can prepare the post and I can filter the wording of that I want to say to my students. While I am preparing the material, and other is quizzes also very easy to develop, and create, and integrated to grading system." (NI, Ln 165)

4 DISCUSSION

Concerning the use of Google Classroom for E-Learning media at the University of Muhammadiyah Malang, ELED lecturers had various perceptions about it. The perceptions expressed by lecturers through interviews tend to be positive found by the researcher. All of the lecturers stated that Google Classroom was useful, easy, and user-friendly. It is supported by previous findings that the usefulness score was 3.13, which indicates that Google Classroom was valuable as an E-Learning media (Asnawi 2018). In addition, it also related to the other findings which stated that Google Classroom users could feel that all the facilities and features provided were easy to use, and readily accessible to ease in completing tasks lectures. Both lecturers and students are familiar with this application (Wijaya 2016).

Moreover, the lecturers admitted that it was easy to use the application because when they uploaded the material, the students could access and understand it easily. The Google Classroom also facilitated the learning process with some features that the lecturers could share information or announcements and assignments for the students. The features were also well-known to the students, so the students were able to access any posts from lecturers. It strengthens the results of the research by another researcher who claimed that participants felt easy to download, install, and run the applications because the features in the application were easy to understand, and the instructions were complete (Rahmawati *et al.* 2020). The use of Google Classroom focused on the online process, so when lecturers were unable to attend the class for some reason, the teaching and learning process could still be done through this application. Then, the existence of Google Classroom was beneficial and valuable if used as E-Learning media.

In addition, based on the results found in the interview, the researcher found that the lecturers gained some benefits from using Google Classroom during their teaching practices. The first benefit was lecturers felt easier to share the explicit material with the students online. Besides, the lecturers also easily divided assignments or tasks and provided a detailed dateline.

So that, it had the potency to save lecturers' time. It was related to Sudarsana *et al.* (2019) when the lecturers used Google Classroom, time would not be wasted in distributing physical documents because the teachers' tasks could be completed on time online.

Then, the utilization of Google Classroom was beneficial because it was integrated with other applications or websites. It was related to the other researcher who stated that Google Classroom was easy to incorporate different applications such as YouTube, Google Drive, Google Forms, Flipgrid, and StoryJumper (Kumar *et al.* 2020). Therefore, the various material was delivered to the students.

5 CONCLUSION

Based on the research conducted by the researcher through interviews and questionnaires, the ELED's lecturers perceive that using Google Classroom as an E-Learning media is easy, useful, and helpful for the teaching process. The lecturers state that students also accept the easiness and usefulness of Google Classroom. In addition, the lecturers who utilize Google Classroom in their teaching practices gain many benefits. Easy to share the material, integrate with another platform, conduct the teaching and learning process without face-to-face meetings, supported by various features, and make it easier for lecturers to do something related to the learning are the benefits that the lecturers felt the most. However, in implementing Google Classrooms, the lecturers still face some issues, such as getting student's attention and connections.

Lastly, the lecturers are also really satisfied with Google Classroom while using it in their teaching practices. The satisfaction is influenced by some reasons, especially in terms of using Google Classroom has many benefits. Therefore, Google Classroom is very suitable to be used as an E-Learning medium in the teaching and learning process.

REFERENCES

Adityo, A. (2015) "Teachnology in digital nativeness: Enhancing technology as invisible media," *Erudio (Journal of Educational Innovation)*, 3(1), pp. 46–54. Available at: https://erudio.ub.ac.id/index.php/erudio/article/view/201 (Accessed: September 4, 2023).

Arsyad, A. (2011) *Media pembelajaran*. Jakarta: PT. Raja Grafindo Persada.

Asnawi, N. (2018) "Pengukuran usability aplikasi Google Classroom sebagai e-learning menggunakan USE questionnaire (Studi kasus: Prodi Sistem Informasi UNIPMA)," *RESEARCH: Computer, Information System & Technology Management*, 1(1), p. 17. Available at: https://doi.org/10.25273/research.v1i1.2451.

Atuahene, S., Kong, Y. and Bentum-Micah, G. (2020) "COVID-19 pandemic, economic loses and education sector management," *Quantitative Economics and Management Studies*, 1(2), pp. 103–109. Available at: https://doi.org/10.35877/454RI.qems162.

Fu, J. (2022) "Innovation of engineering teaching methods based on multimedia assisted technology," *Computers and Electrical Engineering*, 100, p. 107867. Available at: https://doi.org/10.1016/j.compeleceng.2022.107867.

Hartley, D.E. (2001) *Selling e-learning*. American Society for Training and Development. Available at: https://books.google.co.id/books/about/Selling_E_Learning.html?id=jcnh8Vcw0-IC&redir_esc=y (Accessed: September 4, 2023).

Iskandar, A. *et al.* (2020) *Aplikasi pembelajaran berbasis TIK*. Yayasan Kita Menulis. Available at: https://kitamenulis.id/2020/02/17/aplikasi-pembelajaran-berbasis-tik/ (Accessed: September 4, 2023).

Izenstark, A. and Leahy, K.L. (2015) "Google classroom for librarians: features and opportunities," *Library Hi Tech News*, 32(9), pp. 1–3. Available at: https://doi.org/10.1108/LHTN-05-2015-0039.

Jonker, H., März, V. and Voogt, J. (2018) "Teacher educators' professional identity under construction: The transition from teaching face-to-face to a blended curriculum," *Teaching and Teacher Education*, 71, pp. 120–133. Available at: https://doi.org/10.1016/j.tate.2017.12.016.

Kumar, J.A., Bervell, B. and Osman, S. (2020) "Google classroom: insights from Malaysian higher education students' and instructors' experiences," *Education and Information Technologies*, 25(5), pp. 4175–4195. Available at: https://doi.org/10.1007/s10639-020-10163-x.

McShane, S.L. and von Glinow, M.A. (2000) *Orgonizational Behavior*. Boston: McGraw-Hill.

Munir, D. (2009) *Pembelajaran Jarak Jauh Berbasis Teknologi Informasi dan Komunikasi*. Bandung: Alfabeta.

Musianto, L.S. (2004) "Perbedaan pendekatan kuantitatif dengan pendekatan kualitatif dalam metode penelitian," *Jurnal Manajemen dan kewirausahaan*, 4(2).

Parker, A.M., Bruine de Bruin, W. and Fischhoff, B. (2015) "Negative decision outcomes are more common among people with lower decision-making competence: an item-level analysis of the Decision Outcome Inventory (DOI)," *Frontiers in Psychology*, 6. Available at: https://doi.org/10.3389/fpsyg.2015.00363.

Prastiyo, W., Djohar, A. and Purnawan, P. (2018) "Development of Youtube integrated google classroom based e-learning media for the light-weight vehicle engineering vocational high school," *Jurnal Pendidikan Vokasi*, 8(1), p. 53. Available at: https://doi.org/10.21831/jpv.v8i1.17356.

Rahmad, R. et al. (2019) "Google classroom implementation in Indonesian higher education," in *Journal of Physics: Conference Series*, p. 012153. Available at: https://doi.org/10.1088/1742-6596/1175/1/012153.

Rahmawati, B.F., Zidni, Z. and Suhupawati, S. (2020) "Learning by Google Classroom in students' perception," in *Journal of Physics: Conference Series*, p. 012048. Available at: https://doi.org/10.1088/1742-6596/1539/1/012048.

Robbins, S.P. (2005) *Organizational behavior*. Toronto: Pearson Prentice Hall.

Sarker, M.F.H. et al. (2019) "Use of e-learning at higher educational institutions in Bangladesh," *Journal of Applied Research in Higher Education*, 11(2), pp. 210–223. Available at: https://doi.org/10.1108/JARHE-06-2018-0099.

Shaharanee, I.N.M., Jamil, J. and Rodzi, M.S.S. (2016) "The application of Google Classroom as a tool for teaching and learning," *Journal of Telecommunication, Electronic and Computer Engineering*, 8(10), pp. 5–8.

Simbolon, M. (2007) "Persepsi dan kepribadian," *Jurnal Ekonomis*, 1(1), pp. 52–66.

Sudarsana, I.K. *et al.* (2019) "The use of Google classroom in the learning process," in *Journal of Physics: Conference Series*, p. 012165. Available at: https://doi.org/10.1088/1742-6596/1175/1/012165.

Sudiran, S., Kurniawati, D.E. and Adityo, A. (2020) "Designing English teaching materials containing popular culture," *Jurnal Dedikasi*, 17(2), pp. 1–6.

Szymkowiak, A. *et al.* (2021) "Information technology and Gen Z: The role of teachers, the internet, and technology in the education of young people," *Technology in Society*, 65, p. 101565. Available at: https://doi.org/10.1016/j.techsoc.2021.101565.

Turnbull, D., Chugh, R. and Luck, J. (2021) "Transitioning to e-learning during the COVID-19 pandemic: How did Higher Education Institutions responded to the challenge?," *Education and Information Technologies*, 26(5), pp. 6401–6419. Available at: https://doi.org/10.1007/s10639-021-10633-w.

Wani, P., and Dalvi, V. (2013) "Blended learning: Is it required in Human Physiology?," *National Journal of Integrated Research in Medicine*, 4(6).

Wijaya, A. (2016) "Analysis of factors affecting the use of Google Classroom to support lectures," in *The 5th International Conference on Information Technology and Engineering Application*.

Strengthening Professional and Spiritual Education through 21st Century Skill Empowerment in Pandemic and Post-Pandemic Era – Arifin et al. (Eds)
© 2024 The Author(s), ISBN: 978-1-032-45243-2
Open Access: www.taylorfrancis.com, CC BY-NC-ND 4.0 license

Vocabulary acquisition about character education by developing flashcards as a teaching media towards young learners

Kharisma Naidi Warnanda Sabgini*, Triastama Wiraatmaja & Estu Widodo
Universitas Muhammadiyah Malang, Indonesia

ABSTRACT: Character education is deemed equally crucial with vocabulary acquisition to young learners in this day and age. Yet, exciting teaching media was required to pique students' interest to deliver those notions to young learners. Therefore, this research aimed to discover the importance of flashcards as a teaching medium to improve young learners' vocabulary acquisition regarding character education from the teacher's perspective. This research is mixed method research. The data were obtained through questionnaires and interviews. The subjects were two English teachers in a kindergarten. The questionnaires and interviews emphasized the teachers' perspectives regarding the importance of flashcards as a teaching medium while improving students' vocabulary acquisition about character education. The result indicated that using flashcards was deemed necessary since it greatly piqued students' interest in improving their vocabulary acquisition while strengthening their understanding of character education.

Keywords: Character education, flashcards, vocabulary acquisition, young learners

1 INTRODUCTION

The rising issue is character education. This has been a prominent issue for the last decade. Character education is as paramount as any other subject taught in school. The education system could graduate thousands of genii who could invent anything. However, if the character of those graduates is corruptible, it would be meaningless. Character education is paramount to prevent moral degradation due to globalization (Suhasdiwi 2018). In addition, there is a presidential decree number 87, 2017, as the legal basis to instill character education in the education system. Thus, seeing the importance of character education, teachers need to involve character education in every aspect of teaching and learning.

Teaching English to young learners has a similar responsibility to instilling character education. It has more responsibility than any other subject since the students are young. Therefore, the earlier the students are exposed to character education, the better the graduate would be. When the young learners have more exposure to character education, they would likely carry out their character throughout their learning experience. The objective of the national education system would be fulfilled. Besides, educating the young learner character education from the earliest stage of education would achieve the long-life learning objective set by the Ministry of Education and Culture.

Teaching second language vocabulary to young learners possesses an exclusive challenge. The teachers must consider the young learners' characteristics before applying such methods, techniques, or strategies in the classroom. The effect would be adverse. There is no room for error in teaching young learners. The effect of such a shocking, dreadful experience may lead to demotivation or even fossilization. Once the young learners acquire vocabulary mistakes,

---

*Corresponding Author: kharisma.naidi@umm.ac.id

DOI: 10.1201/9781003376125-15

the result would be disastrous. The young learner would carry the mistake for the rest of their life. Young learners learn a new word in a different language than their native. It is a critical instrument in second language learning (Alqahtani 2015). In short, a valiant media, technique, method, or strategy is needed to fill the gap and provide a solution to the caveats.

Teaching vocabulary using flashcards is a growing strategy nowadays. The researcher managed to review seven academic publications regarding the issue. Flashcards are a proven teaching media to improve students' vocabulary mastery based on an experimental study (Elisa and Tuti 2020; Ngarofah and Sumarni 2019; Suryani *et al.* 2022). Flashcards attract the students' attention (Kusumawardhani 2020; Matruty and Que 2021). Based on these findings, flashcards solve the problem of teaching vocabulary to young learners. Even though previous studies provide valid data on the usage of flashcards in the classroom, there is not a single study that discovers the importance of flashcards based on the teachers' standpoint. The teachers are the ones who employ flashcards in the teaching and learning process. The gap in the literature should be filled to provide a balanced viewpoint regarding the issue. Moreover, this paper does not merely discover the importance of sheer flashcards. The researcher puts character education flashcards into the variable.

2 LITERATURE REVIEW

2.1 *Issues on teaching vocabulary for young learners*

Young second language learners must master three thousand high-frequency words to understand utterances in the target language. By mastering ninety-five percent of those required words, the young second language learner will understand basic spoken and written expressions (Hestetræet 2019). The challenge is tangible. The teacher must immediately help the students master at least two thousand and eight hundred high-frequency words.

The theory of teaching vocabulary develops over time. The initial theory of teaching vocabulary is to teach the students word by word, drilling, and memorizing. This is a dull and meaningless teaching method that the students fail to recall any of the words once they leave the class. The mishap of the initial theory is that the students do not see the word in a context. The theory fails to present the vocabulary in use. The current theory of teaching vocabulary proposes to teach vocabulary in context and integrated with other skills. This is a more meaningful teaching method since the students see the vocabulary in context as a whole, not a dedicated subject. The students directly see when, where, why, and how the such word is used in a context.

Brown (2015) proposed four principles in teaching vocabulary based on the modern teaching vocabulary theory. To begin with, the teachers should allocate a specific time to learn vocabulary. The specific time does not necessarily require an hour full of new vocabulary. The specific time could be as simple as once the students finish reading a new reading material. The first meeting of new words needs to be addressed in repetition. It means that the new words should be introduced repetitively in, for example, ten minutes across the teaching and learning process rather than in ten minutes at once.

Secondly, teaching vocabulary is best practice is to teach vocabulary in context. The vast amount of authentic material could provide a real-life experience of a second language. Instead of focusing on word-by-word vocabulary out of context, the teacher could show the vocabulary within the communicative framework. Thus, the students could put the vocabulary in a fruitful context in which the vocabulary could apply. However, the in-context vocabulary teaching may differ across age and level of proficiency. The young learner may learn in-context vocabulary through modeling, picture, and persona to elicit the young learner's understanding of the new word. Teaching language in context has another advantage; the learners comprehend when to use the appropriate word for different occasions.

Next, the students would benefit when the teachers make an unplanned vocabulary teaching. The concept of this principle is to have an impromptu vocabulary class once encounter a new word. Another example is when a student asks about an unknown new word. This is important since the student is entirely focused on the new word, and the knowledge retention would be immense. Finally, urge the students to have customizable vocabulary learning. The basis of the principle is to take individual differences into account. There is no one-size-fits-all method. The students should know themselves and fashion the vocabulary learning based on their characteristics. Zimmerman (2014) proposed asking several questions once the students encounter a new word: whether the word is countable or uncountable, the preposition that follows, whether it is formal or informal and whether it has a positive or negative connotation. The teacher should also motivate the students to master more vocabulary to achieve higher learning achievement or simply understand the second language better.

The principles of teaching vocabulary to young learners are not far from the tenets Brown proposed. Young learners have a balanced approach, implicit and explicit teaching and learning process in teaching vocabulary (Hestetræet 2019). Explicit vocabulary teaching is efficient and most beneficial for high-frequency words. This benefit for the students as high-frequency words are the common words that appear in listening or reading tasks. Moreover, the students need high-frequency words to form basic speaking and writing utterances. Explicit vocabulary teaching is best suited by using media such as pictures, objects, or models to aid the students' memorization. On the other hand, extensive reading is one of the strategies in implicit vocabulary teaching. With less than five percent of difficult words, the students could guess the meaning based on the context. Even though the students are able to guess the meaning based on the context, they are still relatively young and need guidance and support to guess the appropriate meaning. Picture books could be used as well as the media. The media serves two parallel variables in teaching, a picture to attract the students' attention as well as a model and picture itself. The word provides a further understanding of the vocabulary. The last example of implicit vocabulary teaching is by using oral storytelling.

2.2 *Flashcards*

Flashcards have its own meaning in teaching English as a second or foreign language. Flashcards are a card that shows pictures to the students as a powerful teaching media. The picture could be anything, from the basic one, such as an animal or food, to the complex one, such as a story scene. It is a practical and applicable teaching media (Herlina and Dewi 2017). The teachers could simply buy flashcards or make flashcards from scratch. The teacher could merely google the image, print it, and show the picture before the class. The usage of flashcards is limitless. The teacher could simply show the flashcards and ask the students what the picture is in it or the complex one, such as having storytelling by showing flashcards occasionally. Furthermore, flashcards are a media that attract the student's attention and encourage them to learn more as well as improve the student's motivation (Yuliantari *et al.* 2021). Moreover, flashcards are a creative teaching media that help the students to have a higher retention o vocabulary mastery. Using flashcards makes the students imagine and associate the word and the meaning in real-time.

3   METHODS

Alnajjar and Brick (2017) conducted a fusion research method between small-scale surveys and case studies. The study replicated the previous one, sharing several similar characteristics and objectives. This study was non-experimental research. The objective of the survey research was to discover the people's beliefs, opinions, and behavior (Ary *et al.* 2019). On the other hand, the case study focused on a single unit to discover a rich, in-depth data description (Creswell and Creswell 2018). The single unit could be a person, group, or process. The basic theory of the study was mixed-method research. It is a study that combines various elements of both quantitative and qualitative methodology (Cohen *et al.* 2018). The objective of this research method was to discover more of a phenomenon than a single methodology would possibly yield. The mixing was not necessarily in terms of the method; the mixing could be the instrument, data collection, or data analysis. This study employed a Quan à Qual methodology. It meant the researcher conducted the quantitative research as the initial study and conducted the qualitative study at a later stage.

The participants in the study were two English kindergarten teachers. The researcher employed a purposive sampling method. This is the best-suited sampling method for the case study. The teachers have more than five years of experience teaching young learners English. The most crucial factor that affected the sampling method was that the two teachers implemented character education flashcards to teach young learners vocabulary.

The researcher employed two instruments in the study. The first instrument is an open-ended questionnaire. The questionnaire consisted of two parts. The researcher employed a paper-and-pencil direct questionnaire, which meant the researcher was present while the participant answered the questionnaire. The first part was to discover the demographic statistic of the participant. The second part consisted of five open-ended questions discovering the general perception of the teacher when implementing the character education flash card. The questionnaire itself was adapted from Jeon and Hahn (2006). Finally, the researcher conducted a semi-structured interview to gain an in-depth understanding of the issue. The data was collected, organized, and coded before being narratively analyzed.

4 RESULTS AND DISCUSSION

The following Table 1 was the demographic data obtained from the questionnaire. The demographic data was to explain the general pictures of the participant. The researcher took full consideration of the participant's behalf by employing a pseudonym to keep the participants' privacy protected.

Table 1. The demographic data of the participants.

Name	Mawar	Melati
Age	34	27
Gender	Female	Female
Education	Bachelor Degree	Bachelor Degree
Teaching Experience	Eight years	Three years
Duration in implementing Flashcards	1 year	1 semester

The implementation of character education in the flashcards was significantly based on the participants' perspectives. They were five factors implemented in the character education flashcards. The five factors were taken from the five principles of Pancasila. They were (1) The belief in one God, (2) A just and civilized humanity, (3) Indonesian unity, (4) Democracy under the wise guidance of representatives' consultations, and (5) Social justice for all the people of Indonesia. The participants could tell that the students improved their character based on the five principles of Pancasila. The participant could show the students the six religions in Indonesia, and they were all worth respecting. The topic of the first principle was applied when the participants were taught the name of a place material. The participant simply showed a picture of a mosque, church, house, shrine, or temple. The participant taught the second principle of Pancasila by doing self and other introductions. The participants showed flashcards of people doing greetings and self-introduction. The participants simply explained to the students how to introduce themselves or their friends. The third principle was taught by showing the diverse culture of Indonesia. The flashcards have filled the picture of tribes wearing their tribal clothes. The fourth principle was introduced by having group work. The participants assigned group-project-based work to the students. Finally, the participants showed the occupation types for the last principle of Pancasila.

The character education presented in the flashcards during teaching vocabulary positively affected the young learner. The young learner could implement the desired character based on Pancasila's principle during teaching and learning. The participants believed that the character education flashcards were essential. Mawar and Melati, in the interview session, told the researcher that the students were eager to learn more about the principles of Pancasila. They highlighted that using character education flashcards was helpful in teaching. The participants believed that the character education flashcards were essential to delivering the material effectively.

The participants agreed that the flashcards were ready and easy to use. Flashcards did not possess a technical usage issue. Flashcards did not need a particular skill from the participants to operate. The participants were merely required to take the printed flashcards and showed to the students. The flashcards could be employed again and again. The activity of the learning process depended on the participant's imagination and pedagogical skills. The participants admitted that the possibility of using such flashcards in any approach, method, and strategy was limitless. Melati provided an example of using flashcards in teaching and learning. She would divide the class into several groups. Then, she would pick two students from a group to have a guessing game. One person is holding a flashcard, and the other is guessing what is in the flashcard. However, the holder could not say the picture in the flashcard definitively. Mawar stated in the interview session that using flashcards saved her time. She did not need to prepare such a complicated teaching media when flashcards were ready to be used. Based on the pedagogical issue, flashcards helped the participants to deliver material efficiently. The flashcards were suitable for the topic, material, and the students their selves. This was in line with Mutohhar (2009) argument about reliable teaching media. A reliable teaching media should fulfill several requirements: suitable for the topic, material, and students, easy to prepare and practical to use, and used over time for different topics and activities.

Both participants agreed that implementing character education flashcards to improve the students' vocabulary mastery would benefit the students. The students generally had a positive reaction toward using the flashcards as well. The students seemed more motivated when the participants implemented the flashcards. The color, the picture, and the curiosity made the students wanted more and more of the flashcards. The students felt they were challenged to guess or answer questions the participants raised. The participants approved that the usage of flashcards provided a relaxing atmosphere. Melati claimed that the use of flashcards could improve the collaborative learning experience. The students were active during the class in project group work. Mawar, meanwhile, argued that the usage of flashcards could make the students enjoy learning. She claimed that the students paid full attention to the flashcards instead of playing or paying attention to something else. Mawar had undivided attention from the students. Furthermore, delivering the material using flashcards was more accessible than the traditional method. The participants agreed that flashcards provided a positive learning environment regarding class management variables. Flashcards offer a challenging learning environment (Sitompul 2013). Furthermore, using flashcards could improve the students' active participation, improve word memory and attract the students' attention (Nguyen and Nguyen 2019).

The participants agreed as well that the usage of flashcards had a positive effect on vocabulary retention. The participants believed the flashcards could provide better vocabulary learning than memorizing and drilling. Mawar, in the interview section, admitted the findings based on her experience. She used to teach vocabulary to the young learner by preparing and memorizing. However, once the class was over, or she asked about the vocabulary the following day, the students could not recall it. On the other hand, once Mawar implemented flashcards, the students had higher vocabulary retention. The students could recall the vocabulary taught in the middle of the semester in the end. Mawar usually showed identical flashcards at the semester's middle and end. Asa result, the students could recall the word correctly and precisely. Rizwan (2021) supported this finding by arguing that high-frequency and low-frequency words have higher retention when flashcards teach the students. No participants agreed that flashcards brought drawbacks in teaching vocabulary to young learners.

5 CONCLUSION

Based on the findings, the researcher concluded that the character education flashcards to teach vocabulary mastery was essential. The study found that flashcards could develop the young learner into a Pancasila student. Furthermore, the flashcards had other benefits for the students and the teacher. The most notable benefit was the students' vocabulary retention.

REFERENCES

Alqahtani, M. (2015) 'The importance of vocabulary in language learning and how to be taught', *International Journal of Teaching and Education*, III(3), pp. 21–34. Available at: https://doi.org/10.20472/TE.2015.3.3.002.

Ary, D. *et al.* (2019) *Introduction to Research in Education*. 10th edn. Boston: CENGAGE Learning.

Brown, H.D. (2015) *Teaching by Principles*. Pearson.

Cohen, L., Manion, L. and Morrison, K. (2018) *Research Methods in Education*. London: Cohen.

Creswell, J.W. and Creswell, J.D. (2018) *Research Design: Qualitative, Quantitative, and Mixed Methods Approaches*. 5th edn. Los Angles: Sage.

Elisa, H. and Tuti, T. (2020) 'An evaluation of the use of flashcards for teaching vocabulary at Kindergartens in Sintang', *JETL (Journal of Education, Teaching and Learning)*, 5(2), p. 388. Available at: https://doi.org/10.26737/jetl.v5i2.2040.

Herlina, H. and Dewi, R.R. (2017) 'Flashcard media: The media for developing students understanding for english vocabulary at elementary school', *IJER – Indonesian Journal Of Educational Review*, 4(1), p. 116. Available at: https://doi.org/10.21009/IJER.04.01.11.

Hestetræet, T.I. (2019) *Vocabulary teaching for young learners. in The Routledge Handbook of Teaching English to Young Learner*. London: Routledge.

Jeon, I. and Hahn, J. (2006) 'Exploring EFL teachers' perceptions of task-based language teaching: A case study of Korean secondary school classroom practice', *Asian EFL Journal*, 8(1), pp. 123–143.

Kusumawardhani, P. (2020) 'The use of flashcards for teaching writing to English Young learners (EYL)', *Scope: Journal of English Language Teaching*, 4(1), p. 35. Available at: https://doi.org/10.30998/scope.v4i01.4519.

Matruty, E. and Que, S.R. (2021) 'Using flashcard as a media in teaching vocabulary for the eighth grade students of junior high school', *MATAI: International Journal of Language Education*, 2(1), pp. 25–34. Available at: https://doi.org/10.30598/matail.v2i1.5490.

Mutohhar, M. (2009) *Teaching English for Young Learners (TEYL) misunderstanding about teyl in elementary school*.

Ngarofah, S. and Sumarni, A. (2019) 'Teaching vocabulary using flashcards to young learner', *PROJECT (Professional Journal of English Education)*, 1(6), p. 775. Available at: https://doi.org/10.22460/project.v1i6.p775–782.

Nguyen, H.G.T. and Nguyen, H.B. (2019) 'Teachers' perceptions about vocabulary instruction through flashcards at English language centers in the Mekong Delta City', *I-manager's Journal on English Language Teaching*, 9(3).

Rizwan, A. (2021) 'Effect of digital flashcard on low frequency vocabulary retention by graduate students', *International Journal of Infrastructure Research and Management*, 9(1), pp. 7–18.

Sitompul, E.Y. (2013) 'Teaching vocabulary using flashcards and word list', *Journal of English and Education*, 1(1), pp. 52–58.

Suhasdiwi, I. (2018) 'Panduan praktis PPK berbasis budaya sekolah'. Kementerian Pendidikan, Kebudayaan, Riset, dan Teknologi.

Suryani, E.A.A., Majid, A.H. and Suryani, S. (2022) 'Introducing English vocabulary to young learners with flashcards', *English Education Journal*, 13(2), pp. 160–171. Available at: https://doi.org/10.24815/eej.v13i2.25454.

Yuliantari, I.G.A.W., Padmadewi, N.N. and Budasi, I.G. (2021) 'The implementation of learning vocabulary using flashcard for young children through Google Classroom', *Jurnal Pendidikan Bahasa Inggris undiksha*, 9(3), p. 271. Available at: https://doi.org/10.23887/jpbi.v9i3.38289.

Zimmerman, C. (2014) 'Teaching and learning vocabulary for second language learners', in M. Celce-Murcia, D. Brinton, and M.A. Snow (eds) *Teaching English as a second and foreign language*. Boston: National Geographic Learning.

Strengthening Professional and Spiritual Education through 21st Century Skill Empowerment in Pandemic and Post-Pandemic Era – Arifin et al. (Eds)

Early word learning acquired by Selegram Shabira Alula Adnan in terms of vocabulary growth

D. Samal & F. Sabilah
University of Muhammadiyah Malang

ABSTRACT: Language development in children is a unique and extraordinary process that greatly influences children's understanding and their style of language. The style of language in each child, which is the result of language development, is also influenced by various factors, which affect the language style of a child. This paper discusses about the learning style used by young selegram Shabira Alula Adnan and how she learned the standard language. The method used in this study is literary study. To answer the objectives of this research, theories related to language development and language style of children are analyzed. Data related to the development and style of language from Shabira Alula Adnan are obtained through social media, from TikTok, Instagram, YouTube, and other online news sources. The data are analyzed by comparing and analyzing theories related to the development and style of language in children, and then compared with the cases faced by Shabira Alula Adnan. The results revealed that the language style used by Shabira Alula Adnan is a combination between two language styles, namely referential language style and expressive language style. The language styles used by Shabira Alula Adnan are influenced by her age, the parenting style in teaching the language, and also her daily environment. The development and styles of language used by Shabira Alula Adnan are affected by many factors, not only because of age but also the parenting style and the daily environment.

1 INTRODUCTION

There has been a long-standing interest in the theory of language development in children and how children learn a good language. This is because the development of language in children or how they learn a good language also affects the language style used by the child. Many researchers believe that a child's language style is heavily influenced and contributed by other factors, such as parenting patterns, family environment, play environment, or even the broader social environment (Aisyah Isna 2019; Putra *et al.* 2018; Wahyuni 2016). A child will not be able to speak well or use a style of language without the help of others (Alatalo and Westlund 2021). In addition, children who get stimulation or directed teaching in the context of language will develop faster than children who do not or even receive stimulation (Yuniarti and Wildani 2015). Supported by the previous research, even the provision of stimulation in the first three years of a child's life is essential for a child's life because the first three years of the brain is an organ that develops very rapidly (Putra *et al.* 2018).

According to that idea, cases related to language development in children and children's language styles are often in the spotlight in science and have been widely explored worldwide. The language style used by children is believed to be the result of teaching and stimulation from their environment, including parenting patterns, verbal environment, and parental history (Pancsofar and Vernon-Feagans 2006). As stated by Mulyani *et al.*

DOI: 10.1201/9781003376125-16

(2015), parenting style is one of the environmental aspects that significantly influence children's language development. In a similar vein, research result conducted by Safwat and Sheikhany (2014) shows that parents who contingently respond to their children's verbal initiatives (parenting style) tend to have children with advanced phonological awareness and story comprehension skills. This parenting style is a pattern of behavior applied to children that is relatively consistent from time to time (Pancsofar and Vernon-Feagans 2006). Based on the stimulation of the environment, children will tend to use language styles that can be the same as the social environment they are in or use different or distinctive language styles, often known as referential and expressive styles (Eun and Junkyu 2018; Hampson and Nelson 1993). Generally, referential style occurs when children prefer to acquire a language through single words, whereas expressive style happens when children use a language with entire phrases (Eun and Junkyu 2018). The language style used in each of these children has its uniqueness. This is supported by Wahyuni (2016) that different children use different strategies for acquiring speech. For example, some concentrate on overall rhythm and slot in words with the same general sound pattern. Whereas others prefer to deal with more abstract slots and of particular interest is work that looks at how children cope with different languages. This also supports why there are children whose language styles vary, ranging from using the same language style as the surrounding community or even using a standard language, which is unique and different from their social environment.

In view of the previously mentioned research findings and methodology, the research settings are mainly conducted using quantitative research (Joni 2015; Mulyani et al. 2020; Putra et al. 2018) and only focusing on parenting rules in children language development (Hasanah and Sugito 2020; Joni 201; Mulqiah et al. 2017, 2020; Pancsofar and Vernon-Feagans 2006; Safwat and Sheikhany 2014). The focus of previous research on parenting rules in children's language development resulted in the limitation of knowledge obtained by researchers or readers on aspects that influence the development and style of language used by children. In addition, the extensive use of quantitative methods compared to qualitative allows for deficiencies in describing and interpreting research results in more depth. In addition, using quantitative methods can also result in a lack of specific understanding in analyzing the research results obtained. This is because, in the use of quantitative methods, in-depth analysis of research results is not that great compared to qualitative methods. Additionally, there is still reasonably limited study exploring the children's role in language development that focuses on the language style used by the children in their daily lives. The previous studies only explored language styles (referential and expressive) in the form of styles of language learning (Cynthia A. Brock 1986; Eun and Junkyu 2018; Hampson and Nelson 1993; Lieven et al. 1992), not making them into children language styles. Meanwhile, the existence of referential and expressive language is also one of the two language styles used by a child the most (Eun and Junkyu 2018). It even becomes a distinctive feature of the language style used. Therefore, this present research aims to discover the contribution of some aspects to children's language style (inferential or expressive style), not only focusing on the role of parenting style but also other aspects, namely analyzing the children language development in dept, language style that possible used by children, dialog system used, until the environmental rules.

This present study itself aims to investigate early word learning acquired by young selegram Shabira Alula Adnan (Shabira Alula Adnan) as the subject in terms of vocabulary growth. Based on this research results, Shabira Alula Adnan often uses standard language in her daily conversation. The use of the standard language style is also one of the characteristics of the language style used, namely referential and expressive style. Therefore, the main purpose of this research is to find out what language style is used by Shabira Alula Adnan (referential or expressive) and how she acquires that language and style. The result of this present research is also projected as input for language learning development in children, especially to know the factors that affect children's language development.

2 METHODOLOGY

The method used in this research is literary study. This study is descriptive, qualitative, and exploratory. It was descriptive because this research investigates and describes the existing phenomena that happened to Shabira Alula Adnan. Qualitative and exploratory because this research tries to find the relevant literature to investigate the language style phenomena that happened in Shabira Alula Adnan. The main characteristic of this method is that the researcher has no control over the variables and can only report what has happened or what is happening. This study uses a literary approach compared with the phenomena that occur in the research subject (Shabira Alula Adnan). To collect the data, the researcher observed videos and articles that showed and explained the language style used by Shabira Alula Adnan. The data was obtained through TikTok, Instagram, YouTube, and several TV programs. To get answers to the objectives of this study, the data obtained regarding the acquisition of the language or style of language used by Shabira Alula Adnan will then be compared or justified based on existing theories. Later, the results of the research investigation will show the case that happened to Shabira Alula Adnan.

3 RESULTS

3.1 *Language development to children*

Language development in children occurs very quickly between the ages of two to five years and becomes one of the most complex language-learning activities (Mulyani *et al.* 2020). It is complex because children's language development in this phase sometimes only takes a short time, and children can master complex languages at their age (Hasanah and Sugito 2020). In addition, at this age, the vocabulary produced by children can reach 50 to 160 or even 2000 words or more (Mulyani *et al.* 2020). According to Joni (2015), at the age of 2.5–5 years old, children will usually be faster in learning a language and more sensitive to what is being heard. They will be free to express their thoughts or feelings about their environment. This is also supported by the large number of vocabularies that have been obtained and consists mainly of verbs. Children no longer repeat words to be understood because, at this stage, the sentence structure and pronunciation are clearer. The hallmark of this phase is that the child will often ask questions about what they see and hear. Not only asking questions, but children will also often tell things that relate to their experiences. Although sometimes it still stutters, it is normal for children at this stage (Conti-Ramsden and Durkin 2012).

Figure 1.   Sabira Alula Adnan's activities while talking (Tiktok account: @Shabiraalula&Ayah).

Regarding the theoretical basis above, Shabira Alula Adnan (Shabira Alula Adnan) has most of the characteristics of a child's language described in this phase (3–4 years). As reported from several sources, namely TikTok, Instagram, and YouTube, as well as several articles, it appears that Shabira Alula Adnan is a 4-year-old girl and has characteristics when speaking, namely her fluency when speaking, distinctive intonation, and often use of standard words in sentences. Based on the results of the researcher's observations, Shabira Alula Adnan's fluency did not only occur when she was four years old but started to be seen when she was three years old. The language used when speaking often uses standard words, such as "Ayah tidak boleh seperti itu", "baiklah ayah", "Kita tidak boleh bersedih", "Mengapa begitu ayah?", and many more. The sentences issued are also very expressive. She will explain or ask about things she saw or heard with great enthusiasm. Moreover, Shabira Alula Adnan often tells her parents about things she experiences or even her daily activities expressively. Figure 1 shows some pictures from one of the sources related to Sabira Alula Adnan's activities while talking.

Based on the explanation above, it can be concluded that the language skills of Shabira Alula Adnan are commonplace per her current age (3–4 years old). It stated that children aged three to four years have significant language development, such as having the ability to speak using simple sentences, more vocabulary, being active in speaking, and much more. At this stage, parents can also have conversations with the child because of the child's ability to ask questions related to what is seen and heard by using longer sentences and more regular grammar. In addition, the words she used consisted of not only one or two words anymore, but three or more words and were done more fluently (Conti-Ramsden and Durkin 2012; Fatmawati 2015). At age 3, Shabira Alula Adnan could have intense conversations with her parents using simple and complete sentences. She often asks questions about what she saw or heard, such as *"Mengapa seperti itu ayah?", "Mengapa dia seperti itu ayah?", "Tidak boleh begitu ya ayah?".* Her vocabulary is also more numerous and varied. She is more active in speaking, asking questions, and even giving opinions in simple sentences, such as *"Wow, aroma sup ayamnya sedap sekali", "Shabira Alula Adnan tidak mau.", "Gigi ayah bersih sekali.",* and so on. However, there are some unique things that Shabira Alula Adnan does, such as the use of standard words when speaking and the intonation of speech which is quite distinctive. The existence of this is motivated by several aspects, such as the style of parental teaching patterns in terms of language learning and the surrounding environment.

3.2 *Children language style*

Language tends to develop in the same way for most children. However, when first learning or acquiring words, some differences exist, such as children prefer a "referential" speaking style, while others prefer an "expressive" style. Even in some cases, there are children whose language style combines two styles at once. The individual characteristics of various language learners are essential to successful language acquisition (Eun and Junkyu 2018). Therefore, language development in children aged 3–4 years is a significant phase of language development. This is because each child uses various strategies and language styles in terms of speaking and acquiring a language (Hampson and Nelson 1993; Conti-Ramsden and Durkin 2012). Referring to the language style above, several language styles often occur or are used by children, especially children aged 2–5 years. Based on several research results, the language style used in preschool age children (3–4 years) when speaking or acquiring a language is categorized into two: Referential and Expressive (Eun and Junkyu 2018; Hampson and Nelson 1993; Nelson 1973).

According to Eun (2018), referential learning happens when language is preferred to be learned through single words. To be specific, children who speak in a referential manner use vocabulary to make references to objects. They label things and people and organize their speech to be understandable. They frequently interact more with adults than peers. More single words are used, and longer phrases and sentences are gradually added. They might take pleasure in labeling the things and people they see when they look at books or pictures. Furthermore, early words used by referential children frequently denote objects, such as "cat." They use single words in their speech, and their pronunciation is typically more understandable. Supported by Gotzke and Sample Gosse (2007), children who use referential language prefer to label things and people, and their word choices are influenced by their preferences for word structure and sounds. They frequently speak in single words and interact more with adults. From single words, they gradually construct longer phrases and sentences.

Whereas, if referential children tend to enter the language with single words, primarily concrete nouns that are articulated, then expressive children appear to be trying to produce complete sentences (Hampson and Nelson 1993; Eun and Junkyu 2018). For further details, children who speak in an expressive style essentially just talk incessantly without worrying if anyone can understand them. They communicate with both adults and peers while frequently speaking incomprehensibly. They use fewer nouns and more greetings and everyday words like "hi" and "mine." Language is primarily used to socialize and express needs and feelings. The tendency for expressive speech to combine two words into one is known as using "unanalyzed wholes." For instance, "allgone" or "stopit". Longer phrases and sentences are gradually broken down into single words to help these kids learn the language. As stated by Eun (2018), children whose vocabularies contain more than 50% of nouns are referred to as referential style, while those whose vocabularies contain a lower percentage of nouns are referred to as expressive style.

According to the case that happened to Shabira Alula Adnan, she is the type of child who is talkative and has a characteristic in her speech, namely using a standard language when speaking. According to the video uploaded to her TikTok account (@Sabiraalula&Ayah), Shabira Alula Adnan often uses various vocabularies that refer to things and even people around her. In one of video that uploaded in her account, Shabira Alula Adnan was seen explaining some of the things around her, such as *"mana ada Kuda, orang ini Dinosaurus"*, *"Dinosaurusnya jenisnya Trex"*, *"Ini kan mainan, bukannya beneran"*, *"Shabira Alula Adnan jadi Trex"*, and many more. Figure 2 is taken from her TikTok account according to the abovementioned expressions.

Figure 2.   Shabira Alula Adnan expressions (TikTok account: @Shabiraalula&Ayah).

In addition to using vocabulary that refers to objects, what Shabira Alula Adnan says is also very easy to understand. This is because the pronunciation, intonation of speech, and expressions used are obvious as if she wants the other person to understand what she is talking about. It can be seen from her style of speech that she often repeats questions and statements that she gives or is given by her interlocutor. She also always uses long and clear sentences when talking with other people. Quoted from one of the videos on Shabira Alula Adnan's TikTok account, here is Shabira Alula Adnan's conversation with her father.

Shabira Alula Adnan: "Eh kenapa bunyi meleduk. Shabira Alula Adnan jadi takut".
Ayah: "Bukan bunyi meleduk, itu bunyi beleduk"
Shabira Alula Adnan: "Ayah, itu bunyi beleduk (she trying to confirm by repeating her statement before)". (@Shabiraalula&Ayah) (https://vt.tiktok.com/ZSRNLsVnQ/?k=1)
Ayah: "Sabira sudah mandi belum?"

Shabira Alula Adnan: "Ayah lihat deh, aku kan sudah cantik dan wangi".
Ayah: "Masa sih?"
Shabira Alula Adnan: "Iya"
Ayah: "Enggah ah. Emang wangi? Ayah ajah cium tadi bau asem."
Shabira Alula Adnan: "Ayam ciumnya bau asem ya?" (Trying to confirm by asking her father statement)
Ayah: "Iya. Bau asem sama bau ketek, Shabira Alula Adnan"
Shabira Alula Adnan: "Bau ketek Shabira Alula Adnannya ya?" (Asking again to measure her father's mean)
(@Shabiraalula&Ayah) (https://vt.tiktok.com/ZSRNLnHVH/?k=1)

In that conversation, Shabira Alula Adnan is seen using sentences that are a bit long and repeating statements several times or giving back questions so that other people can understand them. Using very clear sentences, her intonation and expressions also support how the sentences spoken are easy to understand.

If examined, the case or language style used by Shabira Alula Adnan has the same characteristics as the characteristics of the Referential Language style, namely, where a child uses vocabulary that refers to things (as mentioned in the example above), the structure of the speech to be understood, and using a clear speech. However, not all the language features of the referential style are presented by Shabira Alula Adnan, which is like using more single words and gradually building up to phrases and then tending to interact more with adults than peers. In fact, according to the videos in Shabira Alula Adnan's TikTok account, Shabira Alula Adnan rarely speaks using only single words and gradually builds it up to phrases, but always or more often uses long sentences (not single words but more than two or three words) instead of a single word. She also often interacts with adults and her peers. From several videos on her TikTok account, it can be seen that Shabira Alula Adnan has the same interest in interacting with adults (Figure 3) and their peers (Figure 4). Here are some documentation of Shabira Alula Adnan's activities.

Figure 3.   Shabira Alula Adnan interacts with her peer (TikTok account: @Shabiraalula&Ayah).

Figure 4.   Shabira Alula Adnan interacts with adults (TikTok account: @Shabiraalula&Ayah).

Although in some of the cases above, Shabira Alula Adnan has several language characters that refer to the Referential style, there are also other cases where she is more directed to the Expressive style. Some of the characteristics or aspects of Shabira Alula Adnan's expressive style relate to interacting with adults and peers and using language to express feelings, needs, and socializing. This is appropriate as happened in the previous case where Shabira Alula Adnan was not only interested in interacting with adults but also with her peers. However, most of the videos displayed on social media show that Shabira Alula Adnan interacts with her parents more often because the video was taken when they were at home. In addition, Shabira Alula Adnan has the same interest in interacting with adults and their peers. In addition to these characters, Shabira Alula Adnan also has a character who very often uses language to express feelings, needs, or even socialize (Expressive style). In several videos uploaded on her TikTok and Instagram accounts, it can be seen that Shabira Alula Adnan very often expresses her feelings, needs, or even socializes, such as *"Ayah kok makannya seperti itu, itu tidak boleh ayah"*, *"Shabira Alula Adnan dimarahi ibu karena Shabira Alula Adnan nakal"*, *"Hati Shabira Alula Adnan hancur"*, *"Shabira Alula Adnan lagi lemah, jantung Shabira Alula Adnan lemah"*, *"Ibu, Shabira Alula Adnan minta susu ibu"*, *"Buaya kemana saja? Aku kangen nih Bersama buaya"*, which those characters are the expressive language style. In addition, one other aspect that Shabira Alula Adnan does not adopt from expressive style is that they speak a lot even though their language is not understood. This is contrary to the case experienced by Shabira Alula Adnan above. As already mentioned, Shabira Alula Adnan has a language style that speaks a lot and is easy for her interlocutors to understand (referential style).

Based on the comparison of the two cases above, it can be concluded that Shabira Alula Adnan's language style is a combination of those two, the Referential and Expressive styles. It can be evidenced by the Shabira Alula Adnan language character, which includes the language styles of the two styles, such as using vocabulary to refer to things, structuring her speech to be understood, and labeling objects and people; those characters refer to referential language style. In addition, Shabira Alula Adnan also adopts or has characteristics of expressive speaking styles, such as interacting with adults and peers, using language to express feelings and needs, and socializing, in which the language character leads to expressive language style. Therefore, it can be concluded that Shabira Alula Adnan has a language style that combines referential and expressive styles.

3.3 *Democratic parenting style*

Language skills in children are influenced by internal factors as well as external factors, such as imitation of parents, family, friends, caregivers, or even other people or things in their environment (Joni 2015b; Sudrajat 2017). The existence of children in the environment is also one of the most influential aspects of the smooth development of children's language or the style of language they use. Among the factors above, parenting style is the factor that has a significant influence on the development or how well a child learns a language (Joni 2015b; Mulyani 2020). The parenting pattern can be interpreted as a pattern of behavior that is applied to children and is relatively consistent from time to time and can be felt by children in both negative and positive terms. What is meant by negative and positive aspects here are related to the development of language and knowledge in children. When children get good and appropriate parenting patterns, then language development in children will also be good. On the other hand, when the parenting style applied to the child is inappropriate, language development will also be affected. For example, when a child is continuously stimulated to use one type of language style, the child will imitate and apply what he or she has been taught or heard and seen from their parents. Children who are often given a stimulus to speak actively will automatically speak actively because of habits that are influenced by the environment and parents (social interactionist theory by Vygotsky) (Sudrajat 2017).

Regarding the parenting style applied to children, Mulyani *et al.* (2020) stated that three types of parenting are often used, namely democratic parenting, authoritarian parenting, and permissive parenting. Democratic parenting itself is a parenting style in which there is interaction and communication between children and parents. Interaction and communication between children and parents here are where children will receive examples of words, language, language style, or intonation from their parents to be imitated and expressed so the language skills can be continuously trained and improved (Mulqiah *et al.* 2017). In addition, among the three parenting patterns, the democratic style is stated to be the parenting style that most support language development in children according to their age stages (Mulqiah *et al.* 2017,2020; Safriana *et al.* 2017; Wijayanti *et al.* 2018).

As mentioned by (Hasanah and Sugito 2020; Mulqiah *et al.* 2017), Democratic Parenting is where parents set an example and give children the freedom to express what is experienced. Not only giving freedom, but parents also continue to control and limit children to what they can and cannot do. In the context of language learning, a good parenting style (democratic) can improve children's language development and speech (Wijayanti *et al.* 2018). Children who are guided democratically learn more actively than children who are raised not democratically. Children are given the freedom to imitate and express what they hear and see from their parents and their environment. Parents with this parenting style will provide examples simultaneously and provide opportunities for the child to imitate and express what has been exemplified. This parenting pattern has also been based on clear targets to be achieved. The child's behavior will also be monitored with logical discipline to improve the child's language, social, and motor development (Putri *et al.* 2017). Therefore, democratic parenting is one aspect of how a child can learn a language well.

Similar to the case of Shabira Alula Adnan, it can be seen that the language style used by Shabira Alula Adnan is the result of a program that her parents planned by democratic parenting. In the case of Shabira Alula Adnan's style of language, reported from several sources (TikTok Accounts, Instagram accounts, and several news reports from TV shows), the standard language style used by Shabira Alula Adnan tends to come from the upbringing of her parents, who have targeted Shabira Alula Adnan to speak using good and correct language, namely by using standard language. In addition, in one of the TV programs, namely "PARENTING (*Seni Mengelola Emosi dan Passion Anak*)" held by Transtv_corp, Shabira Alula Adnan's parents (Adnan Fahmi and Oci Febrina) explained that Shabira Alula Adnan's speaking skills using standard language is not something that instant. Still, it has become a program that has been targeted since Shabira Alula Adnan was a toddler (democratic parenting system). Shabira Alula Adnan's parents also explained that the system they applied to educate Shabira Alula Adnan is not an authoritarian system but a dialogical system (open and communicative). Shabira Alula Adnan's parents will set an example to emulate and provide direction and explanation to Shabira Alula Adnan if there is something good or bad. His parents confirmed this in the PARENTING event held by Transtv_corp that the system used was trained, formed, and assisted (democratic parenting).

Based on the observations, aside from democratic parenting, which is the primary strategy in developing Shabira Alula Adnan's language, several other aspects support Shabira Alula Adnan's language development, including the dialogical system itself. Some aspects that support language development and how Shabira Alula Adnan can speak using standard language are:

3.3.1 *Dialogic system*

Regarding the dialogical system (democratic parenting) applied to Shabira Alula Adnan, this is the leading cause of the language style used by Shabira Alula Adnan at this time. The dialogical approach is one of the methods used to teach language to Shabira Alula Adnan. Reporting from Shabira Alula Adnan's TikTok account (@Shabiraalula&Father), Shabira Alula Adnan's parents often mention that one of the keys to Shabira Alula Adnan's fluency in speaking, whether it's the use of standard language or its expression is to routinely interact and use good and correct language (not baby language or slurred language) (Figure 5).

Figure 5. Information from Shabira Alula Adnan's parents regarding language teaching strategy for Shabira Alula Adnan (@Shabiraalula&Ayah).

The dialogical parenting system applied by Shabira Alula Adnan's parents is open and communicative. It was explained that since Shabira Alula Adnan was a toddler, her parents had routinely communicated and interacted verbally and non-verbally. Even though Shabira Alula Adnan still did not understand what her parents were saying at that age, this was still done to train Shabira Alula Adnan's language, understanding, and expression. The communication carried out is also not one-way (only parents to children) but is two-way (parents and children) (Transtv_corp 2022). When having conversations, as much as possible, they allow Shabira Alula Adnan to practice her language so that there is interaction or reciprocity between Shabira Alula Adnan and her parents (communicative). In addition, not only communicative and interactive aspects are emphasized to Shabira Alula Adnan, but also openness. What is meant by openness here is that Shabira Alula Adnan's parents will explain to Shabira Alula Adnan something that is being experienced at that time.

In addition to giving directions, Shabira Alula Adnan is also allowed to express what she is thinking or wants to convey regarding what her parents explained. This is intended to train Shabira Alula Adnan's language and understanding of what she is dealing with. With the opportunity for Shabira Alula Adnan to express what she is thinking, language skills and Shabira Alula Adnan's understanding of things will also be trained. This can be seen in Shabira Alula Adnan's current language skills. For example, when Shabira Alula Adnan makes a mistake, what Shabira Alula Adnan's parents do is reprimand, but use good and correct language. In addition, Shabira Alula Adnan's parents also explained why what she did was not right. Figure 6 shows screenshots of the video uploaded to Shabira Alula Adnan's TikTok account (@Shabiraalula&Father), which shows how Shabira Alula Adnan's parents reprimanded and told Shabira Alula Adnan's mistakes.

Figure 6. Videos that show Shabira Alula Adnan's expression and response when told by her father (@Shabiraalula&Ayah).

In the video, Shabira Alula Adnan is seen being reprimanded and advised by her father for destroying her friend's toy (two photos on the left). It can be seen in the video that her father reprimanded her and gave advice to her. The advice given is also given by giving and asking Shabira Alula Adnan's opinion, so as seen in the video, Shabira Alula Adnan is also allowed to speak and give her opinion. This is intended so that Shabira Alula Adnan does not feel intimidated by her mistakes and, simultaneously, trains her language and personality. The same thing happened in the second video (two photos on the right), where the father tries to explain something to Shabira Alula Adnan. It can be seen that Shabira Alula Adnan calmly listens to her father's advice and responds to what is explained by her father. As stated by Shabira Alula Adnan's parents, this open and communicative system does not only apply when Shabira Alula Adnan makes mistakes but also applies to them as parents. This system of responding to each other is known as a dialogical system (open and communicative).

The application of the dialogical system serves to shape Shabira Alula Adnan's personality and teach Shabira Alula Adnan how to speak properly and correctly. According to various sources, the standard language used by Shabira Alula Adnan in daily conversation is the result of her parents' teaching process to her to be able to speak in the good and correct language. The vocabulary and expressions used are also obtained from the parents' teaching system results. Based on the observations result on the information provided by Shabira Alula Adnan's parents on her social media account, Shabira Alula Adnan's acquisition of fluency and skills in using standard language is the result of interactions using good and correct standard language (not slurred baby language) which is applied by her parents regularly. Interaction using the standard language applied by Shabira Alula Adnan's parents is a habit or stimulus that is done so that Shabira Alula Adnan can speak using good and correct language. Figure 7 shows some of the statements mentioned by Shabira Alula Adnan's parents.

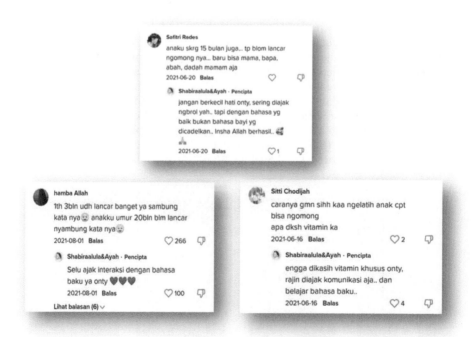

Figure 7. Shabira Alula Adnan's parents' explanation of the acquisition of the standard language used by Shabira Alula Adnan (@Shabiraalula&Ayah).

Based on the explanations of Shabira Alula Adnan's parents above and also on several television shows (Parenting by Transtv_corp, Denny Sumargo Podcast, Rumpi by Transtv), Shabira Alula Adnan has indeed been accustomed and shaped to use good and correct language starting from toddlers. To be able to familiarize Shabira Alula Adnan with the standard language style, Shabira Alula Adnan's parents also use good and correct standard Indonesian language when having conversations with Shabira Alula Adnan. The system to implement these habits is to be trained, formed, and assisted. Therefore, the output obtained is her skill in speaking using a good and correct standard language at this time.

In addition to receiving instruction from her parents, Shabira Alula Adnan's knowledge and language skills are also helped by what she hears and sees on television. Shabira Alula Adnan's parents explained that since she was one year old, Shabira Alula Adnan had been accustomed to not playing on her cell phone and watching children's TV programs that were appropriate for her age. Some children's programs watched are Little Angel, Baby Bus, Coco Melon, and several others. If there is a moral message or new words from what is being watched, Shabira Alula Adnan's parents will educate or explain to make it easier to understand. With a source through what she watched and assisted with her parents' education, Shabira Alula Adnan's language and understanding skills are getting better.

3.4 *Environment*

In addition to the parenting applied, Shabira Alula Adnan's language skills and knowledge are also obtained from the surrounding environment. At the Parenting event held by Transtv_corp, Shabira Alula Adnan's parents explained that apart from teaching and familiarizing Shabira Alula Adnan with standard language, a good environment is also very helpful in learning and acquiring Shabira Alula Adnan's language. In one of the videos uploaded to Shabira Alula Adnan's TikTok account, Shabira Alula Adnan is seen crying and mentioning a few sentences to express her feelings. In the video, Shabira Alula Adnan mentioned that her heart was broken, and Shabira Alula Adnan's parents explained that they had never taught Shabira Alula Adnan such a sentence. When her father asked how she knew about the sentence, Shabira Alula Adnan said that she heard the sentence from her grandmother and her friend she met at her grandmother's house.

This environment not only affects language acquisition but also supports how Shabira Alula Adnan's use of standard language can develop properly. Based on the observations, Shabira Alula Adnan did not have many friends to interact with at the age of 2 to 3 years. Due to this, the teaching and habituation process of using good and correct standard Indonesian language for Shabira Alula Adnan also went well without the distraction of other language styles that might be obtained from her peers (Denny Sumargo Podcast). Her parents also added that because the system they applied is to be trained, formed, and accompanied, when Shabira Alula Adnan gets new vocabulary that they think is not good, they will direct and explain that the vocabulary is indeed not good and should not be used. Therefore, the good and correct standard language Shabira Alula Adnan uses is obtained from the parents' teaching process and the direction of what is heard and seen in her environment.

4 DISCUSSION

The language skills of Shabira Alula Adnan are bland per her current age (3–4 years old). Children aged three to four years have significant language development, such as speaking using simple sentences, producing more vocabulary, and actively speaking (Fatmawati 2015). At age 3, Shabira Alula Adnan could have intense conversations with her parents using simple and complete sentences. She often asks questions about what she saw or heard, such as *"Mengapa seperti itu ayah?"*, *"Mengapa dia seperti itu ayah?"*, *"Tidak boleh begitu ya ayah?"*. Her vocabulary is also more varied. She is more active in speaking, asking questions, and even giving opinions in simple sentences, such as *"Wow, aroma sup ayamnya sedap sekali"*,

"Shabira Alula Adnan tidak mau.", "Gigi ayah bersih sekali.", and so on. However, there are some unique things that Shabira Alula Adnan does, such as the use of standard words when speaking and the intonation of speech which is quite distinctive. This is motivated by several aspects, such as the style of parental teaching patterns in terms of language learning and the surrounding environment. All the phenomena above are supported by several theories (Hasanah and Sugito 2020; Joni 2015b; Mulyani *et al.* 2020; Ramsden and Durkin 2012) that also explain the ideal case of language development faced by children at three to four years.

In the aspect of language style, the results analysis showed that the language style used by Shabira Alula Adnan is a combination of two language styles, namely referential and expressive style. Shabira Alula Adnan has several language characteristics that direct to the Referential style (the use of vocabulary that refers to things, the structure of the speech to be understood, using a clear speech). Yet, other Expressive style characteristics are also used by Shabira Alula Adnan, such as interacting with adults and peers and using language to express feelings, needs and socialize. Hence, it can be concluded that the language style used by Shabira Alula Adnan is a combination of the two types of language styles. These results are in line with theories from (Eun and Junkyu 2018; Hampson and Nelson 1993; Nelson 1973) that explained the characteristics of Referential and Expressive style, namely using vocabulary to refer to things, structuring her speech to be understood, label objects, and people (referential language style). Additionally, Shabira Alula Adnan also adopts or has characteristics of expressive speaking styles, such as interacting with adults and peers, using language to express feelings and needs, and socializing, in which the language character leads to expressive language style.

The language style used by Shabira Alula Adnan itself is also surely supported by several aspects, namely her age, the democratic parenting style used, the dialog system implemented by her parents, and the environment she lived. The results of this study imply that the standard language style used by Shabira Alula Adnan has been planned by her parents and has become a parenting pattern. Stimulation in using standard language is certainly used by Shabira Alula Adnan's parents to communicate with Shabira Alula Adnan and has been done since she was a toddler. Shabira Alula Adnan is used to speaking in standard language with this stimulation. The parenting style that supervises to use of the democratic parenting style and dialogic system also gives Shabira Alula Adnan more space to express herself through her language. This also really helps her fluency in speaking. Supported by the environment in which she is located, other family members and playmates also support the quality of Shabira Alula Adnan's language. Those pacts are in line with the explanation coming from (Hasanah and Sugito 2020; Joni 2015b; Mulqiah *et al.* 2017, 2020; Sudrajat 2017; Wijayanti *et al.* 2018) who stated numerous aspects support the children language development and style, namely coming from the internal aspect (family and parents) and also the external aspects (environments).

5 CONCLUSION

The objectives of this research are to know about the language style used by Shabira Alula Adnan and how she learns the good language and the standard language has been achieved successfully through observation and investigation process. Overall, this study looks at the phenomenon of using standard language as a style of language from Shabira Alula Adnan and how the standard language is obtained at that age. This phenomenon is seen from various aspects based on age, parenting style, and environment. Based on the researcher's review, these aspects are the main causes of Shabira Alula Adnan's use of standard language, especially the parents' parenting style.

Based on the results of this study, the phenomenon that occurred to Shabira Alula Adnan was in accordance with her age at that time, namely a three-year-old child. Based on explanations from various studies, children aged three years have a fairly rapid ability in language learning. Children will be more active in speaking, can communicate, and have significant language development, such as speaking using simple sentences, more vocabulary, being active in speaking, and much more. These characteristics are also in accordance with the phenomena experienced by Shabira Alula Adnan at that time. At the age of 3 years, Shabira Alula Adnan was able to have quite intense conversations with her parents using simple and complete sentences. She often asks questions about what she saw or heard. Her vocabulary is also more numerous and varied. She is more active in speaking, asking questions, and even giving opinions in simple sentences. However, there are some unique things that Shabira Alula Adnan does, such as the use of standard words when speaking and the intonation of speech which is quite distinctive.

Shabira Alula Adnan's use of standard language becomes the style of language she uses in everyday conversation. Concerning the language style, the results of this study indicate that the language style used by Shabira Alula Adnan is not just one but a combination of two language styles at once, namely referential and expressive styles. This is because, in some cases, Shabira Alula Adnan has several language characteristics that refer to the Referential style, such as the use of vocabulary that refers to things, the structure of the speech to be understood, and using a clear speech. However, there are other cases where she is more directed to the Expressive style, such as interacting with adults and peers and using language to express feelings, needs, and socialize. Therefore, the researcher concludes that the language style used by Shabira Alula Adnan is a combination of the two types of language styles.

Apart from age, parenting style and environment are also the biggest influences on Shabira Alula Adnan's language learning. The results of this study indicate that the standard language style used by Shabira Alula Adnan has indeed been intended by her parents and has become a parenting pattern for Shabira Alula Adnan. Stimulation in using standard language is certainly used by Shabira Alula Adnan's parents to communicate with Shabira Alula Adnan and has been done since Shabira Alula Adnan was a toddler. With this stimulation, Shabira Alula Adnan is used to speaking in standard language. The parenting style that tends to use the democratic parenting style and dialogic system also gives Shabira Alula Adnan more space to express herself through her language. This also really helps Shabira Alula Adnan's fluency in speaking. Supported by the environment in which she is located, other family members and playmates also support the quality of Shabira Alula Adnan's language.

Finally, the results of this study can be a source of reference for learning language development in children and contribute to further research on children's language development. In addition, many parents are not too aware of the importance of parenting to children's language development. Therefore, it is hoped that the results of research related to parenting patterns on children's language development from research can be a source of information for the community and future researchers. In addition, researchers encourage future researchers to conduct similar studies to explore more information about standard language styles in children or other language style phenomena deeply.

REFERENCES

@Shabiraalula&Ayah (no date) *Shabira Alula Adnan*. Available at: https://www.tiktok.com/@shabir-aalulaadnan?_t=8VYjfLrOdBC&_r=1.
Aisyah Isna (2019) 'Perkembangan Bahasa Anak Usia Dini', *Al-Athfal*, 2(2), pp. 62–69.
Alatalo, T. and Westlund, B. (2021) 'Preschool teachers' perceptions about read-alouds as a means to support children's early literacy and language development', *Journal of Early Childhood Literacy*, 21(3), pp. 413–435. doi:10.1177/1468798419852136.
Conti-Ramsden, G. and Durkin, K. (2012) 'Language development and assessment in the preschool period', *Neuropsychology Review*, 22(4), pp. 384–401. doi:10.1007/s11065-012-9208-z.

Cynthia A. Brock (1986) 'The Effects of Referential Questions on ESL Classroom Discourse', *TESOL quarterly*, 20(1), pp. 47–59.

Eun, L.S. and Junkyu, L. (2018) 'Learning styles and L2 vocabulary learning: do referential preference learners gain more vocabulary than expressive preference learners?', *The SNU Journal of Education Research*, 27(4), pp. 41–62. Available at: https://hdl.handle.net/10371/168536.

Fatmawati, S.R. (2015) 'Pemerolehan bahasa pertama anak menurut tinjauan psikolinguistik', *Lentera*, 17(1), pp. 63–75. doi:https://doi.org/10.21093/lj.v17i1.429.

Gotzke, C. & Sample Gosse, H. (2007) *No Title*. Available at:.

Hampson, J. and Nelson, K. (1993) 'The relation of maternal language to variation in rate and style of language acquisition', *Journal of Child Language*, 20(2), pp. 313–342. doi:10.1017/S0305000900008308.

Hasanah, N. and Sugito, S. (2020) 'Analisis pola asuh orang tua terhadap keterlambatan bicara pada anak usia dini', *Jurnal Obsesi: Jurnal Pendidikan Anak Usia Dini*, 4(2), p. 913. doi:10.31004/obsesi.v4i2.456.

Joni (2015a) 'Hubungan pola asuh orang tua terhadap perkembangan bahasa anak prasekolah (3-5 tahun) di PAUD al-hasanah tahun 2014', *Jurnal PAUD Tambusai Volume*, 1(6), pp. 42–48. doi:10.31004/obsesi. v1i1.54.

Joni (2015b) 'Hubungan pola asuh orang tua terhadap perkembangan bahasa anak prasekolah (3-5 tahun) di PAUD al-hasanah tahun 2014', *Jurnal PAUD Tambusai*, 1(6), pp. 42–48.

Lieven, E.V.M., Pine, J.M. and Barnes, H.D. (1992) 'Individual Differences In Early Vocabulary Development: Redefining The Referential-Expressive Distinction', *Journal of Child Language*, 19(2), pp. 287–310. doi:10.1017/S0305000900011429.

Mulqiah, Z., Santi, E. and Lestari, D.R. (2017) 'Pola asuh orang tua dengan perkembangan bahasa anak prasekolah (Usia 3-6 Tahun)', *Dunia Keperawatan*, 5(1), p. 61. doi:10.20527/dk.v5i1.3643.

Mulyani, M.K., Sukmandari, N.M.. and Dewi, S.P.A.A.P. (2020) 'Hubungan pola asuh demokratis engan perkembangan bahasa pada anak prasekolah di TK negeri tabanan di kerambitan', *Jurnal Medika Usada*, 3(2), pp. 1–4. doi:10.54107/medikausada.v3i2.68.

Nelson, K. (1973) 'On Behalf of the Fish', *Fisheries*, 38(8), p. 343. doi:10.1080/03632415.2013.813484.

Pancsofar, N. and Vernon-Feagans, L. (2006) 'Mother and father language input to young children: Contributions to later language development', *Journal of Applied Developmental Psychology*, 27(6), pp. 571–587. doi:10.1016/j.appdev.2006.08.003.

Patel (2019) '済無No Title No Title No Title', 2(September), pp. 9–25.

Podcast, D.S. (no date) 'Denny Sumargo dan Shabira Shabira Alula Adnan'.

Putra, A.Y., Yudiemawati, A. and Maemunah, N. (2018) 'Pengaruh pemberian stimulasi oleh orang tua terhadap perkembangan bahasa pada anak usia toddler di paud asparaga malang', *Jurnal Ilmiah Keperawatan*, 3(1). doi:https://doi.org/10.33366/nn.v3i1.828.

Putri, R.A., Murti, B. and Indarto, D. (2017) 'Effect of nurturing at child care center on gross and fine motoric, language and social development in children aged under five years in ungaran barat subdistrict, ungaran', *Journal of Maternal and Child Health*, 02(01), pp. 1–10. doi:10.26911/thejmch.2017.02.01.01.

Ramsden, G.C.- and Durkin, K. (2012) 'Language development and assessment in the preschool period', *Neuropsychology Review*, 22(4), pp. 384–401. doi:10.1007/s11065-012-9208-z.

Safriana, L., Salimo, H. and Dewi, Y.L.R. (2017) 'Biopsychosocial factors, life course perspective, and their influences on language development in children', *Journal of Maternal and Child Health*, 02(03), pp. 245–256. doi:10.26911/thejmch.2017.02.03.06.

Safwat, R.F. and Sheikhany, A.R. (2014) 'Effect of parent interaction on language development in children', *The Egyptian Journal of Otolaryngology*, pp. 255–263. doi:10.4103/1012-5574.138488.

Sudrajat, D. (2017) 'Language development and acquisition in childhood stage: psycholinguistic review', *Intelegensia: Jurnal Pendidikan dan Pembelajaran*, 2(2), pp. 1–18.

Transtv_corp (2022) 'PARENTING (Seni mengelola emosi dan passion anak)'. IndoneSIA. Available at: https://instagram.com/transtv_corp?igshid=YmMyMTA2M2Y=.

Transtv (no date) 'Rumpi'. Available at: https://www.youtube.com/watch?v=tB2EGnEFAAE.

Wahyuni, S. (2016) 'Children's language development', *Getsempena English Education Journal*, 3(1). doi: https://doi.org/10.46244/geej.v3i1.702.

Wijayanti, A., Wekadigunawan, C. and Murti, B. (2018) 'The effect of parenting style, bilingual school, social environment, on speech and language development in preschool children in surakarta, central java', *Journal of Maternal and Child Health*, 03(03), pp. 184–196. doi:10.26911/thejmch.2018.03.03.03.

Yuniarti, S. and Wildani, M.D. (2015) *Asuhan tumbuh kembang neonatus bayi – balita dan anak pra-sekolah, PT Refika Aditama*. Bandung: Refika Aditama.

Strengthening Professional and Spiritual Education through 21st Century Skill Empowerment in Pandemic and Post-Pandemic Era – Arifin et al. (Eds)
© 2024 The Author(s), ISBN: 978-1-032-45243-2
Open Access: www.taylorfrancis.com, CC BY-NC-ND 4.0 license

Scrutinizing grammatical errors found in students' vlog in speaking class

Ema Wafiqah & Triastama Wiraatmaja*
Universitas Muhammadiyah Malang, Indonesia

ABSTRACT: This study examines the grammatical errors found in the students' vlogs in the speaking class at the English Language Education Department at a private university. The research employed mixed methods; the qualitative method was utilized to answer the first research question, and the quantitative method was utilized to answer the second research question. The subject data was obtained through the document of this study. Fourth-semester students in a Speaking Class for Informal Interaction were considered in this study. However, the researchers only involved nine students as the sample of the study. In addition, the researchers conducted observations related to the data from the students, focusing on the basic grammar found and direct observation of the video based on the assignment assigned by the lecturer. The results of this study exhibited that there were minor grammatical errors found in the students' vlogs; article errors, verbs, phrases, prepositions, and others. The major grammatical errors found were that of phrases, prepositions, verbs, and rephrase.

Keywords: Grammatical errors, speaking, vlog

1 INTRODUCTION

To communicate with ease using English, a proper understanding of four language skills is deemed necessary, hence, grammatical aspects are also deemed required to increase communicative competence. As Saputri (2021) claims adequate communicative competence assures that speakers in English to communicate, exchanging news, and ideas between people. Knowing that premises, speaking as a productive skill is a necessity to communicate with others although English has various accents (Purnamaningwulan 2021). In addition, the teaching and learning process in the last few years has to adapt to online or hybrid learning, since technological development also permits us to do so, and the use of technology is also widely implemented in a global context (Hassan 2021). Online learning is also regarded as a method of lifelong learning, and lots of institutions over the globe are encouraging learners to adapt to online learning. Yet, as for Indonesian contexts, both educators and students might have to adjust to online learning and they might be disadvantaged if they fail to adjust to online learning (Nartiningrum and Nugroho 2021). However, although online learning might not be the solution to all issues in education, online learning according to Lekawael (2017), greatly improves learners' communicative competence because it boosts them to be actively accessing materials that suit their interests. Therefore, mastering all aspects of English skills would be a challenging task to do, however, it would be extremely helpful for any learners to master the language they desire since all language skills require to work in unison to fully serve as communicative competencies (Wiraatmaja 2021). In addition, a good understanding of English skills and grammar enhances language learners' comprehension of English, as well as their communicative competencies (Kurniasih 2016; Sadiku 2015).

---

*Corresponding Author: triastama@umm.ac.id

DOI: 10.1201/9781003376125-17

One of the challenges faced by language learners during online learning was grammar proficiency in displaying their speaking prowess. As speaking itself is deemed the most difficult language skill (Leong and Ahmadi 2017), grammar helps language learner observe and understand linguistic aspects, it also requires competence in speaking, and assist the language learner with the arrangement of words and makes it easier for a person to understand a spoken English (Handayani 2013). However, Leacock *et al.* (2014) stated that grammar errors must be addressed in speaking as a means to display effective communication, and as error detection in the language approach model, the error usually lies in a merger language value and becomes a high probability of error. In addition, when displaying or practicing their speaking, language learners might encounter difficulties in delivering and comprehending their intentions if they make any grammatical errors (Lekawael 2017).

Speaking accuracy is the correct and specific communication words that correspond to the sentences being said. Saputri (2021) said a person who babbles can be understood using correct and understandable language. Speaking using the correct verbal language requires confidence and understanding of the vocabulary delivered, especially when speaking in a foreign language. Therefore, an educator needs to provide learning that adapts to the process received by students. (Putri and Rahmani 2019) stated that learners who know mistakes when speaking in pronunciation and the location of grammar make learners learn again from the mistakes, and then correct them so that they will not repeat the same mistakes. There are different types of speaking accuracy or preference. In teaching and learning activities of a second language, a foreign language, in this case, English, has a category for understanding information correctly. According to Heaton as cited by Sukarman and Algiovan (2022) there are two types of accuracy learning, namely pronunciation and grammar.

Sukarno (2016) expressed that grammatical errors in writing include vocabulary, prepositions, word structure, articles, and others. Furthermore, the use of English indicates being careful in using sentences. Minor things can impact mistakes that make readers or those who hear become misinformed even though grammatical errors found are minor and need correction in terms of language rules. The research will focus on basic grammar that introduces detailed sentences from subject, verb, noun, adverb, and adjective. Before getting to know more, students already understood the use of basic grammar studied in the grammar class and began to practice it in their writing and oral activities.

Knowing that grammar is pivotal in language learners speaking competence, research regarding grammatical errors in speaking among students must be conducted. Research about grammatical errors among students on many levels has been done in various schools in Indonesia. However, this research intends to fill the gap by discovering grammatical errors made by university students in a private university in Indonesia. This research involves various numbers of respondents from similar age groups, and the findings of this research aim to provide significant insights for future researchers. The results can be used as future references to conduct research regarding grammatical errors made by university students. Thus, the research questions used in this study were formulated as follows: (a) What are the grammatical errors found in the students' vlog and video presentation at a speaking class? (b) What are the most dominant grammatical errors found on the students' vlog and video presentation in a speaking class?

2 METHODS

This study employed mixed methods, the qualitative method was utilized to answer the first research question, and the quantitative method was utilized to answer the second research question to complete and fulfill information related to the problems of the research. According to Ary et al. (2010) stated that mixed-method research is a method that uses both approaches of qualitative methods and quantitative methods to procedures of research objects. Qualitative and quantitative research provides the answers sought and provides extensive knowledge of each research question, and this method focuses on data that are met in the field.

The total population of the study was nine students who were given the task of making videos. The videos are then assessed to see grammatical errors found on the students' vlog or presentation. In this study, the researchers will only focus on grammatical errors relating to the basic grammar materials, including simple past tense, past perfect tense, and present perfect tense based on the course syllabus.

For collecting the data, first, this study will conduct observations focusing on grammatical errors. The data were collected from vlog assignments at the speaking classes, the researchers were asking permission from the lecturers who taught speaking in the second semester by using document analysis. Then, the researchers asked for permission from lecturers to share Google forms containing students' names, informal interactions in small classes, topics, and vlog video links on social media. After that, the data collection will be continued by data analysis and observation. Finally, the results will be made in the form of a pie chart showing the score of the fourth-semester students' grammatical errors found in the vlog videos.

3 RESULTS

The findings showed that the grammar errors are in a minor category. The most dominant grammatical errors found in the students' vlogs are mostly basic grammar and spelling errors. However, most grammatical errors are in the basic grammar section, among others, the pronunciation of the words and the intended object or the mispronunciation of sentences so that native speakers could immediately justify them (Satria 2020). To sum up, the grammatical errors found in the students' videos can be seen in Table 1.

Table 1. Minor grammatical errors were found in the students' vlogs.

_	Errors Found	Result	Dialogues	Subject
1.	Article	6	I have a homework to make a short video	A
2.	Simple Present Tense	1	Now I studied at the University of Muhammadiyah Malang	A
3.	Prepositional Phrase	1	the second is about my interest in academic	A
4.	Preposition	10	Then I have four months experience as an English tutor	B
5.	Auxiliary Verb	1	Why I interested	A
6.	Punctuation (comma)	1	with writing do you know?	A
7.	Present Perfect Tense	3	This virus has entered Indonesia in 2020	C
8.	Word Order	3	I am starting to think about what would I do next after I graduated	D
9.	Word Choice	1	I also got reworked as the best online teacher at the time, and I don't know how can I get the rewards	B
10.	Present Participle	1	I'm keen on a basketball player	B

(*continued*)

Table 1.　Continued

	Errors Found	Result	Dialogues	Subject
11.	Verb	9	I hope you all good	C
12.	Rephrasing/ Rephrase	8	And now I'm in my fourth semester	C
13.	Overused	1	one of which is a bad network	C
14.	Simple Past Tense	1	So this time, I make a short vlog	D
15.	Awkward Phrasing	2	I am starting to think about what I would do next after I graduated	D
16.	Squinting Modifier	1	That's probably because, during semester 1 to 3	D
17.	Phrase	30	like making proposal and then submitting paperwork to the teacher.	E
18.	Unnecessary	1	I starting to think about what would I do next after I graduated	D
19.	Future Continuous Tense	1	I will continue my study until I get a teaching certificate	D
20.	Wording	2	After I have had enough teaching experience	D
21.	Sentence	1	hope you can enjoy it.	E
22.	Conjunction	4	The happiest day of my life is that I can go on vacation with my friends	E
23.	Adverb	1	The happy moment that I remember also recently happened is when I got a free book from my	E
24.	Word	2	The happiest day of my life was when I was able to go to the tourist spots. I wanted with my best friend for three days, without my parents being accompanied.	E
25.	Pronoun	3	I really wanted to travel here and there with my friends for the holidays, but now I have a car/motorcycle driving license. So, I don't have to worry anymore about will happen to me on the roads, such as raids by the police, and finally, I can travel with my friends on vacation.	E
26.	Past Perfect Continuous Tense	1	It was my dream to be able to participate in the competition. I have to prepare everything, prepare the administration, submit a proposal, and finally, it paid off.	E
27.	Singular	1	my parents also went to the same place with us, but they sat at different table.	E
28.	Adjective	2	B: Yes, I am very happy.	E
29.	Complete Sentence	1	A: Hmm. Maybe, don't look for happiness but create happiness for yourself.	E
30.	Redundant	1	C: I think happiness is earned or given, but you can create your own happiness.	E
31.	Vocab	6	A: Kinda difficult and deep, right? In my opinion, Happiness has a very broad meaning and takes various forms.	E
32.	Subject	1	Is not that I don't want to care for someone or have someone care for me. It's just I get scared. E: The thing that makes me capable is freedom. Because through freedom, I can go to various good places I want, I can try new things that I have never experienced before, and I can have more good experiences.	E

Table 1 shows that students still have difficulty placing the subject and object in the sentences delivered. The table also proves that the difficulty in basic grammar is spotted so that grammatical errors are found in the students' speaking practice.

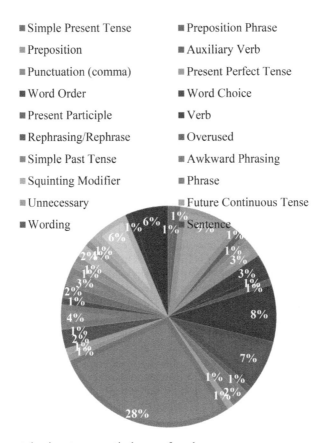

Figure 1. The most dominant grammatical errors found.

From Figure 1, it shows that the use of phrases in speaking is essential. Phrases are made up of many words that become sentences so that grammar is formed. Most students lack understanding of the use of phrases, thus making it challenging to convey a complete idea. The researchers found grammatical errors in the placement of "in," also called a preposition phrase. A preposition is an additional noun or noun phrase to complete the sentence with an additional phrase. The use of verbs in a sentence is essential to describe activities performed in present, past, or future. A rephrase is a repetitive sentence that is long. Sometimes, there are sentences with correct grammar, but it can be challenging to understand what is meant in the sentence.

4 DISCUSSION

Mastering English skills requires lots of effort and time to be taken into account (Wiraatmaja, Sari and Cahyadi 2022). Especially when language learners must maintain extra motivation (Songbatumis 2017), although they encounter technical issues such as grammar. Therefore, the results of this research revealed that many grammatical errors were found in the students' videos. Errors, according to Anggraini and Pradana (2021), occurred due to limited or lack of understanding of the rules of the language. Thus, the researchers discovered that phrase was found as the most dominant grammatical error. Regarding errors found, phrases indicate nouns, verbs, prepositions, and others. (Sabarniati and Zulkarnain

2020) expressed that the students feel the difference when learning English because the mother tongue framework has differences. Therefore, it is necessary to understand the use of the correct structure of word rules, especially in small things that students have learned in previous courses. According to Harmer as cited by Sabarniati and Zulkarnain (2020), learning can be done in any way; for example, by correcting the English use by analyzing any grammatical errors that accidentally interrupted the lesson. Students prefer to speak English without paying attention to minor grammatical errors found.

In addition, the researchers argued that phrases were deemed as the most dominant ones in this study due to various reasons. As Haryanti et al. (2022) stated there were three major reasons; first is the students' motivation, second is the class environment, and lastly the use of outdated and improper references or course books. The researchers also found that students have knowledge of grammar but still have difficulty applying it to practice (Zhang 2020). Grammar studied by teachers and learners is still challenging to learn. In fact, without understanding well through the use of correct grammar, students will find it challenging to learn grammar, either oral or written, correctly. English Language Education students in the fourth semester can speak English reasonably but need increased knowledge in the use of grammar (Setyowati 2020). Grammar helps learners in English speaking skills, both oral and written. Sufficient knowledge of grammar will help students know the rules of every word, object, trait, adverb, and verb according to the liaison used. In the video presentations and video vlogs, there are 32 grammatical errors found (Setyowati 2020). Without grammar, learners cannot speak English properly. Thus, grammar learning efforts need to be increased to facilitate a quick impression impregnated. In addition, students studying grammar need more motivation to improve their knowledge. Zhang (2020) argued that grammar correction will not lead to fossilization, a situation that keeps students stuck at a low level of grammar skills. Lecturers of English classes should provide maximum motivation for teaching grammar to students. Besides, educators also reap the benefits by integrating technology to stimuli as well as providing learning alternatives for students (Sabgini & Triastama Wiraatmaja 2022).

In addition, teachers or educators also possess a responsibility to keep improving their pedagogical skills by adapting to various teaching methods (Harahap et al. 2020). Similarly, students shall have a strong desire to learn and practice English using correct grammar, while the lecturers act as one of the sources of knowledge in the classroom. As Oktaviani and Subekti (2018), also added educators must understand students' interests by choosing specific activities to pique their interest and understand the materials with ease. By understanding that aspect, educators' pedagogical prowess would be deemed effective (Field et al. 2009). Thus, both students and educators must work together to tackle this issue, as stated by Lee and Bozeman (2005) to increase productivity, the modern academic community needs to work together. Because, by combining their heads, the students would be able to increase their ability as well as to develop their skills and accumulate experiences for constant development (Sanyal and Hisam 2018). However, this research is only limited to grammatical issues, meanwhile speaking classes provide various challenges other than grammar; pronunciation, vocabulary, and others.

5 CONCLUSION

The researchers concluded that grammar was deemed a challenging aspect for students in displaying their speaking prowess. The errors found were phrases, prepositions, verb vocabulary, and rephrasing sentences. The researcher will provide advice related to the results of research that has been done. The researcher suggests learners, lecturers, or native speakers to further improve their knowledge of grammar, not only learning the theory but also how to recognize and know each use of grammar in the real context. With the help of environmental motivation or way of learning, students can understand and capture the knowledge learned.

They need to learn grammar not only in the classroom but also outside the classroom to know grammar more broadly. Because to learn every language, there will always be rules that must be followed, including English. In addition, the most dominant errors were; phrase, preposition, verb, and rephrase. The researchers discovered that the errors occurred due to students' lack of grammar understanding. However, further research to discover the cause was needed.

REFERENCES

Anggraini, M.P. and Pradana, S.A. (2021) 'Grammatical errors made by eighth-grade students in speaking english', *Tadris Bahasa Inggris*, 14(1), p. 30. Available at: https://doi.org/https://doi.org/10.24042/ee-jtbi. v14i1.8712.

Ary, D., Jacobs, L.C. and Sorensen, C. (2010) *Introduction to Research in Education Eighth Edition*. 8th edn. Belmont.

Field, S. *et al.* (2009) *Learning for Jobs*. OECD Policy Review of Vocational Education and Training. Paris: OECD Publishing.

Handayani, W. (2013) 'Grammar Usage in Public Speaking', *Polingua: Scientific Journal of Linguistics, Literature and Language Education*, 2(2), p. 81.

Harahap, M.B., Roesminingsih, M. V. and Mudjito, M. (2020) 'Concept of Human Resources Development to Improve Teacher Performance: Multi-Case Study.', *Studies in Learning and Teaching*, 1(3), pp. 140–150.

Haryanti, S., Haryono, P. and Yuwono, S.E. (2022) 'English students' and lecturers' difficulties in teaching and learning of participle phrases', *International Journal of Active Learning*, 7(1), pp. 24–34.

Hassan, M. (2021) 'Online teaching challenges during COVID-19 Pandemic', *International Journal of Information and Education Technology*, 11(1). Available at: https://doi.org/10.18178/ijiet.2021.11.1.1487.

Iskandar, S. and Sabarniati (2020) 'The impacts of grammatical competence towards students' speaking proficiency in learning english as a foreign language', *Getsempena English Education Journal (GEEJ)*, 7(1), pp. 102–112. Available at: https://ejournal.bbg.ac.id/geej/article/view/1029 (Accessed: 28 July 2022).

Kurniasih, E. (2016) 'Teaching the four language skills in primary EFL classroom', *JET (Journal of English Teaching)*, 1(1). Available at: https://doi.org/10.33541/jet.v1i1.53.

Leacock, C. *et al.* (2014) Automated Grammatical Error Correction for Language Learners.

Lee, S. and Bozeman, B. (2005) 'The impact of research collaboration on scientific productivity', *Social Studies of Science*, 35(5), pp. 673–702. Available at: https://doi.org/10.1177/0306312705052359.

Lekawael, R.F.J. (2017) 'The Impact of Smartphone and Internet usage on english language learning', *English Review: Journal of English Education*, 5(2), pp. 255–262.

Leong, L.-M. and Ahmadi, S.M. (2017) 'An analysis of factors influencing learners' english speaking skill', *International Journal of Research in English Education*, 2(1). Available at: https://doi.org/10.18869/acad-pub.ijree.2.1.34.

Nartiningrum, N. and Nugroho, A. (2021) 'English teachers' perspectives on challenges, suggestions, and materials of online teaching amidst the global pandemic', *IJEE (Indonesian Journal of English Education)*, 1(1), pp. 101–119. Available at: https://doi.org/10.15408/ijee.v1i1.17886.

Oktaviani, R.N. and Subekti, E.W. (2018) 'Developing children's supplementary literature book based on character education in sixth grade of elementary school', *Journal of Educational Science and Technology*, 4 (2), pp. 111–118.

Purnamaningwulan, R.A. (2021) 'Video-assisted listening program to improve pre-service EFL teachers' listening skills', *celtic: A journal of culture, English Language Teaching, Literature and Linguistics*, 8(1), pp. 33–43.

Putri, R.N. and Rahmani, B.D. (2019) 'Students perception on using video recording to improve their speaking accuracy and fluency', in *UICELL Conference Proceedings 2019*, pp. 113–122.

Sabarniati and Zulkarnain, S.I. (2020) 'The impacts of grammatical competence towards students' speaking proficiency in learning english as a foreign language', *Getsempena English Education Journal (GEEJ)*, 7(1), pp. 102–112.

Sabgini, K.N.W. and Triastama Wiraatmaja (2022) 'The pre-service teachers' perception on integrating technology in teaching english for young learners', *Project (Professional Journal of English Education)*, 5 (4), pp. 706–722.

Sadiku, L.M. (2015) 'The importance of four skills reading, speaking, writing, listening in a lesson hour', *European Journal of Language and Literature*, 1(1). Available at: https://doi.org/10.26417/ejls.v1i1.p29–31.

Sanyal, S. and Hisam, M.W. (2018) 'The impact of teamwork in work performance of Employees: A study of faculty members in Dhofar University', *IOSR Journal of Business and Management (IOSR-JBM)*, 20(3), pp. 15–22.

Saputri, R.I. (2021) 'The correlation between speaking habit and speaking accuracy in second semester of english department student of UNISMA', *Jurnal Penelitian, Pendidikan, dan Pembelajaran*, 16(5), pp. 1–15.

Satria, V.R. (2020) 'English speaking teaching methods for elementary school student at kampung inggris pontianak', *Celtic: A Journal of Culture, English Language Teaching, Literature and Linguistics*, 7(2), pp. 183–190. Available at: http://ejournal.umm.ac.id/index.php/celtic/index.

Setyowati, L. (2020) 'The role of speaking practices on grammar learning', *English Education*, 7, pp. 18–28. Available at: https://doi.org/10.32682/jeell.v7i1.1519.

Songbatumis, A. Mumary. (2017) 'Challenges in teaching english faced by english teachers at mtsn taliwang, indonesia', *Journal of Foreign Languange Teaching and Learning*, 2(2). Available at: https://doi.org/10.18196/ftl.2223.

Sukarman, E.P. and Algiovan, N. (2022) 'The use of audio-lingual method in improving speaking accuracy of indonesian efl learners', *International Journal of Multicultural and Multireligious Understanding (IJMMU)*, 9(2), pp. 734–740.

Sukarno (2016) 'The analysis on the grammatical err', *Celt: A Journal of Culture, English Language Teaching & Literature*, 16(1), pp. 1–21.

Wiraatmaja, T. (2021) 'Critical Discourse Analysis on Difficulties in Teaching English Skills During Pandemic: Indonesian' s English Lecturers Perspectives', in, pp. 436–443. Available at: https://doi.org/https://dx.doi.org/10.2991/assehr.k.211028.155.

Wiraatmaja, T., Sari, L.K. and Cahyadi, P. (2022) 'How listening deemed as the most difficult english skills during online learning among students?', *Premise: Journal of English Education and Applied Linguistics*, 11 (3), pp. 438–457.

Zhang, J. (2020) 'A review of grammar corrective feedback: The learning experience in China's English Classes', *Studies in English Language Teaching (SELT)*, 8(3), pp. 127–137.

Strengthening Professional and Spiritual Education through 21st Century Skill Empowerment in Pandemic and Post-Pandemic Era – Arifin et al. (Eds)
© 2024 The Author(s), ISBN: 978-1-032-45243-2

Foreign language anxiety and enjoyment performance in classroom: Literature study

Nuruz Zakiyyah Yahya & Agista Nidya Wardani*
Universitas Muhammadiyyah Malang, Indonesia

ABSTRACT: The classroom can affect the emotions of language learners. This study analyzes students' anxiety and enjoyment in the classroom context. This study examines the characteristics of FLA and FLE in the EFL classroom and the components of EFL teaching that support them. This study examines 32 annual limited-issue journals (2018–2022). The data shows that FLA and FLE are influenced by motivation, EI and language proficiency, the causes of which are self-concept and FL achievement. This study shows that the teaching component is one component that contributes to FLA and FLE. Teachers, students, CE, and course design support students' emotions. Under the influence of these interacting components, FLE and FLA self-regulate into a withdrawal state characterized by anxiety and enjoyment. Furthermore, FLE and FLA are responsive to feedback. A simple response such as a teacher explanation, peer assessment, or an unexpected nudge can change it significantly.

1 INTRODUCTION

Studying a foreign language may excite students to experience various emotions to foster the development of students' cognitive and reasoning skills. Thus, emotions are inseparably linked to cognitive ability, crucial variables in language learning. According to research, the positive and negative emotions of language learners are part of a complex and dynamic system (Yang 2021). In recent years, the recent development and expansion of positive emotions (such as enjoyment) in foreign language learning have broken the trend of focusing excessively on negative emotions (such as anxiety) in research on emotions in EFL students, and positive emotions are beginning to attract the attention of researchers (Dewaele and Alfawzan 2018; Dewaele and MacIntyre 2014, 2016; Elahi Shirvan and Taherian 2020; Elahi Shirvan et al. 2020). Therefore, it seems to suggest that it is essential to eliminate the lingering consequences of negative emotional arousal and boost human resilience in the face of adversity.

Positive and negative emotions are essential for learning a foreign language since they are an inherent element of the educational process (Yeşilçınar and Erdemir 2022). The research on emotions in foreign language learners has changed from an exclusive emphasis on negative emotions to a more comprehensive investigation of the mix of positive and negative emotions. Foreign Language Enjoyment (FLE) and Foreign Language Class Anxiety (FLCA) are the two emotions that foreign language students experience most often (Piniel & Albert 2018). According to research in the area of language acquisition, Positive (FLE) and negative (FLCA) emotions are an intrinsic component of classroom practices (Chen et al. 2021a; Dewaele and Dewaele 2020; Jiang et al. 2020; Li et al. 2018; Saito et al. 2018; Yu 2022). Therefore, it demonstrates that the construct of research attention has been

---

*Corresponding Author: agistaward2@gmail.com

DOI: 10.1201/9781003376125-18

established, whereby the researcher not only investigates students' FLCA but also recognizes the importance of integrating the two in the classroom performance of EFL students.

Numerous research has focused on the experiences of FLCA and FLE in language learning and their relationship to various supportive factors. Consequently, this research investigates FLA and FLE in the classroom context and highlights their features and performance supported by learning components during the last five years. To acquire a better knowledge of the emotional performance of EFL students in the classroom, however, only a few research have undertaken literature evaluations about this topic. This research examines the features of FLCA and FLE in the setting of EFL classrooms and the EFL teaching components that promote FLCA and FLE. This study is anticipated to reveal future research opportunities linked to this topic.

2 METHOD

Reviewing the available literature on the characteristics of FLA and FLE in EFL classrooms and the EFL teaching components that support them was done to accomplish the study's purposes. The research presented here provides a review and analysis founded on inquiries into the pertinent literature. To conduct a literature search, the terms "Foreign Language Anxiety" and "Foreign Language Enjoyment" were searched for on Google Scholar. This search produced a total of 41 items, 32 of which were considered to be relevant. Articles must concentrate on a particular sort of question for reasoning evaluation, be written in English, and have been published between 2018 and 2022. The titles and abstracts of the articles determine whether or not they are relevant to the requirements. In order to provide answers to the questions raised by the research, the remaining papers were analyzed. Although the results may have been skewed due to the exclusion of unavailable articles from the complete text, the authors insist that no essential information has been skipped over.

3 THE CHARACTERISTICS OF FLCA AND FLE

Instead of depending on a single positive or negative axis, the link between anxiety and enjoyment is multidimensional according to the two-dimensional taxonomy of control value theory. Foreign Language Enjoyment (FLE) is a multifaceted emotion composed of self-, teacher-, and peer-enjoyment that results from continuous learning activities (Jiang and Dewaele 2020). Meanwhile, Foreign Language Anxiety (FLA) is an emotion that is significantly related to past or future performance or achievement in learning activities or tasks (Dewaele et al. 2019). Thus, FLE is more sociable and associated with others, whereas FLA is more egocentric and associated with self-factors. Changes in FLE were significantly connected to teachers and peers in the classroom (Dewaele and MacIntyre 2019; Dewaele et al. 2019, 2022; Jiang et al. 2020; Saito et al. 2018), whereas FLCA was more strongly predicted by internal student characteristics (Dewaele and MacIntyre 2019). Thus, FLCA is more similar, and FLE is more like a state (Dewaele and Dewaele 2020).

On the other hand, contextual variables can affect the emotional system of EFL students (Bielak 2022; Elahi Shirvan and Taherian 2021). Under certain conditions, the student's emotional system can arouse worry, pleasure, or both (Shirvan and Talebzadeh 2020). The impact of future FLE and FLCA forecasts is unpredictable. However, contextual influences more on FLE than FLCA (Jiang et al. 2020). Due to limited material and context, people are forced to make choices that simplify their rich and complex experiences (Dewaele and Pavelescu 2021). It relies more on social constructs and environmental elements (e.g., quality of teachers and peers) than on individual variables (e.g., traits of intellectual intelligence) (Li et al. 2021). Therefore, the emotional performance of FLCA and FLE can be seen from the causes and factors accompanying them.

3.1 The Cause of FLA and FLE in classroom

3.1.1 Self-concept

FLCA and FLE have a contribution to the self-perception of EFL students. Students with high FLE and low FLCA have more confidence in FL skills (Bensalem 2021; Jiang 2020). They are more accumulated; therefore, sound judgments are closely related to individual self-assessment ability (Dong *et al.* 2022). Students with a healthy self-concept are more likely to be socially responsible, interested in their studies, and self-assured in their abilities and responsibilities. Thus, the emotions of peers and teachers transcend the ego-centred level of Intellectual Humanity (Moskowitz and Dewaele 2020). High degrees of self-assurance are often seen in students' classroom interactions in the form of active participation and linguistic inquiry, which are vital aspects of FLE. As a result, faith in one's intellectual capabilities may act as a protective mechanism against FLCA.

Students with negative self-concepts cannot interact in learning, have a pessimistic view, and are unsure about their future FL acquisition (Fathi and Mohammaddokht 2021). Some students associate anxiety with low self-esteem, fear of making mistakes, and dislike of English (Liu and Hong 2021). Students with significant anxiety levels find it difficult to formulate responses to questions, attend lessons, and participate in discussions with others. As a result, a lack of faith in one's own views and intellectual capacity may prevent a person from engaging in debates within FL and experimenting with various identities. As a consequence, the FLCA may negatively impact the positive self-perception that EFL students have of their own potential to learn FL and use FL in the future.

3.1.2 FL achievements

English Language Achievement (EA) is closely correlated with FLCA or FLE. The consequences of two emotions on EA varied according to student achievement group (Jiang *et al.* 2020). While she is a member of the low achievement category, EA does not suffer any negative emotional effects. On the other hand, those who fell in the middle of the range of accomplishments suffered FLA more often owing to a lack of self-confidence and FL ability, which may have led them to quit. While this is taking place, the impact of FLE at high performance is only slightly more substantial than the effect that FLCA has on EA. Thus, FLCA and lack of self-confidence are negative emotions associated with FLE and self-confidence (Kitaoka 2021). Conversely, reducing FLCA may increase an individual's self-confidence and intrinsic value, but that is all it accomplishes.

While this is going on, an increase in FLE can raise all of the motivational components associated with the anticipated value. The explanation concludes that the cross-sectional and longitudinal facilitative effect of FL is greater than the attenuating effect of FLCA (Dong *et al.* 2022; Jiang and Dewaele 2019; Li and Wei 2022). In this regard, a study looked at how FLE and FLCA work longitudinally (Li and Wei 2022). FLE has the most significant independent effect on future performance, while FLCA can only provide a short-term forecast of future FL accomplishment. Actual and perceived English attainment (global and domain-specific) were positive for FLE and negative for FLCA (Dewaele 2022). As a result, FLE contributed to anxiety, and the successful completion of FL created an essential relationship between the two.

3.2 The factors that contribute to the FLA and FLE performance in the classroom

3.2.1 Motivation

The level of motivation shown by EFL students is connected to English FLE. A happy mindset and strong motivation to learn FL offer a reasonable basis for developing natural emotions such as FLE (Dewaele and Proietti Ergün 2020). However, FLE is a more fleeting emotion (Dewaele and Dewaele 2020). In contrast, FLCA ranges and attitudes/motivation are longer and can affect study and exam preparation (Dewaele and Proietti Ergün 2020). However, lowering anxiety levels may increase functional learning efficiency by boosting learning motivation and a feeling of accomplishment. It indicates a negative relationship between FLE and FLCA (Yang 2021). Therefore, intense sensations of enjoyment and interest increase students' motivation, leading to solid future assessments of their FL self-image (Fathi and Mohammaddokht 2021).

3.2.2 *Emotional Intelligence (EI)*

EI correlates better with FLA than with FLE (Chen *et al.* 2021b; Resnik and Dewaele 2021). Although EI is generally connected with personality, the link between FLA and student personality is much stronger than between FLE and personality. The impact that EI and FLA have on FLE may be considered distinct, additive, and interactive simultaneously. Increasing EI and reducing FLA will increase FLE (Chen *et al.* 2021b). Therefore, Trait Emotional Intelligence (TEI) is essential for FL learners (Li *et al.* 2021). Students with higher TEIs may have a greater capacity to control negative emotions, particularly anxiety, and generate positive learning emotions. TEI partially mediates the predictive value of grit, indicating that students' TEI is influenced by their learning determination, which predicts greater FLE (Resnik *et al.* 2021). Therefore, emotionally competent students have less anxiety when it comes to English. Consequently, increasing EI will increase FLE while decreasing FLA.

3.2.3 *Language proficiency*

If a student is enjoyment, there is a far better chance that they will enhance their English language skills. Anxiety's negative effect is weaker than enjoyment's positive effect on FL ability (Inada 2022). However, proficiency, FLA, and FLE predict many categories of fluency across different settings (Bielak 2022). Overall, FLE was predicted by both general English competence and domain-specific perceptions, notably reading, grammar, and speaking competencies. In contrast, FLCA is predicted by English proficiency, verbal and grammatical competence, and English test scores (Dewaele 2022). Thus, Self-Perceived English Proficiency (SPEP) and FLCA tend to have more influence than FLE (Jiang *et al.* 2020). Therefore, the negative effect that FLCA has on FL proficiency is far more critical than the total benefit that FLE delivers.

4   THE EFL TEACHING COMPONENTS WHICH SUPPORT FLCA AND FLE

The previous discussion shows how FLA and FLE can be predicted through several causes and factors that bind FL students. A study described a three-pull cycle (including students, peers, and teachers) of EFL students' emotions in the classroom (Shirvan and Talebzadeh 2020). In this particular scenario, several students have expressed concerns over the atmosphere of the classroom as well as the educational tools available in English. Some kids like our class activities, while others find them stressful. A vicious cycle of worry is maintained by the lengthy summative examination in English and the competitive nature of group projects. The pull cycle shift is exacerbated by the absence of emotional support provided by the teacher (in the role of a third puller) inside the classroom pull system. Thus, there are three main themes related to the learning component: classroom activities, instructor skills, and personal success/failure in the classroom, which cause pleasure and worry (Bensalem 2021). Therefore, the suggested topic is relevant to the classroom in terms of the teacher, the students, instructional design, and the overall atmosphere of the classroom.

4.1   *Teachers*

Instructors impact the FLE variance in teaching and learning (Dewaele 2019; Dewaele and Dewaele 2020; Dewaele and MacIntyre 2019; Dewaele *et al.* 2022; Jiang *et al.* 2020; Saito *et al.* 2018). However, the teacher gave only a quarter of the FLE to the participants in the class (Su 2022). In this regard, several studies compare the performance of teachers (with different levels of competence) on students' emotions in the classroom (Dewaele *et al.* 2019;

Dewaele and Dewaele 2020). Even though both sets of teachers had the same level of FLCA, the contributions to FLE produced by instructors with higher levels of competency were of significantly more considerable significance than those provided by teachers with lower levels of competence. The lack of pleasure towards lower competency teachers is due to their lack of trust or willingness to use the target language (Dewaele and Dewaele 2020). This is because negative opinions about FL teachers' abilities and teaching abilities can hinder their ability to create a pleasant classroom atmosphere where students are encouraged to use FL to complete a series of relevant, engaging, and challenging learning tasks (Dewaele *et al.* 2019). Thus, teacher quality is an unreliable FLCA factor (Dewaele and MacIntyre 2019). Therefore, teachers with a high level of FL competence can maintain an emotional influence on their students during the teaching and learning process (Dewaele *et al.* 2019).

Despite having a low relationship, teacher-student interaction affects FLCA (Toyama and Yamazaki 2022). Students have a higher level of engagement in the learning process as a direct result of the psychological relationship between the instructor and students that the dean encourages in the classroom. As a consequence, these students absorb more information. On the other hand, cultural influences manifest themselves as an integral component of the teaching and learning process in higher-level pupils and manifest themselves as triggers for FLCA. In collectivist cultures, positive relationships may work, but not in individualist cultures (Toyama and Yamazaki 2022). For example, Chinese culture holds that strict teachers will produce great students (Liu and Hong 2021). FL students have a high FLCA because of the consequences they are subjected to if they do not meet the criteria set by their teachers. As a result, the quality of the instructor affects the feelings of the FL students, which in turn affects their level of academic accomplishment, despite the fact that the FLCA is low.

4.2 *Students*

Students' internal variables strongly predict against FLCA (Dewaele and MacIntyre 2019; Liu and Hong 2021). Fear of failure and the demands of competition are the causes of anxiety in the emotional system of FL students (Shirvan and Talebzadeh 2020). FLCA is driven by the fear of unfavourable evaluations that predict self-assessed FL ability (Dong *et al.* 2022). Students with FLCA are more afraid of unfavourable assessments than test and communication anxiety (Fang and Tang 2021). Most students described the anxious classroom experience as a fear of poor evaluation, whereas obtaining a positive score was the most memorable and enjoyable (Bensalem 2021). Thus, FLCA and FLE are activated for good assessment and test results (Yang 2021). Therefore, anxiety and enjoyment do not alternate between students in FL education (Dewaele *et al.* 2019).

Students' internal and external variables combine to cause these two emotions (Amini and Author 2021). FLE and FLCA do not have dominant elements because they develop gradually, from unique experiences to frequent interactions with instructors and peers to excitement and anxiety (Dewaele and Pavelescu 2021). Students who spend more time in class align obstacles and problem-solving skills. Even if students integrate information internally (for example, when studying alone because of the objectives, materials, procedures, and learning outcomes (Li *et al.* 2021)), then social dynamics cannot be separated from their learning (Yeşilçınar and Erdemir 2022). Students can attain classroom goals through engaging in-class activities, gaining enough knowledge to back their answers, preparing for examinations, exchanging information in pairs or groups, and creating a secure atmosphere (Elahi Shirvan and Taherian 2021). Thus, FLE and external factors (instructors and colleagues) can exceed students' internal variables in FL learning (Dewaele and MacIntyre 2019).

4.3 *Class Environment (CE)*

CE greatly influences students' feelings about FL (Li *et al.* 2021). When taught in encouraging environments, students of FL report feeling happier and less worried. The instructors, students' peers, their traits, and interactions with other students create a pleasant learning environment. Take, for instance, the concepts of involvement and equality, as well as task orientation and collaboration. Students may increase their enjoyment of learning a language by participating in more activities, locating more information, and sharing what they have learned with others. These colorful graphics inspire the study of a second language and creative thought. The children will worry less about their instructor and peers because of this learning environment. Therefore, CE and FLE have a strong relationship that reinforces the environmental dimension of FLE (Li *et al.* 2021).

4.4 *Course design*

The theme of 'teaching methodology' is significant because it has two main points (Yeşilçınar and Erdemir 2022). To begin, the inclusion of Foreign Language teaching and learning activities as emotional facilities (FLA and FLE) has to be a part of the design of the class in order to enhance the overall performance of Foreign Language students. They will be able to communicate in the target language more effectively. For example, games, skits, group work, and crossword puzzles can engage and enhance student learning (Elahi Shirvan and Taherian 2021). Second, teacher development should emphasize enjoyment when combining ideas, tactics, and materials. For instance, using "music" (Dewaele and Proietti Ergün 2020) and "song" (Liu and Hong 2021) may increase student engagement since it incorporates something they like and are familiar with it. Both of these subjects are necessary for the students, and whether or not they have FLE may affect how well they perform in school. On the other hand, students get dissatisfied when the location of the school and its amenities need to live up to the standards they have set for them. For this reason, to enhance the performance of students taking Foreign Language classes, the design and delivery of suitable classroom courses must include the expectations of implementers of teaching and learning activities as facilities for students' emotions (FLA and FLE).

5   CONCLUSION

This study explores the characteristics of FLA and FLE and their performance which is supported by learning components in the classroom context. FLCA has similar features to FL students. In contrast, FLE is a situation that forms attitudes. Several factors influence the emotional condition of EFL students. Self-perception contributed to the success of FL, resulting in FLCA (in the short term) and FLE (in the long term) (in the future). Language skills, motivation, and emotional intelligence influence students' emotions in the classroom. The subjects of FLA and FLE are centred on learning components, which include instructors, students, the learning environment, and course design. FLA and FLE talk about classroom activities, the teacher's skills, and individual success and failure. These findings have repercussions for this research in the field of education. Taking into consideration the fact that several learning elements impact FLA and FLE. Since participants' internal factors, especially language performance, are key for FLE and FLCA, adapting the boring teaching pattern and paying more attention to students' positive and negative emotions when studying English is essential. Positive FL emotions may enhance learning, but negative emotions cause students to reject tasks and lose interest (Dong *et al.* 2022). To support the success of FLCA and FL, EFL teachers and students must cultivate a positive classroom image. This research investigates the characteristics of FLA and FLE in EFL courses and the teaching components that support them. Based on the study, this article looks forward to future research. More emphasis should be placed on widening theoretical views, enriching research themes, and developing research methodologies. The emotions of EFL students (particularly FLA and FLE) are complex, multifaceted systems that demand more investigation and study.

REFERENCES

Amini, D. and Author, C. (2021) 'Relationship between persian as foreign language learners' anxiety, enjoyment and goal orientation', *Journal of Teaching Persian to Speakers of Other Languages*, 10(1), pp. 75–100. Available at: https://doi.org/10.30479/jtpsol.2021.15250.1525.

Bensalem, E. (2021) Classroom Enjoyment and Anxiety among Saudi Undergraduate EFL Students: Does Gender Matter?

Bielak, J. (2022) 'To what extent are foreign language anxiety and foreign language enjoyment related to L2 fluency? An investigation of task-specific emotions and breakdown and speed fluency in an oral task', *Language Teaching Research* [Preprint]. Available at: https://doi.org/10.1177/13621688221079319.

Chen, Z. *et al.* (2021a) 'Interactions of trait emotional intelligence, foreign language anxiety, and foreign language enjoyment in the foreign language speaking classroom', *Journal of Multilingual and Multicultural Development* [Preprint]. Available at: https://doi.org/10.1080/01434632.2021.1890754.

Chen, Z. *et al.* (2021b) 'Interactions of trait emotional intelligence, foreign language anxiety, and foreign language enjoyment in the foreign language speaking classroom', *Journal of Multilingual and Multicultural Development* [Preprint]. Available at: https://doi.org/10.1080/01434632.2021.1890754.

Dewaele, J.-M. (2022) 'Foreign language enjoyment and anxiety: Associations with general and domain-specific english achievement', *Chinese Journal of Applied Linguistics*, 45(1), pp. 32–48.

Dewaele, J., Magdalena, A.F. and Saito, K. (2019) 'The effect of perception of teacher characteristics on Spanish EFL learners' anxiety and enjoyment', *Modern Language Journal*, 103(2), pp. 412–427. Available at: https://doi.org/10.1111/modl.12555.

Dewaele, J.M. *et al.* (2022) 'How distinctive is the foreign language enjoyment and foreign language classroom anxiety of Kazakh learners of Turkish?', *Applied Linguistics Review*, 13(2), pp. 243–265. Available at: https://doi.org/10.1515/applirev-2019-0021.

Dewaele, J.-M. and Alfawzan, M. (2018) 'Does the effect of enjoyment outweigh that of anxiety in foreign language performance?', *Studies in Second Language Learning and Teaching*, 8(1), pp. 21–45. Available at: https://doi.org/10.14746/ssllt.2018.8.1.2.

Dewaele, J.-M. and Dewaele, L. (2020) 'Are foreign language learners' enjoyment and anxiety specific to the teacher? An investigation into the dynamics of learners' classroom emotions', *Studies in Second Language Learning and Teaching*, 10(1), pp. 45–65. Available at: https://doi.org/10.14746/ssllt.2020.10.1.3.

Dewaele, J.-M. and MacIntyre, P.D. (2014) 'The two faces of Janus? Anxiety and enjoyment in the foreign language classroom', *Studies in Second Language Learning and Teaching*, 4(2), pp. 237–274. Available at: https://doi.org/10.14746/ssllt.2014.4.2.5.

Dewaele, J.-M. and MacIntyre, P.D. (2016) 'Foreign language enjoyment and foreign language classroom anxiety: The right and left feet of the language learner', in *Positive Psychology in SLA*. Multilingual Matters, pp. 215–236. Available at: https://doi.org/10.21832/9781783095360-010.

Dewaele, J.-M. and MacIntyre, P.D. (2019) 'The predictive power of multicultural personality traits, learner and teacher variables on foreign language enjoyment and anxiety', in *Evidence-Based Second Language Pedagogy: A Collection of Instructed Second Language Acquisition studies*. Abingdon, UK: Routledge, pp. 338–359.

Dewaele, J.-M. and Pavelescu, L.M. (2021) 'The relationship between incommensurable emotions and willingness to communicate in English as a foreign language: a multiple case study', *Innovation in Language Learning and Teaching*, 15(1), pp. 66–80. Available at: https://doi.org/10.1080/17501229.2019.1675667.

Dewaele, J.M. and Proietti Ergün, A.L. (2020) 'How different are the relations between enjoyment, anxiety, attitudes/motivation and course marks in pupils' Italian and English as foreign languages?', *Journal of the European Second Language Association*, 4(1), p. 45. Available at: https://doi.org/10.22599/jesla.65.

Dong, L., Liu, M. and Yang, F. (2022) 'The relationship between foreign language classroom anxiety, enjoyment, and expectancy-value motivation and their predictive effects on Chinese high school students' self-rated foreign language proficiency', *Frontiers in Psychology*, 13. Available at: https://doi.org/10.3389/fpsyg.2022.860603.

Elahi Shirvan, M. and Taherian, T. (2020) 'Affordances of the microsystem of the classroom for Foreign Language Enjoyment', *Human Arenas*, 5(2), pp. 222–244. Available at: https://doi.org/10.1007/s42087-020-00150-6.

Elahi Shirvan, M. and Taherian, T. (2021) 'Longitudinal examination of university students' foreign language enjoyment and foreign language classroom anxiety in the course of general English: latent growth curve modeling', *International Journal of Bilingual Education and Bilingualism*, 24(1), pp. 31–49. Available at: https://doi.org/10.1080/13670050.2018.1441804.

Elahi Shirvan, M., Taherian, T. and Yazdanmehr, E. (2020) 'The dynamics of foreign language enjoyment: An ecological momentary assessment', *Frontiers in Psychology*, 11. Available at: https://doi.org/10.3389/fpsyg.2020.01391.

Fang, F. and Tang, X. (2021) 'The relationship between Chinese english major students' learning anxiety and enjoyment in an english language classroom: A positive psychology perspective', *Frontiers in Psychology*, 12. Available at: https://doi.org/10.3389/fpsyg.2021.705244.

Fathi, J. and Mohammaddokht, F. (2021) 'Foreign language enjoyment and anxiety as the correlates of the Ideal L2 self in the english as a foreign language context', *Frontiers in Psychology*, 12. Available at: https://doi.org/10.3389/fpsyg.2021.790648.

Inada, T. (2022) 'Levels of enjoyment in class are closely related to improved english proficiency', *English Language Teaching*, 15(5), p. 69. Available at: https://doi.org/10.5539/elt.v15n5p69.

Jiang, G., Li, C. and Dewaele, J.M. (2020) 'The complex relationship between classroom emotions and EFL achievement in China', *Applied Linguistics Review*, 11(3), pp. 485–510. Available at: https://doi.org/10.1515/applirev-2018-0043.

Jiang, Y. and Dewaele, J.M. (2019) 'How unique is the foreign language classroom enjoyment and anxiety of Chinese EFL learners?', *System*, 82, pp. 13–25. Available at: https://doi.org/10.1016/j.system.2019.02.017.

Jiang, Y. and Dewaele, J.M. (2020) 'The predictive power of sociobiographical and language variables on foreign language anxiety of Chinese university students', *System*, 89. Available at: https://doi.org/10.1016/j.system.2020.102207.

Kitaoka, K. (2021) An Empirical Study of Classroom Enjoyment and Negative Emotions: A Model of the Use of Authentic Materials in the Japanese EFL context. Available at: https://www.researchgate.net/publication/352330860.

Li, C., Huang, J. and Li, B. (2021) 'The predictive effects of classroom environment and trait emotional intelligence on Foreign Language Enjoyment and Anxiety', *System*, 96. Available at: https://doi.org/10.1016/j.system.2020.102393.

Li, C., Jiang, G. and Dewaele, J.-M. (2018) 'Understanding Chinese high school students' Foreign Language Enjoyment: Validation of the Chinese version of the Foreign Language Enjoyment scale', *System*, 76, pp. 183–196. Available at: https://doi.org/10.1016/j.system.2018.06.004.

Li, C. and Wei, L. (2022) 'Anxiety, enjoyment, and boredom in language learning amongst junior secondary students in rural China: How do they contribute to L2 achievement?', *Studies in Second Language Acquisition* [Preprint]. Available at: https://doi.org/10.1017/S0272263122000031.

Liu, M. and Hong, M. (2021) 'English language classroom anxiety and enjoyment in Chinese young learners', *SAGE Open*, 11(4). Available at: https://doi.org/10.1177/21582440211047550.

Moskowitz, S. and Dewaele, J.M. (2020) 'The role of intellectual humility in foreign language enjoyment and foreign language classroom anxiety', *Eurasian Journal of Applied Linguistics*, 6(3), pp. 521–541. Available at: https://doi.org/10.32601/ejal.834664.

Resnik, P. and Dewaele, J.M. (2021) 'Learner emotions, autonomy and trait emotional intelligence in "in-person" versus emergency remote English foreign language teaching in Europe', *Applied Linguistics Review* [Preprint]. Available at: https://doi.org/10.1515/applirev-2020-0096.

Resnik, P., Moskowitz, S. and Panicacci, A. (2021) 'Language learning in crisis mode: The connection between LX grit, trait emotional intelligence and learner emotions', *Journal for the Psychology of Language Learning*, 3(2), pp. 99–117. Available at: https://doi.org/10.52598/jpll/3/2/7.

Saito, K. *et al.* (2018) 'Motivation, emotion, learning experience, and second language comprehensibility development in classroom settings: A cross-sectional and longitudinal study', *Language Learning*, 68(3), pp. 709–743. Available at: https://doi.org/10.1111/lang.12297.

Shirvan, M.E. and Talebzadeh, N. (2020) 'Tracing the signature dynamics of foreign language classroom anxiety and foreign language enjoyment: A retrodictive qualitative modeling', *Eurasian Journal of Applied Linguistics*, 6(1), pp. 23–44. Available at: https://doi.org/10.32601/ejal.710194.

Su, H. (2022) 'Foreign language enjoyment and classroom anxiety of Chinese EFL learners with intermediate and low english proficiency', *Journal of Language Teaching and Research*, 13(1), pp. 101–109. Available at: https://doi.org/10.17507/JLTR.1301.12.

Toyama, M. and Yamazaki, Y. (2022) 'Foreign language anxiety and individualism-collectivism culture: A top-down approach for a country/regional-level analysis', *SAGE Open*, 12(1). Available at: https://doi.org/10.1177/21582440211069143.

Yang, B. (2021) 'Predicting efl learners' achievement from their two faces—fle and flca', *Theory and Practice in Language Studies*, 11(3), pp. 275–285. Available at: https://doi.org/10.17507/tpls.1103.07.

Yeşilçınar, S. and Erdemir, N. (2022) 'Are enjoyment and anxiety specific to culture? An investigation into the sources of Turkish EFL learners' foreign language enjoyment and anxiety', *Innovation in Language Learning and Teaching* [Preprint]. Available at: https://doi.org/10.1080/17501229.2022.2063295.

Yu, Q. (2022) 'A review of foreign language learners' emotions', *Frontiers in Psychology*. Frontiers Media S.A. Available at: https://doi.org/10.3389/fpsyg.2021.827104.

Strengthening Professional and Spiritual Education through 21st Century Skill Empowerment in Pandemic and Post-Pandemic Era – Arifin et al. (Eds)
© 2024 The Author(s), ISBN: 978-1-032-45243-2
Open Access: www.taylorfrancis.com, CC BY-NC-ND 4.0 license

The controversial mathematical reasoning process of prospective teachers when solving mathematical problems

A.A.P. Rosyadi*
Universitas Muhammadiyah Malang, Indonesia

C. Sa'dijah, S. Susiswo & S. Rahardjo
Universitas Negeri Malang, Indonesia

ABSTRACT: An important aspect of the learning process is reasoning. One of the studied reasonings is controversial reasoning. Controversial reasoning can be used to determine the understanding of prospective teachers. The purpose of this study is to explain the controversial reasoning of prospective teachers when solving problems. This research is descriptive qualitative. The instruments used are tests and interviews. There are 50 prospective teachers who are given a problem, then their work is analyzed to find out their reasoning. Data analysis in this study is a) reviewing tests and interviews, b) determining the data used, c) analyzing test and interview results, d) making patterns, and e) presenting data. The conclusion of this study is the controversial reasoning process of prospective teachers, namely a) logically concluding, b) explaining the model, facts, and concept relationships, c) determining the conjecture, and d) using the conjecture to analyze the situation and make an analogy with the given problem. Suggestions for other researchers are to develop appropriate instruments for generating controversial reasoning for prospective teachers. In addition, after prospective teachers solve controversial problems, they can explore their critical and creative thinking processes.

Keywords: Mathematical reasoning, prospective teachers, problem

1 INTRODUCTION

Reasoning is one of the goals of the curriculum and an important element in mathematics education (Brumbaugh *et al.* 2020; Herbert and Brown 2020; Martin and Kasmer 2020; Rott 2020). Reasoning is used in solving mathematical problems so that it can facilitate solving (Bozkuş and Ayvaz 2018; Mariotti 2019; Zhou *et al.* 2018). Because of the importance of reasoning in mathematics education, one of the main foundations of prospective teachers must be emphasized (Susiswo *et al.* 2021). Prospective teachers are one of the determinants of the success of the learning process (Fernández *et al.* 2020; Nelson and Hawk 2020; Simon 2020).

The mathematical reasoning of prospective teachers is still relatively low (McCrory and Stylianides 2014; Hohensee 2017). Based on research results (Jeannotte and Kieran 2017) state that prospective teachers have not had the opportunity to learn about how to reason and prove. Research results (Battista 2017) mentioned that prospective mathematics teachers are still weak in reasoning but they still have confidence in the learning process carried out.

Various attempts have been made to correct the weak reasoning of prospective teachers. Many studies have been carried out to improve the reasoning of prospective teachers. Among other things (Karatoprak *et al.* 2015; Kertil *et al.* 2019; Mulenga and Marbán 2020; Thanheiser *et al.* 2016), research (Karatoprak *et al.* 2015) mentioned that training had been carried out for prospective teachers to develop reasoning. Researchers (Thanheiser *et al.*

---

*Corresponding Author: alfi_rosyadi@umm.ac.id

DOI: 10.1201/9781003376125-19

2016) conducted studies on reasoning strategies as the basis of knowledge of prospective teachers. Researchers (Kertil *et al.* 2019) describe the development of covariational reasoning through three categories, namely the identification of variables, how to coordinate variables, and measuring the level of change. However, no one has used controversial reasoning to strengthen the mathematical reasoning of prospective teachers.

Controversial reasoning causes differences of opinion in which there is a process of arguing (Goldberg and Savenije 2018; Mueller and Yankelewitz 2014a; Simic-Muller *et al.* 2015). In controversial reasoning, some arguments give rise to different ideas. This causes a person to be more leveraged in the process of solving a given problem.

Controversial reasoning research has been carried out by Maria Lim (2013), and the result is that the process of controversial reasoning can help someone's thought process. Mueller and Yankelewitz (2014b) explained that students need controversial reasoning so that they are more critical and can explain it to others. Research results (Mueller and Yankelewitz 2014b) mentioned that students' controversial reasoning tends to be below, and further research is needed. Prospective teachers are one of the important aspects of maximizing students' reasoning. This study is a follow-up to research on controversial reasoning but on aspiring mathematics teachers. This is done because no research looks at the controversial reasoning process of prospective mathematics teachers. The urgency of this research is that research on controversial reasoning has never been done even though the results of previous research with controversial reasoning can make prospective teachers more critical. Based on the above background, this study aims to describe the controversial reasoning process of prospective teachers in solving math problems.

2 METHOD

This research is descriptive with a qualitative approach. The research instruments used were tests and interviews. The test is used to find out the process of working with prospective teachers in solving the problems given and seeing the controversial reasoning process. The test consists of one controversial issue that the prospective teacher must resolve. The test was completed within 20 minutes, after which it was seen how his reasoning used the appropriate criteria. Interviews are used to deepen information about the reasoning of prospective teachers.

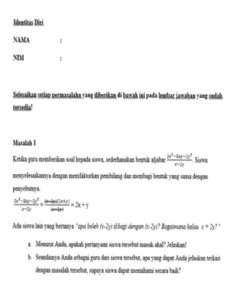

Figure 1. Problems given.

This study involved 50 prospective teachers who had been given problems, then the results of the work of prospective teachers were corrected to find out the controversial reasoning experienced by prospective teachers. The criteria for prospective teachers to experience controversy are the occurrence of cognitive conflicts and arguing during the interview process.

a copy of the problem given:

Problem 1: The form of algebra (implicitly controversial)

When the teacher gives questions to students, simplify the algebraic form $\frac{2x^2-3xy-2y^2}{x-2y}$. Students solve it by factoring in the numerator and dividing the same shape as the denominator.

$$\frac{2x^2-3xy-2y^2}{x-2y}=\frac{(x-2y)(2x+y)}{(x-2y)}=2\mathrm{x}+\mathrm{y}$$

Other students ask, "Can (x-2y) be divided by (x-2y)? How about x = 2y?

3 RESULTS AND DISCUSSION

Based on the results of the study, there was one prospective teacher who experienced controversy, so it could be seen how the controversial reasoning process was. The following are the results of the teacher candidates' answers.

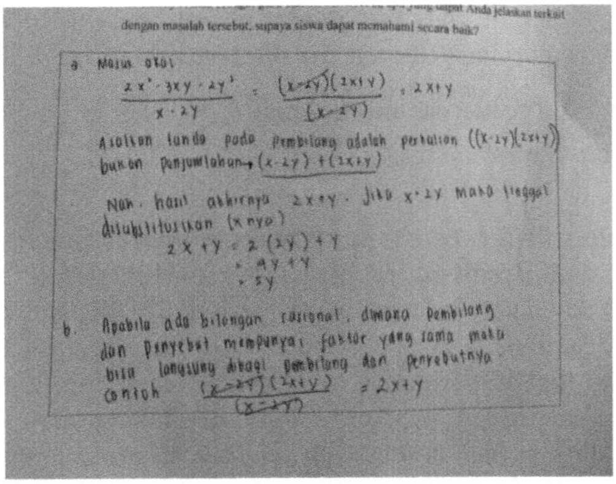
dengan masalah tersebut, supaya siswa dapat memahami secara baik?

a. Maius atau

$\frac{2x^2-3xy-2y^2}{x-2y}=\frac{(x-2y)(2x+y)}{(x-2y)}=2x+y$

Asalkan tanda pada pembilang adalah perkalian ((x-2y)(2x+y)) bukan penjumlahan → (x-2y)+(2x+y)

Nah, hasil akhirnya 2x+y. Jika x=2y maka tinggal disubstitusikan (x nya)

$2x+y=2(2y)+y$
$=4y+y$
$=5y$

b. Apabila ada bilangan rasional, dimana pembilang dan penyebut mempunyai faktor yang sama maka bisa langsung dibagi pembilang dan penyebutnya

contoh $\frac{(x-2y)(2x+y)}{(x-2y)}=2x+y$

Figure 2. Teacher candidate answers.

From the answers of the prospective teachers, each indicator of controversial reasoning can be seen. The following is an explanation:

3.1 *Experiencing controversy when solving a given problem*

This process can be seen during interviews, researchers conduct interviews after prospective teachers work on a given problem. From the results of the interviews, it can be seen that prospective teachers experience controversy. In addition, prospective teachers had time to ask researchers during interviews, the following is an excerpt:

C: Is the question correct, ma'am?
P: Yes, because it is appropriate. Why do you ask that?
C: I think there are additional conditions.

From the snippet of the dialogue, it can be seen that there is a cognitive conflict because prospective teachers ask for additional requirements to solve the problem.

The process of cognitive conflict occurs when a person experiences a conflict within himself (Devine *et al.* 2018). In cognitive conflict, it allows someone to convey their ideas by arguing with others (Bregant 2014). In line with research results (Simic-Muller *et al.* 2015) which state that prospective teachers should be given problems that trigger controversial reasoning (Kuhn 2010).

The problems given can give rise to various arguments, and controversial reasoning that affect the maximum learning process (Aksu *et al.* 2016; Miller and Flores 2012; Oulton *et al.* 2004; Simic-Muller *et al.* 2015). Indicators of prospective teachers are controversial, namely experiencing cognitive conflicts, differences of opinion, and trying to solve the problem (Kello 2016).

3.2 *Concluding logically*

When solving a given problem, prospective teachers draw logical conclusions. The conclusions of prospective teachers can be seen in the answers in Figure 3 as follows.

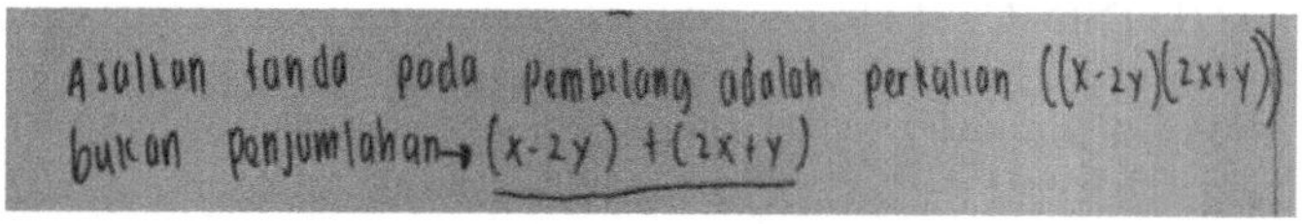

Asalkan tanda pada pembilang adalah perkalian ((x-2y)(2x+y))
bukan penjumlahan → (x-2y) + (2x+y)

Figure 3. Logical conclusion.

Prospective teachers conclude that the operation can be used for multiplication and not addition. Furthermore, researchers deepen the information through interviews as follows.

Q: Why did you write the sign as multiplication?

C: Because addition cannot be used.

Q: Why?

C: Later, the value will not be the sameMaking logical conclusions is one alternative that can be used in solving problems (Simic-Muller *et al.* 2015). Concluding is one of the processes in solving a given problem (Rosyadi *et al.* 2021; Rosyadi and Sa'dijah *et al.* 2022). This is in accordance with the results of the study (Faizah 2009), which states that in deductive and factual reasoning, there is a process of concluding solving the given problem (Rosyadi and Sa'dijah *et al.* 2022). The process of concluding a fact hereinafter referred to as reasoning also occurs in research (Basri *et al.* 2019). Research also mentions that abductive reasoning is also used to solve problems in which conclusions are drawn.

3.3 *Explaining the model, facts, or relationships between concepts.*

From the results of the answers of prospective teachers can be seen models, facts, and the relationship between concepts. Look at Figure 4 below, prospective teachers explain the link between rational numbers, factors, and division of numbers.

b. Apabila ada bilangan rasional, dimana pembilang
dan penyebut mempunyai faktor yang sama maka
bisa langsung dibagi pembilang dan penyebutnya.
contoh (x-2y)(2x+y) / (x-2y) = 2x+y

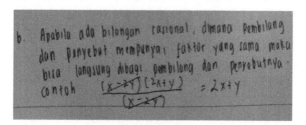

Figure 4. Explaining the relationship between concepts.

Linking between concepts is one alternative to understanding prospective teachers in solving problems (Baroody and Bartels 2020). The facts and models that exist in the given problem can be presented in a relationship between concepts (Blomhøj and Jensen 2003; Vinner and Dreyfus 2020).

An explanation of the interrelationships between concepts is an important part of solving problems (Baroody and Bartels 2020; Hong and Choi 2011; Vanscoy 2019). According to (Baroody and Bartels 2020) The relationship between the two concepts is important in completing the given task (Rosyadi and Sa'dijah *et al.* 2022). By understanding the relationship between concepts, you can solve problems and understand the ideas given (Vanscoy 2019).

3.4 *Making conjectures and evidence*

Allegations and evidence of prospective teachers can be seen from the results of interviews with researchers. The results of interviews with researchers resulted in the following conversations.

Q: What temporary conclusions can you get after working on the problem?
C: Division by the same number can only be done for multiplication operations.
P: okay, then there are others?
C: Oh yes, the number cannot be 0

From the conversation, the prospective teacher can mention two assumptions from the process of solving the given problem. This is in accordance with research (Hariyani *et al.* 2016) which states that the process of making assumptions is one part of the process of solving problems. The process of making guesses is one of the unique phases in the thinking process (Hariyani *et al.* 2016). In making assumptions, the solution strategy chosen will be different from the justification stage (Hidayah *et al.* 2020).

3.5 *Use relationship patterns to analyze situations, make analogies, or generalize.*

The pattern of relationships used by prospective teachers in conducting the generalization process can be seen in Figure 4. *The conversation between researchers and prospective* teachers can be seen as follows.

Q: From the conclusions that have been made, mentioning that division by the same number can only be done for multiplication operations, how do you solve other equivalent problems?
C: I tried to use the material that I got first and relate it to the question
Q: Then what?
C: Suppose I can't finish, I try to use trial and error

The process of making generalizations made by prospective teachers is used to make it easier to understand the problem and be able to solve other equivalent problems (Fensham and Bellocchi 2013; Rittle-Johnson and Schneider 2014). In the generalization process, there is a process of learning, understanding, and manipulating (Saxton *et al.* 2019).

The findings in this study are the stages of reasoning that have been described by Rosyadi *et al.* (2022) and can be used in other relevant studies. In making conjectures and evidence, prospective teachers have not found the right pattern (Ulger 2018). This is because the concept of prerequisites and linkage of the material is not maximized. For further research, appropriate learning methods can be developed for making conjectures and evidence (Martin and Kasmer 2020; Susiswo *et al.* 2021).

The limitation of this research is that it only uses controversial subjects, then it can also be developed for other subjects. Other research can also look at gender and the learning styles of prospective teachers.

4 CONCLUSIONS AND SUGGESTIONS

Based on the results of the study, it can be concluded that the controversial reasoning processes of prospective teachers include: a) there is a controversial process when solving a given problem, b) draws conclusions logically, c) provides explanations about models, facts, or relationships between concepts, d) make conjectures and evidence, and e) use relationship patterns to analyze situations, make analogies, or generalize. Suggestions for other researchers are to develop appropriate instruments in bringing up the controversial reasoning of prospective teachers. In addition, after prospective teachers solve controversial problems, they can explore their critical and creative thinking processes.

REFERENCES

Aksu, Z. *et al.* (2016) "Mathematics self-efficacy and mistake-handling learning as predictors of mathematics anxiety," *Journal of Education and Training Studies*, 4(8). Available at: https://doi.org/10.11114/jets.v4i8.1533.

Baroody, A.J. and Bartels, B.H. (2020) "Using concept maps to link mathematical ideas," *Mathematics Teaching in the Middle School* [Preprint]. Available at: https://doi.org/10.5951/mtms.5.9.0604.

Basri, H. *et al.* (2019) "Investigating critical thinking skill of junior high school in solving mathematical problem," *International Journal of Instruction* [Preprint]. Available at: https://doi.org/10.29333/iji.2019.12345a.

Battista, M.T. (2017) "Mathematical reasoning and sense making," *Reasoning and Sense Making in the Mathematics Classroom: Grades 3–5*, 111(2), pp. 1–19. Available at: https://doi.org/10.1016/b978-0-12-809285-9.00001-6.

Blomhøj, M. and Jensen, T.H. (2003) "Developing mathematical modelling competence: Conceptual clarification and educational planning," *Teaching Mathematics and its Applications* [Preprint]. Available at: https://doi.org/10.1093/teamat/22.3.123.

Bozkuş, F. and Ayvaz, Ü. (2018) "Middle school mathematics teachers' knowledge of mathematical reasoning," *European Journal of Education Studies*, 4(9), pp. 16–34. Available at: https://doi.org/10.5281/zenodo.1287947.

Bregant, J. (2014) "Critical thinking in education: why to avoid logical fallacies?," *Philosophy of mind and cognitive modelling in education*, 61, pp. 18–27.

Brumbaugh, D.K., Moch, P.L. and Wilkinson, M. (2020) "Reasoning and proof," in *Mathematics Content for Elementary Teachers*. Available at: https://doi.org/10.4324/9781410611345-17.

Devine, A. *et al.* (2018) "Cognitive and emotional math problems largely dissociate: Prevalence of developmental dyscalculia and mathematics anxiety," *Journal of Educational Psychology* [Preprint]. Available at: https://doi.org/10.1037/edu0000222.

Faizah, U. (2009) "Keefektifan cerita bergambar untuk pendidikan nilai dan keterampilan berbahasa dalam pembelajaran bahasa Indonesia," *Cakrawala Pendidikan* [Preprint].

Fensham, P.J. and Bellocchi, A. (2013) "Higher order thinking in chemistry curriculum and its assessment," *Thinking Skills and Creativity*, 10, pp. 250–264. Available at: https://doi.org/10.1016/j.tsc.2013.06.003.

Fernández, C., Llinares, S. and Rojas, Y. (2020) "Prospective mathematics teachers' development of noticing in an online teacher education program," *ZDM – Mathematics Education* [Preprint]. Available at: https://doi.org/10.1007/s11858-020-01149-7.

Goldberg, T. and Savenije, G.M. (2018) "Teaching controversial historical issues," in *The Wiley International Handbook of History Teaching and Learning*, pp. 503–526. Available at: https://doi.org/10.1002/9781119100812.ch19.

Hariyani, S. *et al.* (2016) "Math problem solving phases on thinking outside the box," *IOSR Journal of Research & Method in Education Ver. III* [Preprint]. Available at: https://doi.org/10.9790/7388-0604034348.

Herbert, K. and Brown, R.H. (2020) "Patterns as tools for algebraic reasoning," *Teaching Children Mathematics* [Preprint]. Available at: https://doi.org/10.5951/tcm.3.6.0340.

Hidayah, I.N. *et al.* (2020) "Characteristics of students' abductive reasoning in solving algebra problems," *Journal on Mathematics Education* [Preprint]. Available at: https://doi.org/10.22342/JME.11.3.11869.347-362.

Hohensee, C. (2017) "Preparing elementary prospective teachers to teach early algebra," *Journal of Mathematics Teacher Education* [Preprint]. Available at: https://doi.org/10.1007/s10857-015-9324-9.

Hong, Y.C. and Choi, I. (2011) "Three dimensions of reflective thinking in solving design problems: A conceptual model," *Educational Technology Research and Development* [Preprint]. Available at: https://doi.org/10.1007/s11423-011-9202-9.

Jeannotte, D. and Kieran, C. (2017) "A conceptual model of mathematical reasoning for school mathematics," *Educational Studies in Mathematics*, 96(1). Available at: https://doi.org/10.1007/s10649-017-9761-8.

Karatoprak, R., Karagöz Akar, G. and Börkan, B. (2015) "Prospective elementary and secondary school mathematics teachers' statistical reasoning," *International Electronic Journal of Elementary Education* [Preprint].

Kello, K. (2016) "Sensitive and controversial issues in the classroom: Teaching history in a divided society," *Teachers and Teaching: Theory and Practice* [Preprint]. Available at: https://doi.org/10.1080/13540602.2015.1023027.

Kertil, M., Erbas, A.K. and Cetinkaya, B. (2019) "Developing prospective teachers' covariational reasoning through a model development sequence," *Mathematical Thinking and Learning* [Preprint]. Available at: https://doi.org/10.1080/10986065.2019.1576001.

Kuhn, D. (2010) "Thinking as argument," in *Critical Readings on Piaget*. Available at: https://doi.org/10.4324/9780203435854_chapter_7.

Maria Lim, I. (2013) "Teaching historical controversies using the structured academic controversy approach: A case of history teachers in Singapore," in *Controversial History Education in Asian Contexts*. Available at: https://doi.org/10.4324/9780203753491.

Mariotti, M.A. (2019) "Proof and proving in mathematics education," in *Handbook of Research on the Psychology of Mathematics Education*. Available at: https://doi.org/10.1163/9789087901127_008.

Martin, W.G. and Kasmer, L. (2020) "Reasoning and sense making," *Teaching Children Mathematics* [Preprint]. Available at: https://doi.org/10.5951/tcm.16.5.0284.

McCrory, R. and Stylianides, A.J. (2014) "Reasoning-and-proving in mathematics textbooks for prospective elementary teachers," *International Journal of Educational Research* [Preprint]. Available at: https://doi.org/10.1016/j.ijer.2013.09.003.

Miller, H.L. and Flores, D. (2012) "Teaching controversial issues, liberally," in *Effective College and University Teaching: Strategies and Tactics for the New Professoriate*, pp. 155–162. Available at: https://doi.org/10.4135/9781452244006.n17.

Mueller, M. and Yankelewitz, D. (2014a) "Fallacious argumentation in student reasoning: Are there benefits?," *European Journal of Science and Mathematics Education* [Preprint].

Mueller, M. and Yankelewitz, D. (2014b) "Teaching mistakes or teachable moments?," *Kappa Delta Pi Record* [Preprint]. Available at: https://doi.org/10.1080/00228958.2014.931149.

Mulenga, E.M. and Marbán, J.M. (2020) "Prospective teachers' online learning mathematics activities in the age of COVID-19: A cluster analysis approach," *Eurasia Journal of Mathematics, Science and Technology Education* [Preprint]. Available at: https://doi.org/10.29333/EJMSTE/8345.

Nelson, M.J. and Hawk, N.A. (2020) "The impact of field experiences on prospective preservice teachers' technology integration beliefs and intentions," *Teaching and Teacher Education* [Preprint]. Available at: https://doi.org/10.1016/j.tate.2019.103006.

Oulton, C., Dillon, J. and Grace, M.M. (2004) "Reconceptualizing the teaching of controversial issues," *International Journal of Science Education* [Preprint]. Available at: https://doi.org/10.1080/0950069032000072746.

Rittle-Johnson, B. and Schneider, M. (2014) "Developing conceptual and procedural knowledge of mathematics," *Oxford Handbook of Numerical Cognition* [Preprint]. Available at: https://doi.org/10.1093/oxfordhb/9780199642342.013.014.

Rosyadi, A.A.P. *et al.* (2021) "Berpikir kritis calon guru dalam menyelesaikan masalah kontroversial matematika dengan menggunakan high order thinking skills," *AKSIOMA: Jurnal Program Studi Pendidikan Matematika*, 10(4). Available at: https://doi.org/10.24127/ajpm.v10i4.4082.

Rosyadi, A.A.P. *et al.* (2022) "High order thinking skills: Can it arise when a prospective teacher solves a controversial mathematics problem?," in *Journal of Physics: Conference Series*. Available at: https://doi.org/10.1088/1742-6596/2157/1/012038.

Rosyadi, A.A.P. and Sa'dijah, Cholis; Susiswo; Rahardjo, S. (2022) "Critical thinking of prospective mathematics teachers: What are the errors in argumentation?," *Multicultural Education*, 8(3), pp. 80–90.

Rott, B. (2020) "Problem solving in mathematics education," *Research in Mathematics Education* [Preprint]. Available at: https://doi.org/10.1080/14794802.2020.1731577.

Saxton, D. *et al.* (2019) "Analysing mathematical reasoning abilities of neural models," in *7th International Conference on Learning Representations, ICLR 2019*.

147

Simic-Muller, K., Fernandes, A. and Felton-Koestler, M.D. (2015) "'I just wouldn't want to get as deep into it': Preservice teachers' beliefs about the role of controversial topics in mathematics education," *Journal of Urban Mathematics Education* [Preprint].

Simon, M.A. (2020) "Prospective Elementary Teachers' Knowledge of Division," *Journal for Research in Mathematics Education* [Preprint]. Available at: https://doi.org/10.5951/jresematheduc.24.3.0233.

Susiswo, S. *et al.* (2021) "The Development of an Instrument on Negative Fractions to Measure the Cognitive Obstacle Based on Mental Mechanism Stages," *TEM Journal*, 10(3). Available at: https://doi.org/10.18421/TEM103-44.

Thanheiser, E. *et al.* (2016) "Reflective analysis as a tool for task redesign: The case of prospective elementary teachers solving and posing fraction comparison problems," *Journal of Mathematics Teacher Education* [Preprint]. Available at: https://doi.org/10.1007/s10857-015-9334-7.

Ulger, K. (2018) "The effect of problem-based learning on the creative thinking and critical thinking disposition of students in visual arts education," *Interdisciplinary Journal of Problem-based Learning* [Preprint]. Available at: https://doi.org/10.7771/1541-5015.1649.

Vanscoy, A. (2019) "Conceptual and procedural knowledge: A framework for analyzing point-of-need information literacy instruction," *Communications in Information Literacy* [Preprint]. Available at: https://doi.org/10.15760/comminfolit.2019.13.2.3.

Vinner, S. and Dreyfus, T. (2020) "Images and definitions for the concept of function," *Journal for Research in Mathematics Education* [Preprint]. Available at: https://doi.org/10.5951/jresematheduc.20.4.0356.

Zhou, B. *et al.* (2018) "Temporal relational reasoning in Videos," in Lecture Notes in Computer Science (including subseries Lecture Notes in Artificial Intelligence and Lecture Notes in Bioinformatics). Available at: https://doi.org/10.1007/978-3-030-01246-5_49.

Strengthening Professional and Spiritual Education through 21st Century Skill Empowerment in Pandemic and Post-Pandemic Era – Arifin et al. (Eds)
© 2024 The Author(s), ISBN: 978-1-032-45243-2
Open Access: www.taylorfrancis.com, CC BY-NC-ND 4.0 license

Mathematical syntactic and semantic reasoning in trigonometrics

Agung Deddiliawan Ismail
Malang State University, Indonesia
Universias Muhammadiyah Malang, Indonesia

Cholis Sa'dijah, S. Susiswo & S. Sisworo
Malang State University, Indonesia

ABSTRACT: Covid-19 is having an impact on education around the world. The Government and the Indonesian Education Office issued regulations regarding education in this pandemic era. This study aims to describe the syntax and semantics of mathematics students in the pandemic-era Trigonometry material. This research uses a qualitative approach and type of case study research. The research subjects were taken as many as six people based on their level of mathematical ability: high, medium, and low. Data collection techniques used are test or exam techniques and interviews. Based on the results of research and discussion, the number one reasoning used by the subjects tends to be both semantic and syntactic. All subjects use the properties of rectangles and the Pythagorean theorem for right triangles. However, in question number 2, subjects with high abilities use both reasoning, and subjects with moderate and low skills tend to use syntactic reasoning. It can be seen from the answers that only use the formula but do not know its usefulness in solving the problem.

1 INTRODUCTION

The year 2019–2020 is historic and will never be forgotten. The world is shocked by the Coronavirus Disease or Covid-19. This pandemic is very influential on human life. Because of this pandemic, all human activities and cultures have also changed. All life factors are not spared from changes to adapt to this pandemic. Economic, social, government, and cultural factors impact education worldwide. Sasaki *et al.* (2020) stated that the Covid-19 pandemic impacted education worldwide. Many countries were carrying out social and physical distancing, which resulted in the closure of schools for students.

The Government and the Indonesian Education Office issued regulations regarding education in this pandemic era. Through the Circular of the Minister of Education and Culture of the Republic of Indonesia No. 3 of 2020 concerning the Prevention of Corona Virus Disease (COVID-19) in Education Units, the government is trying to prevent educators from completing the material in the curriculum (Mendikbut 2020). The most important thing to do is to ensure that students are still involved in learning the following life skills: health and empathy. In addition, the government also urges that learning be carried out in distance learning, online learning, or data sharing.

Online learning in the pandemic era has advantages and disadvantages. The advantage gained by using online learning is that learning is open to more than space and time. Tezer *et al.* (2019) explain that online learning is online learning, which is learning in an online environment supported by a website. Students who have access or distance to schools that are far away can now study anywhere. Students no longer follow the routine activities that are set by the clock.

DOI: 10.1201/9781003376125-20

Learning can take place at any time. Karaoğlan (2020) explains that with technology in education, the limitations of space and time in the teaching and learning process have become non-existent. Fung *et al.* (2014) explained that learning mathematics online can help students actively learn independently. Online mathematics learning can help students with learning difficulties, and educators can identify students.

Students can access information inside and outside the classroom, for example, by open online courses, video sharing, or social networking communities. Park and Kim (2020) also believe that online classes make learning more flexible and easier to access. On the other hand, online classes also have several shortcomings (Mwenda *et al.* 2019), explaining that online learning in this pandemic era has weaknesses, including the material being taught not following the existing curriculum, and this is following what was conveyed by the Indonesian government. In addition to online learning, it also adds to the spending budget, namely quota or internet access. Not to mention, the internet network quality for all students is different. This becomes an obstacle to learning to take place. Karaoğlan (2020) explains that online classes have weaknesses, namely internet connection problems when taking exams. It is easy to cheat during exams, online exams give students more anxiety, low scores obtained by students can reduce motivation, and students are less focused on studying.

Low scores resulting in decreased motivation are also related to student understanding. As explained by the government, the purpose of learning is that students can understand the material and be able to solve problems. Students are indirectly taught to be independent in mathematics learning (Ichinose and Bonsangue 2016).

Easdown (2009) explains that syntax and semantics are reasoning that is interrelated with one another. Syntactic reasoning is shallow or superficial reasoning in which a person only remembers the form or plot in solving a problem. This reasoning relies on a rule, a simple pattern. Students often use this reasoning when taking exams under pressure and need to answer questions quickly. At the same time, semantic reasoning is the end of learning that relies on strong intuition, experience, and insight. This reasoning is embedded in one's mind and results from practice.

Murphy (2015) states that semantics is reasoning that can be seen from the language used by students. Semantics is an expression of students' knowledge to relate a concept relationship in mathematics. In comparison, Kurzon and Adler (2008) explain that syntax is more directed to the structure used in solving problems. Meanwhile, semantics emphasizes meaning in solving problems. Online learning influences Semantics or meaningfulness to students. Based on the initial observations made on 39 students of the Mathematics Education Study Program in the online class, it was found that 71.9% or as many as 28 students scored below the minimal standard criteria after the exam. From this data, the focus will be the syntax and semantics of students' mathematics in the pandemic era on Trigonometry material.

2 METHODS

This study uses a qualitative approach, and the type of research is descriptive. It is related to the research objective, which is to study the syntax and semantics of students in working on Trigonometry problems. The research subjects were as many as six people based on the level of mathematical ability, namely, high, medium, and low, with each category of 2 people. The selection of this subject used a random sampling technique based on the criteria. For data collection, the technique used is the technique of tests, exams, and interviews. At the same time, the research data is in the form of test answer sheets and interview transcripts. The data analysis techniques used are data presentation, reduction, and collection. The subject was given two problems solving trigonometry to obtain information about applying semantics and syntax. The problem is as follows:

Questions

(1) Suppose it is known that the lengths PQ = QR = 5 cm, RS = 12 cm, and ST = 13 cm, and P,∠R,∠S are right angles. If PQSU is a rectangle, what is the length of PT? (Look at Figure 1)

(2) If you know the lengths of AE = 3 cm, DE = 3 cm, CD = 4 cm, BC = 5 cm, and A,∠D,∠ and C are right angles. Determine the length of AB! (Look at Figure 2)

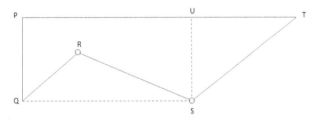

Figure 1. Figure for question 1.

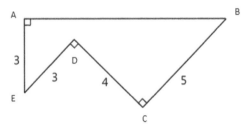

Figure 2. Figure for question 2.

3 RESULTS

The 37 answers will be categorized based on high, medium, and low mathematical ability. After being classified, two subjects will be taken each, so all six subjects will be obtained. These six subjects are selected from the answers that can provide information. Subjects 1 and 2 are subjects who have high mathematical abilities. Subjects 3 and 4 are students who have moderate mathematical skills. While subjects 5 and 6 are students who have low mathematical abilities.

3.1 *Result*

3.1.1 *Subject 1*
Based on Figure 3, it can be seen that subject 1 made a new image accompanied by an additional partition. Besides that, there is also a symbol α at the corner ∠DCE. Syntactic reasoning can be seen using the Pythagorean formula from a length CE search. The following is a snippet of an interview with subject 1.

> Researcher: Why do you use symbols α, and what are they used for?
> Subject 1:   I use the symbol α to name the corner ∠DCE. The point is to find the measure of the angle.

Based on the answers and interviews with subject 1, it can be explained that in working on the questions, subject 1 uses semantic reasoning, which can be seen by looking for values α that aim to find ∠BCE. In contrast, syntactic reasoning is seen from the length of the CE search process.

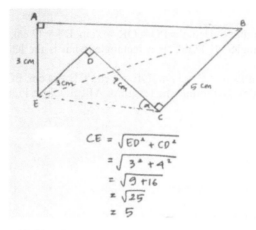

$$CE = \sqrt{ED^2 + CD^2}$$
$$= \sqrt{3^2 + 4^2}$$
$$= \sqrt{9 + 16}$$
$$= \sqrt{25}$$
$$= 5$$

Figure 3.   The answer of Subject 1.

3.1.2   *Subject 2*

From Figure 4, it can be seen that subject 2 uses the Pythagorean theorem to find the length AB. To find the size AB first, subject 2 looks for length EB. Furthermore, we get the length EB = $4\sqrt{5}$ and AB = $\sqrt{71}$. Here is a snippet of the interview.

Researcher: How do you get the score *AB*?

Subject 2:   Initially looking for *BF*, sir. Obtained *BF* = 8 and *EF* = 4 from here can be searched for *EB*. Using the Pythagorean formula, that length *EB* can be used to find the measurement with the help of *AB* and *AE*.

Based on the answers and the results of interviews with subject 2, it can be explained that semantic reasoning can be seen from interviews where subject 2 explains how to find length AB using the Pythagorean theorem where, in the picture, there are several forms of right triangles. For syntactic reasoning, it can be seen from the steps to find the length AB, which starts with finding the size EB, which is then used to find the distance AB.

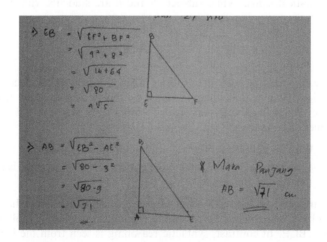

Figure 4.   Answer of subject 2.

3.1.3 *Subject 3*

Figure 5 shows that to find the length EC, subject 1 shows an operation where $\sqrt{4+3}$ equals $\sqrt{16+9}$. In addition, the square image $CE'ED$ looks asymmetrical. The following is an excerpt from an interview with subject 3.

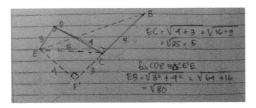

Figure 5. Answer of subject 2

Researcher: How do you find the length, and what is the use of that line length?
Subject 3: How to search EC using Pythagoras using lines 4 and 3 found five, and there is no use, sir.

Based on the answers and interviews, it can be explained that subject two only performs syntactic reasoning as seen from the length EC search, and after knowing the length, it is not used.

3.1.4 *Subject 4*

In Figure 6, it can be seen that subject 4 wrote $\angle C = \cos\theta = \cos(90 + a)$. In the figure in the picture, there is no visible symbol a and. The following is a snippet of an interview with subject 4.

Researcher: What does the symbol $\angle C$ there mean? Then what is it used for?
Subject 4: That angle C is $\cos\theta$. $\cos\theta$ Equal to 90 plus a

Based on the answers and interview results, it can be explained that subject 4 only does syntactic reasoning. We have seen from the search $\angle C = \cos\theta$. Where $\angle C$ is an angle while $\cos\theta$ is an operation.

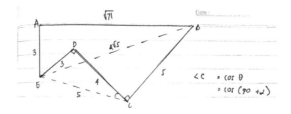

Figure 6. Answer of subject 4.

3.1.5 *Subject 5*

In Figure 7, it can be seen that subject five wrote $\cos(90° + a) = -\sin a$. However, in the figure in the picture, there is no symbol. The following is a snippet of an interview with subject 5.

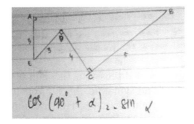

Figure 7. Answer of subject 4.

153

Researcher: Why and what is $\cos(90° + a) = -\sin a$ used to find the length?
Subject 5: That is the formula from the book, sir. Its use is to find the length AB.

Based on the answers and results of interviews with subject 5, it can be explained that the reasoning used is syntactic. Subject 5 just used the formula $\cos(90° + a) = -\sin a$ without knowing where it came from.

3.1.6 Subject 6

Figure 8 shows that in the first line, subject 6 writes $\cos(90° + a)$, and in the second line, it can be seen $-six$. The following is a snippet of an interview with subject 6.

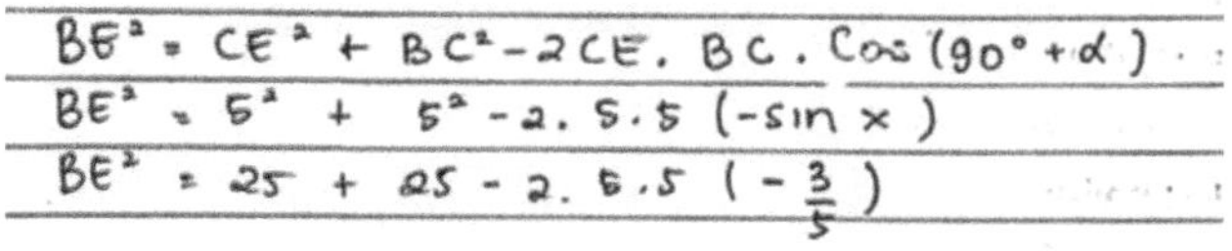

$$BE^2 = CE^2 + BC^2 - 2CE \cdot BC \cdot \cos(90° + \alpha) \cdots$$
$$BE^2 = 5^2 + 5^2 - 2 \cdot 5 \cdot 5 (-\sin x)$$
$$BE^2 = 25 + 25 - 2 \cdot 5 \cdot 5 \left(-\frac{3}{5}\right)$$

Figure 8. Answer of subject 6.

Researcher: Why are angles used in the first row and the second-row angles are used x?
Subject 6: From the formula $\cos(90° + a)$, sir. Which is also from the procedure.

Based on the answers and interview excerpts, it can be explained that the reasoning used by subject 6 in question number 2 is syntactic. It can be seen that subject six only uses the formula in the book but needs to know the angle symbol used.

4 DISCUSSION

In solving problem-solving problems, semantic and syntactic reasoning is needed. A person can solve problems quickly if they can use both reasoning. It might be used if you use semantic reasoning, but it takes more time to work on it. It is different from using only syntactic reasoning. Most likely, the solution or answer made needs to be corrected. Dawkins and Cook (2017) explain that semantic and syntactic reasoning help each other. The skill of using both does require practice. The use of both reasoning requires process and time. In line with research conducted by Easdown (2009) on solving problems, many things could be improved. These mistakes can develop thinking processes and creativity in dealing with other problems.

Based on the study results, some subjects with moderate and low mathematical abilities in working on the second problem use the procedure for working on the first problem. It can be concluded that the reasoning used is syntactic. This incident follows the research conducted by Mejía-Ramos et al. (2015). In his research, it is explained that several research subjects consistently use the method of solving similar problems but not the same. It can also be explained from several subjects that each subject can reason syntactically and semantically, either one or both. All subjects have syntactic and semantic reasoning abilities, but each has a different level (Murphy 2015).

5 CONCLUSION

Based on the results of research and discussion, the number one reasoning used by the subjects tends to be both semantic and syntactic. All subjects use the properties of rectangles and the Pythagorean theorem for right triangles. However, in question number 2, subjects with high abilities seem to use both reasoning and subjects with moderate and low skills tend to use syntactic reasoning. It can be seen from the answers that only use the formula but do not know its usefulness in solving the problem.

ACKNOWLEDGMENT

We want to thank the Faculty of Teacher Training and Education, the Universitas Muhammadiyah Malang and Universitas Negeri Malang, and all parties who have assisted in implementing this research.

REFERENCES

Dawkins, P.C. and Cook, J.P. (2017) "Guiding reinvention of conventional tools of mathematical logic: students' reasoning about mathematical disjunctions," *Educational Studies in Mathematics*, 94(3), pp. 241–256. Available at: https://doi.org/10.1007/s10649-016-9722-7.

Easdown, D. (2009) "Syntactic and semantic reasoning in mathematics teaching and learning," *International Journal of Mathematical Education in Science and Technology* [Preprint]. Available at: https://doi.org/10.1080/00207390903205488.

Fung, J.J.Y., Yuen, M. and Yuen, A.H.K. (2014) "Self-regulation in learning mathematics online: Implications for supporting mathematically gifted students with or without learning difficulties," *Gifted and Talented International*, 29(1–2), pp. 113–123. Available at: https://doi.org/10.1080/15332276.2014.11678434.

Ichinose, C. and Bonsangue, M. (2016) "Mathematics self-related beliefs and online learning," *Learning Assistance Review*, 21(1), pp. 55–70.

Karaoğlan, F.G. (2020) "Investigation of Pre-Service Teachers' Opinions on Advantages and Disadvantages of Online Formative Assessment: An Example of Online Multiple-Choice Exam," 2(June), pp. 10–19.

Kurzon, D. and Adler, S. (2008) *Adpositions Pragmatic, semantic and syntactic perspectives*. Amsterdam: John Benjamins B.V.

Mejía-Ramos, J.P., Weber, K. and Fuller, E. (2015) "Factors influencing students' propensity for semantic and syntactic reasoning in proof writing: A case study," *International Journal of Research in Undergraduate Mathematics Education*, 1(2), pp. 187–208. Available at: https://doi.org/10.1007/s40753-015-0014-x.

Mendikbut (2020) "Edaran Tentang Pencegahan Wabah COVID-19 di Lingkungan Satuan Pendidikan Seluruh Indonesia," 33, pp. 1–5.

Murphy, C. (2015) "Authority and agency in young childrens early number work: A functional linguistic perspective," Mathematics education in the margins (Proceedings of the 38th annual conference of the Mathematics Education Research Group of Australasia), pp. 453–460.

Mwenda, A.B., Sullivan, M. and Grand, A. (2019) "How do Australian universities market STEM courses in YouTube videos?," *Journal of Marketing for Higher Education*, 29(2), pp. 191–208. Available at: https://doi.org/10.1080/08841241.2019.1633004.

Park, C.W. and Kim, D. gook (2020) "Exploring the roles of social presence and gender difference in online learning," *Decision Sciences Journal of Innovative Education*, 18(2), pp. 291–312. Available at: https://doi.org/10.1111/dsji.12207.

Sasaki, R. *et al.* (2020) "The practicum experience during Covid-19 – supporting pre-service teachers practicum experience through a simulated classroom," *Journal of Technology and Teacher Education*, 28(2), pp. 329–339.

Tezer, M. *et al.* (2019) "The influence of online mathematics learning on prospective teachers mathematics achievement: The role of independent and collaborative learning," *World Journal on Educational Technology: Current Issues*, 11(4), pp. 257–265. Available at: https://doi.org/10.18844/wjet.v11i4.4361.

Strengthening Professional and Spiritual Education through 21st Century Skill Empowerment in Pandemic and Post-Pandemic Era – Arifin et al. (Eds)
© 2024 The Author(s), ISBN: 978-1-032-45243-2

The effect of competence and compensation on teacher performance

Umi Farihah*, Ainur Rohma & Abd. Muhith
Universitas Islam Negeri Kiai Haji Achmad Siddiq Jember, Indonesia

ABSTRACT: Teacher performance is one of the most important factors in improving the quality of education, hence finding factors that can significantly affect performance is very important. The purpose of this study is to determine the effect of compensation and competence on teacher performance in State Islamic Junior High School 2 Probolinggo, East Java, Indonesia. This study used a quantitative approach with an associative type of research. Simple random sampling is used as a sampling technique. Data collection techniques use questionnaires. Multiple linear regression tests are used to analyze the data. The results showed that there was a simultaneous effect of compensation and competence on teacher performance, but partially only teacher competence had an influence while teacher compensation did not affect teacher performance. It can be concluded that to maximize teacher performance, the competence and compensation factors must be considered. The conclusion of this study is that teacher competence has the greatest impact in influencing teacher performance.

Keywords: quality of education, teacher compensation, teacher competence

1 INTRODUCTION

Improving the quality of education as well as human resources has become an immense challenge for Indonesians in the era of Society 5.0. The improved quality of both education and human resources are believed to be keys to successful education (Johar *et al.* 2019). Furthermore, one way to observe the success of a national educational system is through teacher performance, as explained by Zahroh *et al.* (2021), who state that teachers have an important role in determining the success of education to develop quality human resources and the quality of education (Habibi *et al.* 2018), particularly on young Indonesians, in which they could be expected as smart and capable generations who can deal with future challenges. In an educational institution, teachers play the central roles whose main function is to improve the quality of education (Jones *et al.* 2006). The better their performance, the better the quality of graduates and the achievement of national educational goals (Sasmito *et al.* 2020). Teacher performance can be influenced by internal and external factors (Muazza 2021; Selasih 2019; Witari and Manuaba 2021). Teachers who have these factors will affect their performance better.

One of the internal factors that can affect teacher performance is competence. Teacher competence is a fundamental ability that every teacher should own (Hakim 2015). Such competence encompasses several aspects, among others values, attitudes, skills, knowledge, and critical understanding (Lenz *et al.* 2022; Pineda-Alfonso *et al.* 2018). Teachers are required to master four competencies namely pedagogical competence, personal competence, social competence, and professional competence. While competence is key to performance, the competencies implemented while performing the duties must follow the expected standard performance, and without competence, teachers will not be able to improve their

---

*Corresponding Author: umifarihah@uinkhas.ac.id

DOI: 10.1201/9781003376125-21

performances (Rahmatullah 2016). The effect of competence on teacher performance has been shown in several studies. But in certain situations, other external factors also influence teacher performance.

Another factor that can affect teacher performance is compensation (external factors) (Witari and Manuaba 2021). According Matriadi *et al.* (2019) explained that compensation is equally important because it directly links to the prosperity and welfare of a teacher that will affect their performance. Additionally, Gary (2019) states that compensation consists of two components, namely (1) direct cash payments in the form of salaries and incentives, and (2) indirect payments in the form of allowances and insurance. Compensation has three dimensions, namely the dimensions of direct financial compensation, the dimensions of indirect financial compensation, and the dimensions of non-financial compensation (Bahtiar and Sudaryana 2020; Vance and Paik 2015). Compensation is very important to improve performance because it is a source of income for teachers and their families and has a psychological impact on teachers in carrying out their duties as educators, for example in increasing morale (Sofi'i *et al.* 2022). The purpose of compensation is as a bond of cooperation, job satisfaction, effective procurement, motivation, employee stabilization, and discipline (Hasibuan 2017). Although compensation is an external factor that generally does not rank at the top in influencing performance, compensation is a very easy factor in influencing the calm and work motivation of teachers which will ultimately affect performance (Hidayatullah 2018).

Madrasah Tsanawiyah Negeri 2 Probolinggo, East Java, Indonesia is one of the educational institutions that has human resources, namely teachers who are quite competent and professional in their fields. There are about 35 teachers with the status of Civil Servants (PNS/Pegawai Negeri Sipil) and 20 teachers with the status of Non-Civil Servants (Non-PNS/Non-Pegawai Negeri Sipil). The difference in status results in differences in the amount of compensation received, where teachers who are civil servants have higher salaries. Even so, based on the observations in Madrasah Tsanawiyah Negeri 2 Probolinggo, East Java, Indonesia is one of the most favorite schools in Probolinggo, Indonesia. Therefore, it is necessary to study more deeply the influence of competence and compensation on teacher performance at Madrasah Tsanawiyah Negeri 2 Probolinggo, East Java, Indonesia which is known as the community's favorite school. In essence, a quality school is not only based on its status as the community's favorite school but also the quality of graduates to achieve the goals of national education itself, which can be realized if teachers as educators have good performance.

Various studies have been conducted to examine the variables that can affect teacher performance. However, the use of two variables, namely competence and compensation to determine their effect on teacher performance, is rarely done. Several other studies have tried to look at several factors that can affect teacher performance, such as Farida, Tippe, and Tunas (2020) who found that teacher competence and motivation simultaneously affect teacher performance at Development Technology Vocational School Bekasi. Meanwhile, Hasibuan and Adi (2020) found that compensation has a significant and positive influence on teacher performance. Competence and compensation variables also have a significant effect on the performance of lecturers at Nahdatul University Cirebon (Bahtiar and Sudaryana 2020). Research at Senior High School 29 Jakarta shows that competence, organizational commitment, and non-financial compensation have a significant effect on teacher performance (Purba *et al.* 2018).

Based on the phenomenon and background of the problem, the purpose of this study is to determine the effect of competence and compensation on performance on teacher performance at State Islamic Junior High School 2 Probolinggo, East Java, Indonesia. In this study, researchers tried to reveal the influence of competence and teacher compensation on teacher performance. This research is very important to do because through this research it can be used as evaluation material in improving teacher performance. Good teacher performance will certainly affect the quality of education so that it can produce quality human resources.

2 METHOD

This study used a quantitative approach with the type of associative research. The population in this study were all teachers at State Islamic Junior High School 2 Probolinggo, East Java, Indonesia, totaling 56 consisting of 34 civil servant-teachers and 22 non-permanent teachers. The number of samples taken in this study were 30 teachers and the sampling technique used is simple random sampling. The data collection technique in this study was in the form of a questionnaire. The research data that has been obtained were then analyzed using multiple linear regression to determine the significant effect of competence and compensation on teacher performance either simultaneously or partially.

Before performing multiple linear regression analysis, it is necessary to test prerequisites which include tests for normality, collinearity, heteroscedasticity, and autocorrelation. The teacher competence questionnaire consists of 40 statement items covering the dimensions of pedagogic, professional, personality, and social competence. The teacher compensation questionnaire consists of 20 statement items which include the dimensions of direct compensation and indirect compensation. Furthermore, the teacher performance questionnaire consists of 50 items covering the dimensions of work quality, work speed/accuracy, an initiative in work, work ability, and communication.

The three questionnaires were tested on 26 teachers in addition to the sample which aims to measure the level of validity and reliability of the instrument. After the validity test was conducted, there were three invalid statement items in the competence questionnaire, two invalid statement items in the teacher compensation questionnaire, and one invalid statement item in the teacher performance questionnaire. Based on these results, the researchers used only valid items to be given to respondents. While the results of the reliability test of the total number of questionnaires on the teacher competence questionnaire were 0.904, the teacher compensation questionnaire was 0.961, and the teacher performance questionnaire was 0.987. From these results, it can be concluded that the questionnaire instrument is very reliable.

The data analysis techniques used consist of two types, namely descriptive analysis and inferential analysis. In the descriptive analysis, interval, frequency, and percentage classes are used. There are five categories used, namely very high, high, medium, low, and very low. Meanwhile, the inferential analysis uses several tools, namely multivariate analysis and bivariate analysis. In multivariate analysis, multiple linear regression is used. Furthermore in bivariate analysis, simple linear regression analysis is used. Before being analyzed using multiple linear regression, all prerequisite tests consisting of normality, collinearity, heteroskedasticity, and autocorrelation must be met. To analyze the data in this study, *the SPSS for Windows version 22 program* was used.

3 RESULT

Teacher The data from this research are in the form of teacher competence, teacher compensation, and teacher performance data. First, the data were analyzed using descriptive analysis to determine the extent of teacher competence, teacher compensation, and teacher performance at State Islamic Junior High School 2 Probolinggo, East Java, Indonesia using the percentage formula. Second, the data were analyzed using inferential analysis, namely multiple linear regression to determine the significant effect of teacher competence and compensation on teacher performance, either simultaneously or partially.

3.1 *Competence questionnaire results*

The teacher competence questionnaire was given to determine the extent of teacher competence at State Islamic Junior High School 2 Probolinggo, East Java, Indonesia. The results of the questionnaire are shown in Table 1 below.

Table 1.   Teacher competence.

Category	Freq.	Percentage
Very High	1	3%
High	28	94%
Medium	1	3%
Low	0	0%
Very Low	0	0%

Based on the results of the study, it was found that the competence of teachers in the very high category was 1 person (3%), the high was 28 people (94%), and the medium was 1 person (3%). Overall teacher competence at State Islamic Junior High School 2 Probolinggo, East Java, Indonesia is in a good category.

3.2   *Headings teacher compensation questionnaire results*

A teacher compensation questionnaire was given to determine the extent of teacher compensation at State Islamic Junior High School 2 Probolinggo, East Java, Indonesia. The results of the questionnaire are shown in Table 2 below.

Table 2.   Teacher compensation.

Category	Freq.	Percentage
Very High	0	0%
High	6	20%
Medium	24	80%
Low	0	0%
Very Low	0	0%

Based on the results of the study, it was found that the compensation of teachers in the high category was 6 people (20%) and the medium category was 24 people (80%). Overall teacher compensation at State Islamic Junior High School 2 Probolinggo, East Java, Indonesia is in the medium category.

3.3   *Teacher performance questionnaire results*

For listing facts, use either the style tag List summary signs or the style tag List number signs. Teacher performance questionnaires were given to determine the extent of teacher performance at State Islamic Junior High School 2 Probolinggo, East Java, Indonesia. The results of the questionnaire are shown in Table 3 below.

Table 3.   Teacher performance.

Category	Freq.	Percentage
Very High	21	70%
High	9	30%
Medium	0	0%
Low	0	0%
Very Low	0	0%

Based on the results of the performance questionnaire, it was found that the performance of teachers in the very high category was 21 people (70%) and the high category was 9 people

(30%). Overall teacher performance at State Islamic Junior High School 2 Probolinggo, East Java, Indonesia is in the very high category.

3.4 *Prerequisite test*

Before performing multiple linear regression analysis, it is necessary to perform prerequisite tests which include tests for normality, collinearity, heteroscedasticity, and autocorrelation.

3.4.1 *Normality test*
From the results of calculations using SPSS for Windows version 22 in this study, it was found that the data were normally distributed, this can be seen in Figure 1 below.

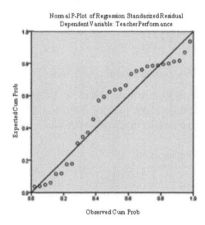

Figure 1. Normality test results of compensation and competence on teacher performance.

Based on Figure 1 above, it can be seen that the normal P-P Plot of regression standardized residual shows that the data spreads around the diagonal line, so it can be concluded that the data is normally distributed. Given such results, the assumption of the normality statement in this regression has been fulfilled.

3.4.2 *Collinearity test*
Based on the results of calculations using SPSS for Windows version 22, the VIF value and Tolerance value are obtained as shown in Table 4 below.

Table 4. Collinearity test results.

Model	Collinearity Statistics	
	Tolerance	VIF
Competence (X1)	,893	1,120
Compensation (X2)	,893	1,120

Table 4 shows that the VIF value for all variables is less than 2, so it can be said that there is no collinearity in this regression or there is no collinearity disorder in this study.

3.4.3 *Heteroscedasticity test*
Based on the results of calculations with the help of SPSS for Windows version 22 Scatterplot independent variables on teacher performance which can be seen in the image below.

160

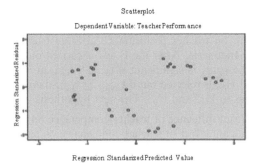

Figure 2.   Heteroscedasticity test results.

Based on Figure 2 above, it shows that there is no clear pattern in the scatterplot, and the points spread above and below the number 0 on the Y axis, so it can be said that there is no heteroscedasticity in this study.

3.4.4   *Autocorrelation test*
Based on the results of calculations with the help of SPSS for Windows version 22, the number D-W = 2,351 which can be seen in Table 5 below.

Table 5.   Autocorrelation test results.

Model	R	R Square	Adjusted R Square	Std. Error of the Estimate	Durbin-Walson
1	0.569	0.324	0.274	21.75429	2.351

Table 5 shows that the number DW = 2.351, then the number lies between 1.56 to 2.43, it can be concluded that there is no autocorrelation or problem in this study. So multiple linear regression analysis to test the hypothesis of this study can be done.

3.5   *Hypothesis test*

Before performing multiple linear regression analysis, prerequisite tests were carried out which included tests of normality, collinearity, heteroscedasticity, and autocorrelation, and the results of the data met the four conditions.

3.5.1   *The effect of simultaneous competence and compensation on teacher performance*
After the prerequisite test is done, the next step is to test the hypothesis, the conclusion of the study is significant if $F_{count} > F_{table}$ then H_a1 is accepted and H_01 is rejected but if $F_{count} \leq F_{table}$ then H_a1 is rejected and H_01 is accepted. The first hypothesis in this study is as follows.

H_a1: There is a significant effect of competence and compensation simultaneously on teacher performance.

H_01: There is no significant effect of competence and compensation simultaneously on teacher performance.

Based on Table 6, it can be seen that F_{count} = 6.478 is greater than F_{table} = 3.340 at the real level = 0.05 or the value of Sig. F = 0.000 which is smaller than the 0.05 significance level, then H_a1 is accepted and H_01 is rejected. In brief, there is a significant effect of competence and compensation simultaneously on teacher performance at State Islamic Junior High School 2 Probolinggo, Indonesia.

3.5.2 The effect of partial competence and compensation on teacher performance

Multiple linear regression analysis can also be used to determine the effect of competence and partial compensation on teacher performance at State Islamic Junior High School 2 Probolinggo, East Java, Indonesia. After the F test is carried out, then the t-test is carried out, the conclusion of the study is significant if $t_{count} > t_{table}$ at a significance level of 0.05 then H_a2 is accepted and H_02 is rejected but if $t_{count} \leq t_{table}$ then H_a2 is rejected and H_02 is accepted, this also applies to H_a3 and H_03. The next hypothesis in this study is as follows.

H_a2: There is a significant influence of teacher competence on teacher performance.
H_02: There is no significant effect of teacher competence on teacher performance.
H_a3: There is a significant effect of teacher compensation on teacher performance.
H_03: There is no significant effect of teacher compensation on teacher performance.

The recapitulation of the results of the first multiple linear regression, the effect of competence and compensation on teacher performance can be seen in Table 6 below.

Table 6. Recapitulation of the first multiple linear regression analysis.

Independent Variables	Dependent Variable	Coefficient Regression b	t count	t table	Sig.	Decision (H_a2)
Competence	Performance	0.923	3.578	2.052	0.001	H_a2 accepted
Compensation	Performance	0.656	0.802	2.052	0.430	H_a3 rejected
Constant	= 4.240					
F count	= 6.478					
F table	= 3.340					
Sig F	= 0.000					
R Square	= 0.324					
α	= 0.05					

Based on Table 6 above, there is one variable that has a significant effect, namely the teacher competence variable, while another variable, namely teacher compensation, has no significant effect on teacher performance at State Islamic Junior High School 2 Probolinggo, East Java, Indonesia. Because there is one variable that is not significant, it means that the estimation of the Y variable with multiple linear regression equations:

$$Y = a + b_1X_1 + b_2X_2.$$

It cannot be done or the contribution of each variable cannot be determined. Therefore, the insignificant variables were excluded. After being calculated with the help of SPSS for Windows version 22, the results of the second multiple linear regression are obtained as shown in Table 7 below.

Table 7. Recapitulation of the second multiple linear regression results.

Independent Variables	Dependent Variable	Coefficient Regression b	t count	t table	r^2
Competence	Performance	0.855	3.532	2.052	0.308
Constant	= 8.843				
F count	= 12.4721				
F table	= 3.340				
Sig F	= 0.000				
R Square	= 0.308				
α	= 0.05				

Based on Table 7 above, the estimation results of the influence of the competence variable can be stated as follows.

$$Y = 8.843 + 0.855\,X_1$$

162

The regression coefficient for the competence variable (X_1) is 0.855. This can be interpreted that if the independent variable X_1 changes by one unit, the variable Y will change by 0.855 units with the assumption that the other independent variables are constant, meaning that if the input of teacher competence is added by one value, it will increase teacher performance by 85.5%. The coefficient of partial determination (r^2) of the X_1 variable is 0,308 or 30.8%, which means that the contribution of the X_1 variable to the ups and downs of the Y variable is 30.8% where the other independent variables are constant. The coefficient of determination of teacher competence is 0.308, which means that the contribution of competence to the rise and fall of the Y variable is 30.8%. In other words, it can be explained that 30.8% of the variation in teacher performance at State Islamic Junior High School 2 Probolinggo can be predicted by teacher competence, while 60.2% is influenced by other variables not examined in this study.

4 DISCUSSION

Based on the results of data analysis show that competence and compensation simultaneously affect the performance of teachers at State Islamic Junior High School 2 Probolinggo, East Java, Indonesia and based on the results of research the performance of teachers is classified in the very high category. This is in line with the results of previous studies which show that the competence and compensation variables simultaneously have a significant effect on lecturer performance (Bahtiar and Sudaryana 2020).

Furthermore, the addition of other variables also shows the same results, such as motivation, competence, and compensation having a significant effect simultaneously on employee performance; competence, training, and compensation simultaneously have a positive and significant effect on the performance variable, and transformational leadership; competence, compensation, and work motivation have a positive, significant, and simultaneous effect on lecturer performance (Hartati 2020; Manurung 2020; Novitasari et al. 2021).

The results of this study also show that competence has a significant partial effect on teacher performance at State Islamic Junior High School 2 Probolinggo, East Java, Indonesia, while one other variable, namely compensation, has no significant effect. These findings are in line with previous studies that explain that competence partially has a significant effect on teacher performance (Novitasari et al. 2021). Competencies that have a more dominant effect on teacher performance are compared to non-financial compensation variables and organizational commitment variables (Purba et al. 2018). These findings are in line with previous studies which explain that competence partially has a significant effect on teacher performance (Yurosma et al. 2021). This can happen because competence is a basic ability that must be possessed by a teacher. Teacher performance also depends on their competence (Millman and Darling-Hammond 1990; House 2013).

As for compensation, although in this study partially it does not have a significant effect on teacher performance at State Islamic Junior High School 2 Probolinggo, East Java, Indonesia, compensation still needs to be considered. According to Sherly et al. (2021), if the compensation received by the teacher is high, the teacher will feel more satisfied. The study shows that a rewarding and productive teacher compensation system can serve to attract well-qualified and highly motivated people to the teaching profession (See et al. 2020). However, other studies show a different analysis. According to Muazza (2021), the reason the compensation received by the teacher does not affect their performance is that compensation does not reflect performance. It is almost definite that compensation will affect teacher performance if the compensation payment system is determined based on work performance.

Although this research has succeeded in showing the facts of how competence and compensation affect teacher performance. However, the writer also realizes that this research has some limitations. This research is limited to only two independent variables, namely competence and compensation. While the dependent variable uses only one variable, namely teacher performance. The results of previous studies show that teacher performance can also be influenced by other factors such as the principal's leadership, organizational culture, work environment, and emotional intelligence (Kanya *et al.* 2021; Mahaputra and Farhan Saputra 2021; Wahyudi 2018).

5 CONCLUSION

Based on the formulation of the problems and hypotheses proposed as well as the results of research based on data analysis and hypothesis testing, it can be concluded that competence and compensation have a simultaneous effect on teacher performance at State Islamic Junior High School 2 Probolinggo, Indonesia. However, the only variable that affects teacher performance is competence. The contribution of competence to the rise and fall of the teacher performance variable is 30.8%. In other words, it can be explained that 30.8% of the variation in teacher performance scores at State Islamic Junior High School 2 Probolinggo, East Java, Indonesia can be predicted by the competence variable, while 60.2% is influenced by other variables not examined in this study.

Through this research, it is known that many factors influence teacher performance. If the teacher's performance is good, it will certainly have an impact on the quality of education. Therefore, prospective teachers must have good competence. Furthermore, the government and educational institutions should pay more attention to teacher compensation.

This research is limited to two independent variables and one dependent variable. It is therefore suggested that future research add independent variables so that other factors that may affect student satisfaction can be identified. In addition, future research can replace the dependent variable other than teacher performance, for example, student learning outcomes because good teacher competence is certainly very related to the quality of education that can be seen from student learning outcomes. Through this study, the author provides recommendations in various education sectors to pay more attention to teacher welfare and provide various pieces of training to improve teacher competence. In addition, teachers as educators are also recommended to take part in various workshops to improve teacher competence, innovate learning, conduct research collaborations, and be active in various activities such as teacher working groups and teacher communities to improve teacher competence and quality.

REFERENCES

Andriani, S., Kesumawati, N. and Kristiawan, M. (2018) "The influence of the transformational leadership and work motivation on teachers performance," *International Journal of Scientific and Technology Research*, 7(7), pp. 19–29.

Bahtiar and Sudaryana, B. (2020) "The effect of competence, and compensation towards the performance of lecturers Nahdlatul University Cirebon," *Indonesian Journal of Social Research (IJSR)*, 2(1), pp. 1–8. Available at: https://doi.org/10.30997/ijsr.v2i1.18.

Farida, I., Tippe, S. and Tunas, B. (2020) "The effect of competence and motivation on teacher performance in development technology vocational school Bekasi West Java," *Asia Pacific Journal of Management and Education*, 3(1), pp. 12–15. Available at: https://doi.org/10.32535/apjme.v3i1.739.

Gary, D. (2019) *Human resource management*. Pearson Publisher.

Habibi, B. *et al.* (2018) "The influence of compensation, academic supervision, pedagogic competency, and work motivation on the performance of Business and Management Teachers of Vocational Schools," *The Journal of Educational Development*, 6(1), pp. 16–24.

Hakim, A. (2015) "Contribution of competence teacher (pedagogical, personality, professional competence and social) on the performance of learning," *The International Journal Of Engineering And Science*, 4(2), pp. 1–12. Available at: http://www.theijes.com/papers/v4-i2/Version-3/A42301012.pdf.

Hasibuan, M. (2017) *Manajemen Sumber Daya Manusia*. Jakarta: Bumi Aksara.

House, E.R. (2013) *New directions in educational evaluation*. Abingdon: Routledge.

Jan, H. (2017) "Teacher of 21 st century: Characteristics and development," *Research on Humanities and Social Sciences*, 7(9), pp. 2225–0484.

Johar, Akbar, M. and Karnati, N. (2019) "Self-efficacy, job design, and work motivation on work effectiviness of lecturer at Institut Transportation and Logistics Trisakti Jakarta," in I.S. Wekke *et al.* (eds.) *International Conference on Environmental Awareness for Sustainable Development in Conjunction with International Conference on Challenge and Opportunities Sustainable Environmental Development.* Kendari: European Alliance for Innovation, pp. 442–450. Available at: https://doi.org/10.4108/eai.1-4-2019.2287250.

Jones, J., Jenkin, M. and Lord, S. (2006) *Developing effective teacher performance.* London: SAGE Publications.

Kanya, N., Fathoni, A.B. and Ramdani, Z. (2021) "Factors affecting teacher performance," *International Journal of Evaluation and Research in Education (IJERE)*, 10(4), p. 1462. Available at: https://doi.org/10.11591/ijere.v10i4.21693.

Lenz, C. *et al.* (2022) *Reference Framework of Competences for Democratic Culture: Teacher Reflection Tool.* Strasbourg: Council of Europe.

Mahaputra, M.R. and Farhan Saputra (2021) "Literature review the effect of headmaster leadership on teacher performance, loyalty and motivation," *Journal of Accounting and Finance Management*, 2(2), pp. 103–113. Available at: https://doi.org/10.38035/jafm.v2i2.77.

Manurung, E.F. (2020) "The effects of transformational leadership, competence and compensation on work motivation and implications on the performance of lecturers of Maritime College in DKI Jakarta," *International Journal of Multicultural and Multireligious Understanding*, 7(6), p. 112. Available at: https://doi.org/10.18415/ijmmu.v7i6.1741.

Matriadi, F. *et al.* (2019) "The influences of compensation and supply chain managemnet towards educatioan system: The mediating role of job motivation," *International Journal of Supply Chain Management*, 8(3), pp. 183–191.

Millman, J. and Darling-Hammond, L. (1990) *The New Handbook of Teacher Evaluation: Assessing Elementary and Secondary School Teachers* 1st Edition. Newbury Park, California: SAGE Publications.

Muazza (2021) "In search of quality human resources in education: professional competency, compensation, working climate, and motivation toward vocational teachers' performance," *Indonesian Research Journal in Education |IRJE|*, 5(1), pp. 175–191. Available at: https://doi.org/10.22437/irje.v5i1.12497.

Novitasari, D. *et al.* (2021) "Teacher performance determinants: competence, motivation, compensation and work environment Turkish journal of computer and mathematics education research article," *Turkish Journal of Computer and Mathematics Education*, 12(12), pp. 2954–2963.

Pineda-Alfonso *et al.* (2018) *Handbook of Research on Education for Participative Citizenship and Global Prosperity.* IGI Global Publisher.

Purba, C.B., Rafiani and Ali, H. (2018) "The influence of competency, organizational commitment and non financial compensation on teacher performance in SMAN 29 Jakarta," *Scholars Journal of Economics, Business and Management (SJEBM)*, 5(3), pp. 227–239. Available at: https://doi.org/10.21276/sjebm.2018.5.3.13.

Rahmatullah, M. (2016) "The relationship between learning effectiveness, teacher competence and teachers performance Madrasah Tsanawiyah at Serang, Banten, Indonesia," *Higher Education Studies*, 6(1), p. 169. Available at: https://doi.org/10.5539/hes.v6n1p169.

Selasih, N.N. (2019) "The knowledge of classroom management as a basis in improving Hindu religious teacher's performance," in K. Saddhono *et al.* (eds.) *SEWORD FRESSH 2019: Proceedings of the 1st Seminar and Workshop on Research Design, for Education, Social Science, Art, and Humanities.* Surakarta: Research Meets Inovation, pp. 318–325. Available at: https://doi.org/10.4108/eai.27-4-2019.2286882.

Sherly, S. *et al.* (2021) "Interpretation of the effects of job satisfaction mediation on the effect of principal supervision and compensation on teacher performance," *Journal of Educational Science and Technology (EST)*, 7(1), pp. 105–116. Available at: https://doi.org/10.26858/est.v7i1.19208.

Sofi'i, I., Mukhoyyaroh and Yunus (2022) *Kepemimpinan Kepala Sekolah dalam Meningkatkan Kinerja Guru.* Indaramayu: Penerbit Adab.

Vance, C.M. and Paik, Y. (2015) *Managing a Global Workforce: Challenges and Opportunities in Intenational Human Resource Management.* Third Edit. New York: Routledge.

Wahyudi, W. (2018) "The influence of emotional intelligence, competence and work environment on teacher performance of SMP Kemala Bhayangkari Jakarta," *Scientific Journal of Reflection: Economic, Accounting, Management and Business*, 1(2), pp. 211–220. Available at: https://doi.org/10.37481/sjr.v1i2.139.

Witari, I.A.K.Y.B. and Manuaba, I.B.S. (2021) "Correlation between pedagogical competence and personality to teacher performance," *Proceedings of the 2nd International Conference on Technology and Educational Science (ICTES 2020)*, 540(Ictes 2020), pp. 405–412. Available at: https://doi.org/10.2991/assehr.k.210407.272.

Yurosma, Lian, B. and Eddy, S. (2021) "The effect of competence and certification on teacher performance," *Proceedings of the International Conference on Education Universitas PGRI Palembang (INCoEPP 2021)*, 565(INCoEPP), pp. 244–249. Available at: https://doi.org/10.2991/assehr.k.210716.044.

Zahroh, A. *et al.* (2021) "Human resources on increasing teacher performance in Islamic Education Institution," *Journal of Instructional and Development Researches*, 1(2), pp. 48–59. Available at: https://doi.org/10.53621/jider.v1i2.62.

Strengthening Professional and Spiritual Education through 21st Century Skill Empowerment in Pandemic and Post-Pandemic Era – Arifin et al. (Eds)
© 2024 The Author(s), ISBN: 978-1-032-45243-2

Muhammadiyah's educational philosophy and contextualization of Islamic moderation: Challenges to religious extremism

Nafik Muthohirin* & S. Suherman
Universitas Muhammadiyah Malang, Indonesia

ABSTRACT: Part of the Muslim community in Indonesia understands the Muhammadiyah's movement of purification paradoxically. They regard this ideology as a foundation of thought that is anti-reform. This puritanical style of Islam is seen as the cause of a number of Muhammadiyah members being exposed to the ideology of terrorism in the last two decades. This study explains that this assessment is very baseless, because it ignores the characteristics of Muhammadiyah as a reform movement (*tajdid*). This article examines the basis of Muhammadiyah's Islamic moderation through the educational principles taught by *Kiai* Ahmad Dahlan contained in his speech and official Muhammadiyah documents. In detail, this paper focuses on two important research objects, namely studying the Muhammadiyah's educational philosophy and contextualizing the principles of Islamic moderation, as well as making it a foundation for resilience from the ideology of religious-based violent extremism. Thus, this article concludes that even though Muhammadiyah adheres to purification of Islam, Muhammadiyah has strengthened its movement ideology and religious thought through the renewal of the Islamic education movement which promotes rational, modern and scientific thinking.

Keywords: Islamic Education, Muhammadiyah, Religious Extremism, Islamic Moderation

1   INTRODUCTION

Muhammadiyah's educational philosophy contains the teachings of Islamic moderation which are epistemologically based on three important documents, namely: First, the speech of Kiai Haji Ahmad Dahlan entitled "The Unity of Human Life" which was published by the Taman Pustaka Assembly of Muhammadiyah with the title "Tali Binding Life (1923)"; Second, Praeadvies HB Muhammadiyah at the Cirebon Great Islamic Congress (1921); Third, the Decree of the 46th Muktamar Muhammadiyah in Yogyakarta (2010) concerning the Revitalization of Muhammadiyah Education (Mulkhan and Abrar 2019).

These three documents contain Muhammadiyah teachings that encourage its citizens to be inclusive, prioritize rationality and knowledge, master technology, and care about education and the economy of the poor. These three documents became the basis for the development of educational philosophy and the foundation for Muhammadiyah's religious moderation from the threat of religious radicalism.

Islamic education (*tarbiyyah*) has been one of Muhammadiyah's areas of work since its establishment in 1912. As an Islamic organization committed to the mission of enlightenment, Muhammadiyah's philosophy of Islamic education is based on Islamic teachings by focusing on moral development, developing one's intellectual, spiritual, and social attitudes. Islamic education is considered as a means to develop individual potential so that they can become individuals who are able to contribute positively to society. Therefore, the aim of Muhammadiyah education is to make someone a perfect human being, namely someone

---

*Corresponding Author: nafikmuthohirin@umm.ac.id

DOI: 10.1201/9781003376125-22

who achieves perfection in all aspects of life. Education is expected to foster religious, scientific, personality and good skills, so that a person can live a prosperous and happy life in this world and the hereafter. In practice, Muhammadiyah Islamic education emphasizes the development of aqidah, morals, knowledge, skills and entrepreneurial spirit. Education is also expected to foster an attitude of tolerance, cooperation, creativity, criticality and independence as well as providing a correct understanding of Islam.

The concept of Islamic education which prioritizes knowledge, rationality and openness becomes the three philosophical foundations for Muhammadiyah. It explains to the public that the Islamic organization which is more than a century old contains moderate Islamic values. In one of Kiai Dahlan's speeches it was stated that Muhammadiyah education should be encouraged to produce progressive *kiai* (Arifin 1985; Rosyidi 1975). Kiai Dahlan's statement through a number of texts of his speech is contradictory to the emergence of various intolerant groups who are anti-science and are closed to new views. This also confirms that Muhammadiyah has no relationship at all with religious fundamentalist groups, either those who aspire to establish an Islamic state through political Islam or those who act by means of violence and terrorism (Muthohirin 2014; Tibi 1998).

2 METHODS

This research was deliberately made to complement the studies on Muhammadiyah educational philosophy which are still very few. The results of this research are expected to contribute to the progress of Muhammadiyah in the field of Islamic education. On the other hand, the author sees that there is a positive potential that through the philosophy of Islamic education which originates from these various documents, Muhammadiyah can elaborate it into a basis for religious moderation from the threat of extremist movements and ideologies.

The design of this study uses a form of qualitative research. Various data sourced from the statements or speeches of *Kiai* Dahlan and a number of important Muhammadiyah documents were analyzed and elaborated by the author to become conceptual formulations capable of contributing as counter-narratives to various dissemination of ideas of religious extremism which is a challenge for Muslims.

According to Bungin, qualitative research aims to understand the social phenomena being studied by utilizing one important keyword, namely how a researcher understands an object of research, so that its nature is in process (Bungin 2003). In relation to this research, a qualitative approach is useful for exploring and understanding the literature that contains the formulation of Muhammadiyah's educational philosophy. In addition, this qualitative research is used to understand a number of empirical facts regarding the occurrence of various acts of religious extremism.

3 RESULTS AND DISCUSSION

This study discusses the educational philosophy of Muhammadiyah which has not been widely practiced. In particular, there are only two main works written by the Higher Education Research and Development Council Team of the Muhammadiyah Central Executive (Mulkhan and Abrar 2019). The first book is the only scientific book that specifically collects evidence of the philosophical foundations of Islamic education in Muhammadiyah which are based on Muhammadiyah's important documents. The book shows the philosophical basis of Muhammadiyah education which emphasizes rationality, science, and divinity. Meanwhile, the second book explains the ethical and philosophical basis of Muhammadiyah education. Through this book, the Muhammadiyah Higher Education Council team succeeded in exploring the philosophical values of Islamic education in Muhammadiyah by presenting various academic arguments based on the philosophical thoughts of medieval Muslim philosophers.

Other works that are also relevant to this research are Mu'ti and Khoirudin's books (Mu'ti and Khoirudin 2019). This book also bases its study on a number of important documents which form the basis of Muhammadiyah's educational philosophy for studying religious plurality and the importance of multicultural Islamic education in Indonesia. According to Mu'ti and Khoirudin, Muhammadiyah is a socio-religious organization that plays an important role in accommodating religious diversity through education. In essence, the book focuses on the implementation of a pluralist Muhammadiyah education.

Mu'ti and Khoirudin's work is considered the closest to this research topic because it makes Muhammadiyah's educational philosophy the basis for multicultural educational values as actualized in various Muhammadiyah educational institutions. However, none of these writers specifically contextualize it in the development of an attitude of religious moderation, especially in dealing with religious extremism movements and thoughts which are problematic challenges for contemporary Muslims.

Ideally, the study of Muhammadiyah educational philosophy (Islam) contains three important aspects which include the foundations of epistemology, ontology and axiology. The basis of epistemology discusses the sources or foundations of knowledge, which in this case is simplified into a question of where the educational philosophy of Muhammadiyah is formulated. Then, on the basis of ontology, this research seeks to explore the nature, objectives, processes, curriculum, management, leadership and all matters relating to Islamic education (Muhammadiyah). In the aspect of ontology, it is also discussed about human nature as a creature of Allah SWT, which naturally is the subject as well as the object of education. While the axiological basis of the philosophy of Islamic education contains the values or benefits of Islamic education. So basically the educational philosophy of Muhammadiyah examines all questions that have relevance to the education that applies in Muhammadiyah. However, this article will only contain the contextualization of Muhammadiyah's educational philosophy and its contextualization of the development of an attitude of Islamic moderation against the threat of religious extremism.

Muhammadiyah has the characteristics of a movement as a socio-religious organization that is oriented towards Progressive Islam. The Progressive Islamic variant is in accordance with the meaning of Islam itself which means rising or progressing. Thus, Progressive Islam according to Muhammadiyah is various efforts to "raise degrees and advance human life, and fight backwardness, poverty, ignorance, and moral decline" (Mughni *et al.* 2022).

One of the forms of implementing the idea of Progressive Islam voiced by Muhammadiyah in the last decade is regarding the urgency of developing an attitude of Islamic moderation. An understanding of the concept and practice of Islamic moderation is very important, especially when society is facing global challenges related to acts of religious extremism (Muthohirin 2015; Wahyudi and Pradhan 2021). Islamic moderation is rooted in the verses of the Koran which mention the existence of ummatan wasathan which means the best of the people (al-Baqarah: 143), and the best role model for the people is Muhammad (al-Imran: 100).

Yusuf Qaradawi, a well-known Islamic scholar and activist with moderate Islamic thoughts, explained that Islamic moderation is a balance between sharia principles and the social and cultural conditions of society. He stressed that Islamic teachings must be applied in a way that is appropriate to the times and social context, and not in a dogmatic and inflexible way. Qardahawi also emphasized that Islamic moderation must be applied in all aspects of life, including politics, economics and social (Qaradhawi 2008, 2009). In interpreting the word "jihad", according to him, it does not always mean war. Jihad can also be interpreted as a struggle to uphold truth and justice. In certain situations, peace can be considered as a form of jihad. In carrying out Islamic teachings, attention must be paid to the context and social situation of today's society. In his book "Fiqh al-Jihad", he explains that social change and scientific developments must be recognized and taken into account in interpreting Islamic teachings (Qaradhawi, tt). Overall, Qaradawi's moderate Islamic view emphasizes the importance of a balanced and comprehensive understanding of Islamic teachings, as well as the need for adaptation to changing times and social contexts.

Meanwhile, Muhammadiyah believes that Islamic moderation is the best people and not exaggerating in religion (*ghuluw*). In the life of modern society, Islam Wasathiyyah must be contextual with democracy, human rights, and modernism. According to Haedar Nashir, Islam Wasathiyyah means choosing a position in the middle of various extremities by upholding the concept of Islamic justice (Nashir 2020). Muhammadiyah understands that Islamic moderation consists of three dimensions, namely doing good (*khair*), not being extreme and not exaggerating, behaving in accordance with applicable science and law, and being fair (Mu'ti 2021).

Moderate as one of Muhammadiyah's eight main values has equivalent words in Arabic, namely *tawasuth*, *i'tidal*, *tawazun* and *iqtisad* which mean in harmony with the concept of justice. Haedar Nashir said that moderate means the opposite of *tatarruf* or *ghuluw* which means towards the periphery, extreme, radical and excessive. Moderate also means the best choice (Nashir 2021). In the *Second Century Statement of Muhammadiyah Thoughts* (Pernyataan Pikiran Muhammadiyah Abad Kedua) it is stated that Muhammadiyah is committed to developing progressive Islamic views and missions as this organization has striven for since its establishment in 1912. As a consequence, Muhammadiyah always pays attention to humanitarian issues at the national and global levels, including the threat of terrorism (PP Muhammadiyah 2010).

In the religious context, Islamic moderation means that Muslims must live in balance. Not excessive and not lacking in carrying out religious orders. Muslims must also find the right balance between faith and good deeds, between worshiping Allah and providing for the needs of the world, and between respecting the rights of others and fighting for personal rights. In addition, Islamic moderation also emphasizes the importance of equality and justice in everyday life. In essence, the main principle of Islamic moderation is to treat all people fairly regardless of their religious, cultural, linguistic or ethnic background. A Muslim must fight for the rights of others, especially the rights of the weak, such as children, women and the elderly.

Islamic moderation is a very important concept in Islam because it shows that this religion not only teaches not to be extreme in everyday life, but rather guides its followers towards a balanced and simple life. In other words, Islamic moderation teaches that Muslims must maintain balance in all aspects of life, both in religious, social and economic matters. In addition, Islamic moderation also teaches that every Muslim must understand and respect the differences that exist in society. Peaceful community life is an entity that consists of various backgrounds, beliefs, and outlooks on life. Therefore, Islamic moderation teaches not only to fight for personal or certain group interests, but also to fight for the interests of society as a whole. However, although the concept of Islamic moderation is very valuable for Muslims, there are several challenges that must be faced in applying this concept, such as facing pressure from groups that teach religious extremism.

Indonesia is in fifth position as a country in Southeast Asia that is most affected by various acts of terrorism (Liang *et al.* 2022). Suicide bombings at three churches in Surabaya (2018) were called the worst terrorist attacks in the last decade. The act of extremism in the name of religion was carried out by a family who recently returned from Syria, is affiliated with the Islamic State of Iraq and Syria (ISIS), and is involved in the Jamaah Ansharut Daulah (JAD) and Jamaah Ansharut Tauhid (JAT) networks (Yuliawati 2018). The suicide bombing also destroyed the cathedral church in Makassar (2021). In addition to successfully transforming its attack strategy through technological sophistication, suicide bombing and lone wolf work (Muthohirin 2021), terrorist groups also recruit and radicalize young minds with extremist understandings through social media (Muthohirin 2015; Bamualim *et al.* 2018; Huda *et al.* 2021).

After 9/11, Islamic extremism has become one of the serious problems faced by the world community in contemporary times (PEW 2021). Extremism is defined as an ideological belief that wants to place religious doctrines into the political system through violent means (Arena and Arrigo 2005). Extremism is also often interpreted as a terrorist movement against the state, such as ISIS in Syria and the Moro Islamic Liberation Front (MILF) in the Philippines. The emergence of various acts of religious extremism is driven by a number of factors, including responses to injustice, oppression, and even misinterpretation of religious doctrines (Tibi 1998; Wibisono *et al.* 2019). The Institute of Economic and Peace in its latest research report entitled *Global Terrorism Index 2022*, notes that terrorism attacks at the world level increased by 5,226 attacks in 2021. Although the resulting death rate decreased to 7,142 people (down 1.1% from the previous year), Extremist groups continue to use advanced technology to carry out precision attacks, including using drones, GPS systems in mobile phones, and encrypted messaging services (Liang *et al.* 2022).

The ideology of Muhammadiyah is very far from these extreme religious-based movements. Muhammadiyah does not teach and does not condone acts of violence, intolerance, ideology of terrorism and disbelief. If a particular case mentions that a terrorist has attended a Muhammadiyah educational institution (Jateng.inews.id 2018), it cannot be the basis for calling Muhammadiyah an organization that teaches the doctrine of terrorism/Wahabism. The minor view that Muhammadiyah contains the doctrine of radicalism for the reason of adopting religious purification is nothing but a misguided thought because it ignores aspects of renewal (tajdid) and the rationality of thought which has been the ideology of Muhammadiyah (Boy ZTF 2016; Bachtiar 2020).

In terms of movement ideology, Muhammadiyah and Wahhabism are similar but not the same (Luth 2013). Both of them refer to the al-Qur'an and al-Hadith, but in the practice of purification of religion, both have different attitudes. Muhammadiyah and Wahhabism use different Islamic propagation methods due to differences in local culture. Arab Muslims are synonymous with tribal fanaticism (tribalism), while in Indonesia they are accommodative to local traditions. Muhammadiyah founder Kiai Ahmad Dahlan never banned cultural activities. In fact, he is very accepting of local Javanese traditions and culture. Ahmad Najib Burhani disclosed several things that indicated Muhammadiyah was open to local culture and traditions. According to him, in the early periods of Muhammadiyah's establishment, Friday sermons at Muhammadiyah mosques were carried out in Javanese. At every major event Muhammadiyah leaders always wore Javanese priyayi batik at that era (Burhani 2016).

In facing ideological infiltration and religious extremism movements, Muhammadiyah continues to move to encourage people to put forward a moderate attitude. This moderate attitude can be fostered through the implementation of Muhammadiyah Islamic educational philosophy which has been practiced so far in various Muhammadiyah schools or colleges. Some of Muhammadiyah's Islamic educational philosophies include: *First*, Muhammadiyah follows a comprehensive education model, which means teaching religious education, academic education, skills education, character education, and general education to students; *Second*, Muhammadiyah schools are always oriented towards building the character of students. Muhammadiyah considers that education is an effective tool in shaping one's character, so that graduates of Muhammadiyah schools are expected to have good character and noble character; *Third*, Islamic educational institutions in Muhammadiyah strive to form independent individuals who can think critically and make their own decisions and can contribute positively to society; *Fourth*, Muhammadiyah's philosophy of Islamic education always prioritizes rationality, inclusiveness and knowledge. Muhammadiyah considers that science-based education is the basis for understanding and practicing Islamic teachings, so Muhammadiyah schools provide quality and science-oriented education.

4 CONCLUSION

Overall, Islamic moderation is a very important concept in Islam because it teaches its followers to be fair, equal and balanced in all aspects of life. By practicing Islamic moderation, Muslims will become a balanced and civilized society. Every individual Muslim will become a community that respects the rights of others and fights for their own rights. By applying the principles of Islamic moderation, it is hoped that it can become a pioneer for the realization of a society that is baldatun tayyibatun wa rabbun ghafur. However, this moderate attitude will not grow if it is not taught through a well-organized educational model.

In this case, the good practice of Muhammadiyah Islamic education can be a medium for the dissemination of understanding of the principles of Islamic moderation. Apart from the number of Muhammadiyah educational institutions which number in the thousands from early childhood to university levels, it is also because of Muhammadiyah's Islamic educational philosophy which contains moderate Islamic doctrines. Since initiating the establishment of Muhammadiyah schools, Kiai Dahlan has wanted Muhammadiyah educational institutions to be managed inclusively, both in terms of thought (integrating religious knowledge with general knowledge) and movement (in collaboration with other religious groups).

Muhammadiyah's educational philosophy focuses on holistic individual development, which includes intellectual, spiritual, social, and physical aspects. Muhammadiyah education also emphasizes the development of noble character and morals adhered to by Islam as the basis for forming people who believe and fear Allah SWT. In addition, Muhammadiyah's philosophy of Islamic education emphasizes the formation of individuals who are independent and creative, and able to adapt to the times and technology. This education also focuses on scientific aspects such as science, technology, arts, and sports.

Muhammadiyah Islamic Education also pays attention to the formation of people who love the motherland and are virtuous, and are able to contribute to the development of society and the state. Muhammadiyah's educational philosophy basically seeks to produce human beings who are prosperous, have strong personalities, and are beneficial to their environment.

REFERENCES

Arena, M.P. and Arrigo, B.A. (2005) "Social psychology, terrorism, and identity: A preliminary re-examination of theory, culture, self, and society," *Behavioral Sciences & the Law*, 23(4), pp. 485–506. Available at: https://doi.org/10.1002/bsl.653.

Arifin, M. (1985) *Gerakan Pembaruan Muhammadiyah Dalam Bidang Pendidikan: Reformasi Gagasan Dan Teknik*. Surakarta: Bagian Penalaran, Lembaga Pembinaan Mahasiswa UMS.

Bachtiar, H. (2020) "Dār al-'Ahd wa al-Shahādah: Muhammadiyah's position and thoughts on negara Pancasila," *Studia Islamika*, 27(3). Available at: https://doi.org/10.36712/sdi.v27i3.11325.

Bamualim, C.S., Latief, H. and Abubakar, I. (2018) *Kaum Muda Muslim Milenial: Konservatisme, Hibridasi Identitas dan Tantangan Radikalisme*. Jakarta: Center for The Study of Religion and Culture (CSRC) UIN Syarif Hidayatullah Jakarta.

Boy ZTF, P. (2016) "Membela Islam murni," *Suara Muhammadiyah*.

Bungin, B. (2003) *Analisis Data Penelitian Kualitatif*. Jakarta: PT. Raja Grafindo Persada.

Burhani, A.N. (2016) "Muhammadiyah Jawa," *Suara Muhammadiyah*.

Huda, A.Z., Runturambi, A.J.S. and Syauqillah, M. (2021) "Social media as an incubator of youth terrorism in indonesia: Hybrid threat and warfare," *Jurnal Indo-Islamika*, 11(1), pp. 21–40. Available at: https://doi.org/10.15408/jii.v11i1.20362.

Jateng.inews.id (2018) *Kecam terorisme, Muhammadiyah tegaskan Dita bukanlagi kader IPM*. Available at: https://jateng.inews.id/berita/kecam-terorisme-muhammadiyah-tegaskan-dita-bukan-lagi-kader-ipm.

Liang, C.S., Velasquez, C.A. and Kfir, I. (2022) *Global Terrorism Index 2022*. Sydney.

Luth, T. (2013). "Wahhabi menyelamatkan, Muhammadiyah tertuduh," *Suara Muhammadiyah*.

Mu'ti, A. (2021) *Moderasi Beragama dalam perspektif Muhammadiyah*. Available at: https://muhammadiyah. or.id/moderasi-beragama-dalam-perspektif-muhammadiyah/.

Mu'ti, A. and Khoirudin, A. (2019) *Pluralisme positif: Konsep dan implementasi dalam pendidikan Muhammadiyah*. Jakarta: Majelis Pustaka dan Informasi Pimpinan Pusat Muhammadiyah.

Mughni, A.S., Boy, P. and Muthohirin, N. (2022) *Risalah Islam berkemajuan: Memajukan Indonesia mencerahkan semesta*. Jakarta: Pimpinan Pusat Muhammadiyah.

Mulkhan, A.M. and Abrar, R.H. (2019) "Jejak-jejak filsafat pendidikan Muhammadiyah: Membangun basis etis filosofis bagi Muhammadiya," *Suara Muhammadiyah*.

Muthohirin, N. (2014) *Fundamentalisme Islam: Gerakan dan tipologi pemikiran aktivis dakwah kampus*. Jakarta: IndoStrategi.

Muthohirin, N. (2015) "Radikalisme Islam dan pergerakannya di media sosial," *Afkaruna*, 11(2), pp. 240–259. Available at: https://doi.org/10.18196/aiijis.2015.0050.240-259.

Muthohirin, N. (2021) "Lone wolf dan transformasi strategi teror," *Koran SINDO*. Available at: https:// nasional.sindonews.com/read/391152/18/lone-wolf-dan-transformasi-strategi-teror-1617887056.

Nashir, H. (2020) *Moderasi berasal dari karakter Islam dan Indonesia itu Sendiri*. Available at: https://suaramuhammadiyah.id/2020/12/30/haedar-nashir-moderasi-berasal-dari-karakter-islam-dan-indonesia-itu-sendiri/.

Nashir, H. (2021) "Pidato Milad ke-109 Muhammadiyah optimis hadapi Covid 19: menebar nilai utama."

PEW (2021) Two decades later: The Enduring legacy of 9/11. Washington DC.

PP Muhammadiyah (2010) *Pernyataan pikiran muhammadiyah abad kedua*. Yogyakarta: Percetakan Muhammadiyah GRAMASURYA.

Qaradhawi, Y. (2008) *Kalimat fi al-Wasathiyah al-Islamiyyah wa Mu'amaaliha*. Kairo: Dar al-Syuruq.

Qaradhawi, Y. (2009) Fiqh al-Wasathiyyah al-Islamiyyah wa al-Tajdid. Kairo.

Rosyidi, S. (1975) *Perkembangan filsafat dalam pendidikan Muhammadiyah*. Semarang: PWM Dikdasmen Jawa Tengah.

Tibi, B. (1998) *The challange of fundamentalism: Political Islam and the new world disorder*. London: University of California Press.

Wahyudi, W. and Pradhan, D. (2021) "Glocalization of religious extremism and terrorism in indonesia," *Sospol: Jurnal Sosial Politik*, pp. 121–132. Available at: https://doi.org/10.22219/sospol.v7i1.15959.

Wibisono, S., Louis, W.R. and Jetten, J. (2019) "A multidimensional analysis of religious extremism," *Frontiers in Psychology*, 10. Available at: https://doi.org/10.3389/fpsyg.2019.02560.

Yuliawati, Y. (2018) "Terduga Pelaku bom Surabaya suami-istri dengan 4 anak & pendukung ISIS." Available at: https://katadata.co.id/yuliawati/berita/5e9a55f6db62a/terduga-pelaku-bom-surabaya-suami-istri-dengan-4-anak-pendukung-isis.

Strengthening Professional and Spiritual Education through 21st Century Skill Empowerment in Pandemic and Post-Pandemic Era – Arifin et al. (Eds)
© 2024 The Author(s), ISBN: 978-1-032-45243-2
Open Access: www.taylorfrancis.com, CC BY-NC-ND 4.0 license

Development of mind mapping-based student worksheet on the nature of science lesson for class III students at UPT SDN 155 Lombok, Masalle District, Enrekang Regency

Dian Firdiani
Universitas Muhammadiyah Enrekangg, Indonesia

Muhammad Wajdi*
Universitas Muhammadiyah Makassar, Indonesia

P. Panitra
Universitas Muhammadiyah Enrekangg, Indonesia

ABSTRACT: In order to improve the quality of education, professional teachers are required to be able to choose and use various types of learning media around them such as student worksheets. On the other hand, mind mapping is one of the learning techniques in form of visual media which is able to help students to understand teaching materials. This study aims to determine the development process and see student responses, all of which were assessed using a questionnaire. This research is development research that adapts the ADDIE model developed by Lee and Owen. There were five main stages in this research consisting of analysis, design, development, implementation, and evaluation stages. The product was validated by teams of media and material experts and then was tested in a small group of 10 third-grade students. The post-test scores were declared "very effective" with a total percentage 82,15%. Based on the results of the feasibility and practicality test, the Mind Mapping-based student worksheet for the material properties of objects for third-grade elementary school students was affirmed as very feasible and practical to be applied to third-grade students at UPT SDN 155 Lombok.

Keywords: mind mapping, science primary school, student worksheet

1 INTRODUCTION

Currently, science and technology are developing very rapidly. The progress of science and technology cannot be separated from changes in the field of education (Jan 2017; Popenici and Kerr 2017). The impact of the development of science and technology on the education sector is the enrichment of learning resources and media, such as textbooks, modules, transparency overheads, films, videos, TV, Slides, Hypertext, Web, and so on (Bower *et al.* 2014; Cheung and Slavin 2013; Kirkwood and Price 2014; Martín-Gutiérrez *et al.* 2017). In the Industrial Revolution Era 4.0 towards 5.0 The education system is required to keep up with the times. This is certainly one of the challenges for educators in providing knowledge to students. In an effort to improve the quality of education, professional teachers are required to be able to choose and use various types of learning media around them (Caena and Redecker 2019; Suprapto *et al.* 2020). Based on some of the facts that have been stated previously, the achievement of quality education in Indonesia is still relatively low, including in the subjects of Natural Sciences.

---

*Corresponding Author: muh.wajdi@unismuh.ac.id

DOI: 10.1201/9781003376125-23

Science learning in elementary schools still has many shortcomings that need to be improved (Acesta 2020; Arifin *et al.* 2018; Yustikia 2019). The process and evaluation of learning have not been maximized and the results have not met the minimum passing mark. According to Khair *et al.* (2022) the teaching materials used still involve more textbooks and the worksheets used are still contained in the books so students are not accustomed to solving problems that require higher-order thinking skills (Ishartono *et al.* 2021; Kosasih *et al.* 2022). The learning method used is still dominated by conventional methods or lectures, which are more teacher-centered (Gunawan 2017). This also happened at UPT SDN 155 Lombok, especially in class III.

The Student Worksheet is a program that contains tasks that must be done and completed which functions to train students' skills and knowledge (Dermawati *et al.* 2019). This study uses Mind Mapping-based worksheets. Mind Mapping is one of the learning techniques that use aids (media) in the form of visual media in the delivery of teaching materials by using mind mapping to make it easier for students to understand teaching materials in a structured manner. With the use of Mind Mapping-based worksheets, it can improve the memory of students. Based on an interview that was conducted on November 15, 2021, in class III at UPT SDN 155 Lombok: Mrs. Nurlina, S.Pd as class III teacher said "in giving evaluations of learning I still use the assignment system to students, when the learning evaluation process takes place there are some students are active but some are passive in responding to the questions presented in the book. There are even those who do not do the evaluation of the learning given. On the other hand, children also have difficulty understanding and recalling lessons that have been taught previously.

The lack of interaction of students in the learning process is the cause of the learning process not running effectively and efficiently in achieving learning objectives, so that science learning outcomes at UPT SDN 155 Lombok are not optimal. This can be seen from the value of student learning outcomes where of the 27 students only 12 students or around 44.4% have met the Minimum Passing Mark while the other 15 students or around 55.6% have not met the Minimum Passing Mark. Based on the description above, the researcher was interested in conducting development research entitled: "Development of Mind Mapping-based Student Worksheets for Class III Students in Science Subjects at UPT SDN 155 Lombok, Masalle District, Enrekang Regency".

2 METHODS

The type of research used in this research is Research & Development (R&D). The development model used in this research is the ADDIE development model which consists of 5 stages, namely: Analyse, Design, Develop, Implement, and Evaluate (Sugiyono 2018). The limited trial was conducted in class III SDN 155 Lombok with Mind Mapping-based The Student Worksheet learning media. There are three data collection instruments used in this study, namely validation sheets, learning outcomes, and questionnaires. The validation sheet is used to measure the validity of the media created by the researcher. The validity of this media was validated by 2 validators, namely expert validators and one practitioner validator. Then the effectiveness is measured by looking at student learning outcomes through learning evaluation tests and seeing the positive responses given by students by filling out questionnaire sheets distributed to students.

2.1 *Analysis*

The analysis is a step carried out to observe in depth and detail a process of decomposition of various components related to the needs of students in the nature of science lessons, in the form of initial observations.

2.2 Design

The design stage in the development of this learning media has several stages, namely: Making the student worksheet Arrangement of material into media, Preparation of Learning Scenarios, preparation of material, and making practice questions.

2.3 Develop

At the development stage, the activities carried out are to realize the concepts that have been made in the previous Design stage. This development activity realizes the framework that has been made in the form of training materials that will be used in evaluation by experts to find out whether the developed learning media is valid or not, if the developed media is not valid it will be revised.

2.4 Implement

The implementation stage is the stage where the program is implemented. The program implemented is a training and planning program under the training method for using learning media development materials that have been made.

2.5 Evaluate

The purpose of the evaluation is to review the implementation, whether it is following the needs or not, if not, a design will be carried out to improve it.

3   RESULTS AND DISCUSSION

The result of the development of this research is The Student Worksheet based on Mind Mapping with the material properties of third-grade elementary school objects. This development uses the ADDIE model which consists of 5 stages, namely: Analysis, Design, Development, Implementation, and Evaluation. The development of the Mind Mapping-based The Student Worksheet was carried out with product validation tests by media experts and material experts which were carried out in two revisions. In a media expert's assessment includes Richard Meyer's 12 media principles.

Validation tests are carried out by validators who are expert lecturers in their respective fields using a validation instrument sheet that has been prepared previously. The validation of this development product is carried out using a questionnaire sheet, so that the data presented is the result data from the validator. In addition to providing an assessment, the validator also provides input in the form of criticism and suggestions on the product being developed. Assessments from this validator will be compiled and produce test data for the validity of the Mind Mapping-based The Student Worksheet.

The results of material expert validation on Mind Mapping-based worksheets with the theme of object properties of third-grade elementary school students are 94% included in the "Very Eligible" category. Meanwhile, for media expert validation, the aspects assessed include the display to assess the carrying capacity of images and illustrations, the selection of images and the display of Mind Mapping-based worksheets, the results obtained are 65.33% with a fairly decent category. The main thing starts from the cover design which must be attractive and adapted to the material in the Mind Mapping-based worksheets. For image use, look for images that are more relevant to the material. And for the use of illustrations, real illustrations must be used and adapted to the students' environment. Finally, the validator suggested not to use too many colours to make it look simple but attractive. Then improvements were made, the results obtained were 89.33% with a very decent category.

After the product has gone through the validation stage by experts in its field, it has been repaired, then the product is tested on 21 third grade students of UPT SDN 155 Lombok. Based on the results of the calculation, it was found that 82.15% belonged to the Very Practical category. Furthermore, after students use Mind Mapping-based worksheets, students will work on Post-Test questions that have been made by previous researchers to determine the effectiveness of the Mind Mapping-based worksheets that have been developed. Based on the calculation results, the results obtained are 84.47% classified in the very effective category.

The final result of this stage is to obtain a Mind Mapping-based The Student Worksheet with the theme of the properties of objects for third-grade elementary school students that are feasible and practical to use. Mind Mapping-based The Student Worksheet is expected to be a new alternative learning media that can help and support the conventional learning process. Through Mind Mapping-based The Student Worksheet, it is also hoped that learning objectives will be easier to achieve and the time used in the learning process and evaluation will be more effective.

4 CONCLUSION

Based on the results of the research conducted, it was concluded that: (1) The Student Based on the results of the research conducted, it was concluded that: (1) The Student Worksheet based on Mind Mapping material properties of objects for third-grade elementary school students was developed using the Research and Development (R&D) method by Sugiyono (2016) which was then limited by researchers to be adapted to the needs of researchers and development carried out. The procedures and development stages in this study are potential and problems, data collection, product design, design validation, product testing, and product revision, (2) Validation results from the 2 validators, namely media experts and material experts to test the feasibility of The Student Worksheet Mind Mapping based on the material properties of objects for grade III elementary school students that was developed was declared "very feasible" to be used in the learning process and evaluation with the percentage of media expert assessment results amounting to 89.33% and material expert at 94%, (3) Response test carried out on 21 third grade students and 1 science teacher response person at UPT SDN 155 Lombok and was declared "very practical" with a total student percentage value of 82.15% and teacher response percentage of 89.33%, (4) Test Post-Test scores were carried out to 21 third grade students at UPT SDN 155 Lombok and were declared "very effective" with a total percentage value of students' Post-Test results of 82.15% and the percentage of teacher responses before 84.47%.

REFERENCES

Acesta, A. (2020) "Analisis kemampuan higher order thingking skills (HOTS) siswa materi IPA di sekolah dasar," *Quagga: Jurnal Pendidikan dan Biologi*, 12(2), p. 170. Available at: https://doi.org/10.25134/quagga.v12i2.2831.

Arifin, M.B.U.B., Nurdyansyah, N. and Rais, P. (2018) "An evaluation of graduate competency in elementary school," in *Proceedings of the 1st International Conference on Intellectuals' Global Responsibility (ICIGR 2017)*. Paris, France: Atlantis Press. Available at: https://doi.org/10.2991/icigr-17.2018.23.

Bower, M. *et al.* (2014) "Augmented reality in education – cases, places and potentials," *Educational Media International*, 51(1), pp. 1–15. Available at: https://doi.org/10.1080/09523987.2014.889400.

Caena, F. and Redecker, C. (2019) "Aligning teacher competence frameworks to 21st century challenges: The case for the European digital competence framework for educators (Digcompedu)," *European Journal of Education*, 54(3), pp. 356–369. Available at: https://doi.org/10.1111/ejed.12345.

Cheung, A.C.K. and Slavin, R.E. (2013) "The effectiveness of educational technology applications for enhancing mathematics achievement in K-12 classrooms: A meta-analysis," *Educational Research Review*, 9, pp. 88–113. Available at: https://doi.org/10.1016/j.edurev.2013.01.001.

Dermawati, N., Suprata, S. and Muzakkir, M. (2019) "Pengembangan lembar kerja peserta didik (LKPD) berbasis lingkungan," *JPF (Jurnal Pendidikan Fisika)*, 7(1), pp. 74–78. Available at: https://doi.org/10.24252/jpf.v7i1.3143.

Gunawan, I. (2017) "Indonesian curriculum 2013: Instructional management, obstacles faced by teachers in implementation and the way forward," in *Proceedings of the 3rd International Conference on Education and Training (ICET 2017)*. Paris, France: Atlantis Press. Available at: https://doi.org/10.2991/icet-17.2017.9.

Ishartono, N. *et al.* (2021) "The quality of HOTS-based science questions developed by Indonesian elementary school teachers," *Journal of Education Technology*, 5(2). Available at: https://doi.org/10.23887/jet.v5i2.33813.

Jan, H. (2017) "Teacher of 21 st century: Characteristics and development," *Research on Humanities and Social Sciences*, 7(9), pp. 2225–0484.

Khair, B.N. *et al.* (2022) "Development of science interactive student worksheets oriented higher-order thinking skills for elementary school student," *Jurnal Pijar Mipa*, 17(1), pp. 41–45. Available at: https://doi.org/10.29303/jpm.v17i1.3087.

Kirkwood, A. and Price, L. (2014) "Technology-enhanced learning and teaching in higher education: what is 'enhanced' and how do we know? A critical literature review," *Learning, Media and Technology*, 39(1), pp. 6–36. Available at: https://doi.org/10.1080/17439884.2013.770404.

Kosasih, A. *et al.* (2022) "Higher-order thinking skills in primary school," *Journal of Ethnic and Cultural Studies*, 9(1), pp. 56–76. Available at: https://www.jstor.org/stable/48710289.

Martín-Gutiérrez, J. *et al.* (2017) "Virtual technologies trends in education," *EURASIA Journal of Mathematics, Science and Technology Education*, 13(2). Available at: https://doi.org/10.12973/eurasia.2017.00626a.

Popenici, S.A.D. and Kerr, S. (2017) "Exploring the impact of artificial intelligence on teaching and learning in higher education," *Research and Practice in Technology Enhanced Learning*, 12(1), p. 22. Available at: https://doi.org/10.1186/s41039-017-0062-8.

Sugiyono (2018) *Metode Penelitian Kuantitatif dan Kualitatif R&D*. Bandung: Alfabeta.

Suprapto, Y. *et al.* (2020) "Design and implementation of self-test learning application to increase competence," in *Proceedings of the International Joint Conference on Arts and Humanities (IJCAH 2020)*. Paris, France: Atlantis Press. Available at: https://doi.org/10.2991/assehr.k.201201.068.

Yustikia, N.W.S. (2019) "Pentingnya sarana pendidikan dalam menunjang kualitas pendidikan di sekolah," *Guna Widya: Jurnal Pendidikan Hindu*, 4(2), p. 1. Available at: https://doi.org/10.25078/gw.v4i2.1053.

Strengthening Professional and Spiritual Education through 21st Century Skill Empowerment in Pandemic and Post-Pandemic Era – Arifin et al. (Eds)
© 2024 The Author(s), ISBN: 978-1-032-45243-2
Open Access: www.taylorfrancis.com, CC BY-NC-ND 4.0 license

Application of teaching module as an implementation of "Curriculum Merdeka" for fourth-grade students at Kuala Lumpur Indonesian School

A.R. Wijayaningputri*, M. Innany & G.D. Murtyas
Universitas Muhammadiyah Malang, Indonesia

ABSTRACT: The problems at the Kuala Lumpur Indonesian School (SIKL) can be seen in the implementation of the curriculum. The results of interviews with fourth-grade teachers and the head of SIKL stated that teachers do not yet have sufficient knowledge about Curriculum Merdeka learning, including the application of learning tools developed in a Curriculum Merdeka. The aims of this study were: (1) to describe the readiness of SIKL teachers in implementing the Curriculum Merdeka, (2) to describe the obstacles to the readiness of SIKL teachers in implementing the Curriculum Merdeka, and (3) to improve the ability of teachers to implement teaching modules as a Curriculum Merdeka implementation. Through direct observation, it is hoped that teachers will understand the application of teaching modules in a Curriculum Merdeka implementation. In addition, each teacher is able to apply and develop Curriculum Merdeka-based learning using teaching modules that can be implemented independently and continuously. This activity can be followed up by solving problems for teachers in understanding the application of teaching modules as an independent curriculum implementation that can be carried out independently and continuously.

Keywords: curriculum implementation, Merdeka Curriculum, teaching modules

1 INTRODUCTION

The presence of a curriculum in education holds significant importance as it serves as the fundamental framework for the execution of the learning process (Wyse 2018). The curriculum also serves as the foundation for a teacher to make decisions tailored to the classroom context and the needs of the students they are instructing (Siuty *et al.* 2018). A well-structured curriculum serves to delineate the path of the educational journey undertaken by students. In the presence of a robust curriculum, the quality of both teaching and learning is heightened, ultimately optimizing the competence of graduates (Chan *et al.* 2017; Ritter *et al.* 2018). Moreover, a sound curriculum ensures that students acquire knowledge, skills, and attitudes that align with the contemporary demands of our evolving world (Acedo and Hughes 2014; Alismail and McGuire 2015).

The problems that exist in the Kuala Lumpur Indonesian School (SIKL) appear in the implementation of the curriculum. Currently, the curriculum used at SIKL is the 2013 curriculum. Based on government policy, the curriculum undergoes changes and developments, namely "Curriculum Merdeka". Based on the results of interviews with fourth-grade teachers and the head of SIKL stated that teachers do not yet have adequate knowledge about learning the "Curriculum Merdeka", including the application of teaching tools developed in the "Curriculum Merdeka", namely the application of teaching modules. The teaching module is a development of the Learning Implementation Plan (RPP) which is equipped

*Corresponding Author: arinta@umm.ac.id

DOI: 10.1201/9781003376125-24

with more detailed guidelines, including student activity sheets and assessments to measure the achievement of learning objectives. By using the teaching module, it is expected that the learning process will be more flexible because it does not depend on the content in the textbook, the speed and learning strategies can also be in accordance with the needs of students so that it is hoped that each student can achieve the targeted minimum competencies. SIKL teachers are fresh graduates and have never received material or training on the application of teaching modules in the implementation of the "Curriculum Merdeka".

Based on the above problems, the Indonesian School of Kuala Lumpur (SIKL) and the implementing team need to improve the ability of teachers to apply teaching modules in the implementation of a "Curriculum Merdeka". Activities that can help solve problems for teachers include the implementation of lecturer assignments in schools. The implementation team will carry out activities using learning practices in 2 meetings. This program for assigning lecturers to foreign schools is intended to develop learning innovations in the international arena which aims to become examples of best practices for teachers. Through direct observation, teachers are expected to understand the application of teaching modules as the implementation of a "Curriculum Merdeka". In addition, every teacher is expected to be able to implement and develop "Curriculum Merdeka"-based learning using teaching modules that can be carried out independently and sustainably.

Based on the explanation of these problems which motivated the researchers to conduct research, the urgency of the research is about teacher readiness in implementing the Curriculum Merdeka, especially at the elementary school level. This study aims to find out how teacher readiness is in implementing the independent curriculum at the Indonesian School of Kuala Lumpur. It is hoped that from the results of this study, institutions can immediately respond to aspects that teachers have not been able to prepare properly. So that the implementation of the independent curriculum at the elementary level can run optimally.

2 METHODS

This research was conducted at the Indonesian Elementary School in Kuala Lumpur. This study is qualitative descriptive research because the results of this research will produce descriptive data in the form of written statements obtained in searching data from data sources that provide an overview of existing events or phenomena, both scientific and human engineering, and pay more attention to characteristics, quality, and interrelationships between activities. The research design used is descriptive qualitative research, that is, what problems are sought, how to conduct research in the researcher's situation, and how the researcher interprets the various information that has been explored and recorded in accordance with the actual conditions that occur in the study field. Based on this, researchers can collect as much data as possible about teacher readiness in implementing the independent curriculum based on lesson plans. The data obtained is used as a reference to describe the teacher's readiness to implement the independent curriculum based on the RPP, which includes aspects of planning, implementation, and assessment in the independent curriculum. In addition, this study also found out what obstacles were obstacles and what efforts or follow-up actions were taken to overcome obstacles in implementing the independent curriculum.

The data collection technique used in this study was carried out in various ways including direct interviews which were used as the main source to obtain data related to teacher readiness in implementing the independent curriculum based on lesson plans. Documents are used as a complement to interview techniques which will complement documents or data that cannot be found in interviews. The validity of the data in this study uses triangulation of sources and techniques. As for what is meant by source and technique triangulation according to Sugiyono (2016), source triangulation means obtaining data from different sources with the same technique, while technical triangulation means that researchers use different data collection techniques to obtain data from different sources. The same.

Data analysis is an attempt to summarize the data that has been collected in a reliable, accurate, reliable and correct manner. The data from this study were analyzed using data collection techniques and analysis strategies. The stages in data analysis include planning, the beginning of data collection, basic data collection, and reduction, closing data collection and presentation, and refinement.

3   RESULTS AND DISCUSSION

3.1   *Lesson planning*

The results of the interview with the principal of SIKL stated that it was necessary to design the Basic Concepts of Teaching Modules. Nowadays, teaching modules are often the subject of discussion by teachers at all levels, both elementary, middle, and high levels. Teaching modules are learning materials that are arranged extensively and systematically with reference to learning principles that are applied by teachers to students. Systematic can be interpreted sequentially starting from the opening, content of the material, and closing, making it easier for students to learn and making it easier for teachers to deliver the material. In addition, according to Sungkono, (2009), teaching modules are unique and specific, which means they are aimed at certain targets in the learning process that are in accordance with their goals. While specific can be interpreted that the teaching module is designed optimally to achieve indicators of success.

Teaching modules are very important in the learning process for teachers and students. Indeed, teachers will have difficulty upgrading teaching effectiveness if they are not paired with a complete teaching module. This applies to students because what is delivered by the teacher is not systematic. The possibility of delivering material is not in accordance with the curriculum that should be applied, therefore the teaching module is the main medium to improve.

3.2   *Curriculum Merdeka*

The curriculum structure is the most important part of the curriculum itself. To be able to analyze the needs and implement the curriculum in accordance with the realities of the field, the independent curriculum prioritizes the development of character through content on learning and student profiles of Pancasila.

The components of the teaching module contain general information, core components, and appendices. General information contains details of school name, subject, school level, compiler name, year, class, initial competence, Pancasila student profile, facilities and infrastructure, learning mode, learning model, target, time allocation, and number of meetings, while the core component contains information on the topic, rationalization, learning objectives, meaningful understanding, trigger questions, preparation for learning, learning activities and assessment (assessment). The assessment section consists of an explanation of the diagnostic problem by giving questionnaires to students, group formative in the form of class discussions, individual formative, summative, and enrichment and remedial programs. The attachment contains information on student worksheets, reading materials for teachers' and participants' education, a glossary, and a bibliography.

The teaching modules are prepared by considering the depth of the material, the competencies, and needs of the students, the interests of the students, as well as the facilities and media needed. The procedure for preparing teaching modules includes: 1) analysis of the needs of students, teachers, and schools; 2) identification and determination of the dimensions of the profile of Pancasila students who will be trained; 3) determining the flow of learning objectives that will be developed in the teaching module; 4) preparation of teaching modules based on the specified components; 5) implementation of learning; 6) evaluation and follow-up. Based on the results of interviews with mathematics teachers, information was obtained that the character of students in SIKL is like a normal curve, meaning that there are students who are at high, medium, or low levels. Regarding this, the data on the characteristics of students is used as a consideration for the preparation of teaching modules to provide appropriate actions during learning. To determine learning materials in the Driving School Curriculum, use ATP (Learning Objectives) which refers to CP (Learning Outcomes) and TP (Learning Objectives). The time allocation itself is shorter than the 2013 curriculum whereas in the Merdeka Curriculum, there are only 4 hours of lessons (3 hours of teaching and learning activities and 1 hour of project lessons) in 1 week. The selection of the learning model applied adapts the learning model from the Ministry of Education and Culture which is adapted to the characteristics of students and learning needs. The learning media that can be used in the learning is PowerPoint. The obstacles felt by teachers in the preparation of teaching modules are that they must adjust to the characteristics of students, and the arrangement is more complex such as assessment, diagnostics, and others.

3.3 *Implementation of learning*

The implementation stage of the learning model is carried out by offline (face-to-face) learning. Offline learning is carried out in class while still following the health protocol. Researchers observe the learning process in the classroom by looking at the suitability of the learning process with the teaching modules that have been made. The implementation of learning is carried out on Indonesian and Pancasila subjects. The Indonesian language subject applies the Project Based Learning (PjBL) learning model, while the Pancasila subject applies the Problem-Based Learning (PBL) model. In the learning process, it appears that students are very enthusiastic about participating in learning so that learning can run conducive and students are also more active in conducting discussion activities. The learning process activities can be seen in Figure 1.

Figure 1.   Application of teaching modules in Indonesian and Pancasila subjects.

The implementation of PjBL has been shown to significantly enhance student competence. Through PjBL, students are guided to undertake project activities that align with real-world challenges. Engaging in contextual projects not only deepens students' understanding but also enhances their 21st-century skills. PjBL stimulates the development of critical (Eldiva and Azizah 2019; Issa and Khataibeh 2021; Sasson *et al.* 2018) and creative thinking skills (Isabekov and Sadyrova 2018; Ummah *et al.* 2019; Yamin *et al.* 2020) as students design projects. Furthermore, collaborative (Lee *et al.* 2015; Kokotsaki *et al.* 2016) and communicative skills (Notari *et al.* 2014; Owens and Hite 2022) are honed during the group-based completion of project activities. Consequently, PjBL enriches students' academic experiences and prepares them to confidently confront the challenges of the contemporary era.

In line with the positive impact of PjBL, the implementation of PBL plays a pivotal role in enhancing student competence. Through the adoption of PBL, the learning environment becomes dynamic, encouraging students to take an active role in addressing real-world problems (Albanese and Dast 2013). Moreover, PBL prompts students to utilize their critical thinking skills to seek innovative solutions collaboratively (Masek and Yamin 2011; Nguyen 2017). Additionally, PBL cultivates a collaborative spirit among students, fostering teamwork and peer learning (Aslan 2021; Yew and Goh 2016). By immersing students in authentic problem-solving scenarios, PBL not only enriches their academic experiences but also nurtures practical skills and competencies that can be applied across diverse facets of their personal and professional lives.

4 CONCLUSION

Conclusions should state concisely the most important propositions of the paper as well as the author's views of the practical implications of the results. Based on the results of the research that has been described, it can be concluded that: 1) The planning stage of the teaching module in the independent curriculum, as seen from the results of interviews and documents for the Independent Curriculum teaching module as a whole, is appropriate, so it can be said to be very good. 2) The implementation phase of the implementation of the teaching modules in the Merdeka Curriculum in the fourth grade of SIKL is in the very good category. 3) The results of student learning mastery after the implementation of the teaching module on the Independent Curriculum seen from the grade 4 SIKL score are in a good category.

Suggestions that can be given for further research include other researchers conducting further research using teaching modules in the "Curriculum Merdeka" covering more aspects and applying them to different learning materials. In learning, teachers should be more creative and innovative in the learning process so that the material and tasks given to students can be understood well even though the allocation of time for learning mathematics in the Merdeka Curriculum is shorter. One of them can use the Learning Management System (LMS) as a media aid. It is very necessary to cover the difficulties faced by students in a more detailed understanding when the teacher implements the independent curriculum. Second, further research is highly recommended to analyze teacher readiness in implementing the independent curriculum with various learning models.

Based on the direct experience of researchers in the research process In this case, there are some limitations experienced and can be several factors so that it can be given more attention to future researchers in further perfecting his research because this research itself of course has deficiencies that need to be continuously improved in research in the future. Some of the limitations in this research are in the data collection process, the information provided by the respondents through a questionnaire sometimes does not show the opinion of the respondent, this happens because sometimes there are differences in thinking, assumptions, and different understanding of each respondent, as well as other factors such as honesty factor in filling out the opinions of respondents in the questionnaire.

REFERENCES

Acedo, C. and Hughes, C. (2014) "Principles for learning and competences in the 21st-century curriculum," *Prospects*, 44(4), pp. 503–525. Available at: https://doi.org/10.1007/s11125-014-9330-1.

Albanese, M.A. and Dast, L.C. (2013) "Problem-based learning," in T. Swanwick (ed.) *Understanding Medical Education*. Chichester, UK: John Wiley & Sons, Ltd, pp. 61–79. Available at: https://doi.org/10.1002/9781118472361.ch5.

Alismail, H.A. and McGuire, P. (2015) "21st Century standards and curriculum: Current research and practice," *Journal of Education and Practice*, 6(6), pp. 150–155. Available at: http://files.eric.ed.gov/fulltext/EJ1083656.pdf.

Aslan, A. (2021) "Problem-based learning in live online classes: Learning achievement, problem-solving skill, communication skill, and interaction," *Computers & Education*, 171, p. 104237. Available at: https://doi.org/10.1016/j.compedu.2021.104237.

Chan, C.K.Y. *et al.* (2017) "A review of literature on challenges in the development and implementation of generic competencies in higher education curriculum," *International Journal of Educational Development*, 57, pp. 1–10. Available at: https://doi.org/10.1016/j.ijedudev.2017.08.010.

Eldiva, F.T. and Azizah, N. (2019) "Project based learning in improving critical thinking skill of children with special needs," in *Advances in Social Science, Education and Humanities Research*, pp. 348–355. Available at: https://doi.org/10.2991/icsie-18.2019.64.

Isabekov, A. and Sadyrova, G. (2018) "Project-based learning to develop creative abilities in students," in J. Drummer *et al.* (eds.) *Vocational Teacher Education in Central Asia: Developing Skills and Facilitating Success.* Cham: Springer International Publishing, pp. 43–49. Available at: https://doi.org/10.1007/978-3-319-73093-6_4.

Issa, H.B. and Khataibeh, A. (2021) "The effect of using project based learning on Improving the critical thinking among upper basic students from teachers' perspectives," *Pegem Egitim ve Ogretim Dergisi*, 11(2), pp. 52–57. Available at: https://doi.org/10.14527/pegegog.2021.06.

Kokotsaki, D., Menzies, V. and Wiggins, A. (2016) "Project-based learning: A review of the literature," *Improving Schools*, 19(3), pp. 267–277. Available at: https://doi.org/10.1177/1365480216659733.

Lee, D., Huh, Y. and Reigeluth, C.M. (2015) "Collaboration, intragroup conflict, and social skills in project-based learning," *Instructional Science*, 43(5), pp. 561–590. Available at: https://doi.org/10.1007/s11251-015-9348-7.

Masek, A. and Yamin, S. (2011) "The effect of problem based learning on critical thinking ability: A theoretical and empirical review," *International Review of Social Sciences and Humanities*, 2(1), pp. 215–221. Available at: https://pdfs.semanticscholar.org/4f47/2dc06281c45f765dc945599e92525b4c5679.pdf.

Nguyen, T.T. (2017) "Developing important life skills through project-based learning: A case study," *The Normal Lights*, 11(2), pp. 109–142. Available at: https://pdfs.semanticscholar.org/d85d/6dbed-f4ebf63c425fca4c929441857409b9b.pdf.

Notari, M., Baumgartner, A. and Herzog, W. (2014) "Social skills as predictors of communication, performance and quality of collaboration in project-based learning," *Journal of Computer Assisted Learning*, 30 (2), pp. 132–147. Available at: https://doi.org/10.1111/jcal.12026.

Owens, A.D. and Hite, R.L. (2022) "Enhancing student communication competencies in STEM using virtual global collaboration project based learning," *Research in Science & Technological Education*, 40(1), pp. 76–102. Available at: https://doi.org/10.1080/02635143.2020.1778663.

Ritter, B.A. *et al.* (2018) "Designing management curriculum for workplace readiness: Developing students' soft skills," *Journal of Management Education*, 42(1), pp. 80–103. Available at: https://doi.org/10.1177/1052562917703679.

Sasson, I., Yehuda, I. and Malkinson, N. (2018) "Fostering the skills of critical thinking and question-posing in a project-based learning environment," *Thinking Skills and Creativity*, 29, pp. 203–212. Available at: https://doi.org/10.1016/j.tsc.2018.08.001.

Siuty, M.B., Leko, M.M. and Knackstedt, K.M. (2018) "Unraveling the role of curriculum in teacher decision making," *Teacher Education and Special Education: The Journal of the Teacher Education Division of the Council for Exceptional Children*, 41(1), pp. 39–57. Available at: https://doi.org/10.1177/08884064 16683230.

Sugiyono (2016) *Metode penelitian pendidikan (Pendekatan kuantitatif, kualitatif, dan R&D).* Bandung: Alfabeta. Available at: http://pustaka.unm.ac.id/opac/detail-opac?id=35458.

Sungkono, S. (2009) "Pengembangan dan pemanfaatan bahan ajar modul dalam proses pembelajaran. Majalah Ilmiah Pembelajaran," *Majalah Ilmiah Pembelajaran*, 5(1). Available at: https://journal.uny.ac.id/index.php/mip/article/view/6154/.

Ummah, S.K., Inam, A. and Azmi, R.D. (2019) "Creating manipulatives: Improving students' creativity through project-based learning," *Journal on Mathematics Education*, 10(1), pp. 93–102. Available at: https://doi.org/10.22342/jme.10.1.5093.93-102.

Wyse, D. (2018) *Creating curricula: Aims, knowledge and control.* Routledge. Available at: https://doi.org/10.4324/9781315530017.

Yamin, Y. *et al.* (2020) "Implementing project-based learning to enhance creative thinking skills on water pollution topic," *JPBI (Jurnal Pendidikan Biologi Indonesia)*, 6(2), pp. 225–232. Available at: https://doi.org/10.22219/jpbi.v6i2.12202.

Yew, E.H.J. and Goh, K. (2016) "Problem-based learning: An overview of its process and impact on learning," *Health Professions Education*, 2(2), pp. 75–79. Available at: https://doi.org/10.1016/j.hpe.2016.01.004.

Strengthening Professional and Spiritual Education through 21st Century Skill Empowerment in
Pandemic and Post-Pandemic Era – Arifin et al. (Eds)
© 2024 The Author(s), ISBN: 978-1-032-45243-2
Open Access: www.taylorfrancis.com, CC BY-NC-ND 4.0 license

Online learning think talk write: Developing communication mathematics skills students

Sonia Marlinda, Yus Mochamad Cholily* & Z. Zukhrufurrohmah
Universitas Muhammadiyah Malang, Indonesia

ABSTRACT: This quantitative descriptive study aims to describe the improvement of mathematical communication in students who applied online learning with the TTW method on the Equations and Inequality Linear One Variable material online. The subjects of this research were 15 students of the class online. The data source used is the test questions' answer sheet, namely pre-test and post-test. This research is divided into three stages, namely, research preparation, research implementation, and data analysis. The researcher hopes for the following achievements: (1) students can reflect pictures into mathematical ideas; (2) students can explain the idea of a situation using written and algebraic methods; (3) students can express everyday events in mathematical language and symbols. The results of research on the application of online TTW learning are excellent (95.15%), and students' mathematical communication has increased in each indicator and number of questions.

Keywords: Online Learning, Think Talk Write, Mathematical Communication

1 INTRODUCTION

An unexpected case brought about a significant change around the world. The government enforces policy recommendations to minimize its spread (Herliandry and Suban 2020). The policy is implemented by changing learning that usually comes to class or campus to being at home, thus making learning change from face-to-face to online (Basilaia and Kvavadze 2020). Due to the current conditions in the education sector, there is a need for fast adaptation and excellent and appropriate innovation by utilizing technology to continue the learning process (Ahmed *et al.* 2020). Online learning can use platforms in the form of applications, websites, social networks, and other supporting facilities (Gunawan *et al.* 2020).

Mathematics is a branch of science that can develop skills, especially for students in the field of reasoning. It is needed today for the development of modern technology from time to time. However, the reality is that the application of mathematics is often made not by way of exploration, students tend to sit and just listen, and students become passive because they only take notes on what the teacher says. So that learning can be maximized, it is necessary to have an effective learning model that is innovative and creative to make students active and more enthusiastic and improve the quality of student learning (Rizal 2018; Yadrika 2019; Yuliana and Muljono 2020). The effective model to use is the Think Talk Write (TTW) model.

Think Talk Write model is a learning model that prioritizes thinking, reflection, and writing that can improve mathematical communication skills, the ability to understand concepts given by teachers to students, and can increase students' desire to express their opinions (Anggraini and Hia 2016; Riansyah and Sari 2018; Supandi *et al.* 2018). In addition, the application of TTW can make students able to express their ideas, think and reflect appropriately (Rahmani and Sutiawan 2020). To achieve students can express their ideas

---

*Corresponding Author: yus@umm.ac.id

DOI: 10.1201/9781003376125-25

and thoughts, it is necessary to have basic abilities that students must have in learning mathematics, namely the ability to communicate.

Mathematical communication has an essential role in utilizing mathematical ideas to help students see various things related to mathematical material, a tool to measure students' understanding of mathematical reflection, a tool to form mathematical knowledge, develop problem-solving, improve reasoning and belief, and improve social skills (Anisah *et al.* 2020). However, their research said that students' mathematical communication skills were still in the poor category (Purnama and Hidayat 2021). The Think Talk Write model is quite effective and can improve mathematical communication (Leutualy *et al.* 2020; Suriyana 2011).

Indicators of mathematical communication skills are: (1) Can model problem situations using methods such as oral, written, real, graphic, and algebraic methods; (2) Can reflect real objects, pictures, and diagrams on mathematical ideas; (3) Can listen, discuss, and write about mathematics; (4) Can read using comprehension from a written mathematical presentation; (5) Can explain and ask about mathematics that has been learned; (6) Can express everyday events in symbols or mathematical notation; (7) Can speculate, organize arguments, formulate definitions, and generalize (Wijayanto *et al.* 2018).

The difference between online and offline TTW lies in its application. In offline TTW, the application is carried out in the classroom, while online, the implementation is using the help of supporting applications and can be done anywhere and is more flexible. Then the steps between online and offline are the same consisting of 3 stages, namely think, talk, write. What distinguishes the step from think to talk. In dividing students into groups if offline students can go directly to the place where the group is. If online students must enter using the breakout room

Based on the descriptions above, the difference between previous research and the research that will be carried out is in its application which is carried out through online learning. So, researchers are interested in describing the improvement of mathematical communication in students who are applying online learning with the TTW method.

2 METHOD

This research is a quantitative descriptive study that aims to describe the improvement of students' mathematical communication skills using online TTW. The data collection technique was carried out with test questions in the form of Pre-Test and Post-Test questions, which were used to measure students' mathematical communication. The test questions used are in the form of essay questions. In addition, the technique used is an observation sheet of learning activities to observe the learning process carried out by the researcher. The research subjects were 15 grade VII students of SMP Negeri II Pungging, Kab. Mojokerto, East Java, for the 2022/2023 academic year. Subject selection is obtained from the choice of teaching teachers who have considered various factors. The place used in this research is online. The research time is in the odd semester of the 2022/2023 academic year. The data analysis technique is data reduction which is done by sorting the data sources that have been obtained. The source of the data obtained is the test answers from the research subjects. Then, the stage of presenting data in the form of activities to analyze the subject's solutions by the achievement indicators that have been determined by the researcher. Furthermore, the results of the analysis are seen as whether they are by the predetermined mathematical communication indicators.

The technique used to determine the criteria for completeness or success of the implementation of learning using online TTW is as follows.

Determine the score of each meeting in a way.

$$TN_n = (4 \times N_1) + (3 \times N_2) + (2 \times N_3) + (1 \times N_4) \tag{1}$$

Next, the meeting percentage is determined using

$$\bar{x} = \frac{TN_n}{NM} \times 100\% \tag{2}$$

Description:
n = The meeting
N_1 = The number of values of N_1
N_2 = The number of values of N_2
N_3 = The number of values of N_3
N_4 = The number of values of N_4
$\bar{x}$ = Average of each meeting
TN_n = Total Value of the Meeting
NM = Maximum Value

After knowing the percentage of the entire meeting, the success criteria for implementing online TTW learning are determined based on Table 1 below.

Table 1. Criteria for completeness of learning implementation.

Percentage	Criteria
$0\% \leq x \leq 49\%$	Very Less
$49\% < x \leq 59\%$	Not Enough
$59\% < x \leq 69\%$	Enough
$69\% < x \leq 79\%$	Good
$79\% < x \leq 100\%$	Very Good

The technique used to analyze the Pre-Test and Post-Test is to group based on indicators and then make conclusions based on the number of indicators met from student answers. And the results of the analysis are in the form of a description of the ability of 3 students who can fulfil all indicators.

3 RESULT AND DISCUSSION

3.1 *Result*

3.1.1 *Description of online TTW learning activities*
In this study, the results of learning using the online TTW method were excellent, with a percentage of 95.15%. This can be seen from the results of thorough observations made by observers, and it is relevant to the results of research conducted by Artayasa *et al.* (2021) said that the online TTW learning model has high effectiveness. The results of the implementation of learning can be seen in the following Table 2 below.

Table 2. Observation percentage result.

The Meeting	Average
1st Meeting	95%
2nd Meeting	96,7%
3rd Meeting	93,75%
Average Number of Meetings	95,15%

In this study, the learning steps with the TTW method used are as follows: In the thinking phase, students independently read and study the problems that have been given and are asked to make possible solutions to the mathematical problems that have been given. Next, students were given small group divisions and asked students to join in the breakout room. In it, students discuss with their group friends the results of the completion of each of their work. In the talking phase, students are asked to present the results of the conclusions from their solutions to their friends. After all group representatives present their results, in the writing phase, the teacher provides reflections and conclusions on the solution to solving mathematical problems, and students write what the teacher says.

3.1.2 Description of students' mathematical communication ability with indicators of being able to express daily events in mathematical language and symbols

The researcher presented information from the answers to the Pre-Test and Post-Test questions to random subjects. Of the 15 subjects, there are three categories of subjects, namely subjects with code S1, namely subjects who can answer questions according to the indicators correctly and completely, S2, namely subjects who answer questions according to indicators but are not correct or incomplete, while S3 are subjects who cannot answer questions. by the indicators correctly and completely.

Of the 15 subjects studied, in the number one Pre-Test question, all subjects were included in the S1 category, which was able to use symbols or notations in stating events completely and correctly. The following results from the presentation of one of the subject's test answers.

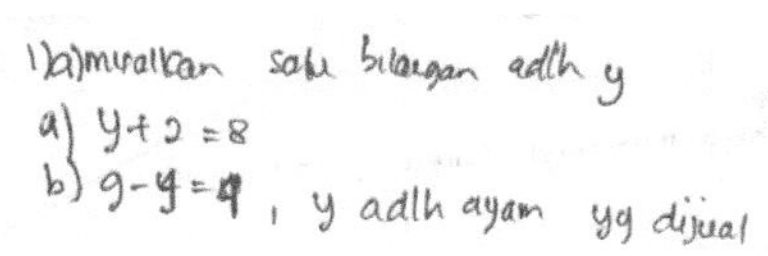

Figure 1.   Answer number $1S_1$ pre-test.

Based on the data in Figure 1, in solving a problem in number one on the Pre-Test question, S1 can use terms, symbols, or notations in expressing daily events completely and correctly. In this case, S1 can describe the problem by first assuming the variables to be used before solving the given problem.

Next, based on Figure 2, in Post-Test question number one, of the 15 subjects, all subjects also belonged to the S1 category, which was able to use symbols or notations to state events completely and correctly. The following is the result of the presentation of one of the subject's test answers.

Figure 2.   Answer number $1S_1$ post-test.

Based on the data in Figure 2, in solving the problem in number one on the Post-Test question, S1 can use terms, symbols, or notations in stating daily events completely and correctly, even though they do not first assume the variables to be used.

Pre-Test question number three in Figure 3, all subjects included in the S3 category could not reflect on mathematical ideas. Here are the presentation results of one of the subject's test answers.

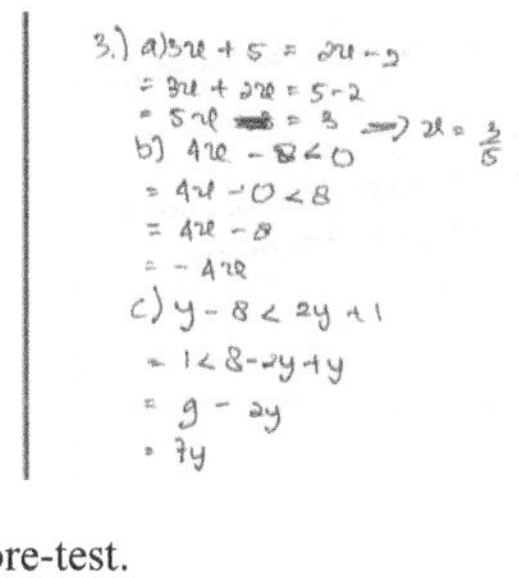

Figure 3.   Answer number $3S_3$ pre-test.

187

Based on the data in Figure 3, in solving problem in number three on the Pre-Test question, S3 in solving it is by the orders and questions asked, so the solution is not appropriate and not appropriate. For example, in a problem asked to solve, make it into a number line, and determine the set of solutions, all subjects did not complete it according to the command requested.

In post-test number three, out of 15 subjects, three are included in the S2 category, which can reflect on mathematical ideas but are still not quite right. The following results from the presentation of one of the subject's test answers.

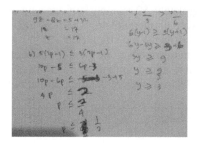

Figure 4.   Answer number $3S_2$ post-test.

Based on the data in Figure 4, in solving the problem in number three on the Post-Test question, S2 can reflect mathematical ideas, but the solution is still not precise and complete. In addition, the answer from S2 is still not by the questions asked in the question. Where in the problem, the solution is asked to use a set of solutions and a number line, but the subject only reaches the completion.

3.1.3   *Description of students' mathematical communication ability with indicators students can explain the idea of a situation by using writing and algebraic methods*

The researcher presented information from the answers to the Pre-Test and Post-Test questions to random subjects. Of the 15 subjects, there are three categories of subjects, namely subjects with code S1, namely subjects who can answer questions according to the indicators correctly and completely, S2, namely subjects who answer questions according to indicators but are not correct or incomplete, while S3 are subjects who cannot answer questions. by the indicators correctly and completely.

Of the 15 subjects studied, in Pre-Test question number two, nine subjects were included in the S2 category and were able to explain the idea of the situation using the written method, but it was still not quite right. The following is the result of the presentation of one of the subject's test answers.

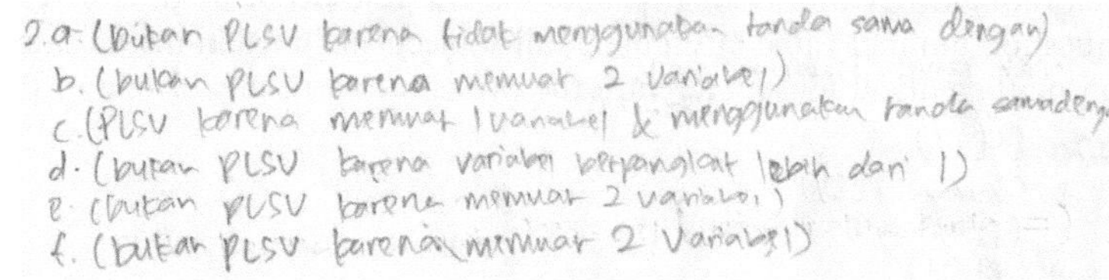

Figure 5.   The answer number 2 of S_2's pre-test.

Based on the data in Figure 5, in solving the problem in number two on the Pre-Test question, S2 can explain the idea of the situation using the written method, but the solution is still not precise and complete. In addition, the answer from S2 is still not by the questions asked in the question. As in the example in 2a, there should be One Variable Linear Inequality, but there are still many who answer Not One Variable Linear Equation.

Then in the Post-Test question Figure 6, number two, of the 15 subjects, all of the subjects were able to explain the idea of the situation using the written method correctly. The following is the result of the presentation of one of the subject's test answers.

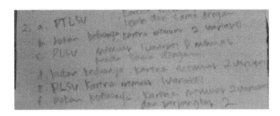

Figure 6.   Answer number 2 S_1 post-test.

Based on the data from Figure 6 in solving the problem in number two on the Post-Test question, S1 can explain the idea of the situation using the written method correctly and completely, as well as the reasons presented.

Next, in Pre-Test question number five, of the 15 subjects, all subjects were classified as S3, which were unable to explain the idea of the situation using the written method and were still not quite right. The following is the result of the presentation of one of the subject's test answers.

5) PLSV : Kalimat terbuka yg memuat 1 Variabel & menggunakan tanda sama dengan

bukan PLSV : Kalimat terbuka yg memuat lebih dari 1 Variabel & tdk menggunakan tanda sama dengan.

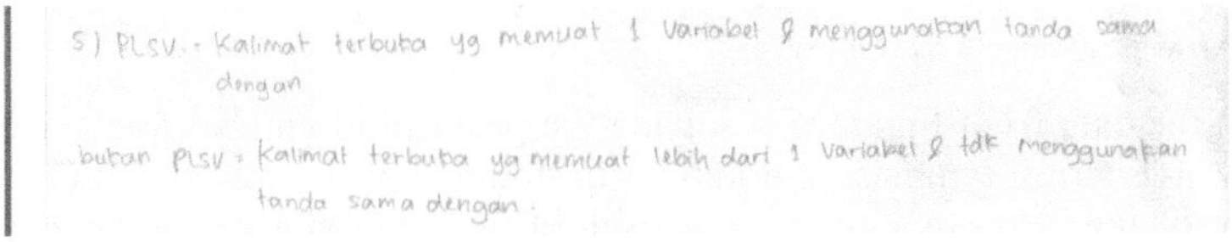

Figure 7.   Answer number 5 S_2 pre-test.

Based on the data from Figure 7 in solving the problem in number two on the Pre-Test question, S3 was not able to explain the idea of the situation using the written method, and the solution was still not precise and complete. In addition, the answer from S3 is still not by the questions asked in the question. For example, the definition of One Variable Linear Inequality should be defined, but the subject wrote it as Not One Variable Linear Equation.

In Post-Test question Figure 8, number five, from 15 subjects, there are three classified as S1, which can explain the idea of a situation using the written method. The following is the result of the presentation of one of the subject's test answers.

5.) PLSV memiliki 1 Variabel & memiliki tanda sama dengan.
PTLSV memiliki 1 Variabel & memiliki tanda lebih dari atau sama dengan.

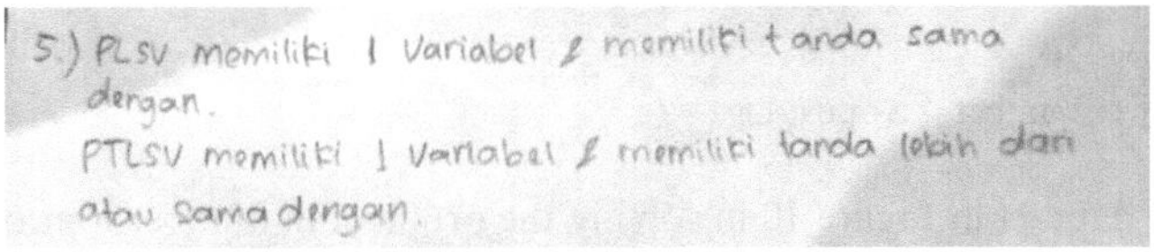

Figure 8.   Answer number 5 S_1 post-test.

Based on the data from Figure 8 in solving the problem in number five on the Post-Test question, S1 can explain the idea of the situation using the written method correctly and completely. For example, in the Pre-Test, all subjects wrote Not One Variable Linear Equation, but in the Post-Test, three subjects were by the requested question, namely Linear Inequality, but others still wrote Not One Variable Linear Equation, and some did not answer.

3.1.4 Description of students' mathematical communication ability with indicators of student's ability to reflect images into mathematical ideas

The researcher presented information from the answers to the Pre-Test and Post-Test questions to random subjects. Of the 15 subjects, there are three categories of subjects, namely subjects with code S1, namely subjects who can answer questions according to the indicators correctly and completely, S2, namely subjects who answer questions according to indicators but are not correct or incomplete, while S3 are subjects who cannot answer questions. by the indicators correctly and completely.

Of the 15 subjects studied, in the number four Pre-Test, of the 15 subjects studied, there were no subjects who were able to solve the problems given by the researchers according to the indicators. However, the subject can use terms, symbols, or notations in expressing everyday events. The following is the result of the presentation of one of the subject's test answers.

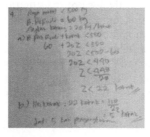

Figure 9.   Answer number 4 S_2 pre-test.

Based on the data from Figure 9 in solving the problem in number four on the Pre-Test question, S2 uses terms, symbols, or notations in stating daily events but not completely and correctly in solving them. In addition, the result of the solution is also not correct.

Then, in Post-Test question number four, out of 15 subjects, there was only one subject who was able to solve the problem, but there were still errors. The following is the result of the presentation of one of the subject's test answers.

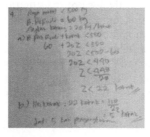

Figure 10.   Answer number 4 S_2 post-test.

Based on the data from Figure 10 in solving the problem in number four on the Post-Test question, S2 uses terms, symbols, or notations in stating daily events but not completely and correctly in solving them. In addition, the results of the completion are also correct, but the use of symbols in describing the results of the solution is not appropriate.

3.2 Discussion

Based on the description of the research results that have been explained, it is found that there is an influence and relationship between increasing mathematical communication skills in students with TTW-type learning. The results of the research conducted say that the application of learning using TTW is quite effective and makes students more active (Suriyana 2011; Yuliana and Muljono 2020). Artayasa *et al.* (2021), in the results of their research, said that the online TTW learning model has high effectiveness compared to conventional learning. The use of zoom in online learning has many benefits for alternative learning processes that are carried out remotely (Monica and Fitriawati 2021). This can be seen in the table of results of mathematical communication with online TTW.

Table 3. Improved mathematical communication based on indicators.

Indicators	Number	Pre-Test	Post-Test
Indicators Can Express Events Into Mathematical Symbols	1	15	15
	3	0	3
Indicators Able to Explain Situation Idea Using Written Method	2	9	15
	5	0	3
Indicators Can Reflect Images Into Mathematical Ideas	4	0	1

In the research results of Sutiawan *et al.* (2020), it was found that learning using TTW is alternative learning to improve mathematical communication skills. This can also be seen in the results of research conducted by researchers that TTW learning online is very well.

Table 4. Improved mathematical communication based on indicators.

Fulfil Indicators	Number of Students
One indicator to 2 indicators	3 Students
One indicator to 3 indicators	2 Student
Two indicators to 3 indicators	5 Students

So, in this study, 15 subjects who were able to fulfil from 2 indicators to 3 indicators were five students, then from 1 indicator to 2 indicators, as many as three students, and from 1 indicator to 3 indicators, as many as two students. So ten students improve in mathematical communication. Therefore, the results of students' mathematical communication with the TTW learning model are increasing and are included in the category of being able to complete according to the indicators. This can be seen from the completion of the Pre-Test and Post-Test that have been given to the subject. So the results of research conducted by researchers are relevant to the results of research conducted by Supandi *et al.* (2017), which stated that TTW learning could improve mathematical communication. This is in accordance with the results of study from Jaohari Effendi and Inganah (2021), which says that an essential skill in mathematics is mathematical communication.

4 CONCLUSION

Based on the results of previous studies, there is a relationship between mathematical communication and TTW learning. It is also proven in the results of this study that students' mathematical communication from the Pre-Test and Post-Test work on each indicator increased in online learning with the TTW method. In the future, learning with online TTW is expected to help teachers in learning to be more flexible not only at school but anywhere. And learning to use TTW online is expected to be developed with the media.

REFERENCES

Ahmed, S., Sbebata, M. and Hassanien, M. (2020) 'Emerging faculty needs for enhancing student engagement on a virtual platform', *MedEdPublish*, pp. 1–5.

Anggraini, D. and Hia, Y. (2016) 'Penerapan model kooperatif tipe think-talk-write untuk meningkatkan kemampuan datar segi empat di kelas vii', *Inspiratif*, 2(1), pp. 63–75.

Anisah, Asikin, M. and Hidayah, I. (2020) 'Mathematical writing ability through Cooperative Learning with Think Talk Write (TTW)', *Unnes Journal of Mathematics Education*, 9(1), pp. 28–36. doi: 10.15294/ujme.v9i1.38097.

Artayasa, I. P. *et al.* (2021) 'Efektivitas penerapan model pembelajaran think talk write (TTW) secara online terhadap literasi informasi siswa SMA', *Jurnal Kependidikan: Jurnal Hasil Penelitian dan Kajian Kepustakaan di Bidang Pendidikan, Pengajaran dan Pembelajaran*, 7(3), p. 641. doi: 10.33394/jk.v7i3.3558.

Basilaia, G. and Kvavadze, D. (2020) 'Transition to Online Education in Schools during a SARS-CoV-2 Coronavirus (COVID-19) Pandemic in Georgia', 5(4).

Gunawan, Suranti, N. M. Y. and Fathoroni (2020) 'Variations of models and learning platforms for prospective teachers during the COVID-19 pandemic period', *Indonesian Journal of Teacher Education*, 1(2), pp. 61–70.

Herliandry, L. D. and Suban, M. E. (2020) '*Jurnal Teknologi Pendidikan Pembelajaran Pada Masa Pandemi Covid-19*', 22(1), pp. 65–70.

Jaohari, T. S., Effendi, M. M. and Inganah, S. (2021) 'Penerapan pendekatan problem solving model SSCS (Search, Solve, Create, and Share) dan kemampuan komunikasi matematis siswa di SMP Muhammadiyah 8 Batu', *Mega: Jurnal Pendidikan Matematika*, 2(1), pp. 1–10.

Leutualy, A. C., Molle, J. S. and Huwaa, N. C. (2020) 'Pertidaksamaan Linear Satu Variabel Melalui Model Pembelajaran Kooperatif Tipe Think Talk Write', 2(2), pp. 2018–2021.

Monica, J. and Fitriawati, D. (2021) 'Efektivitas penggunaan aplikasi google meet sebagai media pembelajaran online pada mahasiswa saat pandemi Covid-19', *National Conference on Applied Business, Education, & Technology (NCABET)*, 1(1), pp. 388–394. doi: 10.46306/ncabet.v1i1.32.

Rahmani, A. and Sutiawan, H. (2020) 'Pengaruh model pembelajaran kooperatif Think Talk Write terhadap pemahaman konsep matematika siswa Smp (the effect of cooperative learning models Think Talk Write of the mathematical concept in the middle school)', 3(1), pp. 1–7. Available at: http://dx.doi.org/10.30656/gauss.v3i1.2168.

Riansyah, F. and Sari, A. (2018) 'Pengaruh penerapan pembelajaran kooperatif tipe Think Talk Write (TTW) terhadap kemampuan pemecahan masalah matematika ditinjau dari kemampuan awal matematika', *JURING (Journal for Research in Mathematics Learning)*, 1(2), p. 119. doi: 10.24014/juring.v1i2.5426.

Rizal, M. S. (2018) 'Pengaruh model pembelajaran kooperatif tipe Think Talk Write (Ttw) terhadap keaktifan belajar siswa dalam pembelajaran matematika kelas Iv Sdm 020 Kuok', *Jurnal Cendekia: Jurnal Pendidikan Matematika*, 2(1), pp. 105–117. doi: 10.31004/cendekia.v2i1.37.

Supandi, Rosvitasari, D. N. and Kusumaningsih, W. (2017) 'Peningkatan kemampuan komunikasi tertulis matematis melalui strategi Think-Talk-Write', *Jurnal Kependidikan*, 1(2), pp. 227–239.

Supandi, S. *et al.* (2018) 'Think-talk-write model for improving students' abilities in mathematical representation', *International Journal of Instruction*, 11(3), pp. 77–90. doi: 10.12973/iji.2018.1136a.

Suriyana (2011) 'Pembelajaran model think tallk write pada materi persamaan linear satu variabel bagi siswa kelas VII SMP negeri 8 pontianak', *Journal of Physics A: Mathematical and Theoretical*, 44(8), pp. 1689–1699. doi: 10.1088/1751-8113/44/8/085201.

Sutiawan, H., Suyono and Wiraningsih, E. D. (2020) 'Pengaruh model pembelajaran kooperatif tipe think talk write terhadap kemampuan komunikasi dan disposisi matematis ditinjau dari kemampuan awal matematika siswa', *Jurnal Penelitian Pembelajaran Matematika Volume*, 13(1), pp. 33–46. Available at: http://jurnal.untirta.ac.id/index.php/JPPM/article/view/2790.

Wijayanto, A. D., Fajriah, S. N. and Anita, I. W. (2018) 'Analisis kemampuan komunikasi matematis siswa smp pada materi segitiga dan segiempat', *Journal Cendikia: Jurnal Pendidikan Matematika*, 2(1), pp. 97–104.

Yadrika, G. (2019) 'Think-Talk-Write: Strategi untuk meningkatkan hasil belajar matematika siswa', *JNPM (Jurnal Nasional Pendidikan Matematika)*, 3(2), p. 294. doi: 10.33603/jnpm.v3i2.1995.

Yuliana, D. and Muljono (2020) 'Penerapan model pembelajaran kooperatif tipe think talk write (Ttw) untuk meningkatkan hasil belajar matematika Smp Negeri 6 Situbondo', *Edusaintek: Jurnal Pendidikan, Sains Dan Teknologi*, 6(2), pp. 64–81. doi: 10.47668/edusaintek.v6i2.37.

Yulianti, Eka Purnama, Y. and Hidayat, W. (2021) 'Analisis kemampuan komunikasi matematis siswa SMP kelas VII pada soal-soal persamaan dan pertidaksamaan linear satu variabel', *Analisis Kemampuan Komunikasi Matematis Siswa SMP Kelas VII Pada Soal-soal Persamaan dan Pertidaksamaan Linear satu Variabel*, 4(1), pp. 73–80. doi: 10.22460/jpmi.v4i1.73-80.

Strengthening Professional and Spiritual Education through 21st Century Skill Empowerment in Pandemic and Post-Pandemic Era – Arifin et al. (Eds)
© 2024 The Author(s), ISBN: 978-1-032-45243-2
Open Access: www.taylorfrancis.com, CC BY-NC-ND 4.0 license

Designing collaborative learning: Shifting learning ownership for students

F.J. Miharja*
Universitas Muhammadiyah Malang, Indonesia

Y. Setyaningrum, Y. Wahyuningtyas, M. Masrudi, F.U. Nurhidayati & M. Mawaddah
Junior High School 1 of Muhammadiyah, Malang, Indonesia

ABSTRACT: Improving the quality of learning is not only seen in how high student learning outcomes are but also in how attached students are to each other in education. This research was conducted to identify how students learn in groups and the impact of these interactions. The subjects involved in this study were 32 students of eighth-grade Junior High School (JHS) 1 of Muhammadiyah, Malang, East Java – Indonesia. The data collection technique used is observation, with video recordings, audio, and pictures during learning. Data analysis was carried out qualitatively using the Miles and Huberman Model. The results show that students have the potential for collaborative learning but are not yet capable enough to initiate discussion and impactful communication, so learning control is still dominant on the teacher's side. This student learning response is a stimulus for us in redesigning collaborative learning that is centered and immerses students in education.

Keywords: Collaborative learning, learning ownership, lesson study for learning community

1 INTRODUCTION

Relations between students in the class are fundamental and are believed to have an impact on the success of the learning process (Binkley *et al.* 2014; Fatimah *et al.* 2018; Lai 2011). The existence of a good relationship provides psychological support and students' confidence in completing their learning assignments (Podschuweit *et al.* 2016; Zhang *et al.* 2021). Logan *et al.* (2017); Malcom (2021); Phillips *et al.* (2022) stated that support from fellow students gives confidence to students that they are not alone in the learning process. Furthermore, this support stimulates the growth of discussions or collaborations that mutually reinforce one another (Lāma and Lāma 2020; Miharja *et al.* 2020). Support in relations between students can be in the form of verbal remarks (Peklaj and Puklek Levpuščcek 2006), gestures (Mas'ud and Wulandari 2020), gazes full of optimism (Zhang *et al.* 2021), or other forms. It is commonly encountered during offline learning.

However, online learning carried out for approximately two years during the pandemic, caused a shift in relations between students (Li *et al.* 2020; Irawan *et al.* 2020; Nikou and Maslov 2021). Students who initially knew each other became unfamiliar, especially new students at each grade level. At least, they only know the name but do not understand each other (Chiu 2022; Domina *et al.* 2021; Vaterlaus *et al.* 2021). This kind of condition makes communication between students stiff. Some researchers say such conditions worsen when teachers do not help connect them during online learning (Calleja and Camilleri 2021; Haavind 2019). These relationship estrangement presents a communication barrier, so many students feel isolated and alone in the classroom (Malcom 2021; Phillips *et al.* 2022).

---

*Corresponding Author: fuad.jayamiharja@umm.ac.id

DOI: 10.1201/9781003376125-26

The isolation of students in learning may be caused by various things such as technical limitations because they do not have equipment support for online learning (Zhang et al. 2020), or other psychological reasons (Chiu 2022; Li et al. 2020). Some researchers note high rates of students who lose motivation (Hira and Anderson 2021; Skar et al. 2021) and feel bored during online learning (Irawan et al. 2020; Phillips et al. 2022). Even though most learning is currently being carried out offline, in reality, the online learning impact is still common and challenging for teachers to design post-pandemic learning that can revive students' collaboration (Ladson-Billings 2021; Schwartzman 2020; Vaterlaus et al. 2021).

The growth of student learning responsibility is one of the solutions to solving problems or post-pandemic impacts. However, researchers believe that the growth of responsibility for ownership of learning can only grow with teacher facilitation. Therefore, this study aims to design collaborative learning to shift student learning ownership for the better.

2 METHOD

This research was conducted at Muhammadiyah Junior High School 1 of Malang from July to December 2022. Researchers involved the school principal and four teachers as a learning community who studied learning during the research period. The subject teachers involved included Science, Indonesian Language, Pancasila and Citizenship Education, and Mathematics (Table 1). The subjects used during the study were 32 eighth-grade students consisting of 17 boys and 15 girls.

Table 1.   The number of cycles and open class activity.

	First Cycle	Second Cycles	Third Cycles	Fourth Cycles
Lesson	Science	Indonesian Language	Pancasila and Citizenship Education	Mathematics
Topics	Motion of objects	Elements of the advertisement	The position of Pancasila and the Preamble of the 1945 Constitution	Coordinate of Cartesius
Date	August 1st, 2022	August 30nd, 2022	September 13rd, 2022	October 18nd, 2022

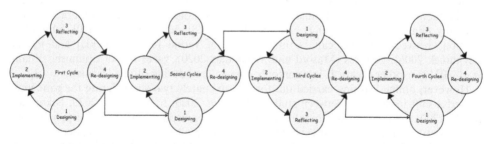

Figure 1.   Four cycles of lesson studies.

Implementation of learning is done in four cycles with the principles of design, implementation, reflection, and re-design (Figure 1). Each evaluation result is a basis for developing a design for the following study. Implementation is carried out using the open class method involving observers to obtain data describing learning. The following is the schedule for conducting open classes during the study. This research's products are lesson designs, predictions of academic dialogue between teachers and students, media, collaborative student worksheets, and learning videos. Data collection using observation instruments and post-learning reflection. The data obtained were analyzed qualitatively using the Miles and Huberman model (Miles *et al.* 2014).

3 RESULT AND DISCUSSION

Implementation of collaborative learning for students begins with designing collaborative learning by teachers in the learning community (Setyawan *et al.* 2019; Shernoff *et al.* 2017). The involvement of teachers from various fields of science is intended to enrich professional discussions and dialogues in each discussion so that the quality of the resulting dialogue is more in-depth and comprehensive (Haavind 2019). The quality of dialogue built in a learning community is fundamental to the achievement of collaborative learning (Barr and Askell-Williams 2020; Jiang and Koo 2020; Ricci 2021). In this case, to design learning for students with varying skills and potential, teachers need to enrich their lesson plans comprehensively. Students may not stand out in a field of science but have advantages in other lessons. If the teacher's preparation misses this, students may experience difficulties in learning without the teacher's scaffolding (Tiantong and Teemuangsai 2013). Teacher assistance in collaborative learning is manifested in selecting models relevant to the material to be delivered. The learning model used is problem-based learning (PBL).

Figure 2. The teachers and their learning community design the lesson plan collaboratively.

Furthermore, the PBL syntax forms the basis for preparing the LKPD used in research. The worksheet design allows students to examine and understand the context of the problem independently before sharing it with peers in their groups (Frisk and Larson 2011; Pluta *et al.* 2013; Monteiro and Morrison 2014). Proportional group division is also an area of concern in collaborative learning (Monteiro and Morrison 2014). In this case, the distribution of eighth-grade students in each learning cycle is different. It is not only based on regrouping but on facilitation according to students' academic ability in each subject. The teacher ensures that each group consists of students with different academic abilities, learning styles, and communication skills. Each group's diversity of student backgrounds is also meant to foster relationships between students after the last two years of studying online (Frisk and Larson 2011).

Figure 3. This girls is isolated in group discussions, but her eyes show her curiosity about the issues being discussed in the group.

At the beginning of offline learning, there were many communication problems in the classroom. Figure 3 shows that Dwi seems isolated from the other three friends. It can be observed from a sitting position between the four. Their sitting positions were far apart and communication limitations, among others, prevented Dwi from joining the discussion. However, she showed great enthusiasm and curiosity about the discussed issues even though his three friends had yet to respond (Figure 4).

Figure 4. The gesture shows learning ownership, even though the group mates have not responded yet.

Collaborative learning with the PBL model allows students to grow their ownership of learning gradually (Gorghiu et al. 2015; Scager et al. 2016). It started from the selection of problems and contexts that are relevant to everyday life (Pluta et al. 2013; Teo et al. 2021). In other words, these problems are problems that are known by students and experienced by students directly, not just problems that students know but are not directly related to students (Tan et al. 2019). Contextualization of material in the form of learning problems is a learning resource that has an attachment to students (Figure 5). It is believed to be fostering student responsibility (Pluta et al. 2013; Scager et al. 2016) and learning ownership (Gorghiu et al. 2015). Professional dialogue grows in the design stage, one of which is aimed at finding the contextualization of the material to be delivered by bringing the context of the problem as closely as possible to students (Figure 6).

Figure 5. Problem and contextualization in problem-based learning.

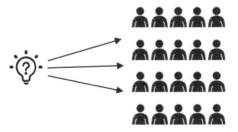

Figure 6.   The context of the problem should be among students.

The consistent implementation of collaborative learning for four months impacted how students learned. In the fourth grade (mathematics), student collaboration seemed more significant than before. In the first two classes, at least students needed more than 20 minutes to start discussions related to how to solve the problems given. In those 20 minutes, dialogue unrelated to the material is even more dominant. The reflection results show that students are still at the guided inquiry level, so they need more scaffolding from the teacher. At the next open class, the time needed by students to start discussions and collaborate is faster (less than 20 minutes).

Furthermore, students' awareness of playing a more significant role in learning is also better. At least this shows a shift in learning ownership from being dominated by the teacher to being more balanced with students. In this context, the teacher cannot shift all learning control over to students but gradually gives a portion of learning control to foster student learning responsibility (Siew and Ambo 2018; Veenman *et al.* 2014).

4   CONCLUSION

Teacher initiation and learning assistance through contextual learning has an important role in collaborative learning. Collaborative learning designs can gradually initiate ownership of learning for students. Furthermore, from the educator side, collaborative learning can strengthen the school learning community so that teachers can improve the quality of learning that is designed contextually. Academic dialogue that grows in the learning community is also a space for teachers and stakeholders to give each other a role in improving the quality of learning.

REFERENCES

Barr, S. and Askell-Williams, H. (2020) 'Changes in teachers' epistemic cognition about self–regulated learning as they engaged in a researcher-facilitated professional learning community', *Asia-Pacific Journal of Teacher Education*, 48(2), pp. 187–212. doi: 10.1080/1359866X.2019.1599098.

Binkley, M. *et al.* (2014) 'Defining twenty-first century skills', in *Assessment and Teaching of 21st Century Skills*. doi: 10.1007/978-94-007-2324-5_2.

Calleja, J. and Camilleri, P. (2021) 'Teachers' learning in extraordinary times: shifting to a digitally facilitated approach to lesson study', *International Journal for Lesson and Learning Studies*. doi: 10.1108/IJLLS-09-2020-0058.

Chiu, T. K. F. (2022) 'Applying the self-determination theory (SDT) to explain student engagement in online learning during the COVID-19 pandemic', *Journal of Research on Technology in Education*, 54(S1), pp. S14–S30. doi: 10.1080/15391523.2021.1891998.

Domina, T. *et al.* (2021) 'Remote or removed: Predicting successful engagement with online learning during COVID-19', *Socius*, 7. doi: 10.1177/2378023120988200.

Fatimah, I., Hendayana, S. and Supriatna, A. (2018) 'Didactical design based on sharing and jumping tasks for senior high school chemistry learning', *Journal of Physics: Conference Series*, 1013(1). doi: 10.1088/1742-6596/1013/1/012094.

Frisk, E. and Larson, K. (2011) 'Educating for sustainability: Competencies & practices for transformative action', *Journal of Sustainability Education*, 2(March), pp. 1–20. Available at: http://www.jsedimensions.org/wordpress/wp-content/uploads/2011/03/FriskLarson2011.pdf.

Gorghiu, G. *et al.* (2015) 'Problem-based learning – An efficient learning strategy in the science lessons context', in *Procedia – Social and Behavioral Sciences*. Elsevier, pp. 1865–1870. doi: 10.1016/j.sbspro.2015. 04.570.

Haavind, S. (2019) 'An interpretative model of key heuristics that promote collaborative dialogue among online learners', *Online Learning*, 11(3). doi: 10.24059/olj.v11i3.1720.

Hira, A. and Anderson, E. (2021) 'Motivating online learning through project-based learning during the 2020 COVID-19 pandemic', *IAFOR Journal of Education*, 9(2), pp. 93–110. doi: 10.22492/ije.9.2.06.

Irawan, A. W., Dwisona, D. and Lestari, M. (2020) 'Psychological Impacts of Students on Online Learning During the Pandemic COVID-19', *KONSELI: Jurnal Bimbingan dan Konseling (E-Journal)*, 7(1), pp. 53–60. doi: 10.24042/kons.v7i1.6389.

Jiang, M. and Koo, K. (2020) 'Emotional presence in building an online learning community among non-traditional graduate students', *Online Learning Journal*, 24(4), pp. 93–111. doi: 10.24059/olj.v24i4.2307.

Ladson-Billings, G. (2021) 'I'm Here for the Hard Re-Set: Post Pandemic Pedagogy to Preserve Our Culture', *Equity and Excellence in Education*, 54(1), pp. 68–78. doi: 10.1080/10665684.2020.1863883.

Lai, E. (2011) Motivation: A literature review, Alwasy Learning.

Lāma, E. and Lāma, G. (2020) 'Remote study process during Covid-19: Application and self-evaluation of digital communication and collaboration skills', in *New Trends and Issues Proceedings on Humanities …*, pp. 124–129. doi: 10.18844/prosoc.v7i3.5241.

Li, S. *et al.* (2020) 'The impact of covid-19 epidemic declaration on psychological consequences: A study on active weibo users', *International Journal of Environmental Research and Public Health*, 17(6). doi: 10.3390/ijerph17062032.

Logan, J. W. *et al.* (2017) 'The effect of individual motivation and cognitive ability on student performance outcomes in a distance education environment', *Journal of Learning in Higher Education*, 13(1), p. 83. Available at: https://files.eric.ed.gov/fulltext/EJ1139727.pdf.

Malcom, D. R. (2021) 'Loneliness as a downstream concern in a pandemic (and post-pandemic) world', *American Journal of Pharmaceutical Education*, 85(4), pp. 251–254. doi: 10.5688/ajpe8456.

Mas'ud, A. and Wulandari, D. A. (2020) 'The student teachers' verbal and non-verbal reinforcement during teaching practice in microteaching class', in *International Conference on English Language Teaching (ICONELT 2019)*, pp. 266–270.

Miharja, F. J. *et al.* (2020) 'Tokkatsu: Initiating students' collaborative activities in lesson study piloting school', *Jurnal Pendidikan Progresif*, 10(1), pp. 63–72. doi: 10.23960/jpp.v10.i1.202008.

Miles, M. B., Huberman, A. M. and Saldana, J. (2014) *Qualitative Data Analysis: A Methodes Sourcebook.* 3rd Ed. Singapore: Sage.

Monteiro, E. and Morrison, K. (2014) 'Challenges for collaborative blended learning in undergraduate students', *Educational Research and Evaluation*, 20(January 2015), pp. 564–591. doi: 10.1080/13803611.2014.997126.

Nikou, S. and Maslov, I. (2021) 'An analysis of students' perspectives on e-learning participation – the case of COVID-19 pandemic', *International Journal of Information and Learning Technology*, 38(3), pp. 299–315. doi: 10.1108/IJILT-12-2020-0220.

Peklaj, C. and Puklek Levpušček, M. (2006) 'Students' motivation and academic success in relation to the quality of individual and collaborative work during a course in educational psychology', in Mateja Brejc (ed.) *31st Annual ATEE Conference*. Slovenia: National School for Leadership in Education University of Ljubljana, Faculty of Education, pp. 146–161.

Phillips, R. *et al.* (2022) 'Student loneliness through the pandemic: How, why and where?', *Geographical Journal*, 188(2), pp. 277–293. doi: 10.1111/geoj.12438.

Pluta, W. J., Richards, B. F. and Mutnick, A. (2013) 'PBL and Beyond: Trends in collaborative learning', *Teaching and Learning in Medicine*, 25(SUPPL.1). doi: 10.1080/10401334.2013.842917.

Podschuweit, S., Bernholt, S. and Brückmann, M. (2016) 'Classroom learning and achievement: how the complexity of classroom interaction impacts students' learning', *Research in Science and Technological Education*, 34(2), pp. 142–163. doi: 10.1080/02635143.2015.1092955.

Ricci, M. C. (2021) *Mindsets in the classroom: Building a growth mindset learning community.* Taylor & Francis. Available at: https://www.routledge.com/Mindsets-in-the-Classroom-Building-a-Growth-Mindset-Learning-Community/Ricci/p/book/9781003236689.

Scager, K. *et al.* (2016) 'Collaborative learning in higher education: Evoking positive interdependence', *CBE Life Sciences Education*, 15(4), pp. 1–9. doi: 10.1187/cbe.16-07-0219.

Schwartzman, R. (2020) 'The (post-)pandemic academic: Re-forming communication studies', *Carolinas Communication Annual*, 36(1), pp. 1–8. Available at: https://doi.org/10.1016/j.solener.2019.02.027%0Ahttps://www.golder.com/insights/block-caving-a-viable-alternative/%0A???

Setyawan, D., Permana, T. and Latifa, R. (2019) 'Lesson study for learning community: A way of collegial participation of teachers and lecturers', *Bioedukatika*, 7(1), pp. 1–10. doi: 10.26555/bioedukatika.v7i1.11936.

Shernoff, D. J. *et al.* (2017) 'Teacher perceptions of their curricular and pedagogical shifts: Outcomes of a project-based model of teacher professional development in the next generation science standards', *Frontiers in Psychology*, 8, pp. 1–16. doi: 10.3389/fpsyg.2017.00989.

Siew, N. M. and Ambo, N. (2018) 'Development and evaluation of an integrated project-based and stem teaching and learning module on enhancing scientific creativity among fifth graders', *Journal of Baltic Science Education*, 17(6), pp. 1017–1033. doi: 10.33225/jbse/18.17.1017.

Skar, G. B. U., Graham, S. and Huebner, A. (2021) 'Learning loss during the COVID-19 pandemic and the impact of emergency remote instruction on first grade students' writing: A natural experiment', *Journal of Educational Psychology*. doi: 10.1037/edu0000701.

Tan, A. L. *et al.* (2019) 'The S – T – E – M Quartet', *Innovation and Education*, 1(3), pp. 1–14. doi: 10.1186/s42862-019-0005-x.

Teo, T. W. *et al.* (2021) 'Centricities of STEM curriculum frameworks: Variations of the S-T-E-M Quartet', *STEM Education*, 1(3), p. 141. doi: 10.3934/steme.2021011.

Tiantong, M. and Teemuangsai, S. (2013) 'The four scaffolding modules for collaborative problem-based learning through the computer network on moodle lms for the computer programming course', *International Education Studies*, 6(5), pp. 47–55. doi: 10.5539/ies.v6n5p47.

Vaterlaus, J. M., Shaffer, T. and Pulsipher, L. (2021) 'College student interpersonal and institutional relationships during the COVID-19 pandemic: A qualitative exploratory study', *Social Science Journal*, 00(00), pp. 1–14. doi: 10.1080/03623319.2021.1949553.

Veenman, M. V. J. *et al.* (2014) 'Assessing developmental differences in metacognitive skills with computer logfiles: Gender by age interactions', *Psihologijske Teme*, 23(1), pp. 99–113. Available at: https://hrcak.srce.hr/index.php?show=clanak&id_clanak_jezik=178355.

Zhang, M., Xin, X. and Li, R. (2021) 'Investigation on psychological health and resilience of clinical nursing students in "Post-Pandemic Era"', *Open Journal of Medical Psychology*, 10(04), pp. 70–79. doi: 10.4236/ojmp.2021.104007.

Zhang, W. *et al.* (2020) 'Suspending classes without stopping learning: China's education emergency management policy in the COVID-19 outbreak', *Journal of Risk and Financial Management*, 13(3), p. 55. doi: 10.3390/jrfm13030055.

Strengthening Professional and Spiritual Education through 21st Century Skill Empowerment in Pandemic and Post-Pandemic Era – Arifin et al. (Eds)
© 2024 The Author(s), ISBN: 978-1-032-45243-2
Open Access: www.taylorfrancis.com, CC BY-NC-ND 4.0 license

Phenomenological study of teacher candidates' perceptions of learning achievement and learning difficulties

Dwi Setyawan* & Wahyu Prihanta
Universitas Muhammadiyah Malang, Indonesia

ABSTRACT: Difficulties in understanding the concept of learning quality by teacher candidates have an impact on their learning and teaching experiences. This study aims to find out through a metaphor how biology education teacher candidates dream of teaching in senior high school, to discuss the concepts of learning achievement and learning difficulties. This qualitative research has a research sample consisting of 153 students (38 in semester I; 40 in semester III; 45 in semester V; and 30 in semester VII) studying at the Biology Education Department, Faculty of Teacher Training and Education, Universitas Muhammadiyah Malang. The research data was collected using a questionnaire that consisted of two questions and content analysis; (1) differences in the perception of teachers about concepts learning achievement variables; and (2) learning difficulties by students are determined by frequency analysis. Results of the study found that the metaphors produced by teacher candidates for learning achievement contained 7 themes; metaphor of learning difficulties 8 themes. It was concluded that each theme that emerged as a result of the analysis of teacher candidates in different semesters contained different perceptions of learning achievement and learning difficulties.

Keywords: Teacher candidates, learning, perception, education concepts

1   INTRODUCTION

Education has a strategic role in determining the history of human life because education can provide the necessary information and anticipate changing times (Ojala 2017; Veidemane 2022). This strategic role of education can be realized if the quality of education components such as; schools, teachers, students, facilities, and infrastructure are well prepared and sustainable (Ajpru *et al.* 2014; Haseena and Ajims 2015). Indonesian education is expected to be able to create superior and competitive human resources, to make it happen, the community continues to improve the supporting components that are of higher quality (Amirudin 2019). The participation of all school components provides a broad perspective on the transformation of learning and teaching as the goal of educational services (Setyawan and Hindun 2020). Thus, the organization of educational services must be improved.

The school works as an educational service organization, where the purpose of teaching and learning is realized by the teacher as the spearhead. On the other hand, the role of teachers and schools is also important in ensuring quality student learning, so schools seek to improve their educational services by recruiting teacher candidates who can actualize their competencies in schools. According to the social system, education and teachers are important interconnected networks to achieve school service goals with the ultimate goal of improving the quality of learning and teaching services (Greenhow and Askari 2017). Teacher candidates are school assets in improving educational services, unfortunately, the competence of teacher candidates is influenced by the learning process they have received. The phenomenon of differences in positive and negative perceptions of teacher candidates towards the concept of school, teacher, and student in the context of educational services can be influenced by the learning environment, learning

---

*Corresponding Author: dwis@umm.ac.id

DOI: 10.1201/9781003376125-27

experience, responsibility for self-development, and awareness of learning needs. (Sadik and Sadik 2014; Soykan *et al.* 2015). Different perspectives produce varied descriptions of schools and their service activities (Ghufron and Hardiyanto 2017).

The perspective of teacher candidates in defining learning outcomes and learning difficulties needs to be identified, this function is important because it can show the role of professionalism in carrying out teaching tasks. The results of defining the relationship between the teacher as the main actor of education with the ability to perceive learning achievement and student learning difficulties have different possible concepts so that the perception of these concepts can change. The teacher must be able to analyze the learning achievements and learning difficulties of their students, this is done to improve the quality of teaching and student learning success (Wahyu *et al.* 2021). According to Budiastuti *et al.* (2021) teacher skills in determining, analyzing, and perceiving learning outcomes can build knowledge and skills. The formation of a positive perception of teacher candidates can help knowledge, as an initial commitment to learning as a professional teacher (Kaban 2020; Kozikoğlu 2017). In line with Casebeer (2015) states that knowing the description of teaching and learning for teacher candidates makes the social process more dynamic. Visualizing the perspectives of teacher candidates can help them to construct positive concepts about teachers and teaching and learning practices (Yüksel 2019). One of the efforts to describe the ideal teacher's qualifications is using the metaphor of perception.

Educational metaphors are widely used for educational practice and research, as one approach to explaining current educational practice (Casebeer 2015; Suleyman 2016; Wahyu *et al.* 2021). The function of metaphor emphasizes profiling and mapping modeling mechanisms to understand individual competence and development (Soykan *et al.* 2015). metaphors are used to reveal practical problems of basic education such as teacher education, and classroom management in finding solutions by gathering information about ideas in various fields (Yüksel 2019). For example, in preparing teacher candidates, a lecturer uses metaphors in the development of action plans or lesson designs to encourage creative thinking in their learning. In line with Sözer and Sel (2020) metaphor has a strong impact on the process of educational analysis. Educational implementation can also be mapped strongly through educational metaphors (Yilmaz 2017). In addition to helping to uncover phenomena that occur in the educational process, metaphors also make it easier to find a point of view on how concepts build individuals (Kozikoğlu 2017), and provide a strong mapping in determining basic perceptions of concepts and conceptual frameworks that are constantly changing (Lavasani and Khandan 2018). So that the educational metaphor can be used as an approach in preparing policies, building teacher training or teaching in the future.

Department of Biology Education, Faculty of Teacher Training and Education, Universitas Muhammadiyah Malang is trusted in preparing professional teacher candidates, a strong mapping effort is needed on future teacher candidate information. Therefore, this study aims to find out through a metaphor how biology education teacher candidates dream of teaching in senior high school, to discuss the concepts of learning achievement and learning difficulties.

2 METHODS

Research Design: This qualitative research, where phenomenology is used to reveal how people give perspective to a phenomenon, how people remember, how people evaluate, and how the perspective relates to other people. Phenomenology is a method for investigating the perspective of life experience (Sadala and Adorno 2002; Østergaard *et al.* 2008). Phenomenology is qualitative research to reveal the perspective of individual experiences in certain fields in life (Neubauer *et al.* 2019).

Population and Sample: The population of this study were all active students in the Biology Education Study Program, Faculty of Teacher Training and Education, University of Muhammadiyah Malang, while the research sample consisted of 153 students from different semesters (38 in the semester I; 40 in the semester III; 45 in the semester V; and 30 in the semester VII), using a random sampling technique. The selection of students in different semesters is done because they are considered to have reached a certain level of awareness of educational concepts through academic and social experiences. The distribution of teacher candidates based on gender and differences in semester levels is presented in Table 1.

Table 1. Distribution of candidate teachers by Gender and semester level.

Variable		Semester I	Semester III	Semester V	Semester VII	Total
Gender	Female	12	11	13	12	48
	Male	26	29	32	18	105
Total		38	40	45	30	153

Data collection tool and data collection: A tool to collect data using a questionnaire consisting of two parts, namely: a question section used to determine gender and a question section posed to teacher candidates to generate a metaphor about the concept; (a) Learning outcomes; and (b) learning difficulties, where they dream of becoming the ideal teacher in high school. In this context, teacher candidates are asked to answer a metaphor which consists of two forms of questions, for example: "The learning achievement that I want in my dream is like … … … . because … … … .". "The teacher's learning difficulty that I don't want to experience is… … … . because … … … ". Each teacher candidate is asked to reflect deeply on his answer so that the meaning given can describe a different perception metaphor. Analysis of data: After the data is collected it is analyzed using content analysis. To get a more detailed explanation of the answers, they were reduced based on grouped themes. To make it easier to interpret/describe, the researcher also uses percentages. According to Sugiyono (2013), data interpretation, data reduction, and conclusion drawing are important to get support for finding data directly, recorded, and in detail to get a clearer picture of the data.

3 RESULTS AND DISCUSSION

3.1 Perceptions of teacher candidates about the concept of "learning achievement in dreams"

Based on the results of the analysis, it was found that from the perceptions of 153 teacher candidates for the concept of learning achievement in their dreams through this metaphor, there were 7 themes. The sample metaphor for teacher candidates' perceptions of the concept of learning achievement is presented in Table 2.

Table 2. Sample metaphors and themes that all participants produced for "learning achievement" in their dreams.

Theme 1. Equality school
EBS120 – "My dream school is like Kihajar Dewantoro's school. Because it provides equality in obtaining competencies and does not compare the competencies obtained by students."

Theme 2. Multifunctional learning objectives
EBS 97 – "My dream school is like an advanced place in terms of socializing. Because social and acquiring social and educational skills will contribute a lot to students, especially in achieving their learning."

Theme 3. Multicultural Learning Goals
EBS 111 – "My dream school is like color. Because it must have many students with different characteristics. These colors have to come together to create new goals to make it easier for him to achieve learning."

Theme 4. Meaningful learning goals
EBS 34 – "My dream school is like nature. Because instead of inside walls, education should be carried out as naturally and in an environment as free as possible with everyday life so that learning is more meaningful."

Theme 5. learning goals initiate the future
EBS 57 – "My dream school is like the school in the Indian movie "thee idiots". Because school must interesting, entertaining, full of activity and also educational while having fun."

Theme 6. Small-scale and complete learning objectives
EBS 89 – "My dream school is like the kind of school that has the goal of learning not to be greedy. Because the more you learn, the more you forget, it's better to have a little but gain a great learning experience."

Theme 7. Modern learning goals with technology
BS 25 – "My dream school is like a technology environment. Because I believe that students will become the goal of learning in the future"

Based on Table 2. The metaphor of teacher candidates' perceptions in producing different concepts about learning outcomes, obtained 7 themes. The most common theme related to the concept of learning achievement when they dream of becoming a teacher at school is "equality school". This finding illustrates that the learning objectives expected by teacher candidates' when they teach in schools in the future are learning outcomes that emphasize equal competencies and do not differentiate the competencies obtained by students. This perception of prospective teachers arises due to the unequal learning outcomes that they have experienced at school. Different learning experiences result in far different competencies achieved between one student and another (Letina 2020). So they hope that when they become teachers in the future, they will have the responsibility to improve it. The evenness of learning achievement designed by the teacher is the basic thing as an indicator of students' success in learning or vice versa. The development of learning achievement policies designed by teachers affects the improvement of student performance (Sirait 2016). Based on the results of research by Ghufron & Hardiyanto (2017), the problem of learning quality, especially learning achievement, occurs because of the aspect of activity dimensions with uneven learning system characteristics.

As for the difference in semester levels, it can be seen from the frequency of the appearance of the theme of teacher candidates'' perceptions of the concept of learning achievement. The percentage of similarities and differences in participants' perceptions of the concept of "learning achievement" dreams of teacher candidates according to semester level is presented in Table 3.

Table 3. Percentage of similarities and differences in the perceptions of participants for "learning achievement" concept in teacher candidates' dreams by their semester level.

Themes	Semester I Number of Metaphors	(%)	Semester III Number of Metaphors	(%)	Semester V Number of Metaphors	(%)	Semester VII Number of Metaphors	(%)
Equality school	17	9.3	26	19.6	15	11.3	10	5.5
Multifunctioal learning objectives	34	18.7	15	11.3	26	19.6	13	7.1
Multicultural Learning Goals	25	13.8	24	18.1	17	12.8	30	23.2
Meaningful learning goals	30	16.5	17	12.8	24	18.1	17	9.3
learning goals initiate the future	42	23.2	27	20.4	27	20.4	42	16.5
Small-scale and complete learning objectives	13	7.1	10	7.5	10	7.5	25	13.8
Modern learning goals with technology	10	5.5	7	5.3	7	5.3	34	18.7
Not prediction	5	2.7	3	2.2	2	1.5	13	2.7
Not prediction	3	1.1	2	1.5	3	2.2	3	1.6
Not prediction	2	1.6	1	0.0	1	0.0	5	1.1

Based on Table 3. The percentage of similarities and differences in participants' perceptions of the concept of "learning achievement" dreams of teacher candidates according to semester level shows that there are similarities in perceptions in several themes, namely; "Multifunction al learning objectives", "Meaningful learning goals", and "learning goals initiate the future". This finding shows that even with the same concept, teacher candidates at different semester levels have the same perception of other themes. This proves that the common perception of teacher candidates is influenced by the learning experience they receive, in other words, the common perception of the concept of learning achievement in schools in the future is more realistic. Yüksel (2014) and

Susilo & Rohman (2020) in their research results state that teachers' perceptions in designing learning achievement goals are influenced by learning and teaching experiences, as well as self-competence development. Meanwhile, the similarity of perceived reality is influenced by the learning environment and professional knowledge (Makovec 2018).

3.2 Teacher candidate's perception of the concept of "difficulty learning in dreams"

Based on the results of the analysis, it was found that from the perceptions of 153 teacher candidates for the concept of learning difficulty in their dreams through metaphor, there were 7 themes. The sample metaphor for teacher candidates' perceptions of the concept of learning difficulties is presented in Table 4.

Table 4.   Sample metaphors and themes that all participants produced for "learning difficulties" concept in their dreams

Theme 1. Teachers are not a source of information
EBS 56 – "My dream teacher is like a lion. Because he must have extensive knowledge, wisdom, and experience to overcome student learning difficulties."

Theme 2. Difficult to learn Teachers are not highly qualified
EBS 51 – "My dream teacher is like Kh. Ahmad Dahlan. students find it difficult to learn because they lack examples such as discipline, hardworking, virtuous and scientific."

Theme 3. Lack of focus on lessons
EBS 143 – "My dream teacher is not like a robot. Because giving lessons is not good for forcing participation and giving a lot of homework."

Theme 4. Lack of self-improvement
EBS 150 – "The teacher whose bicycle brake failed. Because he doesn't find out, how students learn, only think about the end result. So it is difficult for him to become the dream teacher of his students."

Theme 5. Difficulty in learning due to authoritarian teachers
EBS114 – "My dream teacher is like a father. Because he keeps his distance from students and doesn't let students disrespect himself. so that any difficulties are easily communicated"

Theme 6. Not student-centered
EBS 121 – "My dream teacher is like a god. Because he needs to predict and organize an environment where students can meet their needs and realize themselves so that they don't have trouble understanding the lessons."

Theme 7. Interrupted by friends while studying
EBS 45 – "My dream friend is an irresponsible study partner. Because he does not love, there is no love and care like a mother in solving my problems when studying."

Theme 8. It's hard to learn in solitude
EBS 63 – "My study partners are my teacher and my friends. Because I don't want to be alone in studying and completing my assignments, even if I have to be strict with me."

Based on Table 2. The metaphor of the perception of teacher candidates in producing different concepts about learning difficulties obtained 8 themes. The theme that emerged the most was the theme "Lack of self-development". This finding shows that there is a slight difference in the perception of teacher candidates about the concept of learning difficulties. The perception of teacher candidates on learning difficulties consists of two parts, learning difficulties in self-improvement, and difficulties in improving the quality of student learning. Teacher learning in self-improvement arises because of the shock of reality to changes in teacher emotional exhaustion and self-confidence orientation beliefs that are built (Voss and Kunter 2020). The results of the research by Sulisworo *et al.* (2016) stated that the learning difficulties of teachers are also influenced by the qualifications or quality of the input and the personality that does not support their professionalism. Meanwhile, teacher difficulties in providing solutions to student learning difficulties occur due to thinking deadlocks and productivity failures (Lodge *et al.* 2018). The perception of prospective teachers on learning difficulties must be understood as an unavoidable part of the learning process, the existence of learning difficulties encourages teachers to improve self-competence in solving problems.

The existence of differences in semester levels can indicate the frequency of occurrence of themes on the perceptions of prospective teachers regarding the concept of learning difficulties. The percentage of similarities and differences in participants' perceptions of the concept of "learning difficulties" dreams of prospective teachers according to semester level is presented in Table 5.

Table 5. Percentage of similarities and differences in the perceptions of participants for "learning difficulties" concept in teacher candidates' dreams by their semester level.

Themes	Semester I Number of Metaphors	(%)	Semester III Number of Metaphors	(%)	Semester V Number of Metaphors	(%)	Semester VII Number of Metaphors	(%)
Teachers are not a source of information	69	37.7	25	19.2	15	11.3	10	5.5
Difficult to learn Teachers are not highly qualified	19	10.3	31	23.8	26	19.6	13	7.1
Lack of focus on lessons	23	12.5	32	24.6	17	12.8	42	23.2
Lack of self-improvement	26	14.2	7	5.3	24	18.1	17	9.3
Difficulty in learning due to authoritarian teachers	10	5.4	2	1.5	27	20.4	30	16.5
Not student-centered	14	7.6	12	9.2	10	7.5	25	13.8
Interrupted by friends while studying	16	8.7	13	10	7	5.3	34	18.7
It's hard to learn in solitude	2	1.0	3	2.3	2	1.5	13	2.7
Not prediction	4	2.1	4	3.0	3	2.2	3	1.6

Based on Table 5. The percentage of similarities and differences in participants' perceptions of the concept of "learning difficulties" dream of teacher candidates by semester level shows that there are similarities in perceptions in several themes, namely; "Teachers are not a source of information", "Difficult to learn teachers are not highly qualified", "Lack of focus on lessons", "Difficulty in learning due to authoritarian teachers", and "Interrupted by friends while study- ing". This finding shows that even with the same concept, teacher candidates at different semester levels have the same perception of other themes. The perception of teacher candidates in the same concept is possible due to positive thinking about the reality of awareness of one's abilities as teachers who are demanded to always improve themselves. According to Kaban, (2020) and Kozikoğlu, (2017) states that the teacher's efforts to improve self-competence can prove the ser- iousness of self-commitment to the quality of positive mindset changes. Not being able to provide an overview of the factors that cause the emergence of learning achievement statements and learning difficulties in the attitudes and behavior of prospective teachers is a limitation of this study.

4 CONCLUSION

Based on the research findings, it can be concluded that each concept that is different between learning achievement and learning difficulties for prospective teachers has a different perception. Meanwhile, in each of the same themes, prospective teachers have the same perception of other themes, both perceptions of learning achievement and learning difficulties. So that these findings can be suggested as a teaching plan at the university for future teacher candidates.

REFERENCES

Ajpru, H., Wongwanich, S. and Khaikleng, P. (2014) "Design of educational quality assurance system for driving policy of educational reform in Thailand: Theory-based evaluation," *Procedia – Social and Behavioral Sciences*, 116(22), pp. 1416–1422. Available at: https://doi.org/10.1016/j.sbspro.2014.01.408.

Amirudin, M.F. (2019) "Hubungan pendidikan dan daya saing bangsa," *BELAJEA: Jurnal Pendidikan Islam*, 4(1), p. 35. Available at: https://doi.org/10.29240/belajea.v4i1.723.

Budiastuti, P. *et al.* (2021) "Analisis tujuan pembelajaran dengan kompetensi dasar pada rencana pelaksanaan pembelajaran dasar listrik dan elektronika di Sekolah Menengah Kejuruan," *Jurnal Edukasi Elektro*, 05(1), pp. 39–48. Available at: https://doi.org/10.21831/jee.v5i1.37776.

Casebeer, D. (2015) "Mapping preservice teachers' metaphors of teaching and learning," *International Journal of Learning, Teaching and Educational Research*, 12(3), pp. 13–23.

Ghufron, A. and Hardiyanto, D. (2017) "The quality of learning in the perspective of learning as a system," in *1st Yogyakarta International Conference on Educational Management/Administration and Pedagogy (YICEMAP 2017)*. Atlantis Press, pp. 255–259. Available at: https://doi.org/10.2991/yicemap-17.2017.43.

Greenhow, C. and Askari, E. (2017) "Learning and teaching with social network sites: A decade of research in K-12 related education," *Education and Information Technologies*, 22(2), pp. 623–645. Available at: https://doi.org/10.1007/s10639-015-9446-9.

Haseena, A. and Ajims, M. (2015) "Aspects of quality in education for the improvement of educational scenario," *Journal of Education and Practice*, 6(4), pp. 100–106.

Kaban, A. (2020) "Determining teachers', students', and parents' perceptions of distance education through metaphors," *International Journal of Research in Education and Science*, 7(1), p. 245. Available at: https://doi.org/10.46328/ijres.1316.

Kozikoğlu, I. (2017) "Prospective teachers' cognitive constructs concerning ideal teacher qualifications: A phenomenological analysis based on repertory grid technique," *International Journal of Instruction*, 10(3), pp. 63–78. Available at: https://doi.org/10.12973/iji.2017.1035a.

Lavasani, M.G. and Khandan, F. (2018) "High school students' metaphorical perceptions of biology and biology teacher concepts," *Cypriot Journal of Education Science*, 13(1), pp. 41–52.

Letina, A. (2020) "Development of students' learning to learn competence in primary science," *Education Sciences*, 10(11), pp. 1–14. Available at: https://doi.org/10.3390/educsci10110325.

Lodge, J.M. *et al.* (2018) "Understanding difficulties and resulting confusion in learning: An integrative review," *Frontiers in Education*, 3(June), pp. 1–10. Available at: https://doi.org/10.3389/feduc.2018.00049.

Makovec, D. (2018) "The teacher's role and professional development," *International Journal of Cognitive Research in Science, Engineering and Education*, 6(2), pp. 33–45. Available at: https://doi.org/10.5937/ijcrsee1802033M.

Neubauer, B.E., Witkop, C.T. and Varpio, L. (2019) "How phenomenology can help us learn from the experiences of others," *Perspectives on Medical Education*, 8(2), pp. 90–97. Available at: https://doi.org/10.1007/s40037-019-0509-2.

Ojala, M. (2017) "Hope and anticipation in education for a sustainable future," *Futures*, 94, pp. 76–84. Available at: https://doi.org/10.1016/j.futures.2016.10.004.

Østergaard, E., Dahlin, B. and Hugo, A. (2008) *Doing phenomenology in science education: A research review, Studies in Science Education*. Available at: https://doi.org/10.1080/03057260802264081.

Sadala, M.L.A. and Adorno, R. de C.F. (2002) "Phenomenology as a method to investigate the experience lived: A perspective from Husserl and Merleau Ponty's thought," *Journal of Advanced Nursing*, 37(3), pp. 282–293. Available at: https://doi.org/10.1046/j.1365-2648.2002.02071.x.

Sadik, F. and Sadik, S. (2014) "A study on environmental knowledge and attitudes of teacher candidates," in *Procedia – Social and Behavioral Sciences*. Elsevier B.V., pp. 2379–2385. Available at: https://doi.org/10.1016/j.sbspro.2014.01.577.

Setyawan, D. and Hindun, I. (2020) "Lesson study in schools components perception: The challenge of transforming teaching and learning," *Jurnal Pendidikan Progresif*, 10(2), pp. 362–373. Available at: https://doi.org/10.23960/jpp.v10.i2.202019.

Sirait, S. (2016) "Does teacher quality affect student Achievement? An empirical study in Indonesia," *Journal of Education and Practice*, 7(27), pp. 34–41.

Soykan, E., Gunduz, N. and Tezer, M. (2015) "Perceptions of the teacher candidates towards community service learning," *Procedia – Social and Behavioral Sciences*, 197(July), pp. 2468–2477. Available at: https://doi.org/10.1016/j.sbspro.2015.07.314.

Sözer, A. and Sel, B. (2020) "A Metaphoric approach to the conception of the 'teacher-headmaster-school' in different age categories," *International Journal of Progressive Education*, 16(2), pp. 56–71. Available at: https://doi.org/10.29329/ijpe.2020.241.5.

Sugiyono (2016) *Metode penelitian pendidikan (Pendekatan kuantitatif, kualitatif, dan R&D)*. Bandung: Alfabeta. Available at: http://pustaka.unm.ac.id/opac/detail-opac?id=35458.

Suleyman, A. (2016) "An analysis of teachers perceptions through metaphors: Prospective Turkish teachers of science, math and social science in secondary education," *Educational Research and Reviews*, 11(24), pp. 2167–2176. Available at: https://doi.org/10.5897/err2016.3064.

Sulisworo, D., Nasir, R. and Maryani, I. (2016) "Identification of teachers' problems in Indonesia on facing global community," *International Journal of Research Studies in Education*, 6(2), pp. 81–90. Available at: https://doi.org/10.5861/ijrse.2016.1519.

Susilo, H. and Rohman, F. (2020) "Teacher competency and perception in lesson llanning using a software prototype," *International Journal of Innovation, Creativity and Change.*, 13(September), pp. 811–827.

Veidemane, A. (2022) "Education for sustainable development in higher education rankings: Challenges and opportunities for developing internationally comparable indicators," *Sustainability (Switzerland)*, 14(9). Available at: https://doi.org/10.3390/su14095102.

Voss, T. and Kunter, M. (2020) "'Reality Shock' of beginning teachers? changes in teacher candidates' emotional exhaustion and constructivist-oriented beliefs," *Journal of Teacher Education*, 71(3), pp. 292–306. Available at: https://doi.org/10.1177/0022487119839700.

Wahyu, S., Rizal, F. and Syah, N. (2021) "Teacher performance analysis in the learning process," *Journal of Education Research and Evaluation*, 5(1), p. 67. Available at: https://doi.org/10.23887/jere.v5i1.30758.

Yilmaz, N.Y. (2017) "Students and teachers' metaphors about classroom teachers," *Journal of Education and Learning*, 7(1), p. 245. Available at: https://doi.org/10.5539/jel.v7n1p245.

Yüksel, H.G. (2014) "Teachers of the future: Perceived teaching competences and visions of pre-service English language teachers," *International Journal of Human Sciences.| Uluslararası İnsan Bilimleri Dergisi*, (July 2014), pp. 27–39. Available at: https://doi.org/10.14687/ijhs.v11i2.2920.

Yüksel, İ. (2019) "ELT preservice teachers' conceptualization of teaching practice: A metaphor analysis of the dynamics of teaching practice," *International Journal of Higher Education*, 8(4), p. 254. Available at: https://doi.org/10.5430/ijhe.v8n4p254.

Strengthening Professional and Spiritual Education through 21st Century Skill Empowerment in Pandemic and Post-Pandemic Era – Arifin et al. (Eds)
© 2024 The Author(s), ISBN: 978-1-032-45243-2
Open Access: www.taylorfrancis.com, CC BY-NC-ND 4.0 license

Building youth character through the local wisdom culture of Gawai in Malo Jelayan Village, Bengkayang Regency

Subhan Widiansyah*
Sultan Ageng Tirtayasa University, Banten, Indonesia

Iwan Ramadhan & Nining Ismiyani
Tanjungpura University, Pontianak, Indonesia

Muhammad Agus Hardiansyah
Sultan Ageng Tirtayasa University, Banten, Indonesia

ABSTRACT: This study aims to obtain information about community efforts in building the character of youth based on local wisdom through the implementation of Gawai Dayak. In this study, efforts were made to build the character of youth involving the government to achieve the intended community goals. The problem identified was the fading of adolescent character values amid the speed of globalization so the alternative of character planting is carried out through local wisdom in the implementation of Gawai Dayak by the Dayak community in Malo Village. A descriptive qualitative approach was employed in the research. The findings are in the form of descriptions and narratives based on data obtained in the field. The results of the study show the role of Gawai Dayak in shaping the attitudes, behavior, and character of adolescents in every implementation process. There are distinctive functions and meanings between Gawai Dayak in Malo Jelayan Village and that in general in West Kalimantan forming the uniqueness and characteristics as the efforts of the local community and government to build the character of youth based on the values of the nation's personality. It was discovered that there were guidelines for behavior to avoid unwanted things, supervision from parents (the main characters), awareness of human relations, punishment for violations, mutual respect, gratitude, and social and economic aspects helping shape the character of adolescents in the implementation of Gawai Dayak. To conclude, the whole process of the implementation of the Dayak Gawai has social control over the important figures in the Dayak community of Malo Jelayan Village. If the society's rules are violated, there will be punishment given to the teenagers or community according to the procession of Gawai Dayak which has become the tradition carried out for a long time.

Keywords: character building, local wisdom

1 INTRODUCTION

Indonesia is a country that consists of various and diverse tribes and nations, religions, cultures, and languages. The young generation has an important role to play in the resilience and continuation of the nation's independence. Adolescents who have a nationalist and patriotic spirit should be encouraged and continue to study Pancasila values (An'Umillah and Nugraha 2021). The character must be built and shaped to become a dignified nation. A person is said to have a strong character if he has succeeded in absorbing the values and beliefs that society wants to use as a moral force in his life. Local wisdom is closely related to traditional culture in a place, in that local wisdom contains a lot of views and rules so that people have more ground in determining an action such as people's everyday behavior (Rachmadyanti 2017).

---

*Corresponding Author: subhanwidiansyah@untirta.ac.id

DOI: 10.1201/9781003376125-28

Local wisdom is formed as a cultural advantage of the local community and geography in a broad sense and places more emphasis on place and locality (Njatrijani 2018). The values of local wisdom are contained in organizational principles. The main organizational principles are that membership is voluntary and open, management is carried out democratically, and independence (Komariah *et al.* 2018). National character education is a conscious and planned effort to instill values that serve as guidelines and national identity so that they are internalized within students which encourages and manifests in good attitudes and behavior. National character development is carried out through socialization, education and learning, empowerment, and acculturation, one of which is through local wisdom, and cooperation of all components of the nation and state (Ghani 2017). Character education is education related to good habitual values, and positive attitudes that contain knowledge, and aim to provide students with the ability to make decisions appropriately and responsibly so that they can overcome various problems of adolescent character that may arise in the future (Sarbini and Wahidin 2020). Character education given to students aims to fortify attitudes, morals, and behavior so that they are not easily influenced by the flow of globalization and to prepare human resources. The realization of this Indonesian character is a strong foundation as a characteristic of strong Indonesian human beings (Najmina 2018).

National character education aims to form a nation that is tough, competitive, moral, tolerant, cooperative, patriotic, dynamic, and oriented towards science and technology, all of which are imbued with faith and piety to God Almighty as envisioned by the philosophy of Pancasila (Anwar and Salim 2019). Character education, namely religious, honest, tolerant, disciplined, hardworking with creativity, independent, democratic, curios, happy, caring of the motherland, respect for achievement, friendly/communicative, fond of reading, care for the environment and social care, and responsibility. Demanding the quality of human resources in the next millennium certainly requires good character. Character is a key individual goal (Sirnayatin 2017). Local wisdom is a collection of facts, concepts, beliefs, and people's perceptions of their environment. Local wisdom is understood as everything that is based on knowledge, recognized by reason, and in accordance with religious provisions (Rahmi 2016). According to Doan and Grace (2022) differences in beliefs affect differences in getting treatment that shape opinions. The Dayak community is known as a community that is rich in local cultural wisdom. Local genius is also a cultural identity, a national identity that causes the nation to be able to absorb and cultivate foreign culture according to its character.

Local wisdom concerns the relationship between humans and nature, as well as the cooperation within the family, community, nation, and state (An'Umillah and Nugraha 2021). The phenomenon of character change does not only occur in schools but also in adolescents who are the next generation who maintain their cultural traditions. Awareness is needed from village stakeholders such as village heads, traditional heads, and the youth themselves to be able to work together to maintain cultural existence in their respective regions. According to (Melamed *et al.* 2019) humans tend not to realize that each of them has their own unique culture or behavior. Gawai Dayak is one of the cultures of the Dayak ethnicity and each region has its characteristics. Gawai Dayak contributes to fostering social awareness and good solidarity values for the people who carry it out, the gathering event becomes a process that is continuously maintained. The Gawai Traditional Ceremony in West Kalimantan can form solidarity values among the Dayak people. Through a series of Gawai Traditional ceremonial activities, starting from preparation to implementation demanding that the community can work together with one another. Working together to work hand in hand is the community characteristic to prepare all needs and preparations during the Gawai Traditional ceremony. The implementation of the Gawai Dayak ceremony provides and strengthens solidarity values for the Dayak Tribe (Syafrita and Murdiono 2020). According to Reed (2019), the formation of national character also influences national identity. This is because the progress of the times continues, it is necessary to filter new things that enter.

Social capital is formed through local institutions such as cooperation and mutual trust between communities, then Gawai Dayak becomes a bond of friendship, cooperation, togetherness, and mutual care between individuals and communities, and converts into political capital, namely political participation which then becomes the norm and unique local values (Herlan and Elyta 2020). The equipment used is still traditional, showing that the original traditions of the Dayak tribe are still being maintained today (Peterianus and Mastiah 2020). Local wisdom of the Dayak tribe can be seen from two dimensions, namely knowledge and actions that are patterned from generation to generation or across generations to form traditions (Seran and Mardawani 2020).

The purpose of this study was to find out the character of youth through the local wisdom culture of the Dayak Gawai in Malo Village. Research relevant to this research was conducted by (Budiwibowo 2016) with the title "Pembangunan Karakter Generasi Muda Melalui Budaya Kearifan Lokal di Era Globalisasi" (Character Development of the Young Generation through Local Wisdom Culture in the Era of Globalization) with findings in the form of noble values in various local cultural wisdoms, becoming a community weapon to shape the character of young people with research and development. However, this research only examines what noble values are to build the character of young people. The novelty of this research is the direct implementation through the Gawai Dayak tradition to shape the character of the younger generation during the implementation process of this tradition which not only forms the character of local youth, immigrant communities also easily get existing character values while interacting with the youth and the community of immigrant adults. It even has a significant impact on mutual tolerance amongst the non-Dayak ethnic community. Thus, it is necessary to discover the character-building efforts through the cultural values of the local wisdom and the meanings of these values of the Gawai Dayak tradition.

2 METHODS

The research method used in this study is a descriptive qualitative approach by describing and describing the collected data as it is. The research location was in Mesa Malo Jelayan, West Kalimantan, Indonesia. Questionnaires and interviews were employed to collect the data. Primary data sources in the research were conducted through the process of observation and interviews related to the character of adolescents through the local wisdom culture of Gawai. Secondary data sources from literature and research informants were village heads, tribal heads, and elders in Malo Jelayan Village. Community leaders and the surrounding community were those deciding the informants. Documentation tools researchers obtained in the form of relics or tools of the Dayak Gawai tradition in Malo Jelayan Village, Bengkayang Regency. Researchers retrieve the data by reducing them to provide a clearer picture and make it easier to carry out further data collection and look for it when needed. Then the observational data (observations) and interview results were summarized and sorted with a focus on how the local wisdom of the Gawai Dayak tradition can be a character builder for teenagers in Malo Jelayan Village, Bengkayang Regency. Testing the validity of the data was conducted by extending the observations, and then increasing persistence by making more careful and continuous observations. The data in the field were then triangulated with sources by testing the credibility of the source to the responsible or authorized party regarding building the character of youth through local wisdom culture to informants and making observations in accordance with the focus of this research.

3 RESULTS AND DISCUSSION

The Dayak community is known as a community that mostly occupies Kalimantan or Borneo. The Dayak ethnicity includes the Dayak sub-tribes and is spread over the West Kalimantan region in particular. The Dayak tribe is an indigenous tribe on the island of Borneo, Indonesia. There are dozens of names of Dayak sub-tribes and they have a strong unique culture of local wisdom. Each sub-tribe uses its language to communicate with one another within its community. According to Efriani (2021), the experience that the community had in ancient times until now was formed because of people's habits, one of which is the Dayak tribe's habits that become customs or customary law. The Dayak tribes spread across the island of Borneo are quite numerous, consisting of 405 kinship tribes. Malo Jelayan Village is one of the villages in the Teriak sub-district, Bengkayang district. Most of the heads of families in Malo Jelayan Village have elementary and junior high school educational backgrounds.

Gawai Dayak (Naik Dango) is a traditional activity which is held once a year by the Dayak community. According to Shayo (2020), individuals who establish themselves in a community will try to get to know the group they identify with. Dayak community mutually declares themselves as an ethnicity that is very thick with its culture from all aspects of life. A group of people who call themselves Dayak Bakati' are classified in terms of language. They mapped the distribution of the Bidayuhik language family in the western part of Borneo, including in the Bengkayang and Sambas Regencies. The term Bakati' consists of two words, namely "ba", a prefix that is equivalent to "ber-" which means "to have", and "kati", a root word that means "no". In daily conversation, the frequency of the word "kati" appears more often, so it is used to refer to the identity of speakers of that language. So, there are Bakati' and/or Bakati' people. In Bengkayang Regency we find several sub-tribes of the Dayak Bakati' who collectively call themselves "Dayak Kenayatn". However, the term Dayak Kenayatn itself is more popular among the Dayak sub-tribes who speak Banana' and ahe languages, and who live in Landak, Pontianak, Sambas, and Bengkayang Regencies. Gawai Dayak (Naik Dango) is a traditional activity which is held once a year by the Dayak community. Dango in the Kanayatn Dayak language means a hut or hut for shelter which is usually made in fields or rice fields. Dango is also a rice storage barn that is usually built around a residence in a village environment. It is called dango padi (rice house), because according to the beliefs of the Kanayatn Dayak people, rice has a living spirit, and they live in the dango, just like humans. Not only in beliefs, life habits and problems encountered also tend to be related and implicated in their culture which has been passed down from generation to generation. According to Owens *et al.* (2010), strong bonds among tribes will maintain mutual existence and traditions that have existed since their ancestors. Not only that, but inter-ethnic participation also determines the existence of the traditions of each ethnic group that owns the tradition (Sanders 2002). Dango by the Kanayatn Dayak tribe means huts for shelter made in fields or rice fields. A dango is a rice storage area that is usually built around a residence in a village environment. Village community offerings are one of the media or containers as an expression of the abundant rice harvest every year for the Village community. According to Asbari *et al.* (2021) amid globalization, the biggest challenge for the Indonesian people is how to prepare human resources that embrace the national character.

Figure 1. Equipment for the implementation of the Gawai Dayak tradition in Malo Jelayan village.

The Gawai Dayak tradition involves young children in Malo Jelayan village, Bengkayang district. Through the activities of the Gawai Dayak tradition, teenagers interact with each other and this proves that the meaning of rationalization in the social aspect of Malo Jelayan village, Bengkayang district, strengthens social relations among the people in the area. According to Charness & Chen (2020), good interactions start from feelings as part of the many similarities with the group as in the following picture.

Figure 2. Interaction between young people in Malo Jelayan Village as a form of meaning of rationalization in the social aspect.

Figure 3. Village community interaction with guests from outside the village, as a form of rationalization function of mutual respect for fellow human beings.

Besides the young people of Malo Jelayan Village who interacted with each other, the people of Malo Jelayan Village gave a very good welcome and were happy to chat with outside guests who wanted to witness the process of the Gawai Dayak tradition firsthand and the people of Malo Jelayan Village were very enthusiastic about welcoming guests from outside the village. According to Hidayat *et al.* (2022), good character will produce good national morals.

This proves that the function of rationalizing mutual respect still exists or is still being implemented in Malo Jelayan village, Bengkayang district. Rationalization refers to traditions, values, and emotions that motivate people to act and behave rationally and in accordance with the values and norms that exist in society (Purwanto *et al.* 2022). Rationalization can be referred to as individual actions leading to a goal and that goal is determined by value or choice (preference). As for the function of rationalizing the cultural values of local wisdom of the Gawai Dayak tradition in Malo Jelayan village, namely the function of guidelines in behavior, the function of guidelines in behavior means how this Gawai Dayak tradition can become the basis of an individual or society, especially for young people so that they can maintain their attitudes and show good ones. Local wisdom is a collection of facts, concepts, beliefs, and people's perceptions of their environment. Local wisdom is understood as everything that is based on knowledge, recognized by reason, and in accordance with religious provisions.

This function itself has been carried out among adolescents in Malo Jelayan village, Bengkayang district, although there are some habits or behaviors such as consuming wine or palm wine which are still hereditary, making it difficult to eradicate from the life of the Malo Jelayan village community, especially when implementing Gawai Dayak (Browning *et al.* 2018). Next, the function of social control is a very important component in society to limit all attitudes and behaviors that are contradictory in society. This function has been carried out well among adolescents in the village of Malo Jelayan, Bengkayang district, especially during the Gawai Dayak activities where parents keep an eye on all the attitudes and behavior of the youth in the village so as not to violate the norms in the society of the area. According to Schwartz (2008), each social group of cultural entities has its uniqueness in monitoring behavior, in accordance with their respective cultural traditions. This is evidenced by the character of the teenagers in the village who still uphold the attitude of courtesy towards the activities of the Gawai Dayak tradition. Apart from that, teenagers in the village of Malo Jelayan can be said to have good character even though from an educational point of view there are still many who have not experienced college education.

As for the function of mutual respect for fellow human beings, it is an important component in the function of rationalization, where we will see how the attitudes and behavior of a group of people perceive differences among human beings. According to Moll *et al.* (2021) apart from having to have the right religion, humans must also function to interact with other humans by placing themselves and the cultural environment in which they stand. This function has been carried out in the village of Malo Jelayan, Bengkayang district. This was proven when guests or outsiders visited to see firsthand the process of the Gawai Dayak tradition. the high value of tolerance or differences, especially teenagers during the Gawai Dayak tradition. Furthermore, the function of respecting nature is a very important component in building a cultural tradition, especially the Gawai Dayak tradition which is very closely related to the natural surroundings. In the village of Malo Jelayan, Bengkayang district, the function has been carried out well, this is evidenced by how the community uses all materials or offerings that come from nature and the natural conditions there are still very beautiful. Likewise, young people also participate in protecting the nature of Malo Jelayan Village and the function of being grateful to the creator. The Gawai Dayak tradition in Malo Jelayan village, Bengkayang district is one form of the village community's way of giving thanks to the Creator for the blessings bestowed in the form of a bountiful rice harvest. Rational action begins with belief and desire, and then concludes with optimal action to maximize performance and desire, and is conditioned on belief. According to W.J.S Poerwadar Minta in the Big Indonesian Dictionary, that value is defined as (a) Rice (in the sense of estimated price); and (b) The price of something (money for example), if measured or exchanged for another, intelligence score, Content; quality; content value, Characteristics (things) that are important or useful for humanity.

The meaning of rationalization of the cultural values of the local wisdom of the Gawai Dayak tradition in the religious aspect is that the community or youth are grateful for the blessings given by the Almighty through a tradition called Gawai Dayak. In the process, there will be offerings in the form of harvest or other offerings where each item offered has its meaning, especially as an expression of gratitude for the abundant rice harvest. The meaning of the cultural aspect is that it is hoped that future generations of young people in Malo Jelayan village will be able to maintain this culture and pass it to the next generation and remain proud of the culture of the Dayak tribe. Meanwhile, the meaning in the educational aspect shows how the activities of the Gawai Dayak tradition in Malo Jelayan village, Bengkayang district, can provide an education, especially the value of mutual tolerance and divine value, which means that every teenager or younger generation can respect a culture or customs of a society and also it is hoped that teenagers or the people of this village can understand the meaning of the Gawai Dayak tradition, which means an expression of gratitude to God Almighty for the abundant rice harvest. In the economic aspect, the tradition means that by the abundance of rice yielded, the community will be provided with an adequate food supply and not experience difficulties in obtaining food. In addition, the harvested rice can also be sold to meet daily needs or for other needs.

In the village of Malo Jelayan, Bengkayang district, the community usually keeps the harvested rice in their house, which can be sold if needed to generate income. Next, the meaning of the social aspect is that this activity also further enhances interaction or friendly relations between members of the community. According to Li (2020), societies cannot be unrelated to each other, even though they have many tribes and far differences. Furthermore, according to Ashraf & Bandiera (2018), the relationship among humans is horizontal while it is vertical with God. Adolescents also play a role in visiting neighboring homes to simply interact or socialize. This activity took place in the village of Malo Jelayan, Bengkayang district.

4 CONCLUSION

The efforts of the Dayak community in West Kalimantan in building the character of the cultural values of the local wisdom of the Gawai Dayak tradition reveal functions and meanings as forming the character of youth, including the function of guiding behavior, the function of social control, personality characteristics in achieving hopes and expectations among fellow human beings and nature, meaning in religious, cultural, educational, economic and social aspects. Several experts in the social sciences build the character of youth through the local wisdom of the Gawai Dayak tradition from a cultural point of view containing values, functions, and meanings that can be a preventive effort for the younger generation to face the never-ending flow of globalization and the fact that the world is not stagnant. Therefore, the nation's personality continues to refer to the nation's values and morals, and instilling character from an early age is one way to prevent demoralization.

REFERENCES

An'Umillah, A.N.S. and Nugraha, D.M. (2021) 'Pentingnya peran nilai-nilai Pancasila terhadap karakter remaja pada era globalisasi dan disrupsi', *Harmony: Jurnal Pembelajaran IPS Dan PKN*, 6(1), pp. 35–41.

Anwar, S. and Salim, A. (2019) 'Pendidikan Islam dalam membangun karakter bangsa di era milenial', *Jurnal Pendidikan Islam*, 9(2), p. 233.

Asbari, M. *et al.* (2021) 'Does genetic personality and parenting style influence students' character building?', *International Journal of Evaluation and Research in Education*, 10(2). Available at: https://doi.org/10.11591/ijere.v10i1.20483.

Ashraf, N. and Bandiera, O. (2018) 'Social incentives in organizations', *Annual Review of Economics*. Available at: https://doi.org/10.1146/annurev-economics-063016-104324.

Browning, B.R. *et al.* (2018) 'Character strengths and first-year college students' academic persistence attitudes: An integrative model ψ', *Counseling Psychologist*, 46(5). Available at: https://doi.org/10.1177/0011000018786950.

Budiwibowo, S. (2016) 'Membangun pendidikan karakter generasi muda melalui budaya kearifan lokal di era global', *Premiere Educandum: Jurnal Pendidikan Dasar dan Pembelajaran*, 3(1). Available at: https://doi.org/10.25273/pe.v3i01.57.

Charness, G. and Chen, Y. (2020) 'Social identity, group behavior, and teams', *Annual Review of Economics*. Available at: https://doi.org/10.1146/annurev-economics-091619-032800.

Doan, L. and Grace, M.K. (2022) 'Factors affecting public opinion on the denial of healthcare to transgender persons', *American Sociological Review*, 87(2). Available at: https://doi.org/10.1177/00031224221082233.

Efriani, E. *et al.* (2021) 'Eksistensi adat dalam keteraturan sosial Etnis Dayak di Kampung Bonsor Binua Sakanis Dae', *Refleksi Hukum: Jurnal Ilmu Hukum*, 6(1). Available at: https://doi.org/10.24246/jrh.2021.v6.i1.p87-106.

Ghani, Y.A. (2017) 'Pengembangan sarana prasarana destinasi pariwisata berbasis budaya di Jawa Barat', *Jurnal Pariwisata*, 4(1), pp. 22–31.

Hidayat, M. *et al.* (2022) 'Character education in Indonesia: How is it internalized and implemented in virtual learning?', *Cakrawala Pendidikan*, 41(1). Available at: https://doi.org/10.21831/cp.v41i1.45920.

Komariah, N., Saepudin, E. and Yusup, P.M. (2018) 'Pengembangan desa wisata berbasis kearifan lokal', *Jurnal Pariwisata Pesona*, 3(2), pp. 158–174.

Li, J. (2020) 'Humans as social beings-from" People first" to "People-centered"', *Scientific and Social Research*, 2(2).

Melamed, D. *et al.* (2019) 'Status characteristics, implicit bias, and the production of racial inequality', *American Sociological Review*, 84(6). Available at: https://doi.org/10.1177/0003122419879101.

Moll, H. *et al.* (2021) 'Sharing experiences in infancy: From primary intersubjectivity to shared intentionality', *Frontiers in Psychology*, 12. Available at: https://doi.org/10.3389/fpsyg.2021.667679.

Najmina, N. (2018) 'Pendidikan multikultural dalam membentuk karakter Bangsa Indonesia', *Jupiis: Jurnal Pendidikan Ilmu-Ilmu*, 10(1), p. 52.

Njatrijani, R. (2018) 'Kearifan lokal dalam perspektif budaya Kota Semarang', *Gema Keadilan Edisi Jurnal (ISSN: 0852-011)*, Volume 5, (September), pp. 17–18.

Owens, T.J., Robinson, D.T. and Smith-Lovin, L. (2010) 'Three faces of identity', *Annual Review of Sociology*, 36. Available at: https://doi.org/10.1146/annurev.soc.34.040507.134725.

Peterianus, S. and Mastiah, M. (2020) 'Eksistensi suku Dayak Seberuang dalam menghadapi tekanan modernisasi melalui Ritual Gawai Dayak.', *BESTARI: Jurnal Pendidikan dan Kebudayaan*, 1(2), pp. 36–43.

Purwanto, A., Imran, I. and Ramadhan, I. (2022) 'Analisis rasionalisasi nilai-nilai mitos kemponan pada masyarakat etnis Melayu', *Ideas: Jurnal Pendidikan, Sosial, dan Budaya*, 8(1). Available at: https://doi.org/10.32884/ideas.v8i1.642.

Rachmadyanti, P. (2017) 'Penguatan pendidikan karakter bagi siswa sekolah dasar melalui kearifan lokal', *Jurnal Pendidikan Sekolah Dasar*, 3(2), pp. 201–214.

Rahmi, S.A. (2016) 'Pembangunan pariwisata dalam perspektif Kkearifan lokal', *Reformasi*, 6(1), pp. 76–84.

Reed, I.A. (2019) 'Performative state-formation in the early American Republic', *American Sociological Review*, 84(2). Available at: https://doi.org/10.1177/0003122419831228.

Sanders, J.M. (2002) 'Ethnic boundaries and identity in plural societies', *Annual Review of Sociology*. Available at: https://doi.org/10.1146/annurev.soc.28.110601.140741.

Sarbini, M. and Wahidin, U. (2020) 'Pendidikan rabbani', *Jurnal Edukasi Islami*, 9(1), pp. 149–160.

Schwartz, S.H. (2008) 'The 7 Schwartz cultural value orientation scores for 80 countries', *Research Gate*, pp. 1–19.

Seran, E.Y. and Mardawani, M. (2020) 'Kearifan lokal rumah betang Suku Dayak Desa dalam perpektif nIlai folisofi hidup (studi etnografi: Suku Dayak)', *Seri Pendidikan*, 3(1), pp. 167–172.

Shayo, M. (2020) 'Social identity and economic policy', *Annual Review of Economics*. Available at: https://doi.org/10.1146/annurev-economics-082019-110313.

Sirnayatin, T.A.. S. (2017) 'Membangun karakter bangsa melalui pembelajaran sejarah', *SAP (Susunan Artikel Pendidikan)*, 1(3), pp. 312–321.

Syafrita, I. and Murdiono, M. (2020) 'Upacara adat gawai dalam membentuk nilai-nilai solidaritas pada masyarakat suku dayak Kalimantan Barat', *Jurnal Antropologi: Isu-Isu Sosial Budaya*, 2, pp. 151–159.

Author index